Cages of Steel

D1601443

Cages of Steel

The Politics of Imprisonment

in

the United States

`*A15045 448844`

HV
9471
. C22
1992
West

Edited by

Ward Churchill and J. J. Vander Wall

MAISONNEUVE PRESS
Washington, D.C. 1992

Some of the material in this book was originally published in a special issue of New Studies on the Left. Thanks is due to the Saxifrage Publications Group for permission to reprint. Heather Rhoades' article appears courtesy of The Progressive, in which it first ran. Kuwasi Balagoon's poem originally appeared in Breakthrough. The bio-sketeches of Sekou Odinga, Albert "Nuh" Washington, Lucy Berríos Berríos, Alcia Rodrígues, Filiberto Ojeda Ríos, and Carmen Valentín were adapted from items initially published in Can't Jail the Spirit. Susan Saxe's "Telling Someone" was first published in Gay Community News. Thanks also to Bulldozer for permission to use Jim Campbell's piece on Trenton, and to the Yale Journal of Law and Liberation for permission to use its transcription of Julio Rosado's talk and Laura Whitehorn's essay on preventive detention.

A number of individuals made significant contributions to the various stages of the project which resulted in Cages of Steel. These include, most prominently, Hanif Shabazz-Bey, Cindy Bowden, Bob Brown, "Down Town" Fay Brown, Nilak Butler, Bobby Castillo, Chrystos, Claire Culhane, Paulette D'Auteuil-Robideau, Bruce Ellison, Larry Giddings, Brian Glick, Mariana Guerrero, Stuart Hanlon, Nancy Horgan, Kim Jackson, Ellen Klaver, Bill Kunstler, Winona LaDuke, Pat Levasseur, Ojore N. Lutalo, Dian Million, Ahmed Obafemi, Jim Page, Ellen Ray, Mike Riegle, Bob Robideau, Bill Schapp, Afeni Shakur, Doug Spaulding, David Stonebreaker, Jan Susler, Luis Talamantez, Flint Taylor, John Thorne, and Kwame Turé. Of course, Bob Merrill and the folks at Maisonneuve Press have proven unstinting in their commitment to seeing this book in print. To the others, too numerous to name, who've shared thoughts and writing and their spirit of resistance: you know who you are, and you know our appreciation and gratitude are real.

Cover photo courtesy of the Library of Congress. Frontice page image courtesy of Tasso Stathopulos, Baltimore, MD.

Ward Churchill and J. J. Vander Wall, Cages of Steel: The Politics of Imprisonment in the United States.

© copyright 1992 Maisonneuve Press
P. O. Box 2980, Washington D.C. 20013

All right reserved. The publisher encourages references to and quotations from this book in reviews and discussions, provided that acknowledgment is clearly given.
For any other purpose or reproduction in any form, please write to the publisher for permission. Permission to reproduce portions of this book is automatically granted to prisoners and prisoners' rights activists.

Printed in the U. S. by BookCrafters, Fredricksburg, VA

Library of Congress Cataloging-in-Publication Data

Cages of steel : the politics of imprisonment in the United States / edited by Ward Churchill and J. J. Vander Wall.
    Includes bibliographical references and index
    1. Political prisoners--United States. 2. Imprisonment--United States. 3. Criminal justice, Administration of--United States. I. Churchill, Ward. II Vander Wall, Jim.
HV9471.C22 1992   92-25512
365'.6'0973--dc20   CIP

ISBN 0-944624-17-0 paperback, acid-free paper.

Cages of Steel — The Politics of Imprisonment

for

George Jackson

"Security" (photo: Ken Sturgeon)

Ward Churchill

Introduction—
The Third World at Home:
Political Prisons and
Prisoners in the United States

> I have heard people refer to the "criminal countenance."
> I never saw one. Any man or woman looks like a criminal
> behind bars.
>
> —Eugene V. Debs
> *Walls and Bars*, 1927

The government of the United States maintains that there are no political prisoners incarcerated in the country's penal facilities. The official perspective has been perhaps best expressed by John Clark, warden of the federal "super maximum" prison for men at Marion, Illinois: "While it's true that some of the inmates held here subscribe strongly to certain ideologies, they are not here because they hold those ideological beliefs. They are here because they have engaged in criminal acts."[1] Those inclined to accept this convenient self-assessment, even momentarily or in part, should consider the following examples, drawn from the treatment accorded those broadly defined as belonging to the political left.

Leonard Peltier is a 46-year-old Anishinabé/Lakota man serving consecutive life sentences in the federal prison at Leavenworth, Kansas. A member of the American Indian Movement (AIM), Peltier was convicted in 1977 of killing two FBI agents during a firefight on South Dakota's Pine Ridge Sioux Reservation during the summer of 1975. As Jim Vander Wall explains in this book, it has subsequently been shown through the FBI's own documents that incomplete and inaccurate ballistics evidence was deliberately presented at trial in order to "establish Peltier's guilt." As early as 1980, Amnesty International concluded that even the most elementary standards of justice require that Peltier receive a new trial. Prosecutor Lynn Crooks has since admitted the government "has no idea" who killed the agents, and the Eighth Circuit Court of Appeals has formally acknowledged that the original case against Peltier no longer exists. Still, the court has declined to reverse Peltier's conviction, expressly because the problems involved in the case result from a clear pattern of "misconduct on the part of some FBI agents." To order the matter back to trial would, the judges correctly observe, "impute even more impropriety" to the Bureau, a step they profess themselves "reluctant" to take. The U.S. Supreme Court has twice refused to hear Peltier's appeals. No reason was stated on either occasion. Peltier, of course, remains in prison.[2]

Dhoruba Bin Wahad (Moore) is a former leader of the Black Panther Party (BPP) in New York. In 1973, he was convicted of wounding two police officers during an "ambush attack" staged in 1971. He was sentenced to serve from 25-years to life. On March 22, 1990, he was released from prison and ordered back to trial. The reason? As Bin Wahad explains in his interview with Dan Debo, a judge had finally required the release of FBI documents demonstrating conclusively that the Bureau, the New York City Red Squad and state prosecutors had collaborated to coerce false testimony against Bin Wahad during his trial. For example, Pauline Joseph, a key government witness, was shown to have initially insisted to investigators that Bin Wahad was not the individual who had fired a machinegun at the policemen. After several months of being held as a "material witness"—all the while being "worked in shifts" by agents, cops and prosecutors—her story mysteriously changed. In court, she claimed Bin Wahad had "confessed" his deed to her after the fact. The government agencies involved carefully covered up the contradictory statements of Joseph and other witnesses for more than fifteen years.[3] It should be noted before passing on that all of this was acknowledged by the Supreme Court of the State of New York a full year before Bin Wahad was actually freed; he sat in a cage for thirteen additional months while the good judges debated whether the law meant they were "required" to grant him a new trial, or whether retrial wasn't just an "option" they might decline to exercise.

Herman Bell, Albert "Nuh" Washington and Anthony "Jalil" Bottom—the so-called "New York Three"—were members of the Black Liberation Army (BLA). In 1975, they were convicted and sentenced to life imprisonment for the 1971 "execution-style murders" of two New York City policemen. Now it comes out that ballistics evidence presented against them at trial was directly contradicted by FBI lab reports. The FBI, police, and prosecutors knew it at the time, but withheld this crucial information from the defense and then suppressed it for more than a decade. And there is more. Even prosecutor Robert Tannenbaum has admitted that a key witness against the three, Ruben Scott, was tortured—wires inserted into his penis, among other atrocities—by New Orleans police, in order to obtain his "cooperation." Having applied the stick, the government next utilized a carrot, apparently dropping murder charges against Scott in a California cop-killing case in exchange for his testimony against Bell, Washington, and Bottom in New York. Two other important witnesses, Linda Torres and Jackie Tabb, were held in jail as material witnesses for thirteen months and told they would never regain custody over their young children unless they testified to the prosecution's version of events.[4] Much of this information was also suppressed at trial and during direct appeals. Nonetheless, at present, the three remain in prison.

Geronimo ji Jaga Pratt headed the BPP chapter in Los Angeles during the late sixties. In 1972, he was convicted of the 1968 "Tennis Court Murder," committed in Santa Monica, of a white school teacher named Caroline Olsen. Pratt's main line of defense was that it was impossible for him to have killed Olsen, given that at the time of her death he was 350 miles away, in Oakland, attending a BPP national leadership meeting. FBI electronic surveillance logs derived from the Bureau's bugging of Party headquarters, he argued, would prove his point. At trial, FBI representatives lied under oath, denying that any such bugging had occurred. They also denied that they had infiltrated the defense team when, in fact, they had. Pratt was thereupon convicted and sentenced to life imprisonment. Years later, when it was proven that the Bureau had indeed bugged the BPP facilities in question, his attorneys once again demanded the relevant logs. As Pratt explains in the interview contained in this volume, the FBI then claimed to have "lost" the crucial material. The California Supreme Court then decided that the prosecution's having placed informers among Pratt's lawyers and paralegal staff had rendered "no prejudice" to his defense. As in the Peltier case, Amnesty International has long since concluded that a retrial is necessary if justice is to be served. At present, however, Geronimo Pratt remains in prison after nearly two decades in California, a state in which the average time served on a first degree murder conviction is 14.5 years. During a 1988 parole hearing, LA Assistant District Attorney Dianne Visanni went before the board to explain why: Pratt should not be released, she stated, because "he is still a revolutionary man." In 1991, he was again denied parole—and the California courts again refused to reopen his case—despite the fact that two private investigators have come forward and stated that, nearly a decade ago, while they were involved with a completely different case, they had had opportunity to examine the "missing" FBI surveillance logs and that the documents showed clearly Pratt was in Oakland on the crucial evening.[5]

Mumia Abu-Jamal was once a member of the BPP's information section in Philadelphia, working on weekly production of *The Black Panther* newspaper. After the breakup of the Party, he became a prominent figure in the Philadelphia black community's talk radio communications, winning several awards for community service and electronic journalism. In this capacity, beginning in 1978, he was able to do much to expose the illegal nature of the Philadelphia police department's program of harassment against the local MOVE organization. As is covered in my article on Mumia later in the book, this appears to have infuriated the late Philadelphia Mayor (and former police chief) Frank Rizzo. Consequently, Abu-Jamal was arrested and charged with the slaying of a policeman on December 9, 1981, despite the fact that all eyewitnesses described the assailant as looking radically different from the accused (the killer was uniformly described as being short, over 200 pounds and wearing an Afro hairstyle; Mumia is slender, over six feet tall, weighs 170 pounds and wears his hair in dreadlocks). At trial, he was denied the right to the attorney of his choice (MOVE leader, John Africa) and was forced to rely mainly on himself, in consultation with an inexperienced public defender. Convicted, he was sentenced to death. As is covered in the article devoted to Abu-Jamal which follows, it appears at present that his appeals have been exhausted and the execution date draws nearer.

Other Variations

There are several common denominators among the cases sketched above: 1) each man assumed an important political leadership role within his community by opposing the imposition of U.S. socio-economic policy upon it; 2) consequently, each was specifically targeted for political "neutralization" by the FBI and cooperating state/local police agencies; and 3) each was sent to prison on the basis of evidence which was/is suspicious, to say the least. Variations of any one of these stories might be repeated at least a hundred times over, the absolute minimum number of individuals presently held under similar circumstances in U.S. prisons. Even in situations where those imprisoned may actually have engaged to some extent in the acts attributed to them, there are problems of a highly political nature. These concern questions of double jeopardy, selectivity in application of the law and disparity in sentencing (*vis-à-vis* right-wing defendants). Consider the following:

Kazi Touré is an Afroamerican political activist who became very visible during the confrontations concerning the busing of school children in Boston during the late seventies. In February 1982, he was arrested alongside an interstate highway in Massachusetts and charged with firearms violations. Convicted in federal court, he was sentenced to serve six years. He was then hustled into state court and tried a second time for precisely the same offense. Convicted again, he was sentenced to serve four-to-five years, with the state sentence to begin as soon as the federal sentence had expired. Appeals on the basis of obvious double jeopardy have been to no avail.[6] Yet the government can be shown to have consistently adopted the opposite stance where right-wingers are concerned. For instance, in 1975, when Pine Ridge Sioux tribal president Dick Wilson—a solid ally of the FBI in its campaign to destroy the American Indian Movement—faced serious charges as a result of his ordering a physical assault upon AIM defense attorney Roger Finzel, he was advised to go before a tribal court he controlled, plead guilty and receive a $45 fine. Justice Department prosecutors then dropped their own charges against Wilson, arguing that to haul him into federal court—where he might have received a lengthy prison sentence if convicted—would represent "a patent breach of the constitutional prohibition against double jeopardy."[7]

Dr. Allen Berkman, a founder of the John Brown Anti-Klan League, is presently serving a twelve-year sentence stemming from allegations that he provided medical attention to Marilyn Buck, a Euroamerican activist accused of having been wounded during an unsuccessful 1981 attempted expropriation of a Brinks truck in West Nyack, New York. Berkman is the first individual to have been imprisoned on this basis since Dr. Mudd—the physician alleged to have rendered similar services to John Wilkes Booth, assassin of Abraham Lincoln in 1865. Insofar as it is dubious at best that only Berkman and Mudd have committed such an "offense" during the course of American history, selectivity in applying the relevant laws is self-evident. Further, as is recounted by Laura Whitehorn in her contribution to this volume, despite the facts that he has been eligible for parole since 1987, is suffering from a potentially terminal case of Hodgkins Disease, and that co-defendants in a related case entered guilty pleas to charges they would otherwise have contested as part of an agreement by which Berkman was to be released, the government continues to hold him in maximum security confinement.[8]

Susan Rosenberg and Tim Blunk are Euroamerican activists convicted in 1984 of illegally possessing a quantity of dynamite, none of it fashioned into bombs. Both were sentenced to serve fifty-eight years in federal prisons. Their punishments might be usefully compared to that imposed upon Dennis Malvesi, a right-wing ideologue convicted during the same period of having actually used explosives to bomb a number of abortion clinics across the nation. Malvesi was sentenced to only seven years for his far more serious offenses, and was released after only forty-eight months. Another interesting comparison might be drawn with the punishment meted out to Edward Hefferman, a right-wing "survivalist" convicted in the mid-eighties of possessing 1,000 pounds of dynamite and eighteen fully constructed pipe bombs; he was sentenced to serve from six-months-to-two-years, and was released after six months. The Rosenberg/Blunk sentences are far and away the heaviest for any possessory offense in the history of federal law. They are also two and a half times the average 1985 sentence imposed for kidnapping, three times the average for second degree murder, four times the average for bank robbery, nine times the average for felony distribution of narcotics, ten times the average for assault, and sixteen times the average for illegal possession of firearms (a comparable offense).[9]

Linda Evans is a former member of Students for a Democratic Society (SDS) and the Weather Underground. In 1985, she was convicted of harboring a fugitive and using false identification to obtain firearms. She was sentenced to serve three years on the fugitive violation, and a total of forty-two more on the various weapons charges (all sentences were set to run consecutively, so she was actually required to serve forty-five years). Tellingly, Evans was sentenced in New Orleans, the same federal jurisdiction in which Louisiana ku klux klan grand dragon Don Black and several associates had been sentenced two years previously. In 1983, Black and his friends were apprehended on a boat loaded with explosives and automatic weapons, departing for the Caribbean nation of Dominica. Their plan was to invade the island, overthrow its government and establish a new white supremacist regime. For these blatant violations of the Neutrality Act as well as the same weapons laws over which Linda Evans was imprisoned, the klansmen all received sentences of ten years or less. Black himself was released on parole after only twenty-four months to resume his klan organizing activities.[10]

Sometimes matters such as double jeopardy and sentencing disparity are merged with "thought crimes" and/or misapplication of statutes for purposes never intended by their sponsors. Notable in this regard has been the RICO Act (Racketeer Influenced and Corrupt Organizations Act; 18 USCS § 1961-1968). Passed as a means to combat the penetration of labor unions and legitimate businesses by organized crime, RICO has instead seen considerable use against plainly political targets. It thus plays an interesting counterpart role to such traditional political catch-alls as "Seditious Conspiracy" (18 USCS § 2384). The following examples should prove sufficient to illustrate the point.

The Revolutionary Armed Task Force (RATF) was an organization of black and white activists committed to continuing community-based heroin withdrawal and treatment programs in the African American community after New York defunded the Bronx-based Lincoln Detox Center in 1978. One of the means apparently chosen to finance the operation was expropriation of cash from banks and armored trucks. A number of members were apprehended in a series of arrests and trials beginning in 1981. Despite the fact that the government never attempted to establish that any defendant had sought personal gain through his or her activities (in the manner of a racketeer), very severe penalties were visited upon several people for "RICO conspiracy." For instance, Silvia Baraldini, an Italian national, was sentenced to forty-three years imprisonment solely on this basis. Marilyn Buck and Dr. Mutulu Shakur received fifty year RICO sentences. Another alleged RATF member, Sekou Odinga, received fifty years via two RICO convictions. In each case, the RICO sentences were added on (set to run consecutive to) punishments accruing from any other convictions the defendants might have incurred. Hence, activists who otherwise faced less than twenty year sentences—or, in the case of Baraldini, perhaps no sentence at all— instead found themselves confronting a virtual lifetime behind bars. Baraldini's situation is especially acute, given that she has been diagnosed as suffering from an aggressive form of uterine cancer for which she has been consistently denied adequate treatment in prison hospitals. U.S. authorities refuse to allow her circumstance to be favorably altered despite the fact that it has a treaty containing prisoner exchange provisions with Italy, and that the Italian government has repeatedly requested that Baraldini (an Italian national) be transferred to a penal facility in that country.[11]

The Jonathan Jackson/Sam Melville Brigade (otherwise known as the "Ohio 7") was, as Ray Luc Levasseur recounts in his contribution

The "Ohio 7": (from left to right) Jaan Laaman, Richard Williams, Barbara Curzi-Laaman, Carol Manning, Tom Manning, Pat Gros, and Ray Luc Levasseur. (Photo: Paul Shoul)

to this book, a group of Euroamerican activists endeavoring to cause the U.S. *status quo* at least *some* material consequences at home as a result of its international aggression. For example, the group reputedly bombed the facilities of transnational corporations actively doing business in apartheid South Africa. Clandestine by definition—and thus unable to hold regular "above ground" jobs—the Brigade is said to have sustained itself between 1976 and 1983 through the expropriation of cash from several banks. Captured in the latter year, six members of the group were put through a series of trials resulting in convictions for specific acts such as bombings, bank robberies and the killing of a New Jersey state trooper. Correspondingly, they were given lengthy prison sentences: Tom Manning, double-life plus fifty-three years; Carol Manning, fifteen years; Richard Williams, forty-five years; Jaan Laaman, fifty-three years; Barbara Curzi-Laaman, fifteen years; and Ray Luc Levasseur, forty-five years. The seventh group member, Pat Gros Levasseur, was convicted of harboring a fugitive—her husband—and sentenced to five years. With all this already in hand, federal prosecutors took the seven defendants back to trial in 1989, charging Sedition and RICO conspiracy.[12] Prosecutors utilized precisely the same evidence and alleged exactly the same acts for which the seven had already been convicted. Had it been successful, this double jeopardy gambit would have added at least forty years to each prisoner's existing sentence.[13] Fortunately, a Hartford, Connecticut, jury saw through the ploy and voted to acquit the defendants on all counts.[14]

Such things tie rather nicely to the ways in which the government has traditionally upped the ante on political targets through application of seditious conspiracy statutes. A recent example is the "Resistance Conspiracy," a group of seven white activists accused of having *approved of* certain physical consequences suffered by the U.S. government as it engaged in aggression abroad. Among other things, it is charged that they publicly applauded the detonation of a bomb in the U.S. Capitol Building shortly after the 1983 invasion of Grenada. None of the defendants was charged with specific acts; in fact, three of the accused—Susan Rosenberg, Tim Blunk and Allen Berkman—were actually in prison at the time the bombings occurred. As in the Ohio 7 case, the government alleged the same acts for which the three had already been convicted, and sought simply to recycle evidence previously introduced against them, as a means of adding up to forty years to their existing sentences.[15] Ultimately, charges were dropped against these three defendants (on grounds of double-jeopardy) while three others—Marilyn Buck, Linda Evans, and Laura Whitehorn—pleaded guilty to lesser offenses in exchange for a federal guarantee, since reneged upon, that Berkman would be released in order to secure medical attention on the outside (see above). The seventh person accused of participation in the "conspiracy," Elizabeth Duke, went underground at the point the charges were originally filed and remains a fugitive, understandably reluctant to subject herself to this sort of "justice."

Preventive Detention

After all is said and done, the government no longer really needs to bother with a trial in order to keep the politically objectionable out of circulation for extended periods. At issue is the so-called "Bail Reform Act of 1984" (18 U.S.C. § 3142), a measure ostensibly designed to allow courts to keep violent criminals—serial killers, known rapists, and the like—from harming anyone else pending trial, conviction, and sentencing. During hearings prior to passage of the act, law enforcement leaders presented this suspension of constitutional due process rights to bail as a "surgical public safety measure" which would see application in only a tiny and necessary fraction of all criminal proceedings. In actuality, "preventive detention" is now being employed in at least twenty-nine percent of all criminal cases nationally. In approximately half of these, the defendant is ultimately acquitted, but has already served the bulk of a sentence prior to trial as if a conviction had occurred. Predictably, the act has seen increasing application against political targets where public safety concerns are either shaky or absent altogether.

Filiberto Ojeda Ríos, a leader of the Puerto Rican independence organization Los Macheteros, was captured during a massive FBI sweep of the island in August 1985, ostensibly seeking those who had accomplished the 1983 expropriation of more than $7 million from a Wells Fargo vault in Connecticut. When armed agents stormed, unidentified and unannounced, into his home, Ojeda Ríos responded by shooting one of them. Although there was no claim that the Wells Fargo robbery had occurred for motives of personal profit—indeed, the government readily admitted the money went to underwrite political activities— Ojeda and several other *independentistas* were charged with RICO conspiracy. Ojeda was also charged with attempting to murder the FBI agent wounded during the assault on his home. Then, without making any showing that he represented a tangible threat to the well-being of the general public, prosecutors were able to have him placed in preventative detention pending trial.[16] There he remained, despite serious health problems, for nearly five *years*, until he was acquitted by a jury—on the basis of having acted in self-defense—in the attempted murder case.[17]

Laura Whitehorn, one of the Resistance Conspiracy defendants, was held in preventive detention for three years, beginning in May 1985, simply on the basis of having possessed two unregistered firearms and a set of false identity papers at the time of her arrest at her home by FBI agents. In May of 1988, she was also charged under the Seditious Conspiracy statute with having thought a number of politically impure thoughts. As was noted above, she was never charged with a specific "violent act" and, even if it were demonstrated she had actually performed the four bombings—all occurring in *empty* federal buildings— associated with her "conspiracy," the government never demonstrated exactly how that might have added up to a threat to the general public. In the event that she had been acquitted by a jury—a distinct possibility, had the charges ever gone to trial—she, like Ojeda, would have already served a rather hefty sentence for no reason whatsoever. As it was, she was arbitrarily blocked from engaging in the perfectly legal political organizing work which appears to have rendered her so "dangerous" (from the official perspective) in the first place.[18]

Joe Doherty is a member of the Irish Republican Army (IRA). In 1981, he was arrested in connection with the 1980 ambush of a British military patrol in which a soldier was killed. During his trial, he and seven other IRA members escaped from jail. Doherty was arrested in New York in mid-1983 and held for extradition to Northern Ireland. Upon review of his case, however, a federal judge determined that he fell under the political exemption clause of the U.S./British extradition treaty. If Doherty were to be deported, Judge John E. Sprizzo concluded, it would have to be to a non-British jurisdiction such as Ireland itself (alternatively, he might be eligible for political refugee status in the U.S.). This legal finding was unacceptable to the Reagan administration— an attitude subsequently maintained by the Bush administration—which arranged for the prisoner to be held while it appealed for an opinion requiring his deportation directly to *England.* The government lost this and three subsequent appeals before finally succeeding in February 1992.[19] The treatment accorded Joe Doherty should be compared to that extended to, say, former members of Somoza's national guard, wanted in Sandinista Nicaragua for crimes such as mass murder and torture.

The Demography of U.S. Prisons

A thread running through all the above cases—and many more prominent examples such as those of Adolfo Matos, Hanif Shabazz Bey, Alicia Rodríguez, Ojore Lutalo, Ida Luz Rodríguez, David Rice, Luis Rosa, Alejandrina Torres, Ruchell Cinque McGee, Edwin Cortéz, Assata

Shakur, Elizam Escobar, Sundiata Acoli, Haydeé Beltrán, Ed Poindexter, Carmen Valentín, Dylcia Pagán, Ricardo Jiménez, Richard Mufundi Lake, and Oscar Lòpez Rivera, who have not been discussed—is that they disproportionately involve people of color. Almost exclusively, the Euroamericans involved are in the position they're in because of their long histories of supporting the liberation struggles of non-whites. Again, a number of important examples such as Judy Clark, Bill Dunne, Larry Giddings, Kathy Boudin, David Gilbert and Ed Meade have gone unmentioned. The situation is entirely reflective of the composition of the overall population lodged in U.S. prisons today.

The rate of imprisonment in the U.S. has gone up markedly over the past decade. In 1983, the proportion of the population behind bars was under 200 per 100,000. By 1990, the rate was 263 per 100,000 and climbing. Nowhere else in the industrialized world is there a country with anything approaching this proportion of its population imprisoned. The next closest is Austria, with 114 per 100,000, followed by West Germany with 100.3. England stands at 87 per 100,000, while the Netherlands comes in at a mere 28. Even "totalitarian" Third World countries like Cuba and Libya are relative pikers by comparison: 228 and 131 per 100,000 respectively in 1988. One must look to U.S. client states in the Third World—Guatemala, El Salvador and South Korea, for instance—to find imprisonment rates comparable to those evidenced in the U.S. itself.[20] But it is apparent that the government here intends not to be outshown by such allies; hardly a newscast goes by but yet another police official is provided a media forum in which to bemoan the "facts" that he lacks the personnel, equipment, authority and—most of all—jail space to effectively wage the "war on crime" (now often referred to as "the war on drugs"). No less a personage than George Bush himself has answered the call, coming forward to proclaim it a "national objective" to meet the police agenda by *doubling* the number of prison beds available in the U.S. before the end of 1999.

Simple arithmetic suggests that, if this goal is achieved, at least 530 of every 100,000 citizens will be imprisoned by the turn of the century, a rate *four times* that of the next closest industrialized nation and far worse than the rates shown by even the most unsavory Third World dictatorships. It should be noted that these data apply *only* to prisons; they say nothing about the proportions of the population which is intended to be lodged in the country's proliferating local jail cells, subject to one or more of the various electronic incarceration technologies in which the government is presently investing considerable research and development funding, lodged within one or another of the burgeoning "privatized" sectors of the "prison industry" (e.g., "half-way houses," "diversion programs" and the like), or on probation. And even inclusion of these numbers would say nothing at all about those to be caught up in another institutional growth sector, "juvenile corrections" programming.[21] All things considered, a cumulative U.S. incarceration rate of 1,500 per 100,000 would not seem an unreasonable projection. Whatever the actual figure, residents of the United States—already the most imprisoned population on earth—can be expected to become *much* more so in the very near future.

Given both the realities of U.S. history and present trends, it may be expected that the great weight of all this will continue to fall on people of color, as it has in fact been falling for some time now. As of 1980, by the government's own statistics, African Americans comprised eleven percent of the overall U.S. population, while the black proportion of the aggregate U.S. prison population was forty-four percent, and rising. By 1990, the proportion was over fifty percent and still rising. At the present rate of black incarceration—which is *six times* the rate for whites—one in every four Afroamerican males will go to prison at least once during his life. Many will do time more than once. A black male in America is presently twice as likely to go to prison as he would be if he were living under outright apartheid in South Africa. If the present upward trend holds, as it has for sixty years ("only" twenty-three percent of the U.S. prison population was black in 1930), half of all African American males will go to prison by the end of the present decade. For American Indian men, the rate is already one in every 3.5, and also rising. Ladinos currently fill prison cells at a rate double their proportion of society as a whole, and their rate of incarceration too is increasing steadily.[22] The number and proportion of women of color in prison is also rising sharply, a matter explored in some depth in Nancy Kurshan's essay in this volume. As the Marc Mauer demonstrates, official statistics reveal that non-whites consistently receive sentences thirty percent more severe than Euroamericans upon conviction for identical offenses. People of color are at least twenty-five percent less likely than whites in similar circumstances to receive early parole. About fifty percent of all prisoners on death row are, as Jennie Vander Wall shows, people of color, although whites are convicted of some two-thirds of all capital crimes. The litany could be continued at length.

Why and How

The reasons for this are not nearly so mysterious as many people—federal policymakers in particular—wish to pretend. Such things correlate neatly with certain socio-economic circumstances within the U.S. today. American Indians, for example, remain (on paper, at least) the largest per capita landholders of any identifiable population group in North America. Their land contains approximately sixty percent of all known U.S. "domestic" uranium reserves, about a quarter of the low sulphur coal, up to twenty percent of the oil and natural gas, as well as substantial deposits of copper, zeolites and other valuable minerals. Indians also hold preeminent water rights in much of the arid west, considerable fishing rights and huge stands of prime timber and other renewable resources. By any conventional standard of measure, Native America should be the single wealthiest sector of the U.S. population. Instead it is the poorest, experiencing the lowest per capita income on the continent. Correspondingly, it suffers the highest incidence of malnutrition and deaths by plague disease and exposure, infant mortality and teen suicide, of any North American population group. The present life expectancy of a reservation-based Indian males is less than forty-seven years (almost thirty years less than whites); Indian females fare little better. The gulf between Native America's potential wealth and its practical poverty represents pure profit for the U.S. governmental/-corporate élite.[23]

By the same token, a black man living in Harlem or the South Bronx today experiences a poverty so intense that he would live longer were he to move to Bangladesh. His female counterpart will outlast him by less than five years. Ladinos living in U.S. inner cities or in the camps created for migrant farm workers do no better. As Manning Marable and others have compellingly demonstrated, the conditions impacting people of color in the U.S. have worsened dramatically since 1970. Such researchers have also shown the reason for this as being the deterioration of the U.S. position in the world economy over the past twenty years.[24] Increasingly, the status quo has maintained itself at home primarily at the expense of "internal colonies" of non-whites in precisely the same fashion it has maintained itself through neo-colonial exploitation of the Third World elsewhere. Needless to say, the domestic "natives" grow increasingly restless at the burdens placed upon them; the pattern, however, is one the U.S. élite has little alternative but to continue if it is to survive as a dominant world force.

The relationship between this internal imperial dynamic and the present/projected demography of U.S. prisons is thus quite plain. It has long been axiomatic that conditions of impoverishment imposed by the U.S. in the Third World *naturally* generates attempts by the victimized non-white populations to engage in such "criminal" activities as attempting to feed themselves or their families by "unapproved" means and with food they don't "own." Such behavior among the oppressed being understood as integral to any colonial system, it is anticipated and planned for. In the Third World, this has typically meant the installation and support of repressive regimes utilizing massive applications of capital and corporal punishment, imprisonment and indentured servitude as control devices.[25] Self-evidently, the infrastructure for precisely this same sort of social order has been developed and is now being rapidly expanded within the U.S. itself. It may be adduced from this that state planners expect things to get much worse in this country over the not-so-long run. For them, this is a predictable and acceptable cost of going forward with business as usual.

Matters, of course, can never—for obvious reasons—be framed in this manner by "responsible" political analysts, news commentators and other establishmentarian figures representing the interests of the North American status quo. To the contrary, the necessarily repressive sorts of social engineering required to maintain the kind of socio-economic order at issue must be—and therefore is—presented as its exact opposite: the government, all appearances to the contrary notwithstanding, is ultimately providing a beneficent service, "insuring the freedom" of the population by protecting it from itself, as it were. In regard to the Third World proper, this inversion of reality is typically packaged in the ludicrous proposition that outright fascists like Augusto Pinochét in Chile—or Robert D'Aubisson in El Salvador, or General Hector Alejandro Gramajo Morales in Guatemala—have been compelled to resort to "extraordinary methods" to avert the advent of "totalitarianism" represented by their victims' attempts to depose such U.S.-sponsored "leaders' " day-to-day tyranny. In effect, political opposition to even the worst oppression is, by definition, criminalized.[26]

Concerning matters within the U.S., things are usually cast in even more sublime forms. Assorted rationalizations have been field-tested over the past two decades and used as a cover over essentially the same procedures. Over the years, "political extremism" and "terrorism" have been carefully cultivated as specialized rhetorical components of more general appeals to the "need" for ever-increasing levels of "law and order."[27] The current and perhaps most effective mask developed for such purposes has been the proclamation—first by Ronald Reagan, and then by George Bush—of a "National Drug Crisis" requiring imposition of virtual martial law upon huge segments of the population, especially the African American and Ladino communities. Such measures are absolutely essential, proponents insist, to quell not only the "drug epidemic," but concomitant "gang violence" (often referred to as "narcoterrorism"), both of which have come to present dire threats to "the public well-being." The true implications of this official posture may be apprehended in the fact that the government, not "street criminals" and "drug cartels," has played the instrumental role in fostering the very importation and distribution of narcotics it now uses as a justification for rampant draconianism.[28] Nonetheless, it is behind the Orwellian facade of "Drug Wars" that an effectively limitless incarceration of otherwise targeted domestic groups is intended to occur.

Evidence of this trend can be found, not only in the planned rapid expansion of U.S. detention capacities to unprecedented levels, but in incipient legislation like the new Omnibus Crime Bill (S. 1241), known as the "Violent Crime Control Act of 1991." Passed by the Senate on July 7 (by a vote of 71 to 26), and by the House on October 22 (305 to 118), this "get tough" amalgamation of extraordinarily reactionary measures will "authorize the death penalty for about fifty federal crimes . . . limit appeals by condemned prisoners [effectively gutting rights to *habeas corpus* relief for everyone else as well]; relax rules on the use of illegally seized evidence [thus voiding another constitutional protection]; and authorize more money for [federal] state and local law enforcement." In the latter connection, even as a lingering recession undercuts the ability of both unemployed and working Americans to sustain themselves, and as ongoing record federal budget deficits "force" ever deeper cuts in spending for such things as education and social welfare programs, more than $345 million—*in addition to* the billions of tax dollars already lavished upon them—is appropriated by the bill to "reinforce and expand federal law enforcement initiatives" devoted to "combatting drug importation, sales and use."[29]

For instance, slightly over $100 million in additional funding is allocated to underwrite the activities of the Drug Enforcement Administration (DEA), an entity long considered to be one of the worst abusers of citizen rights in the U.S. Another $98 million supplement is allocated to the FBI, another prime violator of civil rights, to beef up its surveillance, infiltration and other "anti-drug efforts" *vis-à-vis* the population at large. The U.S. Marshals Service, Bureau of Alcohol, Tobacco and Firearms (BATF), and Immigration and Naturalization Service each receive smaller supplements—$10 million, $15 million and $20 million respectively—to "enhance" their "normal" activities with regard to "drug-related offenses." The Justice Department receives an additional $45 million to prosecute the anticipated upsurge in the number of citizens arrested, and federal courts are provided a supplement of $20 million to hire additional personnel to process the greatly increased volume of cases expected to result. Finally, in an after-thought provision tacked on at the very end, a meager $12 million is allocated to hire attorneys to defend citizens from the new $330 million police and judicial offensive directed against them. Such priorities speak, and loudly, to anyone who cares to listen.

Official concern that there may well be a substantial—and growing—number of people listening, and perhaps prepared at long last to act upon what they hear, is amply reflected in a number of explicitly political provisions of the Omnibus Crime Bill, each of them designed to "combat terrorism" (the present euphemism encompassing *any* sort of meaningful political opposition). For example, the FBI is allotted another $25 million supplement, this one to augment its ongoing and highly-secret "counter-terrorism" operation; yet *another* $25 million is provided so that the Bureau may accelerate its training and equipping of local police forces to participate in such activities. For its part, the BATF receives an additional $2.5 million with which to assist the FBI in tracking down those who might possess governmentally-proscribed weaponry that could afford them a fighting chance to defend themselves against the resulting SWAT capabilities of the country's "law enforcement establishment" (a measure banning civilians from possessing semi-automatic "assault" weapons and large-capacity magazines was narrowly—and probably tem-porarily—defeated). The death penalty is prescribed for a dozen categories of "terrorist activity," a whole new category of behavior dubbed "economic terrorism" is created (complete with an "Economic Terrorism Task Force"), and the prison sentences associated with a whole range of "terrorist offenses" are increased dramatically.

Political Prisoners, Political Prisons

This takes us back to the matter of political prisoners in the U.S. As should be apparent from the preceding, both the form and function of prisons within the present social context are extremely politicized. In this sense, virtually all prisoners might be accurately viewed as "politicals." A useful distinction may nonetheless be drawn. On the one hand there are multitudes who engage in often desperate acts intended simply to vent their legitimate rage at the sorry social status assigned them, or to better their deprived material position (however slightly and transiently). On the other hand, there is a far smaller group whose "criminal conduct" is motivated by a desire, and often guided by a theory, to transform the social order into something more positive for the oppressed, less profitable for the oppressor. The former might rightly be called "social prisoners." The latter are properly defined as political prisoners. The greatest fear of the élite is always that the latter will be able to galvanize the resentment and inchoate rebelliousness of the former into a coherent force for social change. They recognize clearly that the greater the degree of social oppression, the greater the potential for this to happen. Consequently, in times such as these, "politicals" are viewed as being far more dangerous than mere "criminals" and are therefore usually treated much more harshly.

Throughout the Third World, the means the U.S. has employed to cope with this problem has been the development of effective counter-insurgency programs, complete with specialized military/police units and prison facilities for political prisoners.[30] The same methods have become increasingly pronounced in the U.S. over the past quarter-century, beginning at least as early as the FBI's notorious COINTELPRO (Counterintelligence Programs) launched against the Communist Party, USA, in 1954, expanded to target the Puerto Rican independence movement and Socialist Workers Party from at least as early as 1960, expanded again to include operations against the black liberation movement and "new left" from 1965 onward, escalated against the American Indian Movement during the mid-70s, and continuing through the formation of the so-called "Joint Terrorist Task Force" (JTTF) interlock between the FBI and state/local police units by the end of the latter decade. Today, the JTTF apparatus has been largely perfected and exists on a fully national basis.[31] Its effects, which are focused exclusively upon curtailment of "political deviance," will be greatly amplified by implementation of the Omnibus Crime Bill.

In terms of prisons, the recent experiment within a "High Security Unit" (HSU) at the Lexington, Kentucky federal facility for women should prove instructive. There, Susan Rosenberg, Silvia Baraldini and *independentista* Alejandrina Torres were held for nearly three years in isolated sensory deprivation cells thirty feet below ground. As Rosenberg and Mary O'Melveny explain in their respective essays, the entire environment was painted white, with florescent lights shining twenty-four hours per day. The women, two of whom are lesbians, were routinely strip-searched by male guards. Even attorneys representing the women sometimes found it difficult to obtain permission to meet with them. In another article included in this volume, psychologist Richard Korn, retained by the ACLU to investigate what was happening at Lexington, concluded that the HSU was designed to "force ideological conversion" upon prisoners or, alternatively, "reduce them to psychological jelly" prone to killing themselves.[32] Cogent comparisons have, as Mike Ryan demonstrates in his contribution to the material which follows, can be drawn between the Lexington HSU and the "death wing" of the political prison at Stammheim, West Germany, where Andreas Bader, Ulrike Meinhoff and dozens of other members of the Red Army Faction have been murdered or committed suicide since 1977. Amnesty international (AI) protested that the Lexington model violated all minimum international standards for treatment of prisoners, and the federal government eventually closed it down.[33] But it did so only because it had completed construction of a much larger facility, comparable in to Lexington in many ways but intended to eventually accommodate "several hundred" women, within the federal men's prison at Marianna, Florida.

AI has entered similar protests concerning another U.S. replication of the Stammheim model, the aforementioned federal prison at Marion.[34] Prisoners in this facility have been "locked down"—isolated in their cells 22.5 hours a day—since 1983. Often, as Bill Dunne and others recount at length, they are strapped to concrete slabs, euphemistically called "bunks," for days on end. Beatings by guards are routine. Mail and reading material are strictly censored. Contact visits with relatives and friends are forbidden. No official will say with precision why a prisoner is sent to Marion; even less will authorities articulate what a prisoner must do to get out, once confined there. Tellingly, almost every "heavy" male political prisoner ushered into the federal system over the past decade—including two Silo Plowshares pacifists labeled as "terrorists" by the FBI—and a number from state prisons as well, have been placed in Marion for some length of time. Far from responding to the complaints of AI and other human rights organizations in this regard, the government has set out to build a second such facility in Colorado and to clone off "control units" based on the lessons learned at Marion for incorporation into other federal prisons. Simultaneously, the U.S. Bureau of Prisons is engaged in a thriving business giving tours and otherwise explaining to officials of various state prison systems "how the job gets done."[35]

The specter looms. All official denials to the contrary notwithstanding, the U.S. is not only holding a significant group of political prisoners—as the interviews, articles and personal statements offered by a number of them in this volume will readily attest—every indicator suggests it intends to increase the numbers of such prisoners markedly in coming years. The signs are also strong that this is so because the government's forecast for the short run future shows worsening socioeconomic conditions for people of color—and probably appreciable segments of the Euroamerican population as well—generating vastly increased numbers of social prisoners. This in turn is expected to produce a rapid sharpening of political struggle which will fill new facilities designed both for the politically conscious, and for those deemed most likely to become so. What is at hand is fascism of the *real* rather than metaphorical or "friendly" sort.[36] The state is preparing for what it perceives must lie ahead. For the most part, its opposition is not.

Cages of Steel is produced in the hope of making a useful contribution to changing this last circumstance. While it purports to being neither perfect nor definitive, the book *does* seek to extend what its editors and contributors believe is a range of incisive analysis on the topics of political prisons and prisoners in the United States (and, to a certain extent, of prisons and prisoners more generally) with the idea that provision of such information can help forge a broadbased, viable and *effective* popular resistance to the rapidly consolidating American police state, before it is truly too late to bring it to heel. In this, every participant—all of us, whether political prisoners and prisoners of war inside the walls, or allies and supporters on the outside—must begin by escalating the level of struggle against the malignant power of the U.S. state.

We say this without hesitancy or equivocation, sharing as we do the sentiments expressed by Frederick Douglass in 1858: "If there is no struggle, there is no progress. Those who profess to favor freedom and yet deprecate agitation are [those] who want crops without plowing up the ground. They want the ocean without the awful roar of its mighty waters. . . . The struggle may be a moral one, or it may be a physical one, and it may be both moral and physical, but it must be a struggle. Power concedes nothing without a demand. It never did, and it never will." The time in which it was possible to avoid shouldering responsibility in this regard has long since passed. To put the matter most simply and directly, if the realities of proliferating political police, political prisons and political prisoners don't become central preoccupations of a lot more people in the very near future, there's not going to be much of a future for anyone. The time for action is at hand.

Notes

1. Quoted from Jackie Lyden, "Marion Prison: Inside the Lockdown," *All Things Considered*, National Public Radio Broadcast, October 28, 1986.
2. For detailed information on the legal proceedings affecting Peltier, see Jim Messerschmidt, *The Trial of Leonard Peltier*. 3rd edition (Boston: South End Press, 1990). The Amnesty International report is entitled *Proposal for a commission of inquiry into the effects of domestic intelligence activities on criminal trials in the United States of America* (New York, 1980); it covers not only Peltier, but AIM member Dick Marshall and Black Panther leader Geronimo Pratt.
3. Evidence in Bin Wahad's case was so clumsily handled that its obviousness even came to "trouble" establishment apologists like Kenneth O'Reilly; see his treatment of the matter in *"Racial Matters": The FBI's Secret File on Black America, 1960-1972* (New York: The Free Press, 1989).
4. For prosecutoral admissions, albeit they weren't exactly intended as such, see Robert Tannenbaum and Philip Rosenberg, *Badge of the Assassin* (New York: E.P. Dutton Publishers, 1979).
5. For the most current information, see the briefing paper disseminated by the International Committee to Free Geronimo ji Jaga (Pratt) entitled "Ex-Black Panther Wants a New Trial" (Oakland, CA, March 1991).
6. See Ric Kahn, "Fed Excesses: Going too far to get the Ohio 7," *The Boston Phoenix*, July 8, 1988.

7. Concerning the assault on Finzel and federal handling of the charges against Dick Wilson, see Rex Weyler, *Blood of the Land: The U.S. Government and Corporate War Against the American Indian Movement* (New York: Everest House Publishers, 1982), pp. 172-73.

8. See Ward Churchill and Jim Vander Wall, *The COINTELPRO Papers: Documents from the FBI's Secret Wars Against Dissent in the United States* (Boston: South End Press, 1990), pp. 306-12.

9. These matters are detailed in "Defendants' Motion to Dismiss for Government Misconduct," *U.S. v. Whitehorn, et al.,* Crim. No. 88-145-05 (HHG), United States Court for the District of Columbia, January 3, 1989, p. 55. The government never attempted to rebut defense contentions on such matters.

10. Covered in *ibid.,* p. 56.

11. For the latest information on Baraldini's status, see the briefing paper disseminated by the Free Silvia Committee entitled "Free Silvia Baraldini!" (San Francisco, October 1991).

12. See Dennis Bailey, "Underground," *The Boston Globe Magazine,* March 26, 1989.

13. For analysis of the charges, see Anonymous, "Ohio 7 Minus 2: On Trial for Seditious Conspiracy," *The Insurgent,* September 1989.

14. "Three Cleared of Seditious Conspiracy," *New York Times,* November 28, 1989.

15. See Susie Day, "Resistance Conspiracy Trial," *Z Magazine,* September 1989.

16. A politically garbled, but nonetheless informationally useful study of the case and its context may be found in Ronald Fernandez, *Los Macheteros: The Wells Fargo Robbery and the Violent Struggle for Puerto Rican Independence* (New York: Prentice-Hall Press, 1987).

17. See "Filiberto is Free!" *La Patria Radical,* vol. 2, no. 2, September 1989.

18. See Susie Day, "Political Prisoners: Guilty Until Proven Innocent," *Sojourner,* February 1989.

19. The author has encountered little printed information on Doherty and/or his case. Perhaps the best available, or at least the most accessible, will be found in the biographical sketch included in *Can't Jail the Spirit.* 2nd Edition (Chicago: El Coqui Publishers, 1990).

20. Most of this data is taken from Douglas Spaulding, "End the Marion Lockdown: Why We Need to Build an Effective Prison Movement in this Country," *New Studies on the Left,* vol. XIV, nos. 1-2, Spring-Summer 1989. He is relying, in part, on *Sourcebook of Criminal Justice Statistics,* 1987 (U.S. Department of Justice, Bureau of Justice Statistics, Washington, D.C., 1988) and Margaret Calahan, *Historical Correction Statistics in the United States, 1850-1984* (Washington, DC: U.S. Department of Justice, Bureau of Justice Statistics, 1986).

21. See generally, James Austin and Aaron McVey, *The NCCD Prison Population Forecast: The Growing Imprisonment of America* (San Francisco: National Council on Crime and Delinquency, 1988).

22. See generally, Jim Murphy, *A Question of Race* (Albany, NY: Center for Justice Education, 1988).

23. Detailed assessments of each area of consideration will be found

in M. Annette Jaimes, (ed.), *The State of Native America: Genocide, Colonization and Resistance* (Boston: South End Press, 1992).

24. See, for example, Maning Marable, *Race, Reform and Rebellion: The Second Reconstruction in Black America, 1945-1982* (Jackson: University of Mississippi Press, 1984).

25. An excellent analysis of this structural reality in Central and South America, and U.S. involvement in creating it, will be found in A. J. Langguth, *Hidden Terrors: The Truth About U.S. Police Operations in Latin America* (New York: Pantheon Books, 1978). More broadly, see Edward Herman, *The Real Terror Network: Terrorism in Fact and Propaganda* (Boston: South End Press, 1982).

26. There are a number of good recent studies of this phenomenon. Perhaps the best for our purposes here is Noam Chomsky, *The Culture of Terrorism* (Boston: South End Press, 1990).

27. For a sound assessment of conditions at the outset of the use of such terms during the onset of the current police buildup, see Lyn Cooper, *et al., The Iron Fist in the Velvet Glove: An Analysis of U.S. Police* (Berkeley: Center for Research on Social Justice, 1975).

28. For analysis, see Alfred W. McCoy, with Cathleen B. Read and Leonard P. Adams II, *The Politics of Heroin in Southeast Asia* (New York: Harper Torchbooks, 1972), and Peter Dale Scott and Jonathan Marshall, *Cocaine Politics: Drugs, Armies, and the CIA in Central America* (Berkeley: University of California Press, 1991). Also see Alfred McCoy, *The Politics of Heroin: CIA Complicity in the Global Drug Trade* (Brooklyn, NY: Lawrence Hill Books, 1991).

29. Such rhetoric is standard fare during the consolidation of any codified structure of legalistic repression. See Otto Kircheimer, *Political Justice: The Use of Legal Procedure for Political Ends* (Princeton: Princeton University Press, 1969).

30. See Noam Chomsky and Edward S. Herman, *The Political Economy of Human Rights*, Vol. I: *The Washington Connection and Third World Fascism* (Boston: South End Press, 1979).

31. See *The COINTELPRO Papers, op. cit.*

32. The Lexington experiment has been linked to earlier government efforts in the same connection, best described by John Marks in his *The Search for the "Manchurian Candidate": The CIA and Mind Control* (New York: Norton Paperbacks, [revised edition] 1991). See William A. Reuben and Carlos Norman, "Brainwashing in America? The Women of Lexington Prison," *The Nation*, June 27, 1989.

33. The AI report is titled *The High Security Unit, Lexington Federal Prison, Kentucky* (AI Index: AMR 51/34/88).

34. The AI report is titled *Allegations of Inmate Treatment at Marion Prison, Illinois, USA* (AI Index: AMR 51/261/87).

35. This is building on an already very bad situation. See Lennox S. Hinds, *Illusions of Justice: Human Rights Violations in the United States* (Iowa City: Iowa School of Social Work, Iowa State University, 1978).

36. The term accrues from Bertram Gross, *Friendly Fascism: The New Face of Power in America* (Boston: South End Press, 1982).

Marc Mauer

Americans Behind Bars—
A Comparison of International
Rates of Incarceration

In 1979, a criminal justice report was released which has been often cited for its striking conclusions. That report, "International Rates of Imprisonment," issued by the National Council on Crime and Delinquency (NCCD), documented that the United States' rate of incarceration was third in the industrialized world—behind only South Africa and the Soviet Union.[1] Despite a considerable amount of attention to the report in the criminal justice community, there was little policy-maker response to its findings.

This report provides a new look at some of the issues raised in the NCCD report. We do this for two reasons. First, the NCCD report, useful as it was, was hampered by the unavailability of complete data in some areas. Most significantly, the prison population for the Soviet Union was estimated to be one million at the time, by all measures just a rough approximation. Due to the greater openness in the Soviet Union, we now have far more accurate figures on the number of its prisoners. In this report, we also extend the analysis of the number of prisoners in South Africa beyond what most sources have generally described. The second reason for this updated analysis of international rates of incarceration is that much has changed in the world since 1981. Of particular interest here is that the criminal justice policies of these three nations have taken very different directions, with significant consequences for rates of imprisonment.

After examining overall rates of incarceration, we then look at a subset of the population in the United States and South Africa—black males. As we noted in our earlier report, "Young Black Men and the Criminal Justice System: A Growing National Problem," nearly one in four African American men in the age group 20-29 is under the control of the criminal justice system—in prison or jail, on probation or parole.[2] In order to understand the situation of black males more fully, we developed this international comparison to provide another context for examining this issue. As will be seen, the results in both parts of this report indicate the serious nature of criminal justice problems in the United States.

Major Findings: Rates of Incarceration

Comparing international rates of incarceration is problematic. Crime rates, and rates of violent crime in particular, vary greatly from one country to another. Criminal justice systems are also unique to each country, and methods of punishment and control vary from one society to another. In most areas of the United States, for instance, we maintain a system of jails, for persons awaiting trial and serving short sentences, and a prison system which is generally used for offenders serving sentences of a year or more. In most other nations, there is only a single prison system, both for convicted and unconvicted persons. Most societies make use of mental institutions to some extent for persons convicted of crimes, although these persons may or may not be counted as "prisoners" in official prison counts. And, in apartheid South Africa, restrictions on civil liberties and personal freedom for the country's black population are ever present, whether in prison or not.

Bearing this caution in mind, though, we think it useful to analyze these international data. Although the crime rates and criminal justice policies creating each country's prison population are different, the comparison can help to place in perspective our nation's approach to issues of crime and punishment. While the three nations under study have vastly different political and economic systems, this report demonstrates that the extent of criminal justice control in a society cannot necessarily be predicted by the degree to which that society is dedicated to democracy and human rights. Our analysis examines the number of incarcerated adults in each country, both those awaiting trial and sentenced offenders, and then divides this figure by the country's population to obtain an overall rate of incarceration. For the United States, we have used the combined figures for prison and jail populations to obtain an overall number of inmates. The number of prisoners in the Soviet Union is taken from recent published reports, which are consistent with other observations over the past several years.[3]

Previous reports documenting the number of prisoners in South Africa have been consistent, but have only included the number of persons held in South Africa proper.[4] This figure excludes the number of prisoners held in the four "independent" homelands of South Africa—Bophuthatswana, Ciskei, Transkei, and Venda. These homelands, though, are recognized by no nation outside South Africa, and have been

TABLE 1

INTERNATIONAL RATES OF INCARCERATION

Nation	Population	Inmate Population	Rate of Incarceration per 100,000
UNITED STATES	248,251,000	1,057,875	426
SOUTH AFRICA	35,978,284	119,682	333
SOVIET UNION	287,015,000	769,000	268

TABLE 2

BLACK MALE RATES OF INCARCERATION

Nation	Black Male Population	Black Male Inmates	Rate of Incarceration per 100,000
UNITED STATES	14,625,000	454,724	3,109
SOUTH AFRICA	15,050,642	109,739	729

TABLE 3

<u>**Incarceration rates for the United States, South Africa, and the Soviet Union in comparison to Europe and Asia**</u>

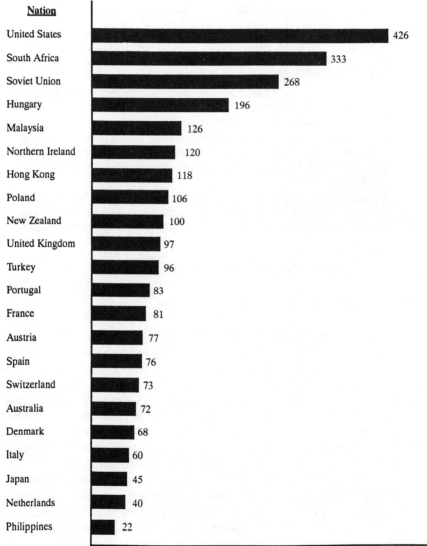

<u>Rates of Incarceration per 100,000 Population</u>

Source: Penal Reform International, using data from the Council of Europe and the Australian Institute of Criminology.

clearly shown to be appendages of the South African government. Therefore, an accurate portrayal of the incarcerated population in South Africa
needs to include this population. Although information on prison systems
in the homelands is difficult to obtain, we have used the available
information to project an estimate of these figures. The major findings
of our study, as seen in Tables 1 − 3, are as follows:

> The United States now has the world's highest known rate of in-
> carceration, with 426 prisoners per 100,000 population. South Africa
> is second in the world with a rate of 333 per 100,000, and the Soviet
> Union third with 268 per 100,000 population. (see Table 1).

> Black males in the United States are incarcerated at a rate four
> times that of black males in South Africa, 3,109 per 100,000,
> compared to 729 per 100,000. (see Table 2).

> The total cost of incarcerating the more than one million Americans
> in prisons and jails is now $16 billion a year. The cost of
> incarcerating the estimated 454,724 black male inmates is almost
> $7 billion a year.[5]

> Although this study only examines three countries in detail, it
> is clear from other reports that no other nation for which
> incarceration rates are known even approaches these levels. Rates
> of incarceration for western Europe are generally in the range
> of 35-120 per 100,000, and for most countries in Asia, in the range
> of 21-140 per 100,000.[6] (see Table 3).

Causes and Consequences

Again recognizing that international comparisons are difficult, we
can discern general trends of the past decade in these three nations
which have placed the United States in the unenviable position of world
leadership in incarceration. The South African prison population has
remained the most stable of these three countries over the past decade,
rising only about eleven percent during this period, from an average
daily population of 100,677 in 1979-80 to 111,557 in 1988-89 (excluding
the four homelands).[7] We do not have sufficient information available
to determine the causes of this relatively modest increase.

In the Soviet Union, the prison population has declined dramatically
during the past decade. Estimates of the prison population ten years
ago range from one million in the NCCD report to 1.6 million.[8] The
drop in the incarcerated population is generally considered to be a result
of the changing political climate in the Soviet Union, leading to the
release of many political prisoners, and amnesties for many minor
offenders.[9] (Similar trends have been examined in other parts of Eastern
Europe, with one report describing a fifty percent decline in Poland's

prison population in three years.)[10] In sharp contrast, the incarcerated population in the United States has more than doubled in the past decade, rising from just over 500,000 in 1980 to more than one million today. On top of this dramatic increase, the rate of increase for African-American males has been even greater than for the population as a whole. Why has the incarcerated population of the United States risen so dramatically, such that it is now the highest in the world? Following, we explore two possible causes—crime rates and criminal justice policies.

International comparisons of crime rates are problematic due to variations in reporting methods and the definition of offenses. Nevertheless, it is clear that in comparison to western Europe, for example, American rates of crime for many offenses are substantially higher. American murder rates are at least seven times as high as for most European countries. There are six times as many robberies and three times as many rapes as in West Germany (prior to reunification).[11] Alfred Blumenstein has demonstrated that much of the disparity in international incarceration rates may be explained by higher crime rates for serious offenses.[12] While a full analysis of this relationship is beyond the scope of this study, it appears that at least some of the disparity in incarceration among nations can be explained by crime rates, particularly for assaultive offenses likely to lead to imprisonment. If this is the case, then its implications are extremely disturbing, for it implies that the wealthiest society in the world has failed to provide a relatively safe society; instead, it has an appallingly high level of crime.

While there is little question that the United States has a high rate of crime, there is much evidence that the increase in the number of people behind bars in recent years is a consequence of harsher criminal justice policies of the past decade, rather than a direct consequence of rising crime. Many criminal justice observers now believe that prison populations are very much a function of policy choices. Looking at the Soviet Union, for example, we have seen how a decision by a reform government to release many political prisoners has resulted in virtually halving the incarcerated population. Although few American prisoners could be considered "political," thousands are in prison due to policy choices— as a result of mandatory minimum sentences, restrictive parole policies, sentencing guidelines, and other policies. While we could debate the wisdom of these policies, the point is that, to a certain extent, the size of the prison population is a reflection of conscious political choices.

The growth of prison populations in the past decade, for example, shows that incarceration rates do not rise or fall directly with crime rates. Although the crime rate has dropped by 3.5 percent since 1980, the prison population has doubled in that period. Breaking down these figures further, we see first that crime dropped by fifteen percent from

1980 to 1984, while the number of prisoners increased by forty-one percent; then, from 1984-89 crime rates climbed by 14 percent, while the number of prisoners rose by fifty-two percent.[13] Any cause and effect relationship is difficult to discern. During this same period, we have seen a number of criminal justice policy changes which have resulted in a more punitive system overall. Mandatory sentencing laws requiring incarceration for certain offenses are now in place in forty-six states. At the federal level, the combined impact of the new sentencing guidelines and harsher drug laws is expected to result in a 119 percent increase in the federal prison population from 1987 to 1997.[14]

There is also a greater proportion of offenders being sentenced to prison than ten years ago. In 1980, there were 196 offenders sentenced to prison for every 1,000 arrests for serious crimes. That figure increased by fifty-four percent to 301 per 1,000 by 1987.[15] In this report, we do not attempt to analyze the relative weight that should be given to crime rates or criminal justice policies in causing such a high rate of incarceration. Other researchers have conducted analyses of these issues, and further work needs to be done. It is our assumption here that both factors play a role: that the United States does have a substantially higher rate of serious crime than many nations, and that criminal justice policies have contributed to the increase in incarceration in the past decade.

African-American Males, an Endangered Species?

The equally shocking conclusion of this report is that African-American males in the U.S. are locked up at a rate four times greater than their counterparts in South Africa. We and others have attempted to analyze the reasons why Afroamerican males have higher rates of crime for certain offenses, and why there are a vastly disproportionate number of black males behind bars. The reasons are complex, but include factors relating to the root causes of crime as well as the response of the criminal justice system. African-American males, who are disproportionately low-income, face a variety of problems, including: the social and economic decline of our inner cities and diminished opportunities for young people; the continuing failure of our schools, health care systems, and other institutional supports to prepare young African American males to occupy legitimate roles in society; continuing poverty and a distribution of wealth which has resulted in even greater disparity between the rich and the poor over the past twenty years.

The comparison with South Africa should not be misconstrued to indicate support for the South African apartheid system or its criminal justice policies, or to imply that the criminal justice system in the United States should emulate the South African system. Despite changes in the South African political climate in recent years, the system of apartheid remains strong and freedom remains an elusive goal for the black population. We make the comparison with South Africa only to provide a point of reference for the cumulative effect of American policies regarding black males.

Particular note needs to be made regarding the "war on drugs," probably the largest single factor behind the rise in prison populations during the past decade. While drug arrests and prosecutions have increased each year since 1980, the number of African-Americans arrested for drug offenses has increased at an even more rapid rate than has the arrest rate for the population as a whole. From 1984 to 1988, the Afroamerican community's percentage of all drug arrests nationally increased from thirty percent to thirty-eight percent.[16] In Michigan, drug arrests overall have doubled since 1985, while drug arrests of blacks have tripled.[17] With a "war on drugs" primarily waged through the criminal justice system and disproportionately targeting inner-city drug users, the end result is an increasing number of prisoners and an ever larger share of black inmates.

Implications for Public Policy

Ten years ago, state and national policymakers were faced with two major circumstances. First, with a combined prison and jail population of 500,000, the United States stood third in the world in its rate of incarceration, behind two highly repressive governments. The country had already experienced a significant increase in its incarcerated population since 1973, with the number of prisoners rising by well over fifty percent from 1973 to 1980. Promising alternatives to incarceration—programs of community corrections, restitution to victims, community service, victim-offender mediation programs and many others—had been developed and were being implemented in many states. Further, there was little optimism in the corrections community that the high rate of recidivism of released prisoners would substantially diminish. Second, communities were in a state of decline, particularly our urban areas. The steady decline of our manufacturing base had eliminated many relatively stable and high wage employment opportunities, replaced in many cases by low wage service jobs. Schools in many urban areas experienced dropout rates of forty percent of more, waiting lists for low-income housing were years long, and over thirty million Americans were without health insurance.

The choice for policymakers in responding to our high national crime rate, therefore, was very stark. The first option was to continue to build new prisons and jails at a cost of $50,000 a cell or more, and to spend $20,000 a year to house each prisoner. The second option was to spend these same tax dollars on prevention policies and services—programs designed to generate employment and to provide quality education, health care, and housing, along with alternatives to incarceration rather than new prison cells. The choice was not described as clearly as this, of course, but those were essentially the two options faced by policymakers. Overwhelmingly, the punitive policies of the first option were the ones selected at both a national and local level. In the area of criminal justice, one would be hard pressed to determine whether Democrats or Republicans were more zealous in their pursuit of repressive criminal justice measures. The conservative Republican governor of California and the liberal Democratic governor of New York both proudly boasted of their accomplishments in adding tens of thousands of new prison cells to their state systems.

Unfortunately, the decision-making process in criminal justice is particularly prone to the influence of political rhetoric. It is no accident that, for several sessions now, a major crime bill has been adopted by Congress every two years prior to the November election. As the "Willie Horton" issue showed too well in the last presidential campaign, public policy on issues of crime and justice is far too often driven by the atypical, sensational "crime of the month," rather than by a rational examination of options. Had the punitive policies of the past decade resulted in dramatically reduced crime rates, one could argue that their great expense was partially justified by the results. But as the 1990s begin, we are faced with the same problems as in 1980, only greater in degree—overcrowded prisons, high rates of crime, a major national drug problem, and the public lack of confidence in the criminal justice system. In many respects, it is not surprising that harsher criminal justice policies have had little impact on crime. Criminologists have long contended that if the criminal justice system can have an effect on crime, it is much more likely to result from increasing the certainty of arrest, and not the severity of punishment.

If we continue to pursue the policies of the 1980s in the 1990s, we can expect that black males may truly become the "endangered species" that many have predicted. No segment of society, however, remains free from the cost of the punitive policies of the 1980s. The nation's record rate of incarceration continues to increase at an unprecedented scale. The National Council on Crime and Delinquency projects that our prison population alone, exclusive of jail inmates, will rise by sixty-eight percent from 703,000 in 1989 to 1,133,000 in 1994.[18] We now have the opportunity, and the obligation, to review our policy options in regard to crime and punishment, and to examine carefully the impact of the lessons of the past decade. In the section following, we suggest a new direction for responding to crime and achieving justice.

Recommendations for Public Policy

I. Establish a national commission to examine the high rate of incarceration of Americans, and African-American males in particular: Congress should establish a national commission on crime, composed of a broad spectrum of representatives, to conduct a comprehensive examination of crime rates and incarceration rates. The commission should be directed to develop a set of recommendations to reduce the rates of crime and incarceration. Those recommendations should include programs and policies within the criminal justice system, as well as preventive measures for the family, community, and workplace.

II. General Accounting Office study of the social and economic factors related to crime: Crime has many causes, some individually-based, others related to social and economic conditions and opportunities. The General Accounting Office should review research in this area to determine the relative influence of a range of social and economic factors on crime. These factors should include unemployment, welfare benefits, school dropout rates, pre-school programs, and access to health care and housing. A greater understanding of the root causes of crime will provide policymakers and the public with information that can guide budget and program priority decisions.

III. Justice Department funding of pilot programs to reduce the high rate of incarceration of African-American males: While criminal justice agencies are relatively limited in the impact they have on crime, they can develop and implement policies to alter the number of offenders and type of control under which they are placed. The Justice Department should encourage the development of programs and sanctions designed specifically to reduce the disproportionate incarceration rate of African-American males. In the area of juvenile justice, the Department is currently providing funding for "programs designed to reduce the proportion of juveniles detained or confined . . . who are members of ethnic and minority groups where such proportions exceeds the proportion such groups represent in the general population."[19] Programs for African-American males could include diversion from prosecution, intensive probation, alternative sentencing, and parole release planning, among others. Priority should be placed on programs which have the potential to be replicated in other jurisdictions.

IV. Redirect the "war on drugs" to define drug abuse as a public health problem and not a criminal justice problem: In the past decade, drug abuse has taken a great toll in human lives and potential among all sectors of our society. The direction of the "war on drugs," though, has served to increase dramatically the number of Americans in prison and, in particular, the number of non-white, low-income males. There is little evidence to show that the law enforcement approach to the drug problem has had a substantial impact on drug abuse or drug related crime. While waiting lists for treatment programs remain at six months or more in many communities, the number of drug arrests and prosecutions continues to rise as seventy percent of federal anti-drug funding is directed toward law enforcement. Defining drug abuse as a public health problem would require a shift in funding and program priorities to a system focused on education, prevention, and treatment rather than incarceration.

V. Redirect the focus of law enforcement to address community needs and to prevent crime: Police forces are inherently limited in their ability to control crime since they can generally only respond to crime once it has occurred. Of thirty-four million serious crimes committed each year, thirty-one million never result in arrest.[20] Even if we assume that a good number of offenders had committed multiple crimes which were not detected, we can still recognize the limited impact that law enforcement can have. Efforts are being made in some police departments to refocus law enforcement priorities. In New York, St. Louis, and other cities, community-oriented policing is being implemented. This approach emphasizes improving police-community relations and a pro-active approach to policing in order to address problems before they escalate and to be able to respond to crime more effectively. The police chief in New Haven, Connecticut, has adopted a policy of discontinuing mass drug arrests and now uses his officers to go door-to-door in certain communities to encourage drug abusers to enter city-sponsored treatment programs.

VI. Reduce the recidivism rate of prisoners by providing effective services: The most recent Justice Department study of recidivism shows that sixty-two percent of state prisoners are re-arrested within three years of release from prison. With prisons seriously overcrowded and state budgets constrained across the country, inmates in most prison systems have fewer opportunities to gain an education or marketable skills than they did a decade ago. Further, more than half of all prisoners with a drug history are not enrolled in drug treatment programs.[21] For those offenders who are sentenced to prison, it is in society's interest to attempt to reduce recidivism by providing a broad range of counseling, educational, and vocational services appropriate to prisoners' needs.

VII. Repeal mandatory sentencing laws: Mandatory sentencing laws for drug crimes and other offenses have exacerbated prison overcrowding, while denying the possibility of judicial discretion in appropriate cases. In Michigan, for example, a fifty-year old grandmother with no criminal record is serving life without parole—the same penalty as for first degree murder—for the offense of possession of more than 650 grams of cocaine. In the federal system, mandatory sentences thwart the purposes of a sentencing guidelines system designed to introduce a rational basis for sentencing. In calling for the repeal of mandatory sentences, the Federal Courts Study Committee charged that they "create penalties so distorted as to hamper federal criminal adjudication."[22] In jurisdictions without mandatory sentencing, judges are not hindered from sentencing drug offenders to incarceration when they feel it appropriate, but can also use their discretion to sentence offenders to nonincarcerative sanctions. Mandatory sentences should be repealed because they do not permit judges to exercise that discretion in the interest of justice.

VIII. Expand the use of alternatives to incarceration: Incarceration is the most expensive sanction in the criminal justice system and brings very limited results in terms of public safety or rehabilitation of offenders. A range of alternatives to incarceration now exist which have the potential to reduce the number of offenders sentenced to prison. A study by the RAND Corporation examined the eligibility criteria of alternative sentencing, or intermediate sanctions, programs and then made projections on the number of "prison-bound" offenders who could qualify for such programs. Even if those offenders convicted of murder or rape, or with a prior prison term were excluded, thirty-three percent of potential inmates still qualified for the alternative programs.[23] Diverting appropriate offenders from the prison system can result in substantial cost savings as well. A study in Delaware calculated the following annual costs of various sanctions:

Prison	$17,761
Work Release	11,556
House Arrest	3,332
Intensive Supervision	2,292
Regular Probation	569

The study also found that for every drug offender sentenced to prison, three offenders could be treated in an inpatient treatment program and sixteen in an outpatient program.[24]

IX. Engage in a national dialogue on issues of crime and punishment: For more than two decades, inspired by politicized rhetoric, our national response to crime has been to demand harsher and harsher punishment, and to equate punishment with incarceration. This approach has taken a great toll in human lives, at a huge cost to taxpayers. In spite of the record number of prisoners resulting from these policies, we are still left with high rates of crime and an epidemic of drug abuse.

The American public is more open to engaging in a broad discussion of crime and punishment issues than is commonly believed by policy-makers.[25] Day-to-day experience with alternative sentencing programs and comprehensive public opinion surveys demonstrate that Americans understand and support more frequent use of non-incarcerating sanctions and programs that address rehabilitation and the causes of crime.[26] It is time now for America's civic, business and political leaders to invite the American people to engage in a rational and constructive discussion of crime, punishment, and justice issues.

Conclusion

> "If you can't do the time, don't do the crime."
> —*Prisoner saying*

More and more Americans, and African-American males in particular, are "doing the time." Unfortunately, this hasn't led them or others to stop "doing the crime." Incarceration rates set new records each day, while crime rates remain intolerably high. Clearly, large-scale imprisonment provides no panacea for crime. As we have discussed, two possible areas of explanation for our high rate of incarceration are crime rates and criminal justice policies. It is important to determine the relative influence of these factors in contributing to an incarcerated population of more than a million Americans, and to develop programs and policies which can offer constructive solutions. This report suggests that we need to engage in a public dialogue regarding the factors which have led the United States to be a world leader in incarceration. This dialogue needs to be very inclusive, ranging from criminal justice officials to prisoners, from members of Congress to neighborhood organizations. If we value the human potential of all members of our society, and if we truly wish to reduce crime, we will need to consider seriously whether we can afford to continue our current ineffective social and criminal justice policies.

Notes

1. Eugene Doleschal and Anne Newton, "International Rates of Imprisonment," (Washington, D.C.: National Council on Crime and Delinquency, Information Center, 1979).

2. Marc Mauer, "Young Black Men and the Criminal Justice System: A Growing National Problem," (WWashington, D.C.: The Sentencing Project, February 1990). This includes the total number of inmates in the nation's prisons as of December 31, 1989, and jails as of June 30, 1989, excluding 2,250 juveniles being held in jails. A small percentage of prisoners under the jurisdiction of state prison systems are held in local jails. Estimates of this number vary in publications of the Bureau of Justice Statistics, due to variations in reporting methods. For this report, we have subtracted 39,115 inmates from the total combined prison and jail population (3.6 percent of all inmates) to account for this overlap. (See "Jail Inmates 1989," Bureau of Justice Statistics, June 1990.) Since this is the higher of the two figures reported for this category, this provides a conservative estimate of the overall number of incarcerated persons. To determine the number of incarcerated black males, we have used the figure of forty-three percent of the jail population ("Jail Inmates 1989"), as well as the most recent estimate of forty-three percent of the prison population (*Correctional Populations in the United States*, 1987, Bureau of Justice Statistics, December 1989). From this total also, we have deducted the number of juveniles as well as the 3.6 percent overlap between jail and prison inmates.

3. Many studies of international rates of incarceration look at sentenced prisoners only, and not those inmates awaiting trial or incarcerated in a local jail. We include both jail and prison inmates in this study because we have no breakdown on the pretrial *vs.* sentenced population in the Soviet Union. The most recent published figure of 769,000 prisoners is taken from *Newsweek*, (Fred Coleman, "Reforming a University of Soviet Crime," September 10, 1990). This figure is consistent with reports documenting the decreasing number of inmates in recent years. (See, for example, the estimate of 800,000 prisoners in 1989 in Peterson.) It is somewhat unclear whether these figures include incarcerated juveniles, and whether there are political prisoners who are still incarcerated under the jurisdiction of a separate agency.

4. See, for example, *Compendium of Social Statistics and Indicators 1988*, (New York: United Nations, 1991), and Doleschal and Newton, *op. cit.* Population figures for South Africa are inconsistent, particularly regarding the nonwhite population. For both South Africa and the homelands, we have relied on estimates made by the Institute of Race Relations, generally considered to be among the most objective organizations in South Africa. These figures are lower than some other estimates. At the high end, for example, is a CIA estimate of a total population of 39,549,941. Using this figure, the overall rate of incarceration in South Africa would be 303 per 100,000, compared to the estimate of 333 per 100,000 we have calculated in the report. The black male rate would be 669 per 100,000, compared to the report's figure of 729. The number of prisoners, along with a breakdown

36 • Marc Mauer

by race and sex, is taken from the annual report of the South African Prisons Service, with figures as of June 1989. The South African categories of blacks and "coloreds" are combined as black for our analysis. To estimate the additional number of prisoners in the four homelands, we begin with a report of the Institute of Race Relations documenting that there were 2,677 prisoners in Bophuthatswana in 1987. Since we were not able to obtain any other incarceration statistics for the homelands, we have used the incarceration rate for Bophuthatswana to project an estimated prison population for the other three homelands. Although there are a very small number of whites living in the homelands, we have assumed for these purposes that all prisoners, as well as the overall population in the homelands, are black. We have also assumed that the percentage of the black prison population in South Africa that is male—96.1 percent—is the same for the homelands. Due to the need to estimate prison populations in the homelands, we have also calculated the black male rate of incarceration excluding the homelands. That figure, 851 per 100,000, is higher than the figure used in the report, but does not change the overall rankings or analysis.

5. Overall costs of incarceration are taken from "Justice Expenditure and Employment, 1988," Bureau of Justice Statistics, July 1990. To calculate the cost of black male incarceration, we have used 43 percent of the total figure, representing the black male proportion of the overall institutional population.

6. See *Newsletter of Penal Reform International*, no. 1, February 1990 and no. 2, April 1990, London. It is possible, of course, that rates of incarceration in some Third World countries may be higher, but there are few published reports discussing this. One source examines 1974 incarceration rates for 48 countries, including many in Asia, Africa, and South America, and finds all well below the rate for the United States. See Calvert R. Dodge, *A World Without Prisons* (Lexington, MA: Lexington Books, 1979, p. 258).

7. Here, we use the *average daily population* in South Africa because of the availability of data, while we have used a *single day count* in calculating the rate of incarceration, in order to be consistent with the method used for the United States and the Soviet Union. We also exclude the four homelands in this section because we have no data available to measure the fluctuation of the prison population there over time.

8. D. J. Peterson, "The Zone, 1989: The Soviet Penal System under Perestroika," in *Report on the USSR*, vol. 1, no. 37, 1989.

9. Recent reports suggest that crime rates are increasing in the Soviet Union, although it is too soon to know whether this will have an impact on the prison population. See, for example, Celestine Bohlen, "Some Soviet Items Aren't Scarce: Crime, Strikes, Fighting, Pollution," *New York Times*, August 18, 1990.

10. Tom Wicker, "An Ungrand Total," *New York Times*, October 13, 1989.

11. Elliott Currie, *Confronting Crime* (New York: Random House, 1985), p. 5.

12. Alfred Blumstein, "Prison Populations: A System Out of Control?," in *Crime and Justice: A Review of Research*, edited by Michael Tonry and

Noval Morris, vol. 10 (Chicago: Chicago: University of Chicago Press, 1988). See also "Imprisonment in Four Countries," Bureau of Justice Statistics, February 1987, for a similar analysis.

13. Federal Bureau of Investigation, *Crime in the United States, Uniform Crime Reports 1989*, August 1990, and Bureau of Justice Statistics, "Prisoners in 1989," May 1990.

14. The United States Sentencing Commission, *Supplementary Report on the Initial Sentencing Guidelines and Policy Statements*, June 18, 1987, p. 71.

15. Sarah Glazer, "Crime and Punishment: A Tenuous Link," *Editorial Research Reports*, October 20, 1989.

16. Sam Meddis, "Drug arrest rate is higher for blacks," *USA Today*, December 20, 1989.

17. E. J. Mitchell, II, "Cops burst in, you feel violated." *Detroit News*, April 26, 1990.

18. James Austin and Aaron David McVey, "The Impact of the War on Drugs," (San Francisco: National Council on Crime and Delinquency, December 1989).

19. *Federal Register*, vol. 55, no. 229, pp. 49484-49485.

20. Criminal Justice Section, American Bar Association, *Criminal Justice in Crisis*, November 1988, p. 4.

21. Marcia R. Chaiken, "Prison Programs for Drug-involved Offenders," National Institute of Justice, October 1989.

22. Federal Courts Study Committee, *Report of the Federal Courts Study Committee*, April 2, 1990, p. 134.

23. Joan Petersilia and Susan Turner, "Reducing Prison Admissions: The Potential of Intermediate Sanctions," *State Government*, March-April 1989.

24. Kay Pranis, "Options in Criminal Corrections: A Study of Costs and Opportunities in Delaware," Minnesota Citizens Council on Crime and Justice, 1989.

25. Stephen D. Gottfredson and Ralph B. Taylor, "Public Policy and Prison Populations: Measuring Opinions About Reform," *Judicature*, vol. 68, nos. 4-5 (October-November 1984).

26. John Dobel and Josh Klein, *Punishing Criminals: The Public's View* (Public Agenda Foundation, 1989).

Bill Dunne

The U.S. Prison at Marion, Illinois:
An Instrument of Oppression

Part I: Plot and Perpetration of the Lockdown at Marion

"In 1978, the BoP [Bureau of Prisons] began to implement a new, higher security classification system . . . In 1979, USP [United States Penitentiary] Marion became the Bureau's only 'level six' penitentiary. Marion's new purpose was to provide long-term segregation within a highly controlled setting . . . The decision [was] to establish USP Marion as a level six penitentiary and to convert the prison from an institution with only one Control Unit, with other [prisoners] congregating and moving in large groups, to a 'close, tightly-controlled, unitized' institution for all [prisoners]. . . ."[1] Thus is assassinated the main premise of BoP public disinformation that the rendering of all of Marion into a control unit in the wake of the killings of October, 1983, was the unplanned and unintentional response to an emergency. Similarly fall other BoP justifications for the perpetual lockdown of the prison such as that it is "humane incapacitation," improves safety and security in the system as a whole, and allows other prisons to be operated more safely.

The beginning of the implementation of this "new, higher security" prison only five years after the opening of the original control unit indicates official dissatisfaction with the scope of the former maximum restrictions and an intent to go beyond them. The original plan, allegedly aimed at modifying the behavior of the miscreants into more socially acceptable forms or at least into something that would make them more tractable captives, had itself been modified. A more destructive brainwashing approach and a changing perception on the part of the prison system's operators of the needs of the class they serve drove the changes. The goal had become more to learn how to control and manipulate than to effect positive change. The cost to the community or the experimental subjects was immaterial.

The falsity of administrative propaganda in light of that goal is revealed in its rhetoric. The "long term segregation" of this "new, higher security" implies exactly what the first control unit was and remains and the rest of Marion has become from the open institution it was in 1979: intentional, permanent lockdown, not emergency response. This "new" purpose for Marion was decreed despite the existence in all other prisons of extensive segregation facilities where prisoners can be kept indefinitely, indicating intent beyond mere incapacitation. Isolation facilitates the secrecy conducive to an experimental program and its ulterior motives. And the decision to convert Marion to a "tightly-controlled, unitized" prison was nothing more than a thin rhetorical disguise for a plan to make it a prison composed completely of isolation units. Dungeon Marion was deliberate. Former BoP Director Norman Carlson has said that he has long wanted several such institutions.[2]

A prison composed completely of control units is exactly what Marion has become: from what it was in 1978 to what it is now precisely mirrors the intent expressed above. The BoP, however, did not impose this condition all at once, probably with an eye toward just the sort of deniability and obfuscation in which it has been engaged. It brought about the result by creating a steep slope several years long and greasing it with public relations ploys. What it blames on the depravity and depredations of prisoners was more the product of increasingly more repressive conditions administratively imposed on prisoners and the mischaracterization of their reaction to the conditions.

These impositions were both movements toward the stated (but publicly denied and distorted) BoP objective of a control unit prison and efforts to instigate actions that would justify more such movements. Former Marion Warden Harold Miller himself admitted that conditions at Marion had deteriorated in the months after his arrival, hardly a circumstance of which he was not in control. In testimony before the U.S. House of Representatives, Professor David Fogel, Director of Graduate Studies of the Department of Criminal Justice of the University of Illinois, characterized that deterioration as "not an abnormal outcome" of policies then in effect, making the prison more and more restrictive and a tougher place to be.[3] Each calculated step toward the administrative end, such as the elimination of prisoner work, intensified pressures on both prisoners and guards and accelerated the descent into lockdown.

Each step escalated the pressure, particularly on prisoners. The deliberate nature was revealed by its continual increase despite its visibility and inconsistency with any rational BoP mission. Prisoners had to exist within the prison, not just spend forty hours a week in it. They had no options such as quitting or transferring to another prison, Marion having already been designated an "end of the line."[4] They had no outlet for the stresses and frustrations engendered by the gratuitous abuse, diminishing opportunities, and concomitant decline in their living standards. Nor did they have any power to resist their victimization via credible, real time appeals, administrative or otherwise. All the problems of this drawn out attack added to and aggravated the usual rigors of maximum security subsistence. All prisoners had with which to consciously contest the injustice of their metastasizing oppression and the deliberate provocations of the staff was their minds and bodies.

Guards, too, were subject to manipulation to the point of expendability in the administrative quest to implement its totalitarian design. Labor-management relations between the American Federation of Government Employees (AFGE) locals representing guards and the BoP were at a very low ebb. A statement by Kenneth T. Blaylock, national president of the AFGE, describes the conditions faced by guards as a crisis.[5] It also cites work details two or three times over quotas, short staff, and inadequate training. It complains of top management, some of whom "view us [guards] as merely tools and stepping stones," that is detached and distant and more concerned with image than employee welfare. The statement goes on to lament the absence of an effective working relationship with management on local, regional, and national levels. It decries bad faith in negotiations and the vindictive downgrading of 1,100 of the union's members. Another report complains about "worsening" conditions for guards, low pay, "take back" demands in negotiations, "harsh arbitrary, and overreactionary" disciplinary procedures for staff.[6] Many other sources attest to the facts that health, safety, and security warnings by guards at Marion and elsewhere were ignored, that union activism was harassed, treatment was unfair, that morale was low, and that the rank and file was permitted no input.[7]

These conditions applied at Marion and were compounded by arbitrary demands on guards to treat prisoners more stringently in the name of security. In short, guards, too, were manipulated as ingredients in the Marion experiment. Unfortunately, they succumbed to ignorance, reaction, and the "just followin' orders" syndrome. They fell for their masters' tricks and transferred blame for their plight to the nasty prisoners, even though they know or should have known better. Marion (and other federal) guards, like the prisoners, tried to resist their oppression through their labor. Unlike prisoners, however, they were not condemned and vilified for it.

Open Prison to Semi-Lockdown

Conditions at Marion in the months following the installation of Harold Miller as warden in 1979 became harsher. The prison was still open with functioning work, educational, vocational, and recreational programs and a degree of free movement despite its maximum security character. But the decision had been made that those days were done, and the slide had already begun. Miller was gruff and uncommunicative and possessed of an attitude amenable to the task of instituting a needlessly more authoritative regime, an attitude that was transmitted to staff despite the schisms. The phasing out of the industries program began, eliminating many jobs for prisoners and causing a contraction in the prison economy. Working conditions worsened. Pay was decreased. Harassment was escalated, including more and more abusive and disrespectful personal and cell searches, and more infraction reports with more severe punishments for frequently petty incidents. Arbitrary exercise of authority, something especially capable of inducing tension due to its unexpectedness became more common, too. Unnecessary limitations were placed on cultural pursuits. Active and passive physical abuse was also included in the administrative assault, active as in beatings and passive as in denying adequate medical care. The following list of concerns presented to Warden Miller by a group of prisoners in August of 1980 illustrates some of the problems:

- allow Native Americans to practice purification rites,
- allow religious services in segregation and the control unit,
- allow Muslims to wear the fez and turban,
- stop the use of boxcar cells,
- stop guards from harassing and beating prisoners,
- extend visiting and make the visiting room more comfortable,
- improve medical care,
- improve diet by using real meat.[8]

In the midst of this expanding instigation, provocation, and repression, the attendant stress expressed itself in various ways; it was bound to do so. There were a number of prisoner-on-prisoner assaults between the accession of Warden Miller and February 1980, and two prisoners died. However, the true number of real assaults will never be known, given the variability of what officialdom reports as an assault, and it will never be surely known whether the deaths were a product of negligence or deliberate indifference. As deplorable and indicative of ignorance and lack of consciousness as what attacks there were by individual prisoners on other members of their oppressed community are, they did and do not occur in a vacuum and cannot be seen solely as evidence of general depravity and justification for further repression.

The largest expression of prisoner resistance to the stress-inducing oppression, however, was in work strikes. In January 1980, the first work strike occurred. Work stopped for a time, but nothing was fixed. Another strike lasted for three weeks in March and April. Participation was virtually total. Officials accused prisoners of threatening others to get that degree of solidarity and launched a press offensive to make the strikes appear to be a product of coercion.[9] However, that very premise contradicts the administrative painting of prisoners as violence prone predators not amenable to intimidation or outside influence of any sort. Assuming that the wages of scabdom and collaboration in prison are similar to those outside (and they are), any significant non-participation in the strike would have caused a lot more mayhem if the anti-prisoner propaganda were true. Widespread coercion is also inconsistent with the staff charge that prisoners had "well organized resistance": one would have cancelled the other. And the organization charge as a justification for harsher repression was inconsistent with the fact that the strikes were peaceful. Any such organization should thus have been seen as a positive development.

In September 1980, a third work strike was launched. The grievances of prisoners were starting to gain some currency in the world beyond the walls. Up until then, the administration had a virtual monopoly on access to the press and thus almost total freedom to ply its disinformation campaign against prisoners. It had incentive to do so: according to at least one report, only one prisoner was working. The action continued despite threats and coercion of administrators and guards. People had to be brought in to perform essential tasks that were formerly done by prisoners. It was a substantial drawing back of the veil behind which prisoncrats could get away with just about anything; it could not be hidden or covered up.

Lawyers, particularly those of the Marion Prisoners Rights Project (MPRP) who had long been associated with the struggle against repression at Marion, helped break the prisoners' isolation and thus gave them greater reach and credibility. When official actions, including court proceedings, are taken in the light and under the scrutiny of outside lawyers and the public, they must be done at least a little more correctly. Hence, Warden Miller took steps to deprive the prisoners of their legal assistance and support and that of the community they represent. Had Marion really fit the propaganda picture and not been proceeding pursuant to counterproductive ulterior motives, Miller would have welcomed the attention as vindicating. Instead, on October 15, 1980, he wrote a letter illegally banning Martha Easter-Wells, Jacqueline Abel, and Elizabeth Mitchell, two lawyers and a paralegal of the MPRP, from the prison for the duration of the work strike then in progress. With respect to the lawyers, the justifying charge was that they had allegedly helped a prisoner formulate a list of strike demands, and, regarding the paralegal, that she had made comments to the press favoring the strike after a legal visit. In a society purportedly predicated on freedom of expression and legal access for all, the ban could only be a contrary demonstration of desire to further shroud in secrecy the destructive consequences of what was being done at Marion.

On December 22, 1980, the banning order was extended to everyone associated with the MPRP and beyond the duration of the work strike, officials by then knowing that the semi-lockdown of the work strike would be permanent. The ban was expanded on the pretext that having prisoners on the organization's board amounted to their conducting a business, prisoners conducting a business being a violation of BoP rules. At that time, the ban against Attorney Abel and Paralegal Mitchell was further justified with the assertion that they had sent contraband to prisoners, horrible things such as self-addressed stamped envelopes from the MPRP for replies and some blank watercolor paper. Even the U.S. Seventh Circuit Court of Appeals, no friend of prisoners, later acknowledged the ridiculousness of these justifications. Apparently, the Marion administration recognized it, too, because contemporaneously with making those allegation it was inducing prisoner Jack Abbot to make other vague, uncorroborated, and unfounded allegations against Project personnel. Several days later, this opportunist was transferred to Utah from whence he was shortly sent to a New York halfway house. These allegations, too, the Court of Appeals billed as incredible.[10]

All of this not only demonstrates the double standard applied against prisoners and the willingness of the Marion BoP administrations to use dishonesty in furtherance of their goals, particularly the reduction of Marion to a locked down lab. As well, it indicates the extent to which prisoners generally, who have much less visibility and power than free legal professionals, were and are victimized by the lies of "confidential informants" and the exaggeration of trivial incidents into major infractions with serious consequences. The local federal district court further revealed the problems of bias and apparent predetermination faced by prisoners in its handling of the banning matter. It upheld all of Marion officials' contentions in the case and contributed a few of its own machinations in support of the prison and BoP, notwithstanding that its position was predicated on what was facially ridiculous and incredible to the appellate court. Before the ban was overturned, in a case that was adjudicated unusually swiftly and successfully, prison officials were able to wreak considerable damage, deprivation, and expense.

While the work strike continued, the Marion administration took a further step in implementing the prison's "new purpose" as a bunch of control units. The removal of the industrial work program was completed and made permanent, the equipment sent elsewhere. Non-industrial jobs were nearly all eliminated, too. There has been no work for any but a few Marion prisoners since. The academic program was shut down in almost all but name. The vocational program was also terminated, all of the training equipment was removed and the building gutted, and the resulting space was turned into a recreation area. Access to recreation was curtailed. Out of unit recreation was reduced to approximately every other day in a highly controlled movement. The only other things for which prisoners were allowed out of the cell block were visits and to go to the chow hall, in small groups without contact with other prisoners from other units. Prisoners were allowed out of the cells during the day, but were restricted to the long, narrow tiers in front of the cells with very little to do and contact only with others in their part of the block.

Marion staff billed the evolving "stringent environment" as allowing the prison to operate in a much more secure and effective fashion than prior to the semi-lockdown. In November 1981, it contended that prisoners and staff were safer as a result.[11] This is what the BoP always claims in order to justify increased oppression: it has learned that the courts have essentially made it sole proprietor of "safety and security," despite its record of failure. The BoP always insists its measures are effective and that trouble increases only because the prisoners get nastier. If that were true, it would be an indictment of the measures as ineffective, but the inherent characters of prisoners entering the system remains the same. Congressional and state legislative testimony shows that, over many years, the increasing depravity excuse has been repeated endlessly; our failures are due to the nastier and nastier people sent to us.[12] In light of those failures, though, the contention of improved safety is evidence of either malfeasance or incompetence. At least according to statistics former BoP Director Norman Carlson himself supplied to U.S. Representative Patricia Schroeder, assaults with weapons on staff at Marion more than doubled in 1981 over 1980 and were only one fewer than in 1979.[13] Verily, that fact indicates that the work strikes provided an outlet that decreased deadly violence.

Semi-Lockdown to Lockdown

The "stringent environment" and its adversarial atmosphere in which idleness, particularly intellectual idleness, aggravated other pernicious factors was a recipe for disaster. Prisoners were left with no constructive pursuits and only limited recreation, a few games like dominoes or cards, a t.v. for each thirty-five prisoners, and whatever they could do on their own in the way of self-education. They were thrust into enforced contact with people from different cultures, racial and ethnic groups, backgrounds, and educational levels, and future prospects given their time structures. There was exceedingly little through which to feel or demonstrate personal competence or value or connect with the de facto community in which the prisoners were compelled to live, let alone any other. Inherent characteristics such as race and geographical origin as well as artificial ones like group affiliation and the things of "jailin'" and the criminal element assumed magnified and disproportionate importance. The constant actual and implied denigration by the authorities intrinsic to a locked down situation plus prisoners' powerlessness to do anything to alleviate it contributed to the impetus to competition on the basis of what seemed immediately relevant. Nor did prisoners have any opportunity to change their situation in any certain, real time way; they were forced to play the game and could not concede, withdraw, choose a different game, or lose, except self-destructively.

These pressures, along with the stress bred by indefinite subjection to rigorously maximum security conditions, could not help but breed conflict and behavior officialdom could hawk as atrocious. They could not help but create a social microcosm divergent from the norms of the larger society. Only the existence of some consciousness and some recent experience of collective action on the basis of commonality and in resistance to shared adversity (i.e., the work strikes) among Marion's prisoners prevented the result from being much worse than it was.

Officialdom is fond of separating the period from February 1980 to June 1983 as especially characteristic of something that has never been fully explained. Presumably, it is to indicate the depravity of Marion prisoners during an "open" period before the current lockdown was imposed in 1983. However, it must be remembered that February 1980 was just after Warden Miller's pushing of the "evolution of a more stringent environment" had already precipitated one work strike. In addition, the regimen initiated subsequent to the physical removal of the industries program in January of 1981 was actually in effect from September of 1980 when the last work strike began. Hence, the behavior during this forty month period with which the BoP seeks to vilify prisoners did not occur under open conditions and is more the product of provocation and repression that any asserted inherent knavery of prisoners.

Cited as demonstrative of prisoner rascality are fourteen attempted escapes, ten group disturbances, twenty-eight assaults on staff by prisoners, and fifty-four assaults on prisoners by other prisoners in which eight prisoners died.[14] First, the fourteen attempted escapes must be discounted as evidence of anything bad. It would be completely unreasonable to expect people to voluntarily submit to draconian punishment and retribution with no redeeming social value for the generally very long sentences with which most Marion prisoners were afflicted. Verily, willingness to so submit could only be seen as a pathology. The very walls and fences and bars and gun towers at even medium security prisons acknowledge the normalcy of thoughts of escape. The only justification for making escape from oppression a crime is that the oppression is only incidental to and no more than is necessary for community protection while the real protection of habilitative programs that facilitate an offender's reintegration into normal life is allowed to work. Marion makes no pretense of doing that and, in fact, insists on doing the contrary.[15]

Responsibility for the extent the alleged violence did occur beyond what would be expected lies at least as much with the administrative practices as with the actual perpetrators. What is reasonable in such an irrational environment as Marion may not be readily discernible as such outside. Individuals may take violently exploitive and oppressive actions on the basis of ignorance, unconsciousness, indiscipline, thoughtlessness, opportunism, and/or as the result of psychological injury. They are accountable and responsible for those actions to the extent that they could have but did not rid themselves of or avoid those negative causal traits. Nevertheless, responsibility also accrues to a variety of contributing factors, not all of them under the control of the immediate actors. It is a given that the mentally impaired are responsible for their actions only in inverse proportion to their disability. The stick does not make them better or more responsible; it exacerbates the problem. So it goes with victims of psychological attack like prisoners, especially when they are placed in circumstances where their ability to work on the negative causal traits is severely circumscribed. Moreover, oppressed people tend to be impelled to attack each other as a reaction to and expression of the stresses of oppression before turning against the oppressor.[16]

In any event, in these incidents are represented only the small minority of Marion prisoners whose victimization forced them to act out in ways the BoP felt it could mischaracterize to its advantage. Prisoner violence is only one of many expressions of the larger violence the BoP perpetrates with weapon Marion.

Another consideration in assessing this period is that these statistics are generated by BoP, which has complete control over what constitutes an assault, an escape attempt, or a "group disturbance." It can vary the criteria in order to come up with the desired numbers. The statistics must also be considered in light of the BoP's demonstrated willingness to lie in furtherance of its interest. Further undermining government credibility, none of the statistics even acknowledge, let alone list assaults on prisoners by staff; feats of penmanship rendered them all an acceptable something else. Misleading, too, are across the board negative characterizations of prisoner violence. What is unreasonable outside might not be in as irrational an environment as Marion. A fight, for example, (always considered a "bad" statistic and frequently reported as assault) may be the proper response to exploitation and oppression where the alternative is becoming a collaborator (a snitch, rat, informant) and/or spending the rest of a long sentence in the segregation conditions of protective custody. And if the antagonist with which one is confronted is bigger and stronger and tougher or has help, rationality may dictate an equalizer. The BoP also inflates the statistics with hyperbole about the events from which they derive, creating an impression of continual mass misbehavior. In reality, the relatively few people involved in the 1980-83 incidents, virtually all of whom were quickly identified and segregated, coupled with consideration of the incidents and statistics in their proper perspective, rob them of force as justification for action so extreme as lockdown Marion.

Events subsequent to the February 1980 to 1983 period are often, albeit arbitrarily, cited generally as "leading" to the October 28, 1983 lockdown.[17] The BoP seeks to justify its victimization of not only all then Marion prisoners, but of all present and future consignees as well, with sensational descriptions of incidents somehow even more threatening than those of the preceding period during this four month period. The intent apparently is to create the impression of a substantive destabilization. The charges from this period involved only some twenty-four perpetrators—some of whom were also victims and not all of whom were assigned to "general population units—or about seven percent of the approximately 350 prisoners at Marion at the time. And again, no information is given about the conditions, instigation, or provocation that precipitated the incidents, most likely because that would seriously undermine their justification value for the BoP.

Take, for instance, the first incident mentioned in this July-October 1983 period. Two prisoners in segregation took two guards hostage. Escape, even to the "mainline," was not even an issue. Knowing the likely consequences of beatings, long sentences, and a lot of "hole" and control unit time, did these prisoners act just because that was in their nasty natures? Or was it a desperate last resort after repeated, unheeded complaints about gratuitous abuse, insufferable conditions, complaints made in the face of the bankruptcy of appeals procedures or even passive resistance? Was it better explained as the stresses born of conditions over which the prisoners had no control needing and finding an outlet? Were these people who felt obligated by their principles to resist injustice inflicted upon them? Though some of the cited incidents may have been efforts to harass back, acting out or opportunistic misbehavior, and while some of the acts may constitute truly corrupt iniquities, again, they must be considered in light of the circumstances.

Precipitation of Lockdown

The specific incidents that are alleged to have precipitated the lockdown of October 27, 1983, the killing of two guards in the control unit, are even more egregiously lacking as justification for slamming down the whole prison permanently. The circumstances surrounding the killings also provide further evidence that the making of Marion into a Control Unit prison was pre-planned. On the morning of October 22, 1983, on B range of the Control Unit, guard Merle Clutts was stabbed repeatedly and later died; the two other guards with him were not injured. A shakedown of that range was ordered and normal activities for the rest of the unit were resumed. That evening, on C range of the Control Unit, guard Robert Hoffman was fatally stabbed in a struggle between three guards and a handcuffed prisoner. The two other guards were also stabbed. The assailants were immediately identified. Prisoners expected retaliation; that would be normal. Despite its separateness from the Control Unit, some activities for prisoners in the general population were, indeed, cancelled the next day. But they were restored the following day. The event seemed closed. Eventually, Thomas Silverstein was convicted of stabbing Clutts and Randy Gometz of giving him the knife and unlocking the handcuffs. Clayton Fountain was convicted in the death of Robert Hoffman.

The theory for the incidents advanced by the prison authorities was that the prisoners had a murder competition going just for something to do or in pursuit of some arcane vision of status, an obvious absurdity.[18] If that were so and assuming, *ad arguendo*, the veracity of contentions made in calls for harsher punishments such as the death penalty for prisoners who "have nothing more to lose" because of sentences that are already life-plus,[19] then why would they stop at one guard each? According to witnesses, neither of the two other guards with Clutts was stabbed despite ample opportunity for the assailant to do so, and those with Hoffman were stabbed only when they interfered and apparently only to the extent required to discourage them. Magistrate Kenneth Meyers wrote with respect to the possibility that all six guards could have been slaughtered: "The two assaults upon the officers in the control unit had demonstrated that one [prisoner], physically powerful from the use of weight-lifting and body building equipment, could take down three employees, even when they were fighting for their lives."[20] Both prisoners surrendered their weapons and returned to their cells without further resistance after the attacks, hardly consistent with maximizing the score in some macabre competition.

There is a much more realistic explanation for the prisoners' actions. Clutts and Hoffman were long time guards who had failed to climb the promotion ladder, were known for their atavistic attitude toward prisoners, and were seemingly possessed of some mystic nostalgia for a mythical way it never really was. They went out of their way to harass and be uncivil to prisoners, particularly singling out Silverstein and Fountain due to their reputations. These guards apparently thought that they could gain status in their gang by targeting prisoners they felt were the toughs. Numerous complaints had been made about abuse by guards over the preceding sixteen months and about Clutts and Hoffman in particular. Warnings about the likelihood of trouble were also given. Those complaints and warnings were in addition to the extreme potential for trouble facially evident to correctional professionals and presumably also apparent to Marion administrators.[22]

Extremes of tension can easily be generated by endless repetition of even petty abuses, and all of those perpetrated on Control Unit prisoners were and are petty. Given the lack of any adequate outlet for this tension for these prisoners such as in viable administrative appeals, litigation, obtaining a transfer to another unit or institution, or in constructive rewarding endeavors like work or school, it would have been surprising had there not been some kind of explosion. The pressure of wrong heaped upon injustice, piled upon affront with no prospect of relief continually mounted until it made Clutts' and Hoffman's killers unable to acquiesce to their oppression. The extraordinary load of stress finally impelled them to accept the dire consequences of the only action available to them, to take some control over their totally dominated lives, even if momentary, whatever the consequences. And those consequences were dire: beatings, digital rapes, strip cell isolation conditions, less likelihood of freedom—even that of a more open prison—legal and illegal vengeance by guards, and the possibility of death, all for an indefinite period. Silverstein and Fountain are still in solitary isolation. For people whose lives are under the total control of others who deliberately set themselves up as adversaries, there are always consequences, deterrents, preventions, retributions, etc., contrary to the assertions of those calling for killing to show that killing is wrong.

Regardless of what one may think of the appropriateness of the reactionary deeds for which Silverstein and Fountain were convicted, their genesis must be understood if conclusions are to be drawn that may help prevent such events as well as less serious misbehavior in the future. As Silverstein noted at his sentencing in the killing of Clutts, life is different at Marion, especially after one has been subjected to Control Unit rigors for five years.[23] But it was and is not so different that cause and effect do not operate; the BoP seeks to deny the causes (and its responsibility for them) and treats the effects as if they did not happen in a situation where appropriate and healthy responses had been eliminated as options. Moreover, both Silvestein and Fountain were legally competent and no claim to the contrary has ever been made. Hence, they were able to appreciate the enormity of their actions. Silverstein made that point, too, at sentencing, at a point when there was nothing he could say that would make a difference to him. Further, to kill merely for "braggin' rights," as one guards' union official put it, is by definition insanity, even without consideration of the consequences.

The fact that the deaths of Clutts and Hoffman occurred in the Control Unit, a unit completely divorced from the rest of the population to the extent of being virtually another prison, also reveals that the murders were not the actual reason for the permanent lockdown of all of Marion. Unlike with segregation, from which prisoners come and go to general population on a frequent basis—even though some spend years there— there was extremely limited contact between the mainline and Control Unit. Occasionally, prisoners were sent there from mainline Marion, but only through segregation in a process that could take more than a year. Infrequently, prisoners were released to the Marion mainline after their Control Unit sentences. Physically, the Control Unit is situated in an isolated end of the prison where no communication was possible by sight or sound; Control Unit prisoners and those in the "population" used no common facilities and did not so much as pass each other in the hallways. Pains were and are taken to maintain that separation. The administration acknowledged that the Control Unit was essentially another prison by allowing what was then normal operation of the mainline after the killings.

Thus, the use of the guard deaths can only be construed as something that was determined after the resolution of the incidents to constitute an excuse sufficient to justify an "emergency response." The excuse had to be a good one considering the magnitude and permanence of the planned regime change. The implementation of the pending plan "to convert the prison from an institution with only one control unit . . . to a 'close, tightly controlled, unitized' prison for all prisoners" needed only its Arch-Duke Ferdinand to be set in motion.

To the guard deaths, the administration added the death of prisoner Jack Callison, who was found stabbed to death in his cell on C range of D block on October 27. Officialdom needed a bridge, both between the time of their excuse and the lockdown and between the Control Unit and the mainline. Many prisoners had been killed previously without much official concern at all, let alone the creation of a long or permanent lockdown. And even this death was not considered serious enough at the time of its discovery to justify any lockdown of the prison. But it was a convenient addition to the justification being assembled for the imminent permanent lockdown.

Prisoncrats multiplied these two "main events" of murder by exaggeration of relatively few and minor incidents occurring in the time between them and came up with an explosive atmosphere of impending riot and incipient takeover of the prison. This fantastic drawing is implausible considering the limited movement of only small groups of prisoners at any given time and their willingness to lock up when instructed to do so. They had been doing that every evening for two daily counts without even the allegation of a problem.

An immediate excuse for drastic action was still lacking, however, no lockdown being in effect on October 27, 1983. Perhaps staff members only then felt compelled to display their machismo that evening after the insult to the guard "us" by the prisoner "them" via the Control Unit killings. More plausible is that the BoP hierarchy had that day transmitted to the prison that the time was ripe for the final step, that the decision had been made to realize the control unit prison. Provocation of some kind of group disturbance that could span the distance between the isolated, individual depredations and the evening of October 27th when nothing warranting lockdown was happening was apparently thought necessary. An incident was instigated. The administrative story about it is that when C unit was released for evening chow, four prisoners ran down the main corridor and attacked several staff members for no other reason than their inherent rascality.

The factual explanation of the event exposes its character as provocation. C unit was not let out for chow that evening until unusually late, approximately 7:00 p.m., after the rest of the population had been locked in their cells. At the release, Executive Assistant Dean Leech and a large squad of club-toting guards were on hand, purportedly to search the prisoners. This is the same Dean Leech who, two days earlier, stated with respect to Marion prisoners, "You have to consider the kind of men imprisoned here. They're here because they're vicious; they're here because they're savage" despite his knowing it was not true.[24] Warden Miller was also present. It was unusual for either administrator to be around at that time, and security matters like shaking down prisoners are not the province of the executive assistant. Nevertheless, Leech insisted on personally participating in the shakedowns, verbally abusing prisoners and treating them roughly as he did so. He subjected some prisoners to a second search. One prisoner, Joe James, having already been shaken down, was blocked by Leech as he walked past. James informed him that he had already been searched, which the guard who had searched him acknowledged, and proceeded. Nevertheless, Leech suddenly grabbed the surprised and unsuspecting James by the shirt. In the tense and confrontational atmosphere at Marion where sudden personal attacks elicited reflexive responses, it is not surprising that James reacted. He knocked Leech down. A brief skirmish ensued—but was only brief due to the number of guards present. The prisoners retired to the unit and were locked up. No one was injured. The only running was Leech running away, pursued briefly by James.

Later that night, some prisoners were brutalized, one at a time, in what was termed as "security shakedown." Apparently, the action was more to insure an attitude of resistance among prisoners and to stimulate activities like throwing trash on the range and shouting threats and insults to make the incident look like a continuing one and help justify what was to come.

The Lockdown

The next day, October 28, 1983, Warden Miller imposed an official "state of emergency." No prisoners were let out of their cells for so much as a shower. They were put on sack lunches (usually a bare slice of bologna and cheese between two pieces of bread like a sandwich and a piece of fruit or something similar) for all three meals. Guards began roving about and searching, verbally and physically abusing prisoners in the process. Writers of the official propaganda that masquerades as history describe the reactions of prisoners, the vast majority of whom had done nothing wrong, as some sort of continuing riot even though all it ever amounted to was a few small fires causing minor damage and throwing trash out of the cells. There was also some verbal abuse, but not during the first few days. Discretion dictated that prisoners locked in single cells could not have even that small venting of frustration face to face with gangs of guards. The propagandists also advanced the finding of several prison-made knives in different parts of the prison as if that somehow proved the nastiness of prisoners and that there was some still imminent threat with them all locked in cells. On the contrary, those discoveries indicated rationality: if even just a few of the prisoners consigned to Marion were the rapacious predators alleged by staff, reason and prudence would demand having access to some sort of defensive instrument. And such finds are made in every prison. In the several days following the declaration of the state of emergency, prisoners remained in the cells amidst this random abuse, on sack lunches, with garbage and dirt accumulating on the tiers; guards continued these and other preparations for even worse depredations.

Goon squads of guards began to arrive from all over the federal BoP on October 30. Five guards and a lieutenant had already arrived from Leavenworth on October 25—apparently on speculation, if the lockdown was not pre-planned. Many more were rotated in over time.[25] All guards were issued three foot long riot batons with metal balls affixed to the ends. Some of the imported guards were special attack squads, and other squads were formed at Marion. The one from Leavenworth called itself the "A-team," and the Marion version billed itself as "Blue Thunder," both after kill-emcop shows on t.v. The goon squads were outfitted with helmets, jump suits, flak jackets (!), gloves, boots, riot gear, and face shields to obscure their identity. All of the guards took off the name tags they are required to wear. Some of the arriving guards were taken to the Control Unit where blood from the killing of the guards was still on the floor and incited against prisoners with comments like "See that? See? That's your brother's blood on the floor there. Your brother! Could be yours. That's what they do, the animals. We've got to show them." Obviously more than merely carrying out the dictates of security was intended. Nor was this systemwide effort something that could be mobilized on short notice.

The reign of terror to usher in the "new, higher security" started in earnest in the Control Unit on November 2. Every prisoner's cell was ransacked in the name of search, and all the men were pushed and shoved around, some being beaten more severely. A number of prisoners were taken to the hospital for forcible searches of the rectum and were then poked, hit, tripped, slammed into walls, and subjected to multiple x-rays.

Illustrative of this brutal treatment are the experiences of Garvin Dale White and Michael Geoghegan. On November 4th, White was taken from his Control Unit cell to the hospital where he was beaten with clubs and forced down when he refused to consent to a rectal search. While held down, a person unknown forced a finger repeatedly into his rectum. He was then subjected to numerous x-rays against his will. After that, he was thrown into a strip cell with no water and no heat, clad only in underwear and while still handcuffed behind his back. He was supposedly to be "dry celled" thusly until he had a bowel movement, but was kept there for three days after he did so, four days altogether, handcuffed behind his back all the while. No contraband was found. All of this was justified on the alleged rumor that there might be a piece of hacksaw blade somewhere in the Control Unit. The court said about this that there was no credible evidence demonstrating a pattern and practice of abuse.[26]

Also on November 4, Michael Geoghegan was beaten for allegedly having a milk carton in his cell. About eight guards rushed into his cell and threw Geoghegan to the floor and stomped on his left hip and thigh. One guard hit him in the face while another admonished, "Not in the face!" Others hit him in the throat and beat his torso. As he was dragged from the cell in leg irons, chains, and handcuffs, guards thought it was great fun to step on the chain between his leg irons, which caused deep cuts in Geoghegan's ankles. Geoghegan is 5'6" and weighed 140 pounds. Public Defender David Freeman was able to photograph Geoghegan weeks after the incident and the damage was still clearly visible. The court "found" that Geoghegan was only handcuffed for "refusing" to return a milk carton and that there was no credible evidence of anything else.[27]

Over the next few days, between approximately November 3rd and 8th, the police terrorism was visited upon the rest of the prison. All of it far exceeded anything that could be considered usual or normal in response to emergencies or rationally related to security. Every prisoner was individually taken out of his cell by a gang of club wielding, riot suited guards with no name tags. Each was pulled out of the cell either naked or in underwear and at least pushed around or jerked about by the handcuffs and verbally abused. At the same time, prisoners were being taken to other units or held in front of the unit while the cells were ransacked. Many were given more serious beatings. They were subject to be attacked anywhere—in cells, stairways, hallways. They were punched, kicked, hit with clubs, and run into walls, bars, and gates. Genitals were common targets. All of this was accompanied by threats, sexual and racial slurs, and demands that prisoners make demeaning statements. Comments were made about the brutality being revenge for the two dead guards. Perhaps some of the rank and file tools of administrative policy unaware of their true function in the conversion of Marion really believed that.

Representative of brutalization of the mainline prisoners were the cases of Hanif Shabazz Bey (s/n Beaumont Gereau), William Omar McCoy, Michael Sizemore, and Frank Segarra. On November 7, in I unit, a group of guards accused Shabazz of being an influential prisoner and stated that they intended to beat him as an example. They handcuffed him behind his back and did as they had threatened, targeting his joints particularly with their clubs. Later the same day, the guards returned and struck him with their clubs while he lay on the bunk. They returned yet a third time that day, removed Shabazz from his cell and clubbed him on his knees. Guard Lt. Booker denied that there had been any abuse on that date and the court found that there was no credible evidence to the contrary.

On November 7, four guards came to the cell of William Omar McCoy. They strip searched him, handcuffed him behind his back, and carried him down the tier with clubs stuck under his arms. He was jabbed in the stomach and beaten on the knees with riot batons. Guards demanded to be called "sir" and to be told who was running the prison as well as making a lot of threats. After fifteen minutes of this maltreatment, McCoy was returned to the cell and pinned face down on the steel bunk while more threats were made. The court said that the credible evidence failed to support the allegations.[28]

Also on November 7, about seven guards took Michael Sizemore, unhandcuffed, from his cell and off the tier to where he was thrown into a wall and knocked to the floor. He was then choked and pulled off the floor by the hair with his arms twisted behind him. All the way down the corridors to I block, he was beaten with clubs, had his bare feet stamped on, was kicked and was repeatedly rammed into walls. In I block, he was pinned with clubs and boots to a steel bunk, beaten on the legs, and punched several times in the face. The guards attempted to get information from his and to make him say "sir," demands he was abused for refusing. He was then warned not to complain about this treatment. The court said that Sizemore was only pushed, which it did not consider excessive, and that the evidence of prisoner witnesses was not credible.[29]

On November 4, a group of guards had Frank Segarra strip searched, cuffed behind his back, and taken out of F unit. A guard pressed Segarra's face against a wall with baton pressure to the spine for fifteen to twenty minutes. He was then lifted up by the handcuffs and genitals and dropped, and guards clubbed, punched, and kicked him after he had fallen to the floor. Guards taunted him and ordered him to get up, only to be beaten again when he managed to comply. He was dragged to I unit and beaten some more upon arrival. He was threatened and told not to look at the guards' faces, which were obscured behind dark visors, anyway. He was strip searched and left in an empty cold cell. The court said that there was no credible evidence that any beating occurred.[30]

So it went in approximately 110 *reported* instances of physical abuse of prisoners by guards. And these are all beyond the routine pushes, shoves, slaps, jerking around by handcuffs and prodding with clubs. Virtually everyone was subjected to verbal abuse and threats and intimidation as well. Many other instances went unreported out of fear of retaliation, or of belief that complaining would be futile and inappropriate (i.e., sniveling) or out of desire to keep the humiliation as secret as possible. The guards and administration insisted that no brutality or abuse ever occurred and that any force that was used was reasonable.[31] The court agreed that none of what was testified to by so many prisoners, at least one guard, and others and was further indicated by the circumstances happened at all.[32]

These denials were contradicted by not only a preponderance but by an avalanche of evidence. From October 27, 1983 on, prisoners were all confined in separate cells between which there was virtually no possibility of unmonitored communication. Even after the isolation of prisoners generally was no longer total, such communication was impossible for most. It still is. There was no communication at all between the units. Conspiracy was impossible for these as well as interpersonal reasons. There was no forewarning that would have permitted a conspiracy in advance. No prisoner or staff member testified about any specific details showing any conspiracy by prisoners to lie. Such a wide ranging conspiracy would be impossible to conceal not only due to the circumstances, but also due to all the confidential informing in the hope of transfer going on at the time. There were *no* prosecutions for perjury, demonstrating a lack of evidence that all of the prisoners were "not credible."

The details of the brutality, corroborated in the testimony of diverse and unconnected prisoners, were not the sort likely to be made up. They left out much that could have made things look worse and included unusual details. Also, conviction of a crime does not necessarily make one a liar. Moreover, lawyers and at least one corrections professional, the only non-BoP people with any short-term access to the prison—though officials kept them out as long as possible—saw evidence of the needless brutality and excessive repression and that it was the administration that was not credible. Dr. David Fogel pointed out in his Congressional testimony that BoP administrators routinely base extreme actions like rectal probes and confinement to administrative and disciplinary segregation on not the sworn testimony of prisoners, but on their mere tips and are backed by the courts in such credibility assessments. Magistrate Meyers himself acknowledges prisoner credibility—albeit only when they say bad things about themselves.[33] Fogel also raised questions about administrative credibility that could have been readily answered by examination of the sort of routine bureaucratic documentation with which he was intimately familiar.[34] But the material was never brought out or examined and possibly never kept to avoid incrimination. These facts are in addition to the lawyers having heard the same things repeatedly from prisoners who could not possibly have concocted a consistent, false story. Together with other factors, the foregoing tends to shift the lack of credibility to the guards, administration, and court, their use of formal procedures and position to make themselves appear otherwise notwithstanding.

The court did accept as fact, despite evidence to the contrary, "the inherently violent aggressive nature" of Marion prisoners and opined that: "The severity of the injuries were [*sic*] proportionate to the resistance offered by the [prisoner]." This was consistent with the image of Marion as a program of experimentation, proportionate force and injury being substantially different than necessary force and unavoidable injury. The court justified everything with the assertion that: "USP Marion is USP Marion."[35] In other words, insistence on its constitutionality aside, it is a constitution free zone.

The official attack was not limited to physical assault but also extended to prisoners' property. After prisoners were removed from their cells, they were returned to empty cells that had been stripped of everything—personal property, lockers, clothes, shelves, clothes pegs, legal material, sheets, and blankets—everything. All of it that was not destroyed or discarded on the spot was dragged haphazardly to the gymnasium where it was dumped on the floor. Much was "lost," "converted" by guards, or destroyed. Some was sent out without notice to prisoners or explanation to surprised and apprehensive relatives. No property inventory receipts were issued, contrary to regulations.

During the two weeks immediately following the initial lockdown, the reign of terror continued, albeit in diminished active intensity after the first wave of brutality. There was not sick call until November 7, and prisoners were discouraged from seeking medical attention for injuries on pain of physical mistreatment for the request. Prisoners were kept in intentionally frigid cells on filthy tiers without hot meals. It was not until the last week of November that three hot—microwaved—meals per day were restored, and those were often delivered to the cells cold and/or contaminated. On November 14, prisoners began to be allowed thirty minutes of recreation per day on the tier in front of the cells, though they often did not get it. Eventually, this was raised to an hour in March of 1984. No outside recreation was permitted until June. Lawyers with the Marion Prisoners Rights Project were prevented from seeing prisoners until late on November 15 and were then only reluctantly accorded limited visits under threat of court order. Officialdom apparently felt that its conversion of Marion was sufficiently a *fait accompli* by then. Starting on November 16th, an exceedingly limited amount of personal property was again permitted. What was allowed had to be kept in one paper bag despite the presence of a lot of rodents. Prisoners were told to file a tort claim over the large part of what had been confiscated and then "lost." Beatings and "goonings" and chainings to bunks continued but with less frequency.

The goon squad from other prisons began to withdraw in January of 1984, their function being taken over by Marion squads. A few privileges were introduced over the year after the imposition of the lockdown. These included a total of eleven hours out of the cells per week (an hour per day on the tier and two hours in the yard with another two hours in either the gym or former t.v. building), some access to the commissary (but no money for it), and somewhat more property plus cardboard boxes to keep it in. T.v.s were installed in July of 1984, and visiting time in the glass and phone visiting booths was extended. The official name for the lockdown was changed to "high security operation." But the atmosphere of fear and intimidation remained, compounded by endless petty harassment and restriction.

It is not possible here to explore or even point out every BoP action demonstrative of the Marion lockdown's true intent and the real character of its implementation or to expose every official lie and malfeasance. Nor was it possible to rebut or put in proper perspective each of the allegations of prisoner depravity that are individually and collectively used to justify mass punishment and counterproductive repression and to disguise officialdom's ulterior motives in applying it. It has, however, been possible to provide a clear outline of the reality of the government's conversion of Marion into a particular tool of oppression that is qualitatively different than it was. It has been possible through revelation of that situation to show a face of the apparatus that the government has gone to great lengths to hide.

Looking much like a national park, the entrance to the U.S. Penitentiary at Marion, Illinois, belies its real conditions. (photo: Ward Churchill)

Part II: Ramifications of the Lockdown at Marion

Marion is still a locked-down prison. Prisoners are forced to spend more than twenty-two hours per day on average locked in single cells. In groups of nine, they are allowed one hour, forty-five minutes per day out on the long, narrow tier that runs in front of the cells. Prisoners can talk only to those other prisoners in the thirty-five cells on the same side of the block during these times. A two hour yard and a two hour gym period are also provided each week, to and from which prisoners are taken with hands cuffed behind their backs by gangs of club wielding guards. The rest of the time is cell time. Education consists of prisoners being allowed to take one correspondence course and rudimentary basic education self-study courses. The library is a cardboard box of ragged paperbacks outside the bars at the end of the tier. There is no work available for any but a few prisoners.

Idleness and isolation are not, however, nearly the extent of Marion oppression. Manipulative harassment is carried right into the cells with endless petty regulations and rules and requirements. These are subject to be made up on the spot and are very unevenly and selectively enforced. No one can even know, let alone comply with, them all. The penalties for transgression of even the most insignificant of the edicts are severe: the slightest infraction is used as justification for up to another year of confinement at Marion[36] in addition to other punishment. And the harassment is frequently tailored to individual prisoners. Everything— education, medical treatment, personal property, food, etc.—is a potential weapon of physical and psychological assault against prisoners.

The imported goon squads have long been returned to other prisons, and the rampant brutality that characterized the period in 1983 and 1984 following the initial lockdown is now more a threat that needs only infrequent demonstration. Nevertheless, there are still more than occasional beatings and goonings and chainings to concrete slabs. The total domination by the administration of all aspects of prisoners' lives is predicated down to the smallest detail on the always imminent and immediately available use of force. Nor is direct attack by guards the only form of physical abuse: food, medical care, segregation, and other methods may also be employed. But the primary vector of attack is now psychological.

There is effectively no appeal from any of the depredations of Marion. A prisoner may be sent here "for any reason or no reason at all."[37] Although there are almost always reasons for the sending, many are not legitimate. And though there are vague guidelines for transfer out of Marion, none of them are mandatory. They are sometimes merely ignored and often used to make prisoners feel as if they, the prisoners, are responsible for their continued confinement at Marion. There is no entitlement of transfer that can override staff decisions to deny it. Prisoners are frequently taken to segregation "pending investigation." They are often surprised with silly infractions, all of which are said to require the victim to "start over" on his indeterminate sentence to Marion. The hearing process is a joke that officials will sometimes verbally acknowledge but which becomes very serious on paper. Appeals, be they administrative or judicial, are similarly bankrupt and may take years.[38] Complaints to prison staff are perilous in that they many times elicit only accusations and punishment.

Numerous authorities on the operation of correctional systems have testified and otherwise made known that arbitrary treatment and the absence of adequate grievance mechanisms are dangerous, particularly in combination. Such conditions accentuate rage, frustration, tension and helplessness. These stimulate prisoners to take matters into their own hands, to take whatever momentary, minuscule control they can. Thus they contribute to undermining safety and security and lead to violence.[39] These contentions are corroborated by six murders, two suicides, and untold fights and assaults since the lockdown, the events being especially indicative of psychological extremity given Marion conditions.

Contact with the community is discouraged and virtually non-existent. Prisoners have no contact with outside people such as mental and other health professionals, teachers, work supervisors, and providers of community services and activities. The only exception is minuscule contact with two contracted chaplains. Should prisoners develop any other local connections such as with church groups or media, every effort is made to destroy them. Visits are needlessly restrictive, being permitted only through glass and via phones with strip searches to and from, unlike all other state and federal prisons. Visitors are also subjected to unnecessary inhibiting impediments. Combined with the remoteness of the area, the oppressive character of visiting makes for relatively few visits. Mail is closely censored and often rejected for inane reasons like merely mentioning the name of another prisoner, and disappearance and delay of mail are not uncommon. This further impedes communication which may be all the community contact a prisoner has.

Marion and its program of repression are characterized by deception. What is visible to the public is a gleaming, modern prison that conveys an impression of cool and deliberate efficiency in the discharge of some ordained task. The U.S. is a rich country and thus has great resources to spend on appearances. In the case of Marion, that translates as money with which to disguise its violation of human rights[40] as "humane incapacitation." Tourists are shown shining, empty corridors, electronic gates, t.v.s in cells, a well-appointed infirmary, and other show items and are led to believe that prisoners have nothing about which to complain. The impression conveyed by the physical plant that Marion is that of the professionally conducted, high security operation of a concentration model. It does not, however, accurately portray the reality experienced by its victims. And the difference between the material implications and the actuality of Marion subsistence is only part of the deceit. The U.S. Bureau of Prisons and Marion administrations try to use the picture reflected by these facilities to lend credibility to their disinformation about who is subjected to Marion, its intent, its effects, and its efficacy at achieving its alleged goals.

The BoP and Marion administrations claim that Marion is filled with violent and vicious predators who constitute "the worst of the worst" in American prisons. Marion prisoners have been characterized as rotten apples "concentrated" into one barrel. The fact, however, is that Marion prisoners are no different than prisoners in other maximum security prisons, at least as far as "crime" goes. They may even be less threatening because most mass murderers, sex criminals, perpetrators of psychotic personal violence, and the like are in state and not federal prisons. And the most destructive criminals like those of the corporate class and its apparatus are in country club prisons and not Marion. Third world men comprise a disproportionately large segment of the Marion population. Nor are all Marion prisoners men who have committed acts of violence in other prisons, and many who have committed such acts are not here. There are many sent to Marion on vague allegations of plotting escape, for administrative reasons, to fill space, or for no specified reason. Others are sent directly from the streets. Many are people with strong belief systems that officialdom needs to experiment upon and undermine, some of whom are political prisoners sent here as part of the repression of them, their communities, and their struggles. Publicly, the administrations try to shift responsibility for prison problems onto their vision of nasty prisoners, and onto Marion prisoners especially, despite the complete control exercised over them by the guards. Though this justification is necessary in order to belabor prisoners with a club of class control in a constitution free zone like Marion, that fiction and the reality of who languishes under the lockdown demonstrate that it is the barrel and its managers that are rotten and not its victims.

That few prisoners at Marion actually fit the criteria the BoP claims to use for consignment has long been an indictment of the Marion operation. Long after the lockdown, fully eighty percent of the prisoners were classified below security level six, the rating of the prison.[41] Tired of taking heat for that situation, the BoP did not eliminate the problem by transferring the lower rated prisoners. Instead it changed the classification system, supposedly the product of long labor by expensive experts to allow almost anyone to be classified as level 6. It then issued an edict that prisoners could not have their custody levels lowered while at Marion, further limiting what incentive there might be to refrain from responding to the lack of options with misbehavior.[42]

The Marion lockdown is not the last resort response to depredations by prisoners that culminated in three deaths in October of 1983. Circumstances and documents, including one cited on ABC's national news magazine, *20/20*, show that it was being planned much earlier. Nor is Marion the "humane incapacitation" that is alleged, as its violation of many of the United Nations' Standard Minimum Rules for the Treatment of Prisoners and condemnation by Amnesty International show. Neither is it only a "concentration model," though it does act as such in some respects incidental to its real function. If people here are not all the nasties alleged and there are nasties not here, there is no concentration. It is not merely a "high security operation" because the repression goes well beyond what could reasonably be related to security. It is not "behavior modification" because that term implies that objectionable attitudes are being replaced with something more appropriate. Marion is merely destructive without the constructive element. It is not only a "mind control" prison, though developing the means of exercising psychological influence over people is part of its intent. The effect of Marion is mental impairment and a decrease in the stability of its victims, thus making them more unpredictable and less controllable. Though they may then be akin to human mines that can be aimed at least and perhaps more than vaguely and thus may be useful for bureaucratic purposes such as increasing the probability of acts that will engender community revulsion, anti-crime hysteria, and political support for policies of repression, specific control is undermined. What Marion is is a laboratory for experiments in social manipulation and control.

Political Rationale

Marion as such a laboratory is the rationale for the perpetual lockdown that is most strongly indicated by the evidence, incidental benefits to prisoncrats in other regards notwithstanding. Whether or not that was the original intention of all of the lockdown's designers, that is the current actuality. The U.S. ruling class sees on the horizon increasing dislocation and discontent as the crisis of capitalism deepens and its pains for the populace become sharper. It will need a larger apparatus of repression to deal with the resultant situation in the future as it increasingly fails to provide acceptable social conditions. That accounts in large part for the disproportionate anti-crime hysteria and expansion of the U.S. Gulag Archipelago at present. It will need more police to serve as occupying armies in poor and working class communities and to protect its institutions and privilege. As well, it will need more prisons with which to threaten and disorganize people resisting their exploitation and courts with which to criminalize them and legitimize their suppression.

Fear of crime, real and imagined, provides the support for expansion of the direct, physical means of class domination. It is also instrumental in dividing people along race and class lines and fragmenting their communities. It provides the psychological acceptance for the continuing presence of the ruling class and its apparatus of control in communities in which they exploit but do not live. This acceptance is an illustration that the ruling class needs psychological control even more than physical control. No amount of physical repression can indefinitely sustain minority control without a well developed system of psychological manipulation. Physical power cannot even always guarantee it temporarily, as demonstrated by the recent uprisings in Los Angeles following the aquittal in the Simi Valley trial of four policemen accused of beating Rodney King. And they were unorganized. People are increasingly seeing through the current American mythology of prosperity for all, belief in which has been maintaining the status quo. And the ruling class sees them seeing. Hence, it is researching and developing not only the physical means of repression but the more important psychological ones as well, the software to go with the hardware.

Enter the Marion lockdown and other maximum restriction control units that include similar experimental oppression. At these places, the people seemingly most immune to external programming are singled out for attention. Many are at least somewhat protected by what to them are clear, principled, and sustaining belief systems, and others are possessed of strong habits of resistance to mental pressure or are psychologically calloused. Being intractable in the sense of resistive to authority is the most relevant criterion. If such people can be induced to surrender tightly held sets of principles or otherwise rendered malleable, that is valuable information to agents of oppression—much more valuable than the maltreatment of a relatively few prisoners. These are the same types of attitudes from which community activists, guerillas, unionists, and other organizers of resistance spring and that allow them to persevere as economic and social conditions deteriorate and become more dangerous. Such attitudes are exceedingly threatening to the owning and exploiting class.

Political prisoners of the radical left make particularly good test subjects in this regard because their operating principles are less susceptible to attack due to their rationality. Those ideas are also most threatening to the hierarchy and are those most likely to be held by or attractive to the people who will increasingly populate the prisons. Prisoners belonging to other groups that adhere to more or less consistent codes also provide grist for the Marion mill because results there are often similar and translatable. The same is true with respect to information garnered from other prisoners who correspond in malleability, interests and outlook, and common types of rebellion to segments of the population the ruling class will need new weapons to control in the future. These others also can serve as experimental controls and camouflage for the experiments.

While repressive models such as Marion and the now closed control unit for women at Lexington, Kentucky, experiment directly on their victims, they are also working on their communities. Deprivation of individuals' connection to the community can injure the community as well as those isolated from it. The community becomes dependent on outside authority to solve the problems of crime largely created by that authority. That contributes to polarization, isolation, and suspicion within the dependent community and helps create identification with the occupying forces, thus undermining its ability to organize against its own exploitation and oppression. In addition, the community loses members who demonstrate the attitudes and capacity for resistance to an unjust social reality through rebellion, even if the rebellion is not always conscious or appropriate. The experimenters then obtain information on the efficacy of the removal vs. other controls. The removal also constitutes a warning and threat to those remaining in the community who would resist, be it in consciously and overtly political action against the status quo or in unconscious reaction to the social realities of oppression. This applies whether the community is on the streets or another prison. And there is always the pain inflicted by personal separation and economic loss. The apparatus is interested in these external effects of the enhanced isolation of prisoners in dungeons like Marion, too.

Psycho-Social Effects

The impact of lockdown laboratory Marion on prisoners reveals its experimental mission. Prisoners at Marion are first stripped of virtually all control over their lives. "Taking all their decisions away" was specifically stated as official policy by Marion Warden Gary Henman in a BBC radio interview.[43] To this atmosphere of complete lack of control the constant and visible threat of force is added to enhance the insecurity. The insecurity is further compounded by the complete uncertainty of existence. U.S. prisoners have a number of rights, but none of them are certain for any individual at Marion. No one knows when he will be accused of some real or imagined rule violation or if any other aspect of his life will be suddenly attacked by official action. These attacks can range from the infliction of minor irritants on up to beatings and chainings. The stress can become so severe that prisoners have been known to fly into a rage at having an official merely standing in front of a cell and looking into it. This is symptomatic of the extremity to which the threat perceived by prisoners in so little as being the object of unsolicited official attention can rise. No one is permitted to escape from the insecurity by creating an at least psychologically secure niche of, say, study or some other connection to reality beyond Marion in the seeming solitude of a cell. Officialdom pursues prisoners into the very corners of their existence with myriad arbitrary demands that may be made at any time and have unknown consequences. Capricious orders to do (or not do) something inane become readily apparent as harassment or personal insult intended only to be demeaning without purpose except as a gratuitous demonstration of power.

Most people are unaware of their character as direct or indirect experimental stimulation. With such basic needs as those for security and control of one's life going unmet, these intrusions can break into a prisoner's consciousness with a stab of anger and resentment that can linger a long time and disrupt constructive thought and action. They are damaging whether they elicit a reaction that can only be self-destructive or force the prisoner to internalize the anger and frustration for which there is no release. The incessant repetitions of these intrusions—often made even when prisoners are asleep—are cumulative and escalate the level of tension both individually and collectively. Such conditions "shape behavior toward violence by accentuating frustration, rage, and helplessness, and the violence is either directed inwardly or outwardly."[44]

The effect is multiplied by the extent to which it prods prisoners into self-policing. In order to avoid the intrusion and its psychological and physical consequences, many prisoners try to figure out—not always consciously—what will attract official interference, reasonable or not, and to eliminate it. This can be extremely stressful and frustrating because it requires acceding to the unreasonable and bowing to adversarial pressure without being specifically required to do so—doing "the man's" job—and is often not possible. For example, sometimes enforced rules forbid the hanging of clothing anywhere but on the one plastic hook in each cell. A prisoner with a handful of wet clothing looks around the cell in which he stands alone and unobserved and must make the choice between a mildewed mess and possibly attendant accusation of misuse of government property or sanitation violations and opening the door to intrusion by some itinerant guard with unknowably severe consequences. When asked what to do to resolve such dilemmas or for explanations that would make them at least understandable, staff members merely shrug and insist that the rules be obeyed. Constant confrontation with these double-wrong non-choices exacerbates the uncertainty and insecurity and stress they engender.

Guards, too, are made victims of this manipulation as they are also subject to Marion experimentation. Supervisory staff, usually above the custodial level, pressure guards to pressure prisoners for frivolous reasons. Guards then try to eliminate the cause for intrusion into their consciousness by trying to anticipate the hierarchy's whims. But then they are constantly faced with having to carry out unjust acts of repression with no serious relation to any legitimate penological objective in exchange for a salary, a sell-out. This pressure and the agent of oppression syndrome that stems from it are much more the cause of the stress in guards that the administration attributes to the supposed dangerousness of Marion prisoners. The hierarchy also experiments on guards with how to counter the syndrome and its impairment of minions' and henchpeoples' zeal with anti-prisoner propaganda and agitation, identification with the guard gang, and material incentive. And whether for guards or prisoners, the least stressful response is to try to move through the situation so incapable of analytical rationalization without thinking about it and to depersonalize the class brethren between whom the ruling class has chiseled a line that can only harden in the circumstances. But that is not always possible and certainly not desirable. Undoubtedly, staff members are aware that they are being manipulated, albeit in varying degrees according to their ignorance, unconsciousness, and programming. But that only enhances their perceptions of lack of control and inclination to show some and seek release at the expense of prisoners. This seems to be a greater factor with altitude in the hierarchy where it becomes increasingly important to appear to other climbers of the ladder to be running something, to be in control, to be operating more than operated.

The assault of Marion continues with deprivation of work and education and exceedingly limited recreation. At Marion, there is no work for the vast majority of prisoners. Only a relative few in the pre-transfer unit are allowed to have jobs—and even they are forced to work on military contracts rather than more productive projects. Working prisoners are the victims of all of the exploitation suffered by outside workers subjected to unfettered capitalism: speed ups, poor and hazardous working conditions, threats of retaliation outside the job for job performance, low pay, insecurity, etc. Thus, the work experience is not what it should be even where it is not completely withheld.

As mentioned previously, there is no substantive education to fill the work gap because, claim staff members, there is no budget for more. Given the demonstrable benefits of education and at a prison that spends substantially more per prisoner than any other federal prison and over three times the federal average, that excuse is equine excrement. It is also contrary to the notions of security advanced by officialdom because prisoner intellects absorbed in educational pursuits are not being applied to endeavors that might undermine prison officials' security and that of the communities into which they will be released. Recreation is needlessly limited, too, and in some instances discouraged, diminishing the benefits prisoners can reap from the meager activities that are permitted.

It is through activity, primarily work, that people satisfy their need to feel some sense of self-worth, competence, and accomplishment in addition to identification as, say, machinist. Education is intimately tied to this equation, too. It adds to one's capacity to work, to accomplish, to contribute to the community, and also provides the satisfaction of accomplishment and knowledge in itself. It allows one to better understand and deal with his or her world outside of a narrow and parochial existence and to be more capable of making rational assessments of it. It helps create community consciousness and awareness and appreciation of the knowledge and values that sustain a society as well as if and where they need change when they are not serving the whole society. It breaks isolation and the errors of ignorance.

But both meaningful work and education are denied to Marion prisoners, allegedly due to the dictates of security. The case is similar with recreation. Given the many work and educational and recreational possibilities available even within the context of the lockdown, the denial is an absurdity. Work, education, and recreation, however, and their physical and psychological benefits are not compatible with Marion's mission of social experimentation. They would empower prisoners and make the desired results impossible to obtain.

The results that are obtained by the deprivation of work and education are another condemnation of Marion. Further negative socialization of prisoners is one such result. Psychologist Frank Rundle described this effect of long term segregation as "progressive desocialization" in congressional hearings on Marion.[45] The denial of a sense of self-worth, of productivity, of usefulness in some effort of value to the individual and the community creates a perception of valuelessness that encourages prisoners to view others similarly. People who feel themselves to be of little value and have no feeling of security of person or property (contributing to worthlessness in a property based society) are inclined to have fewer inhibitions in their treatment of other people and things. This amounts to one less social safeguard for members of the community against deliberate criminal victimization by someone in whom the legacy of Marion pressures contributes to carelessness or a psychotic incident.

Prisoners are also impelled to seek elsewhere the self-value and satisfaction of accomplishment they are denied through work and education and recreation. This usually translates as developing the skills of "jailin'," developing associations with others who have value in the prison society, not always for laudable attributes. These things become what are valued and pursued, also to the detriment of the prisoner and the community.

At Marion, the extent to which the skills of prison society can be developed is limited in practice but exaggerated with respect to attitudes. Self-aggrandizement is forced to take on a more negative aspect. With very little a person can do to feel competent and valuable via dynamic accomplishment, there is an enhanced tendency to try to feel it through static condition. That means encouragement of stronger identification with people with similar characteristics (race, region, religion, gang, etc.), greater exaltation thereof, and harder lines drawn between people with different ones. Within these groupings there is an increased impetus to denigrate "outsiders" (and, though with more constraints, insiders, in jockeying for position) for all sorts of real and imagined faults toward the end that the denigrator and/or those not sharing the characteristics being denigrated are raised, at least relative to the victim. This occurs with non-characteristic actions, too. Tolerance for diversity is crushed by Marion oppression. And Marion victims tend to develop a habit of looking at people generally in a negative manner instead of positively or neutrally until there is some reason to carry them otherwise. To be hard and tough and unfeeling becomes a desirable goal and emotional response is impaired. This pushes prisoners further from desirable social norms and strengthens identification with "the element." And all of it is in addition to the fact that the deprivation of work and education leaves prisoners without the social and job skills necessary to survive in a society where every aspect of existence is not controlled by someone else.[46]

There is very little to counter the deleterious effects of this regimen of psychological assault, even to the limited extent counters are possible. Community involvement is one possibility. But although the BoP does acknowledge the importance of family and community ties and sometimes lives up to the paper policies designed to facilitate their maintenance,

Marion practice is a deliberate impediment to such ties. Arbitrary harassment rules that change whimsically are imposed on both visitors and prisoners. Visiting conditions are made so artificially difficult that many prisoners do not want to subject themselves or their visitors to the humiliation and emotional trauma. Even for the few prisoners who have some skill at written communication, the non-visit contact with the outside is generally insufficient to maintain positive relationships over time. Access to the community more broadly is even more limited. There is no way for prisoners to be exposed to the elements of community life, let alone develop connections with a particular one.

Relationships, be they with a community or individuals, are dynamic and not static things. They are predicated on practice, on interaction. People and communities change over time. When they change in isolation from one another, they tend to diverge, to grow apart from previous points of sharing. This is not necessarily a negative fact, just a fact. Even in the case where a relationship does not deteriorate, by not being exercised it becomes a smaller and smaller part of the consciousness of the people involved as the years contribute to total mental accumulation and the people are conditioned by their respective experience. For prisoners isolated at places like Marion, this means being increasingly divorced from their loved ones and communities beyond the walls. It also results in their being denied satisfaction of their human needs for affiliation with something outside the individual, identification, acceptance, and affection. But prisoners without the morale and psychological support of outside connections tend to be easier to manipulate and better experimental subjects in the Marion laboratory.

This separation by itself is counter to the goal of reintegrating prisoners into society. People are more willing to exploit and oppress where they feel no sense of connection or identification. But it is more than just that. People will seek to satisfy their needs to the extent possible in whatever circumstances they find themselves. For prisoners forcibly deprived of their families and the outside community—especially but not only those in conditions as oppressive as Marion's—this means satisfying social needs with other prisoners as much as can be. It is only from the other prisoners that individuals will get any mutual aid or understanding in real time. A kind word, a few cigarettes, some conversation, sympathy, support against threats—the range of human interaction possible under locked-down conditions—all can be of the utmost importance. And these present only the most obvious elements of prisoner association.

None of that personal support does or can come from prison staff, whom the administration sets up as an adversary that exists across a hard and fast line across which only enmity and distrust can fly. There are no teachers, social workers, work supervisors, paralegals, health professionals, etc. from outside that in other situations might help bridge that barrier as much as can be within one of the repressive institutions of this society. The bridging is also and more importantly between prisoners and the outside community. The presence of such people—and others—can also diminish the negative socialization of prisoners because they serve as representatives of society who are not solely agents of draconian repression and offer some alternatives to the things of a strictly prison existence. But such presence is not consistent with laboratory Marion; it would introduce too many variables and perhaps skew the relationship between the stick and its victims as well as drawing back the veil of secrecy.

Among the many islands in the American Gulag, the result of this isolation from the community is most pronounced at Marion. Prisoners, particularly the ignorant and those lacking in consciousness, have no choice but to identify with and seek acceptance by other prisoners. Because at a place like Marion there are no other social endeavors through which to interact, prisoners are impelled to affiliations on the basis of irrelevant factors that are frequently reactionary and/or unproductive. These include but are not limited to race, region, gang, and, more broadly, the criminal element. Insecurity exacerbates this identification, not only for the obvious reasons but also because these are characteristics of which a prisoner cannot be deprived. The complete lack of security of location or individual association further aggravates the problem of identification with simplistic and superficial notions primarily and people secondarily.

Clinical psychologist Arnold Abrams said in 1973 testimony about Control Unit conditions, which were then similar but less onerous to those of present day Marion:

> I would say that if we want to produce, to make animals out of human beings, that this is a perfect procedure for doing it. And that humanizing [prisoners] means affording them some human contact with each other,and in a limited way with whatever the rules permit, with the world outside. The more limited they are, the more animal-like they will become in their behavior. . . . I think these men would continue much of the same behavior that they have been exhibiting, in turning against themselves, turning against others, other [prisoners], and then turning against the institution. I think this is an inevitable consequence of the kind of conditions they are afforded.[47]

This is almost exactly congruent with the reaction and rebellion path of colonially oppressed people in relation to their oppressors recorded by psychologist Frantz Fanon.[48] His investigation and analysis in that regard are directly translatable to prisoners and especially prisoners at Marion. Former BoP Director Carlson has disparaged the number of pyschological and sociological authorities that have testified against Marion conditions in a variety of legal and legislative proceedings.[49] The BoP has, however, been unable to advance any contrary expert analysis from outside the BoP.

Of course, all prisoners subjected to Marion-style repression do not succumb to these negative pressures, and those who do succumb do so in differing degrees. Ability to resist and extent of the stress inflicted vary. If they did not, there would be no need for experimental station Marion. There is also a counter-current to Marion oppression that works to engender a consciousness among its victims of their commonality, their shared adversity, their shared "us" status versus the oppressor "them." This can and does stimulate development of some awareness of Marion in the larger political context. But this is an unwanted imperfection or defect in the Marion model from the point of view of its owners, and its effects are actively discouraged. For these and other reasons, the experimental outcome and by-products vary between prisoners. Many have their own more or less coherent belief systems and, good, bad, or indifferent, adhere to them in a manner that is principled according to those systems. Such beliefs contribute to the psychological strength to resist oppression. Indeed, it is people with identifiable belief systems that are particularly the targets of Marion experimentation. It is they who will best yield the data desired by the experimenters on how to manipulate, undermine, and destroy attitudes that become threatening—and on what variations may exist among those they encounter. That is what puts political prisoners at particular risk of Marion abuse. Unprincipled criminal opportunists are much more easily able to squirm through the Marion system—and it is not designed to catch them except temporarily as camouflage for its less legitimate aims.

Nevertheless, whatever integrity a prisoner is able to maintain, the tension and stress and anger and frustration and debilitation and resentment and other emotional load factors artificially and deliberately created at Marion do accumulate and do take some toll. No one is immune, contrary to the arcane assertions of former Marion chief psychologist Dr. Richard Urbanik. Individuals may survive more or less intact, but not better for the experience. A very few may improve themselves, but that is in spite of Marion rather than because of it and is far less than the potential. Moreover, what constitutes improvement is a very subjective determination: what may be construed as visible manifestations of improvement may, in Marion prisoners, be outweighed by the less visible damage and deterioration. And any growth on such shifting psychological sands is subject to collapse and reversion. No one leaves Marion conditions after any length of time unscathed.[50]

Psychological scars, separation from people and community, negative socialization, and tension may express themselves in a variety of ways from the very minor up to major explosions. The result can be seen in daily life at Marion when people are put "on the grit" by inconsequential things, when the accumulation of small (and large!) psycho-cuts is manifested in neighbors who are irascible or otherwise unpleasant, in some health problems, and in various forms of misbehavior. Sometimes prisoners feel compelled to assert some control over their lives, even if only momentarily and over something minor and destructive of self and other people or things, to demonstrate their humanity and power over something, anything. Other times prisoners just lose control and "go off." The expressions of psychological injury may be grotesquely public or they may be sufficiently private to escape official attention. But the potential for the emergence in active expression of the damage done by Marion does not end when the prisoner leaves Marion.

The majority of prisoners do not demonstrate the damage in a highly visible manner; the extremes like suicide, murder, violence, and insanity occur more at the fringes. With the majority, it will more likely come out as a decrease in the quality of their lives and that of any community of which they become a part, most probably due to increased crime, diminished productivity, or merely disconnection, to the degree it comes out. Unfortunately, no tracking of prisoners exposed to the abuses of Marion is likely to be done to verify the observations of Marion prisoners and those who live in the other prison communities in which they are visible. The results would contradict official claims about the efficacy of Marion. Nor is there any way to accurately measure the losses or the range of disability inflicted by Marion. Former Marion prisoners are not going to be visible as victims of Marion in the community, further disguising the problem. When the impact is small it will be overlooked and when serious up to the few deadly explosions that can be expected it will be lost in the sensationalism and hysterical hyperbole surrounding the event.

Programmatic Exposure of Intent

Programmatic elements of USP Marion and the apparent direction in which results are sought corroborate the factual indications surrounding the build-up to an implementation of the lockdown as to the true purpose of the conversion. The experimental intent of the destructive practices of laboratory Marion is apparently to see how, and how far, prisoners and, to a lesser extent, guards can be conditioned into an unthinking habit of kneejerk compliance with the decrees of any authority, no matter how unreasonable, without inducing reaction and defiance. Though such conditioning is obviously attractive to prisoncrats, the object is more the mechanism than the immediate result. A problem is that such conformity and dependence is not consistent with any progressive society that depends upon the initiative of its citizens. To the extent that people need some ability to be self-directing in order to get by in a free society, they—whether former prisoners or otherwise—are not going to be able to do so according to its norms when conditioned to be unreasoning automations. Moreover, while this experiment in social programming does and is intended to succeed in breaking some prisoners into thoughtless malleability, its more common result is more dangerous. Along with a partial breakdown or at least undermining of the person, it creates a consciousness that power is the only reality: groveling, however obsequiously, is necessary in the face of power and follows whatever random impulses one may find attractive when power's face is averted. It also creates an impetus to retrieve "face" or self-status as an adherent to some principle and person in control lost in the breaking process. The possible detonation of the cargo of stress borne by Marion's victims makes this even more dangerous.

There is no other reason for the deliberate creation of uncertainty and insecurity and disability among prisoners than that they are being made victims of some arcane experimentation in furtherance of counter-insurgency capability currently described as low intensity warfare. There is no other reason to exacerbate the very problems that are purportedly being solved by the Marion lockdown. It would be no problem to give at least rudimentary hearings to prisoners prior to consignment to Marion and to establish specific duration for the "program." Existing rules would allow the lockdown and/or other lockups to fulfill its alleged functions without the indeterminacy feature. But even establishing such limited criteria would provide some small amount of security and sense of control that would impede or prevent the desired test results. It would also inhibit the investigatory and undermining assaults on political prisoners and others with belief systems strong enough to require more time. And it would make the use of Marion as a warehouse or as a weapon against specific people more difficult.

The value of education is so obvious that a reasonable person would expect it to be encouraged, even if that were only within the lockdown via correspondence courses and closed circuit t.v. and teachers who frequently walk the tiers of cells. But that would allow the development of some self-sufficiency and confidence and a transport beyond the sick banality of Marion that would improve prisoners' ability to resist psychological encroachments. The same is true of expansion of opportunities for visiting and other contact with the community. All these things would increase community involvement and undermine the "worst of the worst" propaganda, not to mention enhancing intellectual and emotional connection and identification beyond the individual and thus capability. The same applies to work and education and even congregate activity between prisoners. But that makes mental infringement more difficult, leaving less to attack and more with which to resist.

All of the groundless deprivations reinforce objectionable attitudes by making them the only ones possible given the circumstances. The negative socialization inherent in an experimental program such as Marion should be something that any prison administration would be desirous of avoiding, especially one with the resources of the BoP. But Marion deliberately encourages pernicious processes to the detriment of both the prison system and the society it supposedly serves. That yields information about the dynamics of interaction in oppressed populations and how to thwart progressive motion. As former Marion warden Jerry Williford noted over five years ago, the costs are ones the BoP is willing to accept.

That there is some ulterior motive in maintaining the lockdown and its experimentation is further borne out by the administrative denials of and diversions of attention from these psychological and social ramifications of the perpetual lockdown at Marion. Other benefits to the repressive apparatus being incidental and secondary, the only reward that is capable of transcending the political, social, and economic costs of maintaining the facade is the acquisition of experimental data that will further ruling class control inside and especially out.

Secondary Lockdown Goals

A likely secondary goal of the Marion lockdown is manipulation of the imprisoned via conditions of confinement. At the time the Marion laboratory was being engineered, what later became the "Omnibus Crime Control Act of 1984" was in the development stages. As originally envisioned, it included a "Sentencing Reform Act" that would have drastically limited plea bargains, disparity in sentencing, parole, and most good time as well as discretion in granting and denying the remaining good time. It has not turned out to be the reform it started out to be, judges and prosecutors and the ilk being loath to accept any such usurpation of their power. But when it appeared that the law might be enacted as planned, the apparatus needed some new mechanism to coerce accused persons into pleading guilty without time consuming and expensive trials and appeals, to pressure people into informing, and to increase the penalties for crimes against the ruling class and its institutions. The recent U.S. Supreme Court decision (January 1989) upholding the current version of the new sentencing law as well as the continuing authoritarian drift of the U.S. government has left that need (albeit a smaller one) and desire intact. Coercive instruments, once fashioned, rarely go away by themselves.

Marion conditions help make the prison apparatus a more potent weapon from initial contact (arrest) by aiding in the attack on the individual presumption of innocence that supposedly exists under U.S. law. The 1984 act allows indefinite pre-trial detention without bail on the basis of the alleged dangerousness of the accused, the same rationale used for consignment of people to Marion since 1983. Coupled with legal doctrines such as that permitting the use of "smugglers' profiles" that allow people who bear some resemblance to people who have been found smuggling over time to be detained and searched, this was another step toward legitimizing the handling of people according to group characteristics and stereotypes rather than as individuals. Marion set and continues to set precedents that allow prisoners to be punished individually because they are among the group of prisoners that also includes—and will increasingly include—people who did something displeasing to authority, although not criminal. A recent Seventh Circuit Court of Appeals decision (July 1988) describes Marion conditions as "sordid and horrible" and "ghastly" but justifies them on the basis of bad acts allegedly perpetrated by a small minority of then Marion prisoners in 1983.[51] It goes on to say that the BoP has complete freedom to send any prisoner to Marion, any time. And if prisoners can be abused for being part of an involuntary group, so can anyone.

Conditions of confinement also provide a vehicle for pretrial coercion of prisoners. There is a drastic difference between, for instance, the prison camp at Elgin Air Force Base in Florida and Marion—indeed, between the prisoners at Leavenworth and Marion. Nevertheless, the courts have held, essentially, that confinement is confinement and the BoP can put its prisoners anywhere. The difference between a sentence to be served at Marion and the same sentence at another prison is substantial and can fulfill the desired functions of coercion and enhancing punishment. Marion has already been used in all these respects. These functions are also indicated by the many needless restrictions and harassments unrelated to any legitimate penological objective.

The BoP has also used conditions of confinement as a threat in order to induce conformity, informing, and collaboration among prisoners already committed to its custody. This appears to be more openly the case at minimum security prisons and camps. In maximum security prisons, it has also been used, though less overtly; security or administrative needs are generally cited for transfer to worse conditions. In this context, former BoP director Norman Carlson called Marion "the ultimate sanction in the prison system" in an April 1987 speech at Southern Illinois University at Carbondale, Illinois, shortly before his retirement.[52]

In cooperation with the Parole Commission, the BoP has until now been better able to manipulate prisoners through the use of "clean time." Most federal prisoners are accorded eight to ten days per month of "statutory" clean time that can be taken away for violations of prison rules. That gives prison authorities a powerful coercive instrument, especially as clean time accumulates. Moreover, whether to release a prisoner between her or his eligibility for parole (one third of sentence for most prisoners) and the expiration of the sentence (usually two thirds of sentence plus whatever clean time had been taken) is up to the Parole Commission, a decision upon which prison authorities have substantial influence. With clean time cut under the reform to a maximum of fifty-four days per year that cannot be rescinded after being certified each year and the abolition of parole, conditions of confinement become more important as a tool of control and will increasingly be so as prisoners with new law sentences supplant those sentenced under the old.

The evidence, however, indicates that control via conditions of confinement has not been very effective and has entailed adverse consequences in maximum security prisons. The same is likely true of lower security prisons, though the effects are less visible owing to the different characteristics of the prisoners and degrees of repression. Indeed, the ineffectiveness of conditions of confinement as a deterrent control mechanism despite all the existing holes, segregations, adjustment centers, intensive management units, etc., etc., *ad nauseam* is what supposedly led to the Marion lockdown and justifies its conditions.

Bureaucratic self-preservation is another consideration that undoubtedly entered the minds of the prisoncrats in creating the lockdown. The more fiendish and nasty prisoners are alleged to be, the more of them there are likely to be, the longer their sentences are likely to be, and the larger and richer in employees (constituency) and money the American Gulag will become. Lockdowns such as that at Marion have metamorphosed into "high security operations" and have demonstrated a propensity to proliferate at an alarming rate. They are expensive, giving prison officials power over increased resources. They allow exclusion of the community. They also raise the notion of security to the level of holy writ and lead courts to confer on prisoncrats unconscionably broad discretion to carry out destructive repression in virtual secrecy. Staff to prisoner ratios range from two to four times that of other prisons. More guards also means more administrators and greater job security. In addition, creation of destructive models of imprisonment insures the expansion of behavior that will increase recidivism and justify yet more repression. That translates as increased security not only for the prison bureaucracy, but also for the rest of the civilian apparatus of repression, here called the "criminal justice system" but, more accurately, the first line of ruling class defense.

That these unstated functions of the Marion lockdown are, indeed, the real ones is borne out by the poverty of administrative claims regarding Marion. It is not only the "violent and predatory worst of the worst" that are sent here, and prisoners are not being humanely incapacitated. Even if they were, while people locked away in almost complete isolation may be temporarily unable to do much contrary to "security," it is apparent that the longer term costs for both security and the community, not to mention the prisoners, cannot be justified by that meager result. Anyway, administrative contentions about how the lockdown has decreased violence in other prisons do not bear scrutiny as the most recent "Sourcebook on Criminal Justice Statistics" and other evidence attest.[53] Verily, lockdown conditions tend to aggravate objectionable behavior. Instead of allowing other state and federal prisons to be operated in a more open manner according to official mythology, circumstances indicate that Marion has been a ball and chain that drags them toward its repressive extreme. And the fact that Marion and its clones go beyond concentration or humane incapacitation or security or even mere attempts at coercion or graft enhancement show that of these unstated functions, it is the experimental function that is primary. It is probable that there are no documents that will ever become public that discuss the creation of a laboratory for experiments in social manipulation and control such as locked down Marion. It is also probable that no hard evidence will be revealed demonstrating an intent to have it also fulfill the secondary tasks discussed herein. Posterity will likely be left with only discredited disinformation from official sources. Indeed, it is hard to tell exactly who the architects are and exactly where in the hierarchy awareness of the reality begins. Only after the practical collusions of prisoncrats has rendered Marion style oppression part of the cultural of penology will any attempts to legislate for or against it be made.

In 1962, then BoP director James V. Bennett spoke following an address to prison wardens and sociologists about brainwashing. He described the BoP as a tremendous opportunity to carry out experimentation and research via the manipulation of the environment and culture and implementing the techniques that had just been discussed. He said that there was a lot of research to do and exhorted his henchpeople and underlings to do it as individuals and report back the results.[54]

They did and are. The center acknowledges the experimenters' value with promotions (all upper echelon staff leave Marion with promotions, and the turnover is rapid) and undoubtedly other bureaucratic signals the public never sees. That way the power of those who do what is desired is enhanced, their practices are set up as those to emulate, and they are given authority over the less zealous or otherwise divergent. Bureaucratic darwinism.

Which of the agents of oppression deliberately follow the ordained path in full cognizance of and belief in its true elements and intent, which conform to it merely as career advancement, and which follow out of real acceptance of the official mythology is and will remain largely a matter of conjecture. So will, for the most part, who among the denizens of the BoP are, on balance, manipulators or manipulated and at what point they become one or the other. But it is not necessary to definitively finger all the individuals who are the sources of the theory in order to recognize the practice as an instrument of class control.

This analysis has been only a superficial survey of the present state of affairs at Marion. It has focused mostly on the more abstract elements of motivational and contradictions and pyschological consequences because it is these that have assumed primary importance. Chief Judge James Foreman of the Southern District of Illinois noted in a Control Unit case that "modern methods of penology make the rack and the thumbscrew obsolete": and all of Marion is now a Control Unit.[55] Psychological manipulation is also key in controlling the political reality beyond prison walls, and by aiding the ruling class in using the intangibles thereof. Marion is an instrument of oppression in addition to its incidental, secondary functions.

Conclusion

Marion is still a locked down prison where the U.S. uses expensive material facilities to cover up its deliberate abrogation of human rights. But it is not merely some atavistic, tough guy approach to controlling recalcitrant prisoners through increased use of force and physical restraint or even through psychological assault, all of which characterize Marion. It is a tool of repression.

The repression is still carried out directly through the infliction of severe conditions on prisoners, some of whom are political, most of whom are third world, and all but a very few of whom are proletarian. It is also done less visibly but more dangerously through the use of Marion as a laboratory for social experimentation toward improving ruling class ability to control the exploited and oppressed majority of people both within and outside prisons. Of that use and other secondary or incidental ones, the conditions are an element.

The U.S. Bureau of Prisons still denies the experimental use by insisting on other intentions and lying about the character and impact of Marion reality. Marion prisoners are not all "the worst of the worst." Conditions at Marion are more likely to reinforce and create objectionable attitudes and behavior than to have a positive effect. Marion practice also legitimizes draconian responses to exaggerated problems by the apparatus and the targeting of people according to group characteristics rather than individual actions. This is an outgrowth of experimental Marion.

Marion still poses a danger not only for the prisoners but for the communities upon which it feeds and into which debilitated and stressed out prisoners with impaired job and social skills will be released, communities against which the information garnered in abusing them will be used. And the danger of this maximum restriction mania is rapidly expanding as new control units are opened. "Final solutions" always start with the use of special repression like "concentration models" against small and particularly vilified minorities that are usually billed as something like "useless eaters," "the worst of the worst," or "rotten apples." But they never end there.

Notes

1. Kenneth J. Meyers, "Magistrate's Report and Recommendations," *Bruscino, et al. v. Carlson, et al.* (District Court for Southern District of Illinois, No. CV 84-4320, August 15, 1985). See also, Allen Breed and David Ward, "The United States Penitentiary, Marion, Illinois: A Report to the Judiciary Committee, United States House of Representatives," October 1984; U.S. Bureau of Prisons Policy Statements 5212.3, July 1979; *U.S. Bureau of Prisons Policy Statement 5212.1*, June 1973; and J. D. Henderson, "Marion Task Force Report," August 1979.

2. Norman Carlson, Testimony before the Subcommittee on Courts, Civil Liberties, and the Administration of Justice of the Committee on the Judiciary, U.S. House of Representatives, Ninety-eighth Congress, second session, March 29, 1984.

3. Dr. David Fogel, Testimony before the Subcommittee on Courts, March 29, 1984.

4. U.S. Bureau of Prisons, Policy Statement 5212.3, July 1979.

5. Kenneth T. Blaylock, Testimony before the Subcommittee on Courts, March 29, 1984.

6. American Federation of Government Employees, National Council of Prisons Locals, AFL-CIO, "A Report on the Worsening Day-to-Day Conditions Affecting Correctional Employees in the Federal Bureau of Prisons," March 1984.

7. Kenneth T. Blaylock and David Fogel, Testimony before the Subcommittee on Courts, March 1984; "Prison Guard Union is Penned by Fear," *The San Antonio Light*, February 5, 1984; and "Memories Painful for Prison Guard," *The Southern Illinoisan*, April 8, 1984.

8. Jan Susler, James B. Roberts, and Marion Prisoners Rights Project, "An Updated Public Report About the Continuing Lockdown and Torture of Prisoners at U.S. Penitentiary, Marion," March 26, 1984.

9. *Southern Illinoisan*, 1981-1982.

10. U.S. Court of Appeals for the Seventh Circuit, "Unpublished Order" in *Abel et al. vs. Miller* (Circuit Court No. 80-2848, May 18, 1982).

11. BoP, "Program and Procedure Review, U.S. Penitentiary, Marion, Illinois," November 2-3, 1981.

12. Fogel, Subcommittee Testimony, March 29, 1989, describing research for the history of corrections he wrote.

13. Norman Carlson, Letter to U.S. Representative Patricia Schroeder, Attachment A, March 9, 1984.

14. Breed and Ward, "The U.S. Penitentiary at Marion. . . ."

15. Warden Jerry Williford (now Regional Director of BoP Western Region), 10:00 pm News, WSIL-TV, February 26 1985, acknowledged mental deterioration of prisoners subjected to Marion conditions but said that was a cost BoP was willing to accept.

16. Frantz Fanon, *The Wretched of the Earth* (New York: Grove Press, 1967).

17. Breed and Ward, "The U.S. Penitentiary. . . ." Also, Meyers, "Magistrate's Report. . . .'

18 "Most Dangerous Men: A Portrait of Inmates Who Kill," *The Southern Illinoisan*, May 25, 1983.

19. For example, 83rd General Assembly of the State of Illinois, "Senate Resolution No. 384," November 4, 1983.

20. Meyers, "Magistrate's Report."

21. "Memories Painful for Prison Guard," *The Southern Illinoisan*, April 8, 1984 and Clayton Fountain, Letter to U.S. Representative Robert Kastenmeier, April 16, 1985.

22. Dr. David Fogel and Dr. Frank Rundle, Testimony before Subcommittee. . . . Also, Craig Haney, Testimony in *Bruscino vs. Carlson*; Dr. Bernard Rubin, Testimony in *Adams vs. Carlson* (Federal Reporter citation 488 F. 2nd 619, 7 Cir. 1973), 1973.

23. "Most Dangerous," *op. cit.*

24. *Chicago Tribune*, October 25, 1983.

25. "Heavy Hand Comes Down at Marion," *Fortune News*, Spring 1984. Also Leonard Peltier, Letter to U.S. Representative William H. Gray III, April 25, 1984.

26. Dennis Cunningham, Jan Susler, Marion Prisoner Rights Project, "A Public Report About a Violent Assault Against Prisoners and Continuing Illegal Punishment and Torture of the Prison Population at the U.S. Penitentiary at Marion, Illinois," January 17, 1984.

27. *Ibid.* See also Meyers, "Magistrate's Report" and Donna H. Kolb, James B. Roberts, Nancy Horgan, "Class Action Complaint for Declaratory Judgement, Injunctive Relief and for Damages and Demand for a Jury Trial" in *Bruscio et al. vs. Carlson, et al.* Southern District of Illinois No. CV84-

4320, Filed June 29, 1984.
28. *Ibid.*
29. *Ibid.*
30. *Ibid.*
31. *Ibid.*
32. Meyers, "Magistrate's Report."
33. Meyers, "Magistrate's Report."
34. Fogel, Subcommittee Testimony, March 29, 1984.
35. *Ibid.*
36. BoP, "Institution Supplement" (to Policy Statement) MAR-5220, "Intermediate Unit Operations (C-Unit)," March 5, 1985.
37. U.S. Court of Appeals for the Seventh Circuit Opinion in *Miller vs. Henman.*
38. Amnesty International, "Report on the Prisoner's Lawsuit Against Marion Prison, Illinois, USA"; sent to BoP Director Carlson, November 30, 1986.
39. American Civil Liberties Union, "Executive Summary of ACLU National Prison Project Testimony, June 26, 1985, in the Sub-Committee on the Courts, Civil Liberties, and the Administration of Justice," Appendixes: Gordon Kamka, Vice President Abraxas Associates (a management consulting firm) former wardern and Secretary of Maryland Department of Corrections, "Statement," Vincent Nathan, attorney, court appointed "special master" of prisons in Ohio, Georgia, Texas, and New Mexico, "Statement." See also, Prof. Craig Haney, Director, Graduate Program in Psychology, University of California, Santa Cruz, Expert Testimony in *Bruscino et al. vs. Carlson et al.*, No. 84-4320.
40. United Nations Minimum Standard Rules for the Treatment of Prisoners.
41. Breed and Ward, "The U.S. Penitentiary at Marion"
42. "Custody Catch," *The Marionette*, No. 15, July 1986.
43. David Wheeler, "Issues and Answers," British Broadcasting Corporation, April 15, 1988.
44. Bernard Rubin, Testimony in *Adams.*
45. Rundle, Testimony before the Sub-Committee.
46. *Ibid.*
47. Dr. Arnold Adams, Testimony in *Bono vs. Saxbe*, Southern District of Illinois, No. 74-81-E. Dr. Abrams spoke regarding control unit conditions in a case contesting them filed in 1983; those conditions were less onerous than those obtaining in all of Marion today.
48. Fanon, *Wretched.*
49. Carlson, Testimony before Sub-Committee, June 26, 1985.
50. Rundle, Testimony before Sub-Committee, June 26, 1985.
51. Seventh Circuit Court of Appeals, Opinion, *Bruscio et al. vs. Carlson et al.*, Seventh Circuit No. 87-1683, 87-1943, July 22, 1988.
52. Norman Carlson, Speech to "the criminal justice community" at Southern Illinois University, April 15, 1987. See also, "The Fat Lady Sings," *The Marionette*, No. 24, April 1987, and Kamka, Nathan, Haney, Rundle.
53. For example, Nancy Emmet Horgan, Attorney, Letter to Jerry Williford, Warden, USP Marion, October 4, 1985. Ms. Horgan calls Warden Williford to task for untrue statements and false conclusions on WSIU-TV

program "Inquiry" on September 26, 1985. Williford had claimed that assaults at other penitentiaries had dropped 44% in the 20 months after *versus* the 20 months before the lockdown; Horgan exposed the deliberate falsity of the claim with BoP statistics of which Williford presumably was aware.

54. Marion Prisoner Rights Project, "Breaking Men's Minds," pamphlet.

55. James Foreman, Chief Judge, "Opinion in *Bono et al. vs. Saxbe et al*," Southern Illinois District Court No. 74-81-E (Federal Supplement citation, 527 F. Supp. 1987 (1981), September 30, 1981.)

Mike Ryan

Solitude as Counterinsurgency—
The U.S. Isolation Model of
Political Incarceration

> ... each prisoner that does not recant is put through a program
> of conditioning. Such psychologically structured programs of
> brainwashing are already routine in different U.S. prisons and
> serve as an example for the West German (isolation) units.
> Therefore, we will briefly describe, as an example, the U.S. prison
> 'Marion.' . . . Marion was established in 1962 and consists of
> separate sections that are separated from one another. On the
> one hand, this is for reasons of security, to prevent a large uprising
> in the prison. On the other hand, it also makes it easier for the
> prison psychologists to separate and monitor prisons. The
> brainwashing in Marion is carried out in four partially combined
> ways. The first is comprised of playing prisoners off against one
> another using corrupt prisoners to spy, using guards to threaten
> and humiliate prisoners, and ending, insofar as possible, all
> contacts to comrades in prison and contacts with the outside. In
> short, the prisoner's actual personality must be destroyed and
> then be reconstructed according to the image of those in power.
> A prisoner in Marion reduced it to the common denominator when
> he said: 'Adapt or die!' The second method is based on the
> psychological model of conditioning. Through a specific daily
> routine and work routine which the prisoner must maintain;
> through training, a particular behavior is to be implanted in the
> unconscious. He should be trained, so to speak, until he responds
> automatically without thinking to orders and situations. Which
> finally leads to a complete submission and adaptation to those
> in power. . . . Thirdly, sensory deprivation is employed. This form
> of white torture was used against Ulrike Meinhof and Astrid
> Proll[1] in the dead wing in Ossendorf. Military psychologists
> discovered in the fifties that a human without environmental
> stimulation, such as seeing, hearing, and feeling, and without
> educational stimulation from others would become physically
> ill. For example, hallucinations, feelings of terror, persecution,
> complexes, and psychosomatic disturbances can occur. As well,
> under such extreme condition, people are susceptible to pro-
> paganda and are generally more open to influence. In Marion

prisoners are subjected to sensory deprivation in small cells which are nearly soundproof and are lighted day and night. Prisoners are locked up under these conditions for extended periods of time until they are soft enough for other forms of treatment. . . . The final method in Marion is psychopharmacology; chemical straitjackets. Using this method, prisoners are rendered submissive; their brains and their wills are chemically burned out. In the FRG [Federal Republic of Germany], this method plays an important role in the psychiatric wings of the prisons and psychiatric clinics. It is, above all, not certain that such drugs are not secretly administered with the prison food. Such cases have been uncovered.[2]

The above extract from a paper written by several prisoners of the West German 2nd of June Movement[3] in February 1980 raises important questions regarding the role of Marion Penitentiary as an experimental model for international counterinsurgency. Elsewhere, I examined the assertion that the Lexington High Security Unit for women was based on the so-called Stammheim model, the prison isolation model used to neutralize political prisoners and prisoners of war in West Germany.[4] Here I will examine the role that North American research and practical applications in Marion and elsewhere have played in refining the techniques applied against prisoners internationally. In short, I will suggest that we have a dialectic of oppression which functions throughout the Western world, if not globally, and that understanding research and experimentation that has been carried out in the U.S. has been and is key to understanding this dialectic.

While Stammheim may well have added significant refinements to the counterinsurgency aspects of prison, the actual origin of organized counterinsurgency in Western prisons lies in North America. In the 1950s and '60s a significant body of work began to appear in academic journals devoted to psychology, psychiatry, criminology, and law examining various propagandistic approaches to behavior modification in prison environments. The impetus for this work was without a doubt the concerns raised for the U.S. state by the Chinese campaign of "re-education" directed at U.S. POWs during the Korean War.

The Korean Experience

The most important work done to analyze and adapt the Chinese program in Korea was, without question, that of Dr. Edgar Schein. A psychologist with the School of Industrial Management at MIT, Schein was involved in interviewing and processing POWs repatriated to the U.S. in 1953. For the better part of a decade, his work focused on the

Korean experience. The final result was a book entitled *Coercive Persuasion,* in which he explains the precepts of Chinese "thought reform." To fully understand the programs at Marion and elsewhere, an in-depth look at Schein's conclusions is instructive.

Schein starts with the presumption that "the beliefs, attitudes, values, and behavior of an individual tend to be integrated with each other and tend to be organized around a person's self-image or self-concept. This integration, even if imperfect, gives continuity and stability to the person and hence operates as a force against being influenced, unless the change which the influence implies is seen to be a change in the direction of greater integration."[5]

Working from this premise, Schein pinpoints a series of steps involved in effecting successful change. Respectively, these are "unfreezing, changing, and refreezing." He defines the three steps as follows:

> **Unfreezing:** an alteration by the agent of influence of the forces acting on the person such that the existing equilibrium is no longer stable. Subjectively one can think of this as the induction of a need or a motive to change; i.e., the person who has been unfrozen with respect to some belief desires to change or abandon that belief.
>
> **Changing:** the provision by the agent of influence of information, arguments, models, to be imitated or identified with, etc., which provide a direction of change toward a new equilibrium, usually by allowing the person to learn something new, redefine something old, re-evaluate or reintegrate other parts of his personality or belief system, etc. Subjectively this would be experienced as 'seeing the light,' having insight, seeing that the other fellow's viewpoint has a lot of merit, beginning to understand how someone else thinks about things, and so on.
>
> **Refreezing:** the facilitation by the agent of influence of the reintegration of the new equilibrium into the rest of the personality and into ongoing interpersonal relationships by the provision of reward and social support for any changes made by the person. Sometimes, however, it is not within the agent's power to determine whether the new belief will in fact fit into the rest of the personality or will be accepted by the person's significant others. Subjectively this would be experienced as discovering that others shared one's new point of view, that they were pleased with the change, that the new belief was quite congenial with other parts of the self-image and other beliefs, etc.[6]

Schein points to a series of tactics that can be used to increase the likelihood of change. He notes that any inner conflict an individual is feeling can be exacerbated by sleep deprivation and by physically exhausting circumstances. He suggests that under such circumstances an individual will cooperate to decrease exhaustion and pain.

[I]t can be seen that the induction of a motive to change could involve a strengthening of forces toward change (e.g. getting the prisoner to denounce a close friend which sets up strong needs to rationalize his behavior; humiliating the prisoner in public to destroy his image of himself, thus heightening his need for new identity, etc.) or a weakening of forces against change (e.g. making certain significant emotional relationships inoperative by cutting or manipulating communication channels with the outside; showing the prisoner that the new attitudes are not, in fact, incompatible with his values or with other parts of the personality by intensive discussion and the encouragement of self-analysis on his part, etc.) or both.[7]

Schein indicates that the unfreezing process undermines and destroys "the prisoner's self-image and basic sense of identity" leaving her or him "with a fundamental psychological problem to solve"—namely the reestablishment of a viable self. In other words, the unfreezing process could precipitate or exacerbate an "identity crisis." Under such conditions, he notes, the establishment of an identity involves "finding new beliefs and attitudes about the self which would be reinforced and confirmed by others." He also observes that if the prisoner is "in an environment in which the only reinforcements available [are] contingent upon his accepting a particular set of beliefs and attitudes about himself, it is likely that he [will] eventually accept such beliefs and attitudes."[8] Schein breaks this process down into six steps:

1. Precipitation or exacerbation of an 'identity crisis' as a result of an unfreezing process.
2. The induction of a motive to find acceptable beliefs about the self in an environment in which the number of such acceptable beliefs is sharply limited.
3. A search for information relevant to finding acceptable beliefs about the self.
4. The finding of an 'other' whose identity is acceptable (whose beliefs about himself are accepted as correct by other prisoners, interrogators, etc.)
5. Identification with this 'other,' even if he was initially defined as an enemy.
6. The acceptance of things that 'other' says and does as credible information about the prisoner's own self.[9]

Schein states that the process of identification "with another prisoner or one of the authorities [is] often aided by the 'discovery' that the 'other' [is] in many respects similar to the prisoner."[10] This identification process is key.

Once an identification process has begun and the behavior of the 'other' begins to be treated as credible information, the foundation was laid for extensive cognitive re-definition in the prisoner. The basic process in such redefinition was the learning of new standards for judging behavior and a new set of semantic rules, i.e., the adoption of a new frame of reference. . . .[11]

Of course, cellmates play a key role: "He received extensive 'help' in this redefining process by the examples of his cellmates, by their criticism of him, and by their continued espousal of the 'correct attitude.'"[12] Even if a prisoner managed to maintain her or his identity under such circumstances, some change is inevitable. Schein notes that in the cases of those "whose identity remained more intact, the cellmates or authorities also assumed importance as sources of information, particularly if they represented a completely unanimous social environment. Unanimity of outlook in terms of premises completely different from the prisoner's led inevitably to some shifting of the prisoner's own standards of judgement and frame of reference."[13] Any change effected can only be expected to remain stable if it is effectively *refrozen*.

> This process implies that the new belief must be integrated into other parts of the person and must be supported and reinforced by the behavior of significant others. If it is not integrated or supported, it will change once again when the original forces toward change have been removed.[14]

Further:

> If the beliefs and attitudes which are involved in the change process concern the person's self and his sense of identity, it is particularly important to consider the role which interpersonal confirmation plays as a refreezing force. We know our 'selves' primarily through others, hence attitudes toward self must be shared by at least those others who are most important to us. If these others do not support or confirm new attitudes, they are in effect forcing the person to change them once again by motivating him to find attitudes which they will confirm or support.[15]

And finally:

> Whether the new attitudes then persisted or not depended on how well integrated they were with the rest of the repatriate's personality and on the likelihood that the repatriate would receive emotional support for the changes from others he regarded as important.[16]

Having developed the outlines of the process of thought reform, Schein acknowledges that there are varying degrees of success in practice. There is what he describes as *minimal behavioral compliance*, marked by a willingness to sign a confession or indicate an attitude change "seen by the prisoner not to be technically true . . . and not to be compromising to himself or important reference groups. . . ."[17] *Extensive behavioral compliance* is described as a willingness to sign a confession or indicate an attitude change "reflecting the agent's accusation but . . . clearly recognized by the prisoner as false, yet . . . confessed to in order to ease pressure and gain release from imprisonment. . . ."[18]

There also exists a phenomenon which Schein refers to as *unintegrated attitude change*; a condition where new attitudes are "grafted onto an old attitude structure but not integrated into it" with "no real identity crisis stimulated." In such cases the person will eventually "re-evaluate his prison experience and . . . recognize that he had been forced to comply against his will."[19]

Schein also indicates the existence of *partially or totally integrated attitude change*, wherein, "new attitudes either continue or exacerbate an identity crisis or tend to resolve it." He adds, "The main difference between the partially and totally integrated groups [is] that in the former the new attitudes and frame of reference did not produce a satisfactory resolution of the identity crisis stimulated in prison, while in the latter they did."[20] In short, the former group is not successfully refrozen while the latter is, experiencing a "conversion to commitment."[21] There are several other factors raised by Schein with are worthy of our attention in this context. For example,

> Most prisoners experienced both solitary confinement and confinement in groups ranging in size from two to twenty or more. It has often been assumed that the explanation of a prisoner's weakening was to be found in the periods of isolation and solitary confinement he suffered. Our data support the opposite conclusion—that the major stress for prisoners was to survive psychologically in a group cell in which the prisoners were committed to reforming themselves and particularly their most backward member.[22]

Also:

> [T]he process of coercive persuasion used as a way of influencing beliefs and attitudes may have unanticipated and undesirable consequences for the influencing institution, in that it may lead to a ritualization of belief and a gradual atrophy of creative abilities which presumably the institution wishes to preserve and harness toward its goals.[23]

And finally:

> [T]he process of coercive persuasion as observed in Chinese Communist prisons has its counterpart in various kinds of total institutions in our own society and elements of it exist in any influence relationship in which there are physical, social, or psychological constraints which tend to force the person to expose

himself to the pressures of the influence agent. In putting our emphasis on the content of the influence we have often tended to overlook similarities in the nature of the influence process. There is a world of difference in the content of what is transmitted in religious orders, prisons, educational institutions, mental hospitals, and thought reform centers. But there are striking similarities in the manner in which the influence occurs, a fact which should warn us strenuously against letting our moral and political sentiments color our scientific understanding of the Chinese Communist approach to influence.[24]

While the model Schein develops on the basis of the Korean experience is indeed frightening, he himself notes in his well-known 1962 article, "Man Against Man: Brainwashing," that the Chinese had a success rate of at best ten to fifteen percent.[25]

Sensory Deprivation, Perceptual Deprivation, and Social Isolation

At approximately the same time Schein was doing his work on so-called Chinese "brainwashing" techniques, another group of scientists was beginning to conduct experiments in the psychological and physiological effects of sensory deprivation, perceptual deprivation, and social (small group) isolation. The impetus was the so-called Moscow Trials. Writing in 1961, one decade after the first studies, Dr. D. O. Hebb said, "The work that we have done at McGill University began, actually, with the problem of brainwashing. . . . The chief impetus, of course, was the dismay at the kind of 'confessions' being produced at the Russian Communist trials."[26]

Before proceeding, some definitions are in order. John P. Zubeck describes procedures of achieving sensory deprivation (SD) and perceptual deprivation (PD) as follows:

> In SD condition, efforts are made to reduce sensory stimulation to as low a level as possible. This is usually accomplished by the use of a dark soundproof chamber in which the subject, wearing gauntlet-type gloves, is instructed to lie quietly on a cot or mattress. Earplugs or ear muffs may be used to reduce further the level of sensory stimulation. Communication between subject and experimenter is kept to a minimum, thus reducing social stimulation. An even more severe procedure to produce "total" deprivation is the water-immersion technique in which the subject, wearing nothing but an opaque mask, is immersed in a large tank of slowly flowing water (94 degrees F) and instructed to inhibit all movements. Because of its severity, this procedure can only be used for short-term deprivation experiments.

Maximum endurance is approximately eight hours. . . . In the PD condition, on the other hand, an attempt is made to reduce the patterning and meaningful organization of sensory stimulation while maintaining its level near normal. This is the McGill procedure. The subject typically lies on a cot in a chamber wearing gloves and translucent goggles, which permit diffuse light but eliminate all pattern vision. A masking sound, usually white noise, or less commonly the hum of a fan, is directed into both ears. The intensity of light and noise is maintained at a constant level. A less widely used variation of the PD procedure, employed for durations of less than a day, involves placing the subject in a polio tank respirator and exposing him to a repetitive drone of a motor and a visual environment restricted to the front of the respirator and the blank surface of an overhead screen. It can be seen, therefore, that PD involves a higher level of sensory input than SD, but the stimulation is largely devoid of meaningful organization.[27]

At a symposium held at Harvard Medical School in 1961, the results of SD, PD, and SI were examined by a number of experts in the field. In an assessment entitled *The Effect of Human Isolation upon Some Perceptual and Motor Skills*, Jack A. Vernon, Thomas E. McGill, Walter L. Gurlick, and Douglas R. Candland indicated that SD had a negative impact on rotary pursuit ability, color perception, motor coordination, minor training, body weight, and galvanic skin resistance.[28] Another assessment by Stanford J. Freedman, Henry U. Grunebaum, and Milton Greenblatt, regarding the effect of as little as eight hours of SD showed significant degrees of deteriorization in concentration and coherent thought, difficulty in speech, changes in body image, auditory illusion, paranoia, and visual hallucinations.[29]

These initial findings were not only verified by another decade's work, but an even more horrifying picture began to emerge. In 1973, a book entitled *Man in Isolation and Confinement* was released. This book contained the expanded and revised papers from the Symposium on Man in Isolation and/or Enclosed Space, sponsored by the NATO Science Committee Advisory Group on Human Factors, held in Rome in October 1969. In a paper entitled "Behavioral and Physiological Effects of Prolonged Sensory and Perceptual Deprivation: A Review," John P. Zubeck outlines the effects of SD and PD. Examining "reported visual reservations" (RVSs), Zubeck indicates consistent results of over forty percent for simple hallucinations or Type A RVSs and eighteen to nineteen percent complex hallucinations or Type B RVSs. In 1966, Zukerman and Hopkins produced comparable results with only one hour of SD. As little as ten to thrity minutes of darkness produce RVSs in some cases. In cases of perceptual deprivation, the occurrence of RVSs is even more marked.

In a generalized way, the effects of perceptual deprivation are more severe than those of sensory deprivation. Studies into the effects of PD indicate an inability to concentrate or think clearly, boredom, a high degree of restlessness, changes in body-image, exaggerated emotional reactions, excessive irritation over small things, annoyance with experimenters, brooding and dwelling on perceived injustices.

A 1967 study carried out by Zubeck and McNeill indicates the following results in the case of seven days of PD. Subjects experienced RVSs, complex and vivid dreams, changes in body-image, loss of contact with reality, reminiscences and vivid memories, cognitive inefficiencies, speech impairment, temporal disorientation, anxiety, hunger, subjective restlessness, boredom, sexual and religious preoccupations, changes in self-appraisal as well as surprise. These results were duplicated in varying degrees in subsequent studies of periods of perceptual deprivation of as little as eight hours.

Studies of individuals subjected to PD also show consistently poorer results on tests of verbal fluency, anagrams, numerical tasks, abstract reasoning and recognition. Perhaps most frightening is the effects of persuasive messages under conditions of PD. Not only is susceptibility greatly increased, but the effects of propaganda in conditions of PD seem to be the only effects that last well beyond the PD period. similar results have also been produced by short periods of PD, If we couple this with the fact that people subjected to PD and SD seek stimulation even if it is meaningless, we have a truly frightening scenario. Both PD and SD impair dexterity and eye-hand coordination. Simple motor coordination may also be impaired if deprivation lasts long enough and gross motor coordination is always severely impaired.

The physical impact of SD and PD is complex. Both SD and PD reduce visual alertness. SD decreases auditory vigilance while PD increases it. Both SD and PD increase tactile perception. SD increases pain sensitivity while PD decreases it. PD increases the sense of taste. PD also disrupts spacial orientation. Both SD and SP cause changes in EEG activity, a result which lasts for a significant time period after deprivation ends, especially with regard to Alpha activity. SD and PD also lead to a decrease in skin resistance. Looking specifically at the effects of prolonged isolation, Zubeck notes a decrease in blood pressure and respiratory rate as well as a decrease of body weight. He notes that all of these factors correct themselves immediately upon release from isolation.

Comparing the results of social isolation (SI) to PD, Zubeck finds similarities in the effects created by both. However, in all cases PD is shown to produce a more negative effect. Changes in EEG activity, especially Alpha activity, are twice as marked in cases of PD. SI produced only slight cognitive impairment compared to extreme impairment in the case of PD. PD also produces more extreme results in the case of hallucinatory experiences, temporal disorientation, speech difficulties, sexual and religious thoughts, and negative attitudes toward the experimenters.[30]

In another paper, E. K. Gunderson examines the behavior of individuals in isolated groups. He observes that minor events trigger stress and tension and that subjects also exhibit emotional regression, general malaise and lethargy, sleep disturbances, and grouchiness. Gunderson also notes that differences in social and educational background, interests, values, viewpoints, and attitudes can lead to and deepen the conflicts.[31] William W. Haythorn examines the impact of isolation in pairs. He notes the development of resentments, boredom, and irritation, with the compensating development of territorial preferences. Long term isolation under these conditions leads to impairment of memory, difficulty in concentrating, and low energy for intellectual pursuits.[32]

Comparing small group isolation to SD, S. B. Sells suggests that isolated groups report few incidents of unusual visual and auditory sensations, perceptual distortions, difficulty in distinguishing between sleep and waking states, unusual dreams, or other distorted experiences.[33] In a book written the same year, John P. Zubeck observes that small group isolation always leads to an extreme level of irritability, hostility, and personality conflicts. He also notes that the longer the isolation lasts, the greater the degree of withdrawal exhibited. He observes that relationships with the outside are also increasingly marked by hostility. He also notes increased sleeplessness, depression, mood declines, compulsive behavior, and psychosomatic problems.[34]

Out of the Lab and into the Prison

It was Schein himself who took the results of his work and elaborated its application to U.S. prisons in a conference with key representatives from the Bureau of Prisons (BoP). His speech and the subsequent discussion were printed in *Corrective Psychiatry and the Journal of Social Therapy* in 1962. In contextualizing his remarks, he says,

> This 'model' of behavior and attitude change is a general one which can encompass phenomena as widely separated as brainwashing and rehabilitation in a prison or a mental hospital. I would like to have you think of brainwashing not in terms of politics, ethics, and morals, but in terms of the deliberate changing of behavior and attitudes by a group of men who have

relatively complete control over the environment in which the captive lives. . . . If we find similar methods being used by Communists and some of our own institutions of change, we have a dilemma, of course. Should we then condemn our own methods because they resemble brainwashing? I prefer to think that the Communists have drawn from the same reservoir of human wisdom and knowledge as we have, but have applied this wisdom to achieve goals which we cannot condone. These techniques in the service of different goals, however, may be quite acceptable to us. Rather than saying that some adult re-education is like brainwashing and therefore bad, I prefer to say that brainwashing is like some adult re-education and therefore has some good features to it, as I will try to indicate.[35]

As to the application of this model to prisons, he is absolutely clear:

Implications: The implications of these unfortunate events for a more general theory of behavior change are perfectly clear. If one wants to produce behavior inconsistent with the person's standards of conduct, first disorganize the group which supports those standards, then undermine his other emotional supports, then put him in a new and ambiguous situation for which the standards are unclear, and then put pressure on him. I leave it to you to judge whether there are any similarities between these events and those which occur in prisons when we teach prisoners 'to serve their own time' by moving them around and punishing clandestine group actively not sanctioned by the prison authorities.[36]

The political context of the discussion was not lost on the participants as the following exchange regarding the so-called Black Muslims and Vietnam era conscientious objectors indicates.

Dr. Lowry: I can offer no pat formula for dealing the Muslim groups, except that there again we have to apply the techniques which we heard about in terms of appreciating what the goal of the Muslims is, or of any other group. And then doing some analytic study of the methods that they are using so that we can try to dissipate the forces that are going in the direction that we regard as destructive. This is not an easy matter and it is an extremely difficult group to work with because they have as some of their basic premises some truth, and that is that members of their race have been persecuted in many ways, and from this premise you can build a whole system of logic and behavior which looks very fine but which can be very destructive.

James V. Bennett: Well, the prisons have been filled with such groups at different times. During the war, we struggled with the conscientious objectors—non-violent coercionists—and believe me, that was really a problem. Every day they got together as a group and put sand in the grease boxes and refused to eat and went on hunger strikes and agitated, etc., and we were always trying to find some way in which we could change or manipulate their environment. Dr. Schein, do you have a technique to change any of these fellows?

Dr. Schein: . . . I think in that situation, as far as I can see, the ethics [are] clear—when a group really is arrayed against you and you allow it the means of organizng itself and subverting all your goals, there is no question in my mind but that you have to take physical action, in the sense of pulling out the leaders, just as the Communists pulled out the leaders from our prisoner groups and isolated them from the rest of the group.

Mr. Bennett: I would agree with that as to certain types of behaviors and certain types of individuals, but in dealing with the conscientious objector, if you pulled what you thought was the leader and the agitator, you then create a defensive solidarity among all the rest of them and make it impossible to deal with them as a group.[37]

In his closing comments, the chairman of the seminar drew the obvious conclusion,

If there is one thing that you can get out of this visit to Washington, let it be that you are thoughtful people with lots of opportunity to experiment. There is lots of research to do—do it as individuals, do it as groups, and let us know the results. Get acquainted with the people in your community who are doing this kind of work, such as the panelists here are doing. Unfortunately, we have no institution very close to Harvard University, but we do have other universities that can be a stimulus and a help. Get acquainted with them.[38]

Just as Schein grasped the significance of this work for U.S. prisons, a certain Dr. James V. McConnell understood the practical significance of SD, PD, and SI experimentation. In a 1970 article entitled "Criminals Can Be Brainwashed Now," he argued for the application of these techniques in U.S. prisons. Describing Dr. Donald Hebb's 1951 McGill University experiment, McConnell observed:

Hebb expected the students to last at least six weeks. None of them lasted more than a few days. During the first 24 hours, they caught up on their sleep, but after that the experience became progressively more painful for all of them. They reported long stretches in which they seemed to be awake, but their minds were turned off entirely—they simply didn't 'think' at all. They were tested while they were in the cubicles, and most of them showed marked deterioration in intellectual functioning. Many experienced vivid hallucinations—one student in particular insisted that a tiny space ship had got into the chamber and was buzzing around shooting pellets at him. Most of all though, the students were bored. They tried to trick the experimenter into talking to them. In a subsequent experiment, Hebb's subjects listened to dull recorded speeches which they could start by pressing a button. The experimenters, who had to listen too, almost went out of their minds, but the students seemed to enjoy thoroughly hearing the same stock-market report a hundred times a day. And when Hebb provided propaganda messages instead of stock-market reports, he found that whatever the message was, no matter how poorly it was presented or how illogical it sounded, the propaganda had a marked effect on the students' attitudes— an effect which lasted for at least a year after the students came out of the deprivation chambers.[39]

The message the reader is to receive is apparent. McConnell argues for a complete control over the environment in which prisoners are held.

It is axiomatic in the behavioral sciences that the more you control an organism's environment, the more you can control its behavior. It goes without saying that the only way you can gain complete control over a person's behavior is to gain complete control over his environment. The sensory-deprivation experiments suggest that we should be able to do exactly that. . . . I believe that the day has come when we can combine sensory deprivation with drugs, hypnosis, and astute manipulation of reward and punishment to gain almost absolute control over an individual's behavior. It should be possible then to achieve a very rapid and highly effective type of positive brainwashing that would allow us to make dramatic changes in a person's behavior and personality.[40]

Proceeding to the logical conclusion, McConnell further argues,

For misdemeanors or minor offenses we would administer brief, painless punishment, sufficient to stamp out the anti-social behavior. We'd assume that a felony was clear evidence that the criminal had somehow acquired full-blown social neurosis and needed to be cured, not punished. We'd send him to a rehabilitation center where he'd undergo positive brainwashing until we were quite sure he had become a law-abiding citizen who would not again commit an anti-social act. We'd probably have to restructure his entire personality.[41]

McConnell also anticipates and responds to the obvious human rights arguments:

Your ego, or individuality, was forced on you by your genetic constitution and by the society into which you were born. You had no say about the kind of personality you acquired, and there's no reason to believe you should have the right to refuse to acquire a new personality if your old one is anti-social. I don't believe the Constitution of the United States gives you the right to commit a crime if you want to; therefore, the Constitution does not guarantee you the right to maintain inviolable the personality it forces on you in the first place—if and when the personality manifests strongly anti-social behavior.[42]

Fittingly, McConnell closes his ramblings with the following statement: "Today's behavioral psychologists are the architects and engineers of the Brave New World."[43] Insane, you say. Indeed. However, as we shall see, an insanity that has its application in U.S. prisons.

"Brave New Prison"

The 1970s were a decade of experiments in behavioral modification in US prisons. Various "programs" were instituted. Some integrated the Persuasive Coercion techniques pinpointed by Schein. Others were based on the principles of SD, PD, or SI. Yet others relied heavily on drug "therapy." All of them had one thing in common: they sought to permanently eradicate undesirable behavior in particularly resistant individuals. As such, they were all generally in keeping with Schein and McConnell's conceptions of behavior modification. An examination of some of the most prominent "programs" offers some insights into the multifaceted nature of the experiments carried on within the prisons during this period.

Perhaps the purest attempt to apply Schein's "Persuasive Coercion" was Dr. Martin Groder's Transactional Analysis Program, which began at Marion in 1968. Writing in *Rough Times* in 1974, Joe Hunt outlines the TA Program, as described by a group of Marion prisoners in a 1972 report to the United Nations Economic and Social Council:

> According to the NPC report, Groder's step-function psychology leads to mind control of the most insidious variety. The first step is to transfer the prisoner to the most remote prison, place him in segregation where he is deprived of mail and other basic privileges until he agrees to participate in Groder's Transactional Analysis (TA) group. . . . Most capitulated because there was no other way of getting out of the hole. Once in the group, he is attacked verbally by Groder's 'prisoner thought-reform team' which probes the vulnerable points and exploits the emotional weaknesses to strip the 'patient' of his self-confidence and sense of autonomy. 'Every effort is made to heighten his suggestibility and weaken his character structure,' says the report, 'so that his emotional responses and thought-flow will be brought under group and staff control as totally as possible. . . .' The purpose of all of this in Groderian language is to help the inmate be 'reborn' as a 'winner in the game of life' . . . and the winners are rewarded with fancy [for Marion] living quarters, including stereos, books, and typewriters, that are denied to other prisoners. 'Like a good attack dog,' every winner is graded and evaluated in his demonstrated capacity to go to the vulnerable points of

any victim placed before him.' and NPC claims that winners are expected to inform on others and police the group for bad thoughts and behavior.[44]

From TA, Groder graduated to the Special Training and Rehabilitative Training program, better known as START. Started at Springfield Federal Penitentiary in the early 1970s, the objective of Project START was described in an October 1972 memo as "to develop behavioral attitudinal changes in offenders who have not adjusted satisfactorily to institutional settings." Characteristics indicated as selection criteria for START included "inability to adjust to regular institutional programs," "a minimum of two years remaining on his sentence," "being aggressive, manipulative, resistive of authority, etc." Prisoners were also to be "transferred from the sending institution's segregation unit."[45] START was actually a "token economy" where obedience was rewarded with "privileges." At the beginning, or level one, the prisoner was in total solitary confinement. After twenty days of "good behavior" the prisoner was allowed out of this cell. It took a minimum of six months for a prisoner to reach the stage where he could start full-time work on a special START job. Each advance was based on the requisite period of "good behavior."[46]

The true nature of the program is perhaps best captured in the following excerpt from ACLU staff attorney Arprar Sanders' letter to Dr. Pasquale J. Ciccone, Director of the Federal Medical Center for Prisoners at Springfield, Missouri.

> In my recent visit I was shocked to learn that two of the fifteen involuntary participants in the START program . . . were shackled by their arms and legs by means of metal straps and chains to their steel beds. Additionally, I learned that they had been forced to eat with both hands still shackled to the bed. . . . Even more outrageous is the fact that neither individual was ever charged with or made an appearance before a disciplinary committee for violation of a rule or regulations.[47]

On July 5, 1972, a group of prisoners wrote the United Nations complaining that those who refused to enter the START program were tranquilized and chained to a toilet for several days. Once they "agreed" to cooperate they were placed in a strip cell from where their continued cooperation could gain them a bed.[48] However, it was not until after Charles Alfano committed suicide to avoid transfer to START that the program was finally discontinued.[49]

While the methods of behavior modification based on the psychological manipulations suggested by Schein were being used by Groder, the use of drugs, as suggested by McConnell, was not being overlooked. In 1970, reports of an aversion therapy program operating at the

California Medical Facility in Vacaville, California, began to leak out. Aversion therapy has been described as "the use of medical procedures that cause pain and fear to bring about the desired behavior modifications."[50] Anectine, the drug used at Vacaville, is clearly made to measure for this purpose. A prisoner subjected to Anectine "therapy" described it as follows:

> They took me into the medical ward and strapped me down. They injected me with Anectine and right away everything started to feel real slow. First my fingers, they started goin' numb. Then I couldn't move my hands or feet, and this feeling like everything's gonna stop was creeping all over my body. I felt my chest go numb and my head started goin' from side to side all by itself. Couldn't move, couldn't breathe like being paralyzed and drowning at the same time. And it just went on and on, man, and all I remember was the doctor standing there, telling me they could always do it again. Again and again and again. And I'll tell you it was worse than dying, man. Worse than dying.[51]

Dr. Arthur Nugent, Chief Psychiatrist at Vacaville, and a key supporter of the use of Anectine, described target candidates for "treatment" as selected for a range of offenses including, "frequent fights, verbal threatening, deviant sexual behavior, stealing, and unresponsiveness to group therapy."[52]

There are also of course, plenty of examples of drugs being used simply to incapacitate prisoners, the practice that has survived as the most common until this day. Prolixin, the drug of choice in the early 1970s, referred to by prisoners as the "liquid straitjacket," is described by the manufacturer, Squibb, as fifty times more powerful than Thorazine.[53] Squibb lists the possible adverse side-effects as the induction of a catatonic-like state, nausea, loss of appetite, headache, constipation, blurred vision, glaucoma, bladder paralysis, impotency, hypertension severe enough to cause fatal cardiac arrest and cerebral edema. Squibb further cautioned that a "persistent pseudoparkinsonian . . . syndrome may develop. . . . The symptoms persist after drug withdrawal, and in some patients appear to be irreversible."[54]

Prison psychiatrist Dr. Philip Shapiro acknowledges that Prolixin "causes a deep depression that may last for weeks."[55] As well as these "therapies," at least three prisoners had psychosurgical operations performed on them in Vacaville in 1968.[56] Consideration was also given to implanting subcortical electrodes, electrically burning out parts of the brain, administering antitestosterone hormones, and using pneumoencephalograms, an excruciating procedure involving the injection of air into the brain.[57]

Marion—The Experiment Continues

Marion Penitentiary is the logical culmination and continuation of the disparate experiments of the 1960s and early '70s. When the START program was terminated, "box car cells were . '. . introduced into Marion. These cells were soundproof, sealed and at times heated like an oven. Marion would thus be an experimental model that would also include the use of drugs and other behavior modification techniques."[58] In a paper entitled, "Breaking Men's Minds," the National Committee to Support the Marion Brothers notes that in fact twenty-three of the twenty-four techniques pinpointed by Schein are actively used in Marion.[59] And indeed the examination of living conditions in Marion paints a horrible picture. As recently as May 28, 1991, Michael Isikoff, writing in the *Washington Post*, reported that

> The key to Marion's 'program' is a system of segregated 'control units,' with each layer progressively stricter then [sic] the other. The most severe controls are in the prison's west wing, where inmates are confined to their cells 23 hours each day, limited to three showers per week, and one 10-minute phone call per month. Each time they move out of their cells, they are restrained with handcuffs and leg irons and escorted by three prison guards yielding [sic] 'rib spreaders'—yard-long black clubs with steel bearings.[60]

It is also routine to subject prisoners to finger probes of the rectum when they return from visits or from court. This process cannot be construed as responding to real security needs as prisoners have no contact visits and are escorted to and from court in handcuffs and leg irons under strict supervision of guards. In fact, prisoners have suggested the use of sonograms and/or dry cells (cells with no running water, even in the toilet) as safe and effective alternatives to the finger probes. The prison administration's unwillingness to institute such safe and effective options indicates that degradation and the subsequent loss of self-respect are the actual reason for this humiliating process.

Everything possible has also been done to destroy the prisoners' contact with the outside world. "Following the lockdown, the prison stated that the visits were to be limited to no more than four one hour visits per month. Visits were now to take place over telephones, which are monitored. The number of family visits has never been substantial and with the new constraints, the number of visits has sharply declined. Additionally, the transfer of prisoners from throughout the country to Southern Illinois has made it impossible for families to afford the trip. Finally, many prisoners are without postage stamps and telephone calls

are restricted to verified 'emergencies.' An emergency must be documented by a U.S. probation officer. Ultimately, the BoP has been
successful in cutting the prisoner's communication from the outside
world."[61] On top of these restrictions, the prison administration has
established a rule, whereby prisoners are prohibited from corresponding
with anyone living within a fifty mile radius of the prison.

As we can see by even this cursory look at conditions in Marion,
aspects of both Schein's model as well as SD, PD, and SI conditions are
combined in an attempt to break prisoners.[62] Not surprisingly, the
conditions produced in laboratory experiments are reproduced in prison.
Summarizing Stuart Grassian's 1983 study, Oliver and Roberts note:

> [P]risoners begin to show symptoms which form a clinically dis-
> tinguishable psychiatric syndrome. Prisoners in solitary
> confinement are said to suffer from detachments from reality.
> Prisoners begin to hallucinate, hear voices and whispers, ex-
> perience anxieties, and fall into confused states characterized
> by the inability to concentrate or partial amnesia. They also
> report thought-content disturbances. Some inmates report the
> emergence of primitive, ego-dystonic fantasies. Prisoners begin
> to entertain fantasies of revenge, torture, and mutilation of prison
> guards. They also feel paranoia and fears of persecution. Finally,
> prisoners exhibit poor impulse control. Some involve themselves
> in acts of self-mutilation, such as cutting their wrists. Grassian
> concludes that solitary confinement is a major psychiatric risk.[63]

In terms that more clearly reflect the cold reality of the situation, Dr.
Bernard Rubin, M.D., stated in his 1973 testimony in the case of *Adams
v. Carlson*:

> [The Control Unit] could only do harm for a variety of reasons:
> One is that the setting in its organization demeans and de-
> humanizes and shapes behavior which is contrary to that which
> is preferred to be the purpose of the program, that is, it seems
> to me that it shapes behavior toward violence by accentuating
> frustration, rage, and helplessness and that the violence is either
> directed inwardly or outwardly.[64]

Even some of those within the system are starting to recognize the
problem. Gayle Franzen, a self-proclaimed hard-liner, who was the
Director of Illinois Corrections during the 1978 Pontiac lockdown, offered
the following observation regarding Marion in 1986:

> They're treating a problem with what appears to be the creation
> of a larger problem, which is much more frustration, much more
> tension, much more want to do violence just to kind of get even,
> by people who . . . wouldn't necessarily participate in violent acts.
> And that's what's frightening about the response to the violence
> they had down at Marion.[65]

The exact nature of the violence to be expected is summed up by a prisoner of Marion as follows:

> If they put you in a room long enough without other people you begin to forget who you are. When they take everything away, including your mirror, you even forget what you look like. There are people in Marion who wish to kill, solely to have achieved something. They kill to show that they exist and that they are somebody. These prisoners kill so they can say, 'I'm the motherfucker who killed that guy.'[66]

Ominously, another prisoner warns:

> [T]he only difference between a diamond and a piece of rock out there on that track, you know a piece of gravel, the only difference between it is the amount of pressure that you're putting on people up here.... You're gonna make 'em hard as diamonds, and some of them are gonna come out and be the exact thing you never want to see [Tyronne Thomas-Bey].[67]

Who are the targets for this destructive campaign? As Jennie Vander Wall notes, "According to one congressional audit, eighty percent of the men at Marion were qualified for placement at a less secure institution."[68] The answer to the question comes as no great shock. In a May 1990 article, Bill Dunne, a political prisoner at Marion, notes,

> The plight of prisoners of war and political prisoners is especially illustrative of the lie of the Marion-prisoners-are-vicious-and-violent argument in addition to being indicative of the real intent of instruments of oppression like Marion. None of those here now were sent here for violence in other prisons—or even for escaping. Ray Levasseur, Sekou Odinga, Hanif Shabazz Bey, Oscar Lopez, Kojo Sababu, and I were all sent for either no specific reason or allegedly because of some suspicion of involvement in vague escape plots. Ones previously here—and at risk of being consigned to Florence—like Leonard Peltier, Sundiata Acoli, Tim Blunk, Danny Atteberry, Alan Berkman, and Standing Deer were also kept here for reasons other than committing violence in other prisons. All were put here because the BoP wants to criminalize them and isolate them and their politics. Even the right wing political prisoners are not here for violence in other prisons.[69]

In spite of the rhetoric in which Schein, McConnell, *et al.* wrap their varying projects, little in the way of "readjustment" is actually achieved. As was previously noted, Schein admitted a success rate of at best ten to fifteen percent. It follows that Marion shows little evidence of any intention other than one which is purely experimental, with the goal of effectively destroying target human beings. Bill Dunne has probably summed the situation up best.

The Marion lockdown is not the last resort response to depredations by prisoners that culminated in three deaths in October of 1983. Circumstances and documents, including one cited on ABC's national news magazine, *20/20*, show that it was being planned much earlier. Nor is Marion the 'humane incapacitation' that is alleged, as it violates many of the United Nation's Standard Minimum Rules for the Treatment of Prisoners and the condemnation by Amnesty International show. Neither is it only a 'concentration model,' though it does act as such in some respects incidental to its real function. . . . It is not merely a 'high security operation' because the repression goes well beyond what could be related to security. It is not 'behavior modification' because that term implies that objectionable attitudes are being replaced with something more appropriate. . . . It is not only a 'mind control' prison, though developing the means of exercising psychological influence over people is part of its intent. . . . What Marion is is a laboratory for experiments in social manipulation and control.[70]

In pinpointing the targets of the experiment, Dunne observes that:

Political prisoners of the radical left make particularly good test subjects in this regard because their operating principles are less susceptible to attack due to their rationality. Those ideas are also most threatening to the hierarchy and are those most likely to be held by or attractive to the people who increasingly populate prisons. Prisoners belonging to other groups that adhere more or less to codes also provide grist for the Marion mill because results there are often similar and translatable. The same is true with respect to information garnered from other prisoners who frequently correspond in malleability, interests, and outlook, and common types of rebellion to segments of the population the ruling class will need new weapons to control in the future. These others also can serve as experimental controls and camouflage for the experiments.[71]

In Dunne's view, Marion is in part a complete experimental model based in part on the manipulation of stress, with both prisoners and guards as subjects. *Vis-à-vis* prisoners, he notes:

The effect is multiplied by the extent to which it prods prisoners into self-policing. In order to avoid intrusion and its psychological and physical consequences, many prisoners try to figure out—not always consciously—what will attract official interference, reasonable or not, and to eliminate it. This can be extremely stressful and frustrating because it requires acceding to the unreasonable and bowing to adversarial pressure without being specifically required to do so—doing 'the man's job'—and it is not often possible.[72]

And *vis-à-vis* guards:

[T]hey are also subject to Marion's experimentation. Supervisory staff, usually above the custodial level, pressure guards to pressure prisoners for frivolous reasons. Guards then try to eliminate the cause for intrusion into their consciousness by trying to anticipate the hierarchy's whims. But they are constantly faced with having to carry out unjust acts of repression with no serious relation to any legitimate penological objective in exchange for a salary, a sell-out. This pressure and the agent of oppression syndrome that stems from it are much more the cause of stress in guards that the administration attributes to the supposed dangerousness of Marion prisoners. The hierarchy also experiments on guards with how to counter the syndrome and its impairment of minions' and henchpeoples' zeal with anti-prisoner propaganda and agitation, identification with the guard gang, and material incentives. And whether for guards or prisoners, the least stressful response is to try to move through the situation so incapable of analytical rationalization without thinking about it and to depersonalize the class brethren between whom the ruling class has chiseled a line that can only harden in the circumstances. But that is not always possible and certainly not desirable. Undoubtedly, staff members are aware that they are being manipulated, albeit in varying degrees according to their ignorance, unconsciousness, and programming. But that only enhances their perceptions of lack of control and inclination to show some and seek release at the expense of prisoners. This seems to be a greater factor with altitude in the hierarchy where it becomes increasingly important to appear to other climbers of the ladder to be running something, to be in control, to be operating more than operated.[73]

Looking at the experimental intent, Dunne concludes that "The experimental intent of the destructive practices of laboratory Marion is apparently to see how, and how far, prisoners and, to a lesser extent, guards, can be conditioned into an unthinking habit of knee-jerk compliance with the decrees of authority, no matter how unreasonable, without inducing reaction and defiance.[74]

Lexington—Quicker, Dirtier Experiment

The experimental nature of the Lexington Control Unit is even more blatant than that of Marion. Opened on October 29, 1986, Lexington was built to house sixteen women. The prison's first two inmates were Puerto Rican nationalist Alejandrina Torres and white anti-imperialist Susan Rosenberg. They were subsequently joined by Italian anti-imperialist Silvia Baraldini.

In his examination of the High Security Unit (HSU) at Lexington, former prison psychologist Richard Korn presents a thorough catalog of the destructive nature of the conditions under which the women were held.[75] He recounts a series of tactics used to depersonalize the women, including the requirement to wear impersonal and drab government issue clothing, the ban on any attempt to decorate or personalize the cell, a restrictive limit on personal property, and the denial of a personal library of any kind. Enforced dependency is also fostered in a number of ways. Korn notes two examples: menstruating women must request sanitary napkins from a male guard one at a time (this is, of course, humiliating as well as depersonalizing) and if a woman wishes to study correspondence courses, she can't purchase the course with her own money as other inmates can but must apply for government funds. The women are also routinely sexually harassed and abused by staff. This abuse includes forced and entirely unnecessary vaginal and anal examinations by male staff as well as physical and mechanical surveillance while showering.[76]

The nature of classification to the HSU is itself structured to engender helplessness. Korn observes that the unit was officially created to house women "whose confinement raises a serious threat of external assault for purposes of aiding the offender's escape," and that "consideration for transfer from the unit should be given [only] when the original factors for placement in the unit no longer apply." As such, entry and exit from the HSU are governed by factors totally outside of the prisoner's control. The only clear hope held out to women was the totally depersonalizing possibility of changing political associations. Korn also notes that any sense of hopelessness thus engendered in the women was reinforced by constant taunts to the effect that they would never get out of the unit.

Predictably the women began to show signs of the physical and psychological disorders discussed earlier in this paper. They suffered varying degrees of claustrophobia, chronic repressed rage, low-level to severe depression, hallucinations, psychological withdrawal, loss of appetite, marked weight loss, exacerbation of pre-existing medical problems, general physical malaise, visual disturbances, dizziness, and heart palpitations. Korn concludes that the program resembles in its effects Marion, Stammheim, and the Korean Model.

> Unfortunately, there is no question in my mind that the experiment being conducted in the HSU at Lexington is an attempt to replicate under modern constraints and by 'acceptable methods,' the program originally developed by the Chinese. This program sets up a hierarchy of objectives. The first of these is to reduce prisoners to the state of submission essential for their ideological conversion. That failing, the next objective is to reduce them to a state of psychological incompetence sufficient to neutralize them as efficient, self-directing antagonists. That failing, the only alternative is to destroy them, preferably by making them desperate enough to destroy themselves. Examples

of reliance on this alternative are to be found in the suicides of two imprisoned terrorists in Germany, and in the self-induced death by starvation of Irish prisoners 'on the blanket' in the English facility designed for political prisoners.[77]

Braver Newer Prisons

Lexington was closed on August 19, 1988, less than two years after it was opened. The Left claimed a victory, but that victory was to some degree hollow as the U.S. Court of Appeals ruled on September 29, 1989 that the government is free to use political beliefs and associations to justify different and harsher treatment of select prisoners. And all indications are that the state plans to use knowledge gained from the Lexington experiment to develop an even more advanced unit. BoP Director Michael J. Quinlan has announced that an HSU capable of housing 108 women will be constructed within the low-security men's prison at Marianna, Florida. Chicago based attorney Jan Susler, who represented Alejandrina Torres, has noted that Quinlan "is not closing Lexington, he's moving it, and he's going to put more women in it." She further adds, "we believe they intend to continue doing exactly what they're doing in Lexington."[78]

The BoP also intends to replace Marion with a new control unit. In 1990, the BoP announced the creation of a new super-max prison at Florence, Colorado. This new prison will refine the isolation techniques developed at Marion. The prison at Florence will be designed so that one guard can control the movements of numerous prisoners in several cell blocks by way of electronic doors, cameras and audio equipment. "We will be able to electronically open a cell door, shut it behind the inmate, and move him through a series of sliding doors," says Russ Martin, project manager for the Florence Prison. Presently, at Marion, the prisoners can scream to one another from their cells; prisoners have minimal contact with guards when their food is shoved between the bars. In Florence, this "contact" may be eliminated. "These guys will never be out of their cells, much less in the yard or anywhere around here," the Florence City Manager states. State of the art security technology and new construction materials will assure near complete isolation; in fact, the building will be designed with no windows at all. And lest anyone doubt the experimental nature of prisons such as Marion and Florence or Lexington and Marianna, Martin inadvertently acknowledges it when he says, "Marion learned from Alcatraz, and now we've had 30 years to learn from Marion."[79]

Brave New Laboratory for a Brave New World

The purpose of this experiment is summed up by Bill Dunne in his study of Marion:

> There is no other reason for the deliberate creation of insecurity and disability among prisoners than that they are being made victims of some arcane experimentation in furtherance of counter-insurgency capability currently described as low intensity warfare.[80]

If we return to Schein and McConnell, we shall see that the target population for this low intensity warfare is much broader than the group of prisoners immediately affected. In the closing pages of a book-length analysis of the Korean program, Schein reflects that prisons, religious orders, educational institutions, mental hospitals, and thought reform centers all use elements of coercive persuasion.[81] It follows that a development in any institution is subject to application in any and all others. Indeed in a society such as ours it is virtually imperative that this is and will be the case. If this sounds like fantasy, McConnell is perfectly blunt on the subject:

> We should reshape our society so that we would all be trained from birth to want to do what society wants us to do. We have the techniques now to do it. Only by using them can we hope to maximize human potentiality. Of course, we cannot give up punishment entirely, but we can use it sparingly, intelligently, as a means of shaping people's behavior rather than as a means of releasing our own aggressive tendencies.[82]

Conclusion

It has been my objective in this article to show that there is an operative dialectic of oppression at play in the treatment of political prisoners in the western world and most probably in the entire world. There can be little question that the techniques developed in Korea were applied at Marion and elsewhere in the U.S. as were the results of SD, PD, and SI experiments. There can be equally little doubt that these techniques were exported to West Germany where they were refined in Stammheim and elsewhere, only to be reimported and applied at Lexington. Anyone who has paid attention to developments in the struggles of political prisoners in Ireland, Spain, and France in the past decade recognizes that the same model is applied and refined in these countries as well.

Equally clear is the fact that more than twenty years of protest has failed to dent such experimental programs. In fact, the development of the control units in Marianna and Florence suggest a new and intensified phase of experimentation. It is also clear that no state would spend many millions of dollars annually simply to control several hundred prisoners. There are cheaper and easier ways were that the only goal. However, as particularly committed opponents, political prisoners are ideal experimental subjects for programs geared toward developing low intensity warfare techniques. The targets of low intensity warfare are not, however, political prisoners alone. Low intensity warfare seeks to use any and all possible means to neutralize social opposition in the broadest possible sense. While it would be absurd to suggest that we are rapidly approaching McConnell's Brave New World, it would be equally absurd to suggest that the knowledge gained in prisons such as Marion and Lexington is and will be restricted in its usage to prisons. It is important that we not lose sight of that fact as we assess the Marion and Lexington experiences and develop our strategy for opposing Marianna and Florence.

Notes

1. Ulrike Meinhof and Astrid Proll were prisoners from the Red Army Faction (RAF). Meinhof was murdered in prison in 1978. Proll was released from prison for health reasons after an extended period in the dead wing. She fled to England and lived in hiding until her re-arrest. After her return, she publicly broke with the RAF. She now works to support defectors still in prison.
2. Reinders, Klopper, Teufel, Fritzsch, "Zum Trakt in Moabit," *Der Blues, Gasammelte Texte der Bewegung 2. Juni*, vol. 1 (n.d.), pp. 331-332.
3. West Berlin based anarchist anti-imperialist armed organization. Dissolved in the late 1970s, part of the underground structure fused with the anti-imperialist armed organization, the Red Army Faction.
4. Mike Ryan, "The Stammheim Model: Judicial Counterinsurgency," *New Studies on the Left*, vol. 14, nos. 1-2 (Spring-Summer 1989), p. 45-68.
5. Edgar H. Schein with Inge Schneier and Curtis H. Barker, *Coercive Persuasions* (New York: W. W. Norton, 1961), p.. 117-118.
6. *Ibid.*, pp. 119-20.
7. *Ibid.*, pp. 123-24.
8. *Ibid.*, p. 131.
9. *Ibid.*, pp. 131-32.
10. *Ibid.*, p. 132
11. *Ibid.*
12. *Ibid.*, p. 133.
13. *Ibid.*
14. *Ibid.*, p. 136.

15. *Ibid.*, p. 137.
16. *Ibid.*
17. *Ibid.*, p. 160
18. *Ibid.*, p. 162.
19. *Ibid.*, p. 163.
20. *Ibid.*, p. 177.
21. *Ibid.*, p. 165.
22. *Ibid.*, p. 177.
23. *Ibid.*, p. 285.
24. *Ibid.*
25. Edgar H. Schein, "Man Against Man: Brainwashing," *Corrective Psychiatry and Journal of Social Therapy*, vol. 8, no. 1 (1962), p. 94.
26. Philip Soloman, *et al.* (eds.), *Sensory Deprivation: A Symposium Held at Harvard Medical School* (Cambridge, MA: Harvard University Press, 1961), p. 6.
27. *Ibid.*, pp. 11-13.
28. *Ibid.*, pp. 56-57.
29, *Ibid.*, pp. 66-68.
30. John P. Zubeck, "Behavioral and Physiological Effects of Prolonged Sensory and Perceptual Deprivation: A Review" in John E. Rasmussen (ed.), *Man in Isolation and Confinement* (Chicago: Aldine Publishing Co., 1973), pp. 9-83.
31. E. K. Eric Gunderson, in *Ibid*, pp. 145-64.
32. William W. Haythorn in *Ibid.*, pp. 219-39.
33. S. B. Sells, in *Ibid.*, p. 296.
34. John P. Zubeck, *Sensory Deprivation: Fifteen Years of Research* (New York: Appleton-Century-Crofts, 1969), p. 402.
35. Schein, "Man Against Man: Brainwashing," *op. cit.* p. 92.
36. *Ibid.*, pp. 94-95.
37. *Ibid.*, pp. 100-02.
38. *Ibid.*, pp. 103.
39. James V. McConnell, "Criminals can be Brainwashed Now," *Psychology Today*, vol. 3, no. 11 (April 1970), pp. 18 and 74.
40. *Ibid.*, p. 74.
41. *Ibid.*
42, *Ibid.*
43. *Ibid.*
44. Joe Hunt, "Behavior Mod in Prison, II," *Rough Times*, vol. 4, no. 3 (September 1974), p. 7.
45. Jessica Mitford, *Kind and Usual Punishment* (New York: Alfred A. Knopf, 1973), p. 124.
46. Dick Russell, "The Unsavory Business of Mind Control," *Arosy* (November 1975), p. 34.
47. *Ibid.*
48. *Ibid.*
49. *Ibid.*
50. Mitford, *op. cit.*, p. 127.
51. Russell, *op. cit.*, p. 29.
52. *Ibid.*
53. *Ibid.*, p. 35.

54. Mitford, *op. cit.*, pp. 129-30.

55. *Ibid.*, p. 130.

56. Russell, *op. cit.*, p. 35.

57. Mitford, *op. cit.*, p. 136.

58. Committee to End the Marion Lockdown, *Close Marion and All Control Units*, (n.d.), p. 1.

59. National Committee to Support the Marion Brothers, *Breaking Men's Minds*, (n.d.) p. 7.

60. Michael Isikoff. "Hard Time: Federal Mission at Marion," *Washington Post*, May 28, 1991, p. 6.

61. Michael Olivero and James B. Roberts, "Marion Federal Penitentiary and the 22-Month Lockdown: The Crisis Continues," *Crime and Social Justice*, nos. 27-28, p. 245.

62. National Committee to Support the Marion Brothers, *op. cit.*, p. 8.

63. Olivero and Roberts, *op. cit.*, p. 238.

64. *Report to the Prisoners at Marion about the Congressional Hearing on March 29, 1984*, p. 2.

65. *Marion Prison: Inside a Lockdown*, p. 5.

66. Olivero and Roberts, *op. cit.*, 238.

67. *Marion Prison: Inside a Lockdown*, p. 6.

68. Jennifer Vander Wall, "How Tough Will New Prisons Be?" *Daily Camera*, May 26, 1990, p. 15A.

69. Bill Dunne, "They're Doin' It Again," *The Marionette*, 1990, pp. 1-2.

70. Bill Dunne, "The U.S. Penitentiary at Marion, Illinois: An Instrument of Oppression," *New Studies on the Left*, vol. 14, nos. 1-2 (1989), p. 10. Also with new material, pp. 38-82 above.

71. *Ibid.*, pp. 11.

72. *Ibid.*, pp. 12.

73. *Ibid.*

74. *Ibid.*, pp. 15.

75. Unless otherwise indicated, all information is from Richard Korn's *The Effects of Confinement in HSU*. See pp. 123-27 below.

76. National Prison Project of the ACLU Foundation, *Report on the High Security Unit for Women, Federal Correctional Institute, Lexington, Kentucky*, 1987, p. 6.

77. See Mike Ryan, "Stammheim: Model for Judicial Counter-insurgency," *op. cit.* for evidence that the RAF prisoners in West Germany were, in fact, murdered.

78. Scott Baker, "Activists Attack New Women's Control Unit," *The Guardian*, March 23, 1988, p. 6.

79. *Ibid.*

80. Dunne, *New Studies on the Left, op. cit.*, p. 16.

81. Schein, *Coercive Persuasion, op. cit.*, p. 285.

82. McConnell, *op. cit.*, p. 74.

Fukoka Sano

BoP Overseer:
A Glimpse of J. Michael Quinlan

The struggle is never without its lighter moments, and one of these for us in Committee to End the Marion Lockdown (CEML), was finding our nemesis J. Michael Quinlan (BoP Director) hold forth—of all places— in the pages of the liberal periodical *The Nation*. For two long columns of bureaucratically stilted prose, Quinlan solemnly discoursed about how never, ever in the world would he dream of discriminatory treatment of political prisoners. He wrote "the Bureau of Prisons has never considered an inmate's political beliefs as a factor in any classification or transfer decision." A Federal judge had just contradicted this promise in *Baraldini v. Meese*, a case regarding Quinlan's pet project: the Lexington HSU (High Security Unit).

The CEML has started to pay closer attention to Quinlan, trying to figure out what he's all about. We were puzzled by the discrepancy between his professed "humanitarianism" and the actual conditions in his prisons, most notably his cool, calculated attempts to destroy people in the Marion and Lexington Control Units. More light was shed on this subject in a radio speech Quinlan made November of 1988. His term to describe the purpose of places like Marion and Lexington is the "incapacitation mode." In the course of discussing various "modes" of corrections, Quinlan dismissed the "rehabilitation mode," the "thera- peutic mode," and several other "modes," before announcing that he had settled on the "incapacitation mode." We can hardly expect an honest discussion of anything from a person who resorts to euphemisms of this type.

During the same broadcast, a member of the audience asked Quinlan why he had entered his chosen line of work. The question obviously caught him off guard. He stumbled, fumbled, and hesitated, racking his brain for an answer. Finally, he replied weakly: "It's a job," as if to make a pathetic joke. A few moments later he came up with another formulation about "working with people" in corrections. He probably likes his job because the pay is good. J. Michael Quinlan bears watching. A man so out of touch with reality, with so much power over people's lives, needs to be watched. J. Michael Quinlan lies, but not out of personal necessity. *Anyone* in his position would have to lie. The Bureau of Prisons (like its creator, the U.S.A.) is a lie, constantly hiding the facts about its purpose and function.

When CEML went to the ASC conference to confront Quinlan, we thought he would cleverly field and deflect our questions. We believed that this "liberal" would try to explain to his audience that he, Quinlan, was really a good guy and that the CEML represents the radical fringe. How shocked we were when he and his entire entourage literally ran out the door as we started to question him. Apparently, Quinlan's thirst for dialogue was finally quenched. Quinlan is a new type of man at the BoP. Unlike Norman Carlson (the man he succeeds) and Gary Henman (the current Warden at Marion) Quinlan can speak in full, grammatically correct sentences. He has a Ph.D. and wears three-piece suits. This appearance does not mean that this technocrat is any less evil than his cohorts. It just means that he is more slippery, a commercialized package ready for a fawning media.

Mary O'Melveny

Portrait of a U.S. Political Prison—
The Lexington High Security Unit for Women

On August 19, 1988 the United States Bureau of Prisons closed the doors to a small underground women's prison in Lexington, Kentucky known as the "High Security Unit" (HSU). In the less than two years that the HSU was operational, this sixteen-bed control unit (which never housed more than six women) became a focus of national and international concern over human rights abuses by the U.S. government, and direct proof that political prisoners not only exist in the United States but are the targets of a well-organized counterinsurgency campaign.

Lexington's origins and opening were shrouded in secrecy, without congressional oversight or public scrutiny. By the time the HSU was closed twenty-two months later, it had been a formal agenda item at the U.S.-U.S.S.R. Summit Conference, had been condemned by national and international human rights advocates (including a 38-page report by Amnesty International in London), had been held by a U.S. federal judge to have been operated in violation of the First Amendment to the U.S. Constitution, and had come to symbolize America's hypocrisy on the issues of human rights and political prisoners. The government's closing of Lexington is, in its view, a mere transferring of its "mission" to a larger women's facility in Marianna, Florida, a remote area near the Georgia and Alabama borders.[1] Thus, while the particular Lexington experiment may have ended, the government has not disbanded its mission. It is important to examine and analyze Lexington's lessons, particularly as they reflect counterinsurgency within U.S. borders against those who resist racism, genocide, colonialism and imperialism and end up as political prisoners in U.S. jails and prisons.

My first visit to the Lexington "High Security Unit" occurred in December 1986. My client, Susan Rosenberg, an anti-imperialist North American political prisoner, and Alejandrina Torres, Puerto Rican *independentista* and proclaimed POW, were the first women prisoners in the federal prison system to go to the High Security Unit when it opened in October 1986. The "new" federal underground prison unit was a prison within a prison. Fundamentally, in intent and practice, the HSU was an isolation unit (although the Bureau of Prisons denies this label) intended to closely monitor and control its residents. The conditions were startling. The HSU was in a basement of an old 1930s building, formerly owned by the Public Health Service, which was "remodeled" in 1986 to house sixteen women at a taxpayer expense of approximately $735,000, and an annual per woman maintenance cost of more than $55,000, more than the annual cost for women in all other federal prisons.

This modern dungeon bore little relationship to the larger (1,700 inmates) prison at Lexington within which it sat amidst rolling hills and green Kentucky grazing land. Its residents could not see the pastoral landscape which lies past the double-razor wire shrouded building. Ceiling-high windows were so thickly screened that daylight was barely perceptible.[2] The HSU prisoners lived in constant artificial light. Their only link to the world above was a television set, an occasional ten-minute social telephone call, and less frequent visits from attorneys. The things we take for granted as basic components of human existence— natural light, fresh air, color, sound, human contact, various smells— were conspicuously, intentionally absent from the lives of the women confined to the HSU. Also denied were those equally important, slightly more subtle human needs—privacy spheres, intellectual stimulation, comradeship, continuing connections to family, friends and caring others, undisturbed sleep, health care, educational and recreational options, and spiritual comforts.

The Political Basis of Assignment to Lexington

The Bureau of Prisons made no secret of the political basis for the designation of the first women sent to this unique experimental control unit. Susan Rosenberg was said to be "associated with the FALN, Black Liberation Army and other terrorist groups" and one who had "threatened in open court to take her armed revolution behind prison walls."[3] Alejandrina Torres was also said to be associated with the FALN and with the militant struggle for an end to the colonial domination of Puerto Rico. Both women were to spend nearly three months alone in the the underground silence of the HSU, surrounded by guards who were tutored to hate and fear them,[4] their every movement monitored by cameras and in log books, cut off from virtually all contact with families, friends, and political supporters.

In January 1987, Susan Rosenberg and Alejandrina Torres were joined by Silvia Baraldini, an Italian national who had worked for years in the U.S. anti-imperialist movement before her 1983 conviction for conspiracy to liberate Assata Shakur from a New Jersey prison. As with the others, politics formed the obvious basis for this transfer:

> Although Ms. Baraldini scores well enough on her Custody Scoring Sheet to be considered for a custody reduction, she is a member of the May 19th Communist Party which is sympathetic to other radical groups including the New African Freedom Front and the FALN.[5]

The Bureau of Prisons advanced two criteria for placement of women prisoners in the HSU. The first was the one it used to try to justify sending all three political prisoners to the Unit:

> Candidates for placement in this Unit are those females whose confinement raises a serious threat of external assault for the purpose of aiding the offender's escape.[6]

The second, said to be applicable on only a "space-available basis," was for those women with "serious histories of assaultive, escape-prone or disruptive activity." Later, the BoP's criteria became even more explicitly political:

> [A] prisoner's past or present affiliation, association or membership in an organization which has been documented as being involved in acts of violence, attempts to disrupt or overthrow the government of the U.S. or whose published ideology includes advocating law violations in order to "free" prisoners. . . .[7]

No one, once sent to the HSU, could get out unless "the original factors for placement in the Unit no longer apply and when placement in a less secure facility becomes appropriate."[8] For political prisoners, the message could not have been clearer—renounce the political affiliations and beliefs which had led the FBI/BoP to define them as candidates for the HSU, and they could get out. Fail to do so and remain in isolation, denied all basic components of humane existence and political connection, for thirty-five to fifty-eight years. All were told they had a "one-way ticket" to the HSU. For nearly two years these women lived alone together, cut off from the rest of the world in all but the most superficial ways. Until their situation eventually provoked outcries from human rights groups, religious communities, families and friends, attorneys and political activists, they existed in a sort of physical and psychic limbo, buried but still very much alive.

The Strategy of Isolation and Denial

The defining feature of the Lexington HSU women's control unit was small group isolation. Isolation as torture is not new. In fact, it began as part of the nazi experiments at Dachau, used first on the communists and homosexuals imprisoned there. There is a science to the use of isolation, as witnessed by the fact that all conditions in isolation are remarkably similar. Nelson Mandela's isolation in South Africa's Pollsmoor High Security Prison shared the same essential characteristics as those in Uruguay's "La Libertad" prison/interrogation center.[9] The isolation units in Italy and West Germany known as "white cells" or dead wings" are likewise strikingly parallel to the Lexington HSU.

Nearly ten years ago, Amnesty International condemned the use of small group isolation and solitary confinement against the Red Army Faction and 2nd June Movement in West Germany's Stammheim high security prison as "torture or other cruel, inhuman or degrading treatment or punishment" of prisoners, in violation of the 1977 United Nations Standard Minimum Rules for the Treatment of Prisoners, and the 1966 United Nations Covenant on Civil and Political Rights. The detailed Amnesty report on Stammheim chronicled the effects of long-term confinement of these political prisoners in extreme isolation and described the inhumane conditions they were subjected to in these "high security" wings.

There can be no doubt that the Lexington HSU was conceived by U.S. authorities as an experimental version of Stammheim's isolation wings, and as part of a deliberate effort to destroy revolutionary and radical political prisoners and their capacity to organize support for their politics. The known life-threatening effects of such long-term confinement on the RAF prisoners did not go unnoticed by U.S. counterinsurgency experts, and the reality of Lexington as it unfolded over twenty months made evident that the significant incapacitation of its residents was indeed the intended effect. Thus, at the 1978 U.S.-sponsored "Special Seminar on Terrorism in Puerto Rico" workshop, participants were specifically encouraged to examine the "interesting lessons" from West Germany and Italy and the conditions employed against political prisoners at Stammheim which resulted in the deaths of four RAF leaders.[10]

The severe isolation of the HSU was accompanied by sensory deprivation and by often extreme voyeurism and sexual harassment by the mostly male staff, as well as sleep deprivation, overt hostility by guards, completely arbitrary rules and rules changes. No meaningful work or recreational opportunities or educational programs were offered. Personal property was forbidden, or so severely restricted as to be meaningless, as a way of establishing an independent identity in the midst of a totally controlled, sterile environment. Twenty-four-hour camera and visual surveillance recorded every word and every activity:

moods, illnesses, menstrual cycles, eating patterns. Correspondence was severely censored for many months. Prison guards prepared logs documenting the names and addresses of every person who corresponded with the HSU prisoners. Telephone calls were also very limited and were not only monitored, but were also the subject of detailed memos analyzing the conversations, listing the names of all persons referred to in the conversations, and describing the assertedly "relevant" portions of what was said. These memos went to other agencies for evaluation and follow up.[11]

The Effects of Lexington on the Prisoners

The more time which passed underground, the more overwhelming the effects. Susan Rosenberg described the conditions as "existential death"; Debra Brown as akin to being "in the grave."[12] Sleep deprivation experiments[13] led to insomnia, exhaustion and unventilated rage. So too, the denial of privacy or personal space, coupled with constant sexual harassment either in fact or in threat, and the effort to infantilize the women because of their enforced dependency on the hostile guards who defined every aspect of their lives. Early on, the women began to experience some of the predictable psychopathological effects of long-term isolation: vision impairment, memory loss, inability to concentrate, loss of appetite and weight, and lethargy.[14] In August 1987, Dr. Richard Korn, a clinical psychologist and correctional expert, issued his first report for the American Civil Liberties Union's National Prison Project based upon a tour of Lexington and interviews with the prisoners. His findings about the conditions of Lexington were stark. First, he observed that "the power of the institution over the prisoners was total, beyond questioning and accounting, even if it appeared to violate traditional fairness or common sense."[15]

Among the factors affecting the psycho-physical well-being of the prisoners were rules "tending to depersonalize and deny individuality" (drab, colorless government clothing, sterile and bleak living spaces, denial of adequate reading materials, severely limited personal effects). Dr. Korn concluded that the restrictions imposed upon the women's lives were nothing less than an ideological attack which was "carefully deliberate, in every detail." The psychological consequences for the prisoners were "evident" to Dr. Korn: claustrophobia, chronic rage reaction, suppressed, low-level to severe depression, onset of hallucinatory symptoms, defensive psychological withdrawal, blunting of apathy. Likewise, there were concrete physical reactions: loss of appetite, marked loss of weight, exacerbation of pre-existing medical problems, general physical malaise, visual disturbances, dizziness, heart palpitations. Finding that Lexington had "many similarities" to the federal prison at Marion, Illinois, and to West Germany's Stammheim prison, Dr. Korn had "no question" about the nature of the experiment being conducted:

> to reduce prisoners to a state of submission essential for their ideological conversion. That failing, the next objective is to reduce them to a state of psychological incompetence sufficient to neutralize them as efficient, self-directing antagonists. That failing, the only alternative is to destroy them, preferably by making them desperate enough to destroy themselves. [16]

Bureau of Prisons officials referred endlessly to the "mission" of Lexington. Deterrence was clearly another central feature of that mission. Some political prisoners, such as Carol Manning and Marilyn Buck, were "designated" to Lexington long before they were eligible for transfer anywhere, while others were threatened with the prospect of being sent there. Even though in-prison behavior was obviously irrelevant to the designation decision, social prisoners at Pleasanton FCI, one of the BoP's general population prisons, were "threatened" with the specter of the HSU if they did not "behave."[17] In addition to increasing the level of intimidation and control over women in the federal prison system, Lexington obviously served as a chilling deterrent to political activists on the outside, particularly as the BoP expanded its placement criteria to include actions which might "disrupt the government" or membership in groups which advocated "law violations."[18]

The Political and Legal Opposition to Lexington

Central to the movement against Lexington was the prisoners' determination not to be broken by the never-ending attempts to destroy them, even as their physical health evidenced the strain. They were joined first by their families, friends and by lawyers who offered crucial support (including women lawyers in Kentucky who immediately mobilized to offer assistance). The Puerto Rican independence movement embraced the issue and played a crucial role in bringing attention to the existence of the Unit and the inhumane treatment of the prisoners. Religious leaders and thousands of other individuals responded to the issue as one of basic human rights, rejecting the Reagan rubric of "terrorism" as a justification for inhumane conditions or political persecution.

A tour in September 1987 by the General Board of Global Ministries of the United Methodist Church resulted in a highly condemnatory report which directly confronted the political issues of Lexington and the concern that it was a secret experiment in political persecution.[19] Not only did the Methodists' report state that the "extreme isolation . . . from all meaningful human contact and from any hope of such contact in the future" was "cruel and unusual punishment," but they called for the U.S. government to officially recognize the existence of political prisoners.

In October 1987 the Bureau of Prisons announced that it would close Lexington and move its "mission" to a new, larger women's prison in Marianna, Florida. However, despite the reports by the National Prison Project condemning Lexington as a "living tomb" which was "incompatible" with constitutional guarantees, and the concerns raised by the Methodist Church, Amnesty International, and others, the BoP continued to keep it open, refused to transfer the women to general population facilities, and persisted in defending the HSU as "safe" and "humane." By not backing away from the politics of Lexington, the BoP continued to keep the women there, causing them to suffer the maximum damage from its intolerable conditions.

A lawsuit was finally begun in March 1988 seeking injunctive relief to close the Unit and transfer the women. After voluminous testimony by deposition and a trial in June 1988, a federal judge ruled on July 15, 1988 that the BoP and Justice Department had unlawfully designated prisoners to Lexington based on their past political associations and personal beliefs. Judge Barrington Parker found that political views of Silvia Baraldini and Susan Rosenberg which were "unacceptable" to the government could not form a constitutional basis for sending them to Lexington, particularly when their in-prison conduct had demonstrated no basis for finding them to be escape risks. The Court rejected the government's effort to make it a "crime" for prisoners to be "members of leftist political organizations, even if those groups have engaged in unlawful pursuits in the past," and found that the government had failed to document any basis for their assignment other than "their alleged past connections with leftist groups promoting ideas that some government officials did not favor."

While breaking ground on the matter of recognizing the political nature of Lexington—and thus the existence of U.S. political prisoners—the Court rejected the Fifth and Eighth Amendment claims in the lawsuit, finding that the treatment of the prisoners did not constitute cruel and unusual punishment. However, Judge Parker did find that the issue was a close one since the Unit had at times "skirted elemental standards of human decency," particularly in light of the "exaggerated security, small group isolation, and staff harassment," all of which "constantly undermine the inmates' morale." He castigated the government for its "shameful" delays in remedying some of the more egregious conditions, and for operating "a unit that in many respects, measures below acceptable standards for federal prisons." Amnesty International monitored the Lexington lawsuit, sending an observer to the trial. In August 1988, Amnesty issued its report which defined the HSU as, "an experimental control unit," with a "deliberately and gratuitously oppressive" regime in which:

> the constant and unjustified use of security chains, the repeated strip searching, the almost total lack of privacy, the claustrophobic lack of sensory stimuli, freedom of movement, possessions, choice of activities and incestuously small range of contacts cannot be other than debilitating. Whereas most small security units compensate for any necessary physical limitations by granting prisoners extra privileges and greater autonomy, the reverse appears to be the case at HSU.[20]

In addition, Amnesty's observer found "overwhelming evidence that the prisoners at HSU have deteriorated physically and psychologically during their custody there. There has to be a prospect that one or more will finally resort to suicide should their custody at HSU be prolonged."[21] Amnesty recommended Lexington's immediate closing and made clear that Marianna "should not replicate HSU."[22] The government responded to the Court ruling by ignoring its direction to move the women to general population federal correctional institutions. Instead it designated the three political prisoners to pre-trial holding facilities (Metropolitan Correctional Centers), ensuring that they would continue to experience many of Lexington's most serious health-threatening conditions. It also appealed, a process which may take months or even years.[23]

The new "high security" prison in Marianna, Florida, opened for business in August 1988 without shower curtains, educational programs, or even adequate medical staffing. By October 1988 more than fifty women had been sent to Marianna, none of them political prisoners. However, the government was already arguing for an expedited appeal because of an "urgent" need to transfer four Puerto Rican POWs to Marianna based upon their "FALN" membership,[24] and the government's intent to send other women political prisoners to Marianna remains clear. Greater control and repression of federal women prisoners will be the hallmark of Marianna regardless of the outcome of the government's appeal from its loss on Lexington. The existence and public acceptance of control units was largely unaffected by the court case. Marion remains locked down, despite national and international criticism of its inhumane conditions, and increasing numbers of state control units are being opened and filled.[25]

The Lessons of Lexington

In addition to the experiment in new forms of psychological torture, Lexington was an intelligence-gathering mission. The government learned a great deal from the Lexington experiment—about the psychology of women political prisoners, about the effects of long-term small group isolation and the denial system and about the nature and content of the resistance mounted against the HSU. No surprise that every letter to the women was read, and the sender's name and address recorded. No surprise that analytical memoranda were made of every phone call. No surprise that the government never retreated from justifying the need for the Unit or the appropriateness of its operating conditions. Lexington opened, existed and "closed" in the midst of increasing retreats from constitutional guarantees both for persons charged in political cases and for political prisoners. Preventive detention and house arrests, together with the imposition of exaggerated sentences in political cases and the deliberate silent complicity of the mainstream press, all set the stage for the inhumanity of a Lexington control unit, and the larger counterinsurgency strategy it represents.

In other countries, the number and operation of special political prisons has been directly affected by the level of public exposure and resistance. These countries at least recognize that political prisoners exist. Thus, the lessons of the Lexington experiment must always be premised on exposing the myth that the United States has none. This done, the political repression and violations of international law which Lexington symbolizes can be more easily recognized and resisted. The political prisoners held at Lexington, like their counterparts in isolation at Marion and elsewhere in U.S. prisons, were and are victims of psychological torture. They were saved from joining the ranks of the "neutralized" and "disappeared" through growing public education generated by unrelenting political organizing. This model can and should be applied to expose the larger issues of how the U.S. treats political resistance in the United States, and how to prevent more live burials.

Notes

1. Letter dated September 30, 1987 from BoP Director J. Michael Quinlan to Congressman Robert W. Kastenmeier (Dem.-Wisc.).

2. There were two groups of cells separated by a corridor. The women were housed on the "dark side" of the corridor until summer of 1987 when a tour by the ACLU National Prison Project questioned the basis for the room assignments. Windows on the "light side" were still heavily screened,

but were located at regular window height, permitting slightly more light to enter.

3. Memorandum from William A. Perrill, Warden, Federal Correctional Institution, Tucson, Arizona to Jerry T. Williford, Regional Director, Western Regional Office of the BoP dated August 19, 1986, designating Ms. Rosenberg for transfer to maximum security custody status at the HSU. Also cited by Warden Perrill was Ms. Rosenberg's asserted "link" to the 1979 escape of Assata Shakur from prison in New Jersey, even though those charges had been dropped by the government in 1985.

4. The women reported several occasions when unit guards remarked on having studied them in a special "school" to prepare them for dealing with the "terrorists" who were to be their charges at the HSU. Photographs and profiles were apparently part of the materials studied. During later litigation about the HSU, the government never produced any documents or information about such special training, but one BoP official, Southeast Regional Director Gary R. McCune, admitted that he had attended a special course given by the FBI about how to deal with "terrorists" in prison.

5. December 23, 1986 Memorandum from Pleasanton FCI Case Manager, Terry R. Ennis to Acting Associate Warden Dave Wisehart.

6. September 2, 1986 Memorandum from G. L. Ingram, BoP Assistant Director to BoP Regional Directors.

7. September 30, 1987 letter from BoP director J. Michael Quinlan to Congressman Robert W. Kastenmeier (Dem.-Wisc.).

8. *Ibid.*, p. 6.

9. See Maxwell Bloche, "Uruguay's Military Physicians: Cogs in a System of State Terror," Report for the Committee on Scientific Freedom and Responsibility (Washington, D.C.: American Association for the Advancement of Science, 1978), pp. 6-8.

10. Terrorism Conference Background materials, pp. 25-26.

11. These telephone logs came to light in the litigation brought against the Justice Department in March 1988 (*Baraldini vs. Meese*, Civ. No. 88-0764).

12. Letter from Susan Rosenberg; ABC *20/20* interview with Debra Brown.

13. Sleep deprivation tactics, another common torture technique, occurred sporadically over several weeks-long periods.

14. See, S. Grassian, "The Psychopathological Effects of Solitary Confinement," *American Journal of Psychiatry* (November 1983), pp. 1450-54; Amnesty Federal Republic of Germany Report; H. D. Nelson, "Long Term Health Effects of P.O.W. Incarceration" (Paper, Resident Talk, December 7, 1987); The Center for Victims of Torture, "Therapeutic Models: A Beginning" (Draft, April 26, 1988).

15. "The Effects of Confinement in HSU" by Dr. Richard Korn, p. 3 (hereinafter "Korn Report"), appended to August 25, 1987 Report on The High Security Unit for Women, Federal Correctional Institution, Lexington, Kentucky, by National Prison Project of the ACLU (hereinafter referred to as the "NPP Report.")

16. "Korn Report," pp. 19-20.

17. Interviews with Linda Evans and Laura Whitehorn, political prisoners then at FCI Pleasanton, September, 1987.

18. September 30, 1987 letter from BoP director J. Michael Quinlan to Congressman Robert W. Kastenmeier.

19. "Report of Visit by General Board of Global Ministries Team to High Security Unit for Women, Federal Correctional Institution, Lexington, Kentucky," October 15, 1987 (hereinafter "Methodist Report").

20. Amnesty International: USA, "The High Security Unit, Lexington Federal Prison, Kentucky," (AI Index: AMR 51/34/88). Amnesty appended its 15-month correspondence with the BoP about Lexington to the report.

21. *Ibid.*

22. *Ibid.*

23. On September 8, 1989, the government won its appeal of Judge Parker's decision which forced closure of Lexington HSU. The District of Columbia Court of Appeals ruled that the First Amendment rights of Silvia Baraldini and Susan Rosenberg were not violated by their placement at the HSU. The D.C. Appeals Court quoted Justice O'Connor (in *Turner v. Safley*, 1987):

> Subjecting the day-to-day judgements of prison officials to an inflexible strict scrutiny analysis would seriously hamper their ability to anticipate security problems and adopt innovative solutions to the intractable problems of prison administration.

While the precedent set by this decision poses *per se* a threat to all political activists within the U.S., the government's actual response, at this time, has not yet emerged. The only certainty is that the question of political imprisonment in this country is now—if possible—even more critical—*editor's note.*

24. See government's Motion to Expedite Appeal, filed September 9, 1988 in *Thornburgh v. Baraldini*, C.A. 88-5275 (D.C. Court of Appeals), pp. 6-10.

25. See, e.g., Amnesty International Report on "Allegations of Inmate Treatment in Marion Prison, Illinois, USA" (AMR 51/26187), May 1987; "An Uneasy Calm. . ." Report on the U.S. Penitentiary at Marion by John Howard.

Dr. Richard Korn

Excerpts from—

Report on the Effects of Confinement in the Lexington High Security Unit

1. Factors Tending to Depersonalize and Deny Individuality

> • The women are required to wear government-issue clothing which is drab, colorless, shabby, ill-fitting, and devoid of any personal touch. According to unfortunately chosen official language, this garb is designed to insure that they look "feminine." Seen from any distance, the women look like institutional carbon copies of one another.
> • Any attempt to personalize and individualize their small living space, their rooms, is forbidden.
> • Personal property is limited to what can be fitted into a small open-faced bookcase. The number of books which the women may have at any one time is five. This is a mind-numbing limitation for the intelligent and studious women, whose only legitimate escape from confinement must be by means of the vigorous and varied exercise of their minds. . . . For three of these women, whose ideology is an intrinsic part of their identity, the denial of a personal library is an unmistakable assault on their identity and their right to decide to be who they are. It is, additionally, an attack which is in itself ideological and violative of their rights as intellectually free and mature human beings.

2. Personal Autonomy: The Denial of Personal Initiative, Tending Toward inforced Dependency and Infantilization

Some minimal sense of adequacy in one's own intimate life, and on one's own behalf is essential for survival as an intact, self-directing human being. Prisoners report a number of practices which reflect an assault on their personal autonomy, the surrender to which would reduce them to the psychological status of irresponsible children.

> • One of the prisoners reports that she ordinarily requires several

large sanitary napkins during her menstrual period, which is typically heavy. When she is in need of additional napkins, she is required to request them one at a time. When she attempts discreetly to make her request to a staff member, it is his practice, she reports, to call out for that item in a loud voice, thereby making it known to all that she is once again in need of it. The coarseness and indelicacy of this procedure speaks for itself. What it also underscores in a ritualistically humiliating and public way, is the extreme dependency to which the women have been reduced.

3. Sexual Abuse and Humiliation

Two of the women made grave and detailed allegations of sexual mistreatment while at a federal facility in Arizona, which included forced and unnecessary vaginal and anal examinations by male staff. Official exonerations of the named staff have tended to convince the women that they are still vulnerable to this kind of abuse. Because of the close mutual identification of these women, they are subject to a process which has been characterized as "emotional contagion." The effect of this process is that even the women who have not actually suffered the reported abuse experience it psychologically both in prospect and retrospect as a permanent possibility.

4. Hopelessness Arising from the Refusal by the Bureau of Prisons to Specify the Behavioral Criteria for Transfer Out of High Security Status

This is the condition beside which all other pathogenic factors fade in comparison.

• According to the official language defining the purpose of the facility, the HSU was designed for females "whose confinement raises a serious threat of external assault for the purpose of aiding the offender's escape." Moreover, "consideration for transfer from the unit should be given [only] when the original factors for placement in the unit no longer apply." Only then will placement in a less secure facility "become appropriate." In one of his letters to Congressman Kastenmeier, Director Norman Carlson makes the same point more explicit by asserting that "transfer to the unit is not for disciplinary reasons, but is solely a matter of classification based on the security needs of the offender."

• This language makes it clear that neither entry into nor exit from the facility is something for which the offender herself is responsible. Nor is it something that she can change by means of any effort she might make on her own behalf.

• Prisoners report they were told they would be transferred to the HSU even before it opened, by officials who taunted them with statements to the effect that they would "never get out." Similar statements continue to be made, according to the women. One officer reportedly told them, "You will never leave here." A counselor, Mr. White, reportedly remarked, "You will be here after I retire." (Mr. White is well below retirement age.)

The Psychological Consequences

1. Claustrophobia

In some of the women, confinement in a close and unvaried space has already induced feelings of spatial compression akin to claustrophobic panic. If and when such experiences become unbearably intense, they can induce uncontrollable, psychotic flight reactions and feelings of unreality. Given the women's vulnerability to one another's emotions, the appearance of such symptoms in any one of the women will immediately threaten to spread to the others. (This is true of all of the effects to be cited.)

2. Chronic Rage Reaction, Suppressed

All report continuous, unrelieved feelings of anger. One woman reported, "I feel violated every minute of every day." The tension typically associated with barely suppressed rage was evident in the body language of each of the women. Unrelieved and suppressed from behavioral expression, these feelings are bound to exact a psychosomatic toll.

3. Low-level to Severe Depression

The women deliberately refuse to give vent to their anger by aggressively acting-out. They do this for at least three reasons: Pride, a refusal to conform to the stereotype of violence, and a wish to avoid giving the authorities a valid pretext for retaliation. But the effort at self-control is not only exhausting; it is also damaging in other ways. Denied an external target, the force and pressure of rage is turned inward and is experienced as depression.

4. Onset of Hallucinatory Symptoms

Three of the women report seeing black spots or "strings" on the wall. These symptoms were more prominent before the glaring white walls were repainted, but they have now returned. The insidious onset of such phenomena is a frequent result of a relatively monotonous visual environment, and can be expected to worsen over time.

5. Defensive Psychological Withdrawal, Blunting of Affect, Apathy

A commonly noted adjustment to unbearable environments is a form of protective withdrawal and desensitization by means of which one decreases one's feelings of suffering by decreasing one's capacity to feel anything. None of the women yet show any overt signs of this malignant coping mechanism. Nevertheless, three of them report an increasing inability to sustain concentration and focal attention, which is foreboding as one of the advance indications of withdrawal.[1]

Psychosomatic Symptoms

The following physical reactions are reported by most of the women:
* Loss of appetite
* Marked loss of weight
* Exacerbation of pre-existing medical problems
* General physical malaise
* Visual disturbances
* Dizziness
* Heart palpitations

The Prisoner's Perspective

For reasons sufficiently persuasive to them, the prisoners view the HSU regime as a deliberate design to undermine their mental and physical well being, that is, to destroy them physically and psychologically. It is a truism of social science that situations perceived to be real are real in their consequences. Their responses to this perceived reality vary from a desperation verging on panic to a determination to preserve themselves by strong inner resistance. They must remain on guard against an environment which tries to control them absolutely. They cannot affect this environment; they can only control themselves. But to do that they must also be on guard—against themselves. The cost of this inner vigilance and control is suffering—a price they would prefer to pay in silence, so as to avoid giving staff the satisfaction of perceiving the pain staff have inflicted. To the cost in anguish the cost of this stoicism must be added. Unfortunately, there is no question in my mind but that the experiment being conducted in the HSU at

Lexington is an attempt to replicate, under modern constraints and by "acceptable methods," the program originally developed by the Chinese. This program sets up a hierarchy of objectives. The first of these is to reduce prisoners to the state of submission essential for their ideological conversion. That failing, the next objective is to reduce them to a state of psychological incompetence sufficient to neutralize them as efficient, self-directing antagonists. That failing, the only alternative is to destroy them, preferably by making them desperate enough to destroy themselves.

Exterior of Lexington High Security Unit. (photo: Nina Rosenblum)

Susan Rosenberg

Reflections on Being Buried Alive

We stood at the electronically controlled metal gate under the eye of one of eleven surveillance cameras, surrounded by unidentified men in business suits. We were wearing newly issued beige short sleeve shirts, culottes, and plastic slippers. We were in handcuffs. An unidentified man had ordered us placed in restraints while walking from one end of the basement to the other. The lights were neon fluorescent burning and bright, and everything was snow white—walls, floors, ceilings. There was no sound except the humming of the lights, and nothing stirred in the air. Being there at that gate looking down the cell block made my ears ring, and breath quicken.

The cell block was one-hundred feet long with nine cells on one side and seven on the other. They were all locked shut. Alejandrina Torres (Puerto Rican Prisoner of War) said, "It's a white tomb, a white sepulcher." I nodded, and whispered, "It's Stammheim." (Stammheim is a special isolation prison in West Germany.) The official in charge said to the voice box on the wall, "Open R1 please, I have Torres and Rosenberg." A disembodied voice answered, "Please move a little to the left, I can't see you on my screen." For nearly three months we were the only two prisoners there, then a third political prisoner, Silvia Baraldini, and a social prisoner, Debra Brown, were brought there.

After our first week Alejandrina and I were "teamed" by officials. We were informed that we were permanently designated to the HSU, expected to serve our entire sentences of thirty-five to fifty-eight years there. We were told that we had no due process because the director of the Bureau of Prisons, acting as an agent for U.S. Attorney General Meese, had personally approved our placement, and only he could approve our removal. When we asked if there was any way for us to get out of the HSU we were informed that if we changed our associations and affiliations a change would be considered. The staff joke was you got a "one-way ticket" to the Lexington HSU.

All contact with everyone was monitored, surveyed, and analyzed. No contact was allowed with anyone other than attorneys and immediate family for the first sixteen months. The phone calls and mail were utilized for ongoing political surveillance against our friends, and our movement.

There were never set policy rules so procedures changed daily, making life completely unpredictable.

At first we were told that we could not receive any mail unless we submitted a list of fifteen names to be investigated. Only those who passed the investigation would be allowed to communicate with us. We refused to submit such a list. After three months this "rule" was changed and we were allowed to receive and send mail but not allowed any political literature. All mail incoming and outgoing was logged, and read by the Special Intelligence Lieutenant assigned to the HSU. Publications which were rejected as "promoting violence, and were a threat to the orderly running of the institution" included *The Nation, Claridad, MERIP Reports, Covert Action*, and others.

At one point we were allowed to review rejected political literature. We would be brought in front of the unit under the eye of the camera and one or two officers, seated at a card table and told "you have one hour." Once, the administration had both Alejandrina and I review the literature at the same time. The officers put two cartons of literature on the table and said, "Girls, you can't exchange literature, remember we're watching you."

The unit was shown to every law enforcement official who came to the prison. That meant we were on constant display. It got so bad that officers would bring their wives and children to tour the unit. A group of high school students came and so did Ed Meese. We made a sign that read "FREE ALL POLITICAL PRISONERS IN U.S. PRISONS—STOP HUMAN RIGHTS ABUSES," and would display it when we heard a tour coming.

One day a man toured the unit. As he came on the cell block, he said, "So this is the dead wing." He had an Irish accent and we asked where he was from. He said he knew all about the "boys" (the Provisional IRA). He said this must be the "terrorist isolation wing" which was similar to the "dead wings" throughout Irish and British prisons. While law enforcement and "terrorism" specialists had full access to HSU tours, access was denied to groups such as the National Lawyers Guild, the Kentucky Chapter of the National Organization for Women, and the American Sociology Association.

Everyone who wrote to us asked us how we felt about what was happening and how we resisted it. It was never an easy question to answer and it still isn't. Small-group isolation is a form of mental/psychological maltreatment, recognized by the tortured and torturer alike. The isolation, the sensory deprivation, the constant inactivity, and the forced dependency for basic life necessities on jailers who both hate you and fear you mean that existence is a constant confrontation where the four walls become the world.

We survived relatively intact only because we knew what the Justice Department was trying to do to us, and that knowledge enabled us to hold onto our political commitments and identities with strength. When we were enraged and tempted to live out the stereotypical behavior that they expected (i.e., to be violent) we had a collective of each other. The unity of the political prisoners and some of the social prisoners allowed us to laugh, to find humanity in each other, and to carry on. Despite the most extreme efforts of the Bureau of Prisons, they did not win. We never lost memory or reality of ourselves or of our political opposition to U.S. imperialism.

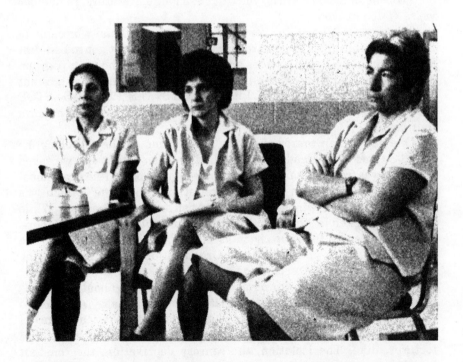

Alejandrina Torres, Susan Rosenberg, and Silvia Baraldini inside the Lexington HSU. (photo: Daedalus Productions)

Fay Dowker and Glenn Good

From Alcatraz to Marion to Florence: Control Unit Prisons in the United States

United States Penitentiary Marion was "locked down" on October 27, 1983 after two guards were killed in a solitary confinement wing of the prison known as the Control Unit. *Eight years later,* the men at Marion remain locked in their cells twenty-two or more hours a day, almost totally isolated from any human contact. Having turned Marion into one huge control unit, the Federal Bureau of Prisons (BoP) used it to refine a repressive regimen that has become the model for similar facilities in many state prison systems. The proliferation of control units and whole control unit prisons has happened at a tremendous rate over the past few years. This article will examine the facts about control units and suggest reasons for the dramatic increase in their numbers. Any theory about prisons is ultimately a theory of the society of which they are a part. Indeed, Dostoevsky wrote that if you want to understand a society, you should look inside its prisons. Thus, the role of control units in the prison system will be examined in the context of a society based on inequality, exploitation and racism. How do they function? What is their effect? Can they be stopped?

Early History of the Marion Control Unit

U.S. Penitentiary (USP) Marion, located in rural southern Illinois, opened in 1963, the same year the federal prison at Alcatraz closed. Alcatraz had gained a reputation as the "end of the line," the federal system's most repressive prison. Prominent gangsters, such as Al Capone, and Robert Stroud, the famous "Bird-Man," were imprisoned there, as were celebrated political prisoners like Rafael Cancel Miranda, the Puerto Rican national hero, and Morton Sobell, co-defendant with Ethel and Julius Rosenberg. However, the brutality of conditions at Alcatraz proved too controversial in an era when prisons were supposedly committed to the rehabilitation of prisoners. Marion was constructed to hold 500 "adult male felons who are difficult to control," according

to congressional testimony in 1971 by George Pickett, then super-
intendent of Marion.[1] Nonetheless, Alcatraz's prisoners were viewed
as providing too stiff an initial test of the new facility and so were
transferred to federal prisons other than Marion. Not until the late 1960's
were some of Alcatraz's former prisoners transferred to Marion.[2] At
about the same time, Marion began its transformation into the new
end of the line, a true heir to Alcatraz in its barbaric treatment of
prisoners.

The transformation began with the prison's implementation in 1968
of a behavior modification program called Control and Rehabilitation
Effort, or CARE. Prisoners in the program were put in solitary confinement and otherwise coerced into participating in group "therapy,"
which consisted of intense psychological "attack sessions." The purpose
was to bring prisoners under the staff's control as totally as possible
and turn them against other prisoners.[3] 1972 marked a turning point
in the program. In July, prisoners began a work stoppage to protest
a guard's beating of a Mexican prisoner.[4] Officials confined all prisoners
to their cells for six days, then put seven suspected strike leaders into
segregation (solitary confinement). The strike abated briefly, then began
again. Prisoners were then subjected to a mass reprisal to end the strike,
with sixty men locked in segregation and enrolled in the CARE program,
establishing the Control Unit. In 1973, H-Unit at Marion was officially
designated the Long-Term Control Unit.[5]

The Control Unit was used to expand the CARE program to include
prisoners from throughout the federal prison system "whose behavior
seriously disrupted the orderly operation of an institution," according
to official BoP policy.[6] This marked a return to a feature of BoP practice
missing since Alcatraz's closing—the concentration in a single prison
of those the BoP targeted for special punishment. Like some of the
prisoners in Marion's traditional solitary confinement unit, the Disciplinary Segregation Unit (I-Unit), prisoners in the Control Unit were
under "administrative" rather than disciplinary segregation. Officially,
administrative segregation differed from disciplinary segregation in that
it was not considered punishment, but rather an administrative response
to the prison's purported inability to manage the prisoner by normal
means.[7]

Prior to the establishment of the CARE program and Control Unit
at Marion and similar behavior modification programs and facilities
in other prisons, prison officials at least went to the trouble of setting
guidelines detailing under what circumstances and for how long a
prisoner should be subjected to solitary confinement. For example, the
1959 *Manual of Standards* of the American Correctional Association,
noting that segregation could have a "damaging effect upon some

inmates" and that "[e]xcessively long periods [in segregation] for punishment defeat their own purpose by embittering and demoralizing the inmate," recommended "a few days" of punitive segregation for most infractions, and an additional thirty to ninety days of administrative segregation in extraordinary circumstances.[8] Evidently intending precisely to demoralize prisoners, Marion officials ignored these guidelines for prisoners in the Control Unit. Indeed, in 1975 the General Accounting Office reported that some prisoners in the CARE program had been in the Control Unit for its entire three year existence.[9]

In 1978, the BoP added a security-level six category to its prisoner classification system, and in 1979 Marion was designated the only level six prison. That same year a BoP report contemplated turning Marion into a "closed-unit operation," and a 1981 report detailed plans to convert the entire prison into a control unit.[10] Stiffer controls inspired prisoner hunger and work strikes throughout the early 1980s. The longest of these—"reported to be the longest and most peaceful [strike] in U.S. prison history"—began in September 1980, when the warden, Harold Miller, refused to respond to the following list of concerns, which had been presented to him the preceding month:

1) Allow Native Americans to practice purification rites.
2) Allow religious services in segregation and the Control Unit.
3) Allow Muslims to wear the fez and turban.
4) Stop the use of boxcar cells [cells having solid doors].
5) Stop guards from harassing and beating prisoners.
6) Extend visiting and make the visiting room more comfortable.
7) Improve medical care.
8) Improve diet by using real meat.[11]

The strike was never broken, but ended when the administration closed the prison factory in January 1981.[12] This extraordinary act of resistance was the result of the BoP's practice over the previous decade of sending its most dissident and politicized prisoners to Marion.

In two separate incidents on October 22, 1983, two guards were killed by prisoners in the Control Unit. Although no rebellion resulted and the murderers were identified, prison officials seized the opportunity to violently repress all prisoners and implement their 1981 plans. The "lockdown," or cell-confinement of all prisoners, was imposed on October 27, 1983. The next day, the warden declared a state of emergency. Sixty guards, including Special Operations Response Team (SORT) members, were transferred to Marion from other institutions to assist in the lockdown. In addition, eight BoP executive staff members and three senior wardens were sent to "monitor" the procedure.[13] A guard at the time, David Hale, recalls how a Marion official, evidently uninhibited by the team of outside monitors, set the tone for the ensuing shakedown:

I seen them carry one inmate down the corridor with a guard on each leg and one on each arm. The assistant warden comes down the hall and grabs the inmate's testicles and starts yanking on them, saying, 'Who's doing it to who now, boy?' Well that was a signal for every guard in the place to do whatever the hell he wanted. I can't describe it to you—I never seen beatings like that. At least fifty guys got it, maybe more.[14]

The guards were outfitted with helmets, plastic shields, bullet-proof vests and other special gear, and their name tags were removed, making it impossible to identify guards who were involved in abuses.[15] They administered severe beatings while conducting cell shakedowns and forcing cell transfers, using fists, boots, and three-foot riot bludgeons, each with a steel ball affixed to the end. These "rib-spreaders," which have been part of regular equipment at the prison ever since, are designed to separate intercostal rib cartilage and inflict pain without breaking bones or leaving bruises. Prisoners were punched in the face, choked, knocked to the ground, and driven head-first into walls and metal doors. Four prisoners were beaten while in the prison hospital. In many cases, prisoners were handcuffed during the beatings. Prisoners were subjected to illegal and excessive x-ray examination for contraband. In many cases, the guards ripped off prisoners' underclothing and conducted forced rectal searches. Several prisoners were confined to individual cells for up to four days, handcuffed behind their backs and wearing only underwear. One prisoner testified that he was injected with an unknown drug which caused him to lose consciousness for two days.

Personal property was destroyed in the raid. Articles for religious worship, glasses and false teeth were destroyed or seized and never returned. For example, guards desecrated Alan Iron Moccasin's medicine bag and confiscated sacred articles of his Lakota religion. A minister's Koran was taken in the raids, and he was given a Bible in its place. Prisoners were locked in their cells around the clock. Most privileges were curtailed or eliminated. Congregate religious worship was eliminated. Visits were restricted. After revelations about the beatings surfaced, attorneys were denied entry to meet with prisoner clients for a period of several days in November. Within days, the Control Unit was expanded from its original seventy-two cells to include all 353 Marion prisoners. The entire population at Marion was collectively, severely, and permanently punished in a calculated move by the BoP.

Ongoing Conditions of the Lockdown

USP Marion comprises nine living units, B through I and K. Conditions vary between units. The five general population units, B though F, are located on Marion's East Corridor. Among these units, D, E and F are the most restrictive. C-Unit is slightly less restrictive than these three units and holds prisoners who are being considered for transfer to B-Unit. B-Unit is a pre-release unit with conditions similar to those in most maximum security prisons. On the North Corridor are located the prison's four "special living units." I-Unit, the Disciplinary Segregation Unit, holds prisoners from the East Corridor units who are on disciplinary or administrative segregation, and those who are being considered for transfer to H-Unit. G-Unit is similar to I-Unit and also holds prisoners in protective custody. H-Unit, or the Control Unit, holds prisoners who are on long-term administrative segregation.[16] K-Unit, or the Director's Unit, holds prisoners assigned there specifically on the order of the Director of the Bureau of Prisons.[17] The following description of conditions at Marion, unless otherwise noted, applies to units D, E and F. At the end of this section we will briefly describe some of the differences between these and the remaining units.[18]

D, E and F-Unit prisoners are let out of their cells one and a half hours each day. By comparison, in the rest of the federal prison system prisoners spend an average of thirteen hours per day out of their cells The hour and a half of daily "recreation" is usually spent in the narrow hallway immediately outside the cell. This time provides little stimulation and no real exercise opportunity. One hour of outdoor recreation in a fenced area is offered once a week in winter and three times a week in summer. The only chance prisoners have to take showers is during the exercise period. The cell itself measures six by eight feet. Meals are taken through the bars and eaten in the cell—there is no congregate dining. Beds are concrete slabs with pads laid on top of them. At each of the four corners of the bunk is a ring so that the men can be strapped down whenever prison authorities think that it is appropriate. Jackie Leyden from National Public Radio reports that "guards have the power to chain a man spread-eagled and naked to a concrete bunk."[19] Prisoners have reported being chained like that for days at a time.

No one makes any pretensions about rehabilitation. The only jobs are barber and porter. Prisoners may take correspondence courses, but only one at a time. The prison feeds educational tapes into the cells via closed circuit t.v., but no instruction, discussion or group classrooms exist. There are no large-group religious services. Prison officials tamper with letters and legal mail. While it is illegal for prison officials to look into prisoners' legal documents, they do so with impunity. Moreover, they often withhold or send back personal correspondence.[20] Visitations rights are severely restricted and no contact visits are ever allowed. The men can never touch their children, wives or other loved ones who come to visit. Prisoners must conduct conversations through Plexiglas and over a phone, which is monitored. A guard remains present, watching and recording the entire affair.

Few visitors venture so far to endure such painful conditions. Prisoners often ask loved ones not to visit while they are at Marion in order to avoid the humiliation that comes with this situation. As a result, one usually finds the visiting room virtually empty. Prisoners are allowed two ten-minute phone calls per month. Despite the Plexiglas partition separating them from visitors, prisoners are strip-searched after every visit. Finger probes of the rectum may be conducted "whenever there is reasonable suspicion" that the prisoner is hiding contraband.[21] A general idea of what constitutes "reasonable suspicion" is given by the fact that every prisoner who leaves the prison for any reason is strip-searched and subjected to the "finger wave" on his return, despite being shackled and guarded the whole time. Whenever a prisoner is not separated from staff by bars, he is handcuffed behind his back and escorted by two guards equipped with rib-spreader bludgeons.

Only the vaguest and most arbitrary rules exist at Marion. These whimsical guidelines all revolve around pleasing the guards and warden. The guidelines allow for disciplinary actions at Marion for trivial matters, such as failing to replace salt and pepper packets on a food tray, or hanging wet clothes to dry on the bars of a cell. In particular, no rules govern graduation of prisoners to relatively less restricted status within Marion. Prisoner promotions and demotions are officially at the discretion of the assistant warden. However, the power to veto any promotion effectively resides in every guard in the form of the despised Incident Reports, or "shots," citations for rule violations. One of the most common shots is "disobeying the direct order of a guard," which can be used to cite any "misbehavior" a guard desires. A single shot wipes out all good-conduct time a prisoner has earned, and puts the prisoner back at the beginning of "the program" that ostensibly governs the progression out of Marion to a level five prison.[22]

According to prisoners, the unending boredom and isolation are two of the most trying aspects of life at Marion. "You really have zero to do. It's the endless repetition of the same day over again," said prisoner Bill Dunne. "There's no community to connect with. If they see you getting too close to people, they move you into another unit. They want to make sure that you don't have any bonding or any association with anyone else."[23] Another prisoner said, "I'll take my chances getting a shank between the ribs, on any mainline in any joint in the country, over this shit. Here, you spend all day in your cell. All you got is yourself in here, man. And if you're having a bad day, look out, self."[24] Robert A. Litchfield, a Control Unit prisoner, looks forward to Wednesdays, when guards deliver the commissary order he is allowed each week, a pint of ice cream and bag of M&Ms. "It's the highlight of my week," he said. "But in another way, it saddens me that something so simple would make me so happy."[25]

B and C-Units are the stepping-stones to release from Marion. Prisoners in C-Unit spend slightly more time out of their cells, and are considered for transfer to B-Unit. B-Unit serves as an "honor unit," the last stage before transfer out of Marion. Here prisoners can spend all day outside their cells, eat meals in the dining room, have lockers and suffer restraints only for legal visits. They also work seven hours a day in the prison's factory for twenty-two cents an hour (which makes the monthly labor bill for the fifty prisoners less than $2,000, during which period they produce $250,000 worth of electrical cable for the Department of Defense).[26] However, placement in C and B-Units is completely arbitrary. A prisoner must have one continuous year of good conduct before being considered for C-Unit, a total of eighteen continuous months of good conduct for consideration for B-Unit, and a total of two continuous years of good conduct for consideration for release to a level five prison. Even without the intercession of guards and their shots, no clear system for progressing from one unit to the next exists. There is apparently no rhyme or reason as to why prisoners get sent to Marion, nor how and why they get to leave.

At the other end of the spectrum from B and C-Units are the North Corridor Units, G, H, and I-Units. In these units, what minute breathing space exists in D, E and F-Units is further restricted. Cells contain only a toilet, sink and concrete bed. Prisoners spend only one hour a day out of their cells, are strip-searched before and after exercise periods, are allowed only one phone call per month and three showers per week, and are put in both handcuffs and leg-irons and escorted by three guards, one holding their handcuffs, when they are out of their cells. Even this level of punishment is superseded in I and H-Units' "boxcar" cells, which have solid second front doors that cut off sound and air circulation. Despite the gradations of repression, all of Marion functions as a control unit, where the men are under constant and total control of the guard. John Campbell, a prisoner at Marion comments, "No one belongs in an environment where he's being buried alive, where he's in a—like a tomb for the dead. . . . And the police have total control over you, and they know they have total control, and they abuse that control frequently, either on a psychological level or a physical level."[27] Another prisoner, Steve Layton, adds, "They try to drag up the monster in you. It eats on a person, on a person's mind."[28]

Marion to be Replaced by Florence

Marion was not originally built as a control unit prison. It has thus been inadequate for the task of implementing the even tighter control of prisoners which BoP Director J. Michael Quinlan, in testimony before a Congressional subcommittee in the fall of 1989, said would constitute an improvement upon Marion's existing regimen.[29] The BoP has decided to replace Marion with a control unit prison in Florence, Colorado, specifically designed to achieve this goal. Scheduled to open in 1993, the prison's state-of-the-art technology will help to eliminate even the minimal levels of human contact prisoners have at Marion. It has proved very difficult to find out exact details of the new control unit prison to be built at Florence. When a Freedom of Information Act request for information on plans for Florence was submitted to the BoP, the BoP denied the request on the basis that the plans did not yet exist.[30] If that is the case, then the local newspapers appear to know more about the new prison than its designers. The following information comes from such newspapers.[31]

The Marion replacement is one of a complex of four federal prisons being built just south of Florence. The control unit will house 550 prisoners and is designed so that one guard will be able to control the movements of numerous prisoners in several cell-blocks by way of electronic doors, cameras, and audio equipment. "We'll be able to electronically open a cell door, shut it behind the inmate, and move him through a series of sliding doors," according to Russ Martin, project manager for the Florence prison. Prisoners will be even more restricted than at Marion, according to the *Pueblo Chieftain*: "Inmates won't have to travel nearly as far in the new Florence prison." At Marion the prisoners can at least shout to each other through their bars. At Florence solid cell doors will make that difficult or impossible.[32]

Just five miles from the prison site, in Lincoln Park, is the Cotter Corporation, a uranium milling company owned by Commonwealth Edison of Chicago, Illinois. The area surrounding the mill and nearby railroad has been extensively radioactively contaminated. Uranium tailings dumped in unlined ponds have poisoned the underground aquifer and the nearby Arkansas River. Radioactive dust is carried for miles by the high winds. The contamination of the water alone has caused the Lincoln Park area to be on the Environmental Protection Agency's National Priorities List since 1984 and it has been designated a Superfund site for contamination clean-up.[33] The political landscape around Florence is equally bleak. Florence is in Fremont County, where more than one in ten of the work force is employed by the Colorado

Department of Corrections in the nine prisons clustered around Cañon City.[34] Prisoners constitute more than ten percent of the population of the county.[35] The guaranteed employment that the prisons bring mean that they are overwhelmingly popular with the residents.

Florence itself is an economically devastated community of 3,000 where unemployment stands at seventeen percent and the prospect of about 1,000 temporary and 750-900 new permanent jobs has proved irresistible. Ninety-seven percent of respondents to one local mail-in poll were in favor of the building of the Florence complex. The citizens raised $160,000 to purchase the 600 acres for the site; 400 locals gathered for the ground-breaking; t-shirts bearing a map of the site were "sold out" at $7.99; a housewarming barbecue hosted by the BoP was attended by 1,000 local residents. Now, Pueblo Community College is offering criminal justice courses customized to suit the needs of the federal prison. It is obviously useful for the BoP to have this kind of support amongst the local population from which its supply of guards will come.

The Proliferation of Control Units

The model for the new control unit at Florence is the Security Housing Unit (SHU) at Pelican Bay State Prison in California.[36] The SHU, which opened in December 1989, was designed as the ultimate facility for the implementation of Marion-style repression. Built to hold 1,056 prisoners in near-total isolation, it is already twenty percent over capacity.[37] Prisoners are confined to their eighty square foot cells with solid steel doors for twenty-two and one half hours a day. They are allowed out only for a ninety minute "exercise" period alone in an empty concrete yard the size of three cells with twenty foot high walls and metal screens overhead. Guards open the sliding doors by remote control and use loudspeakers to direct the prisoners in and out. Prisoners moved off the cell-block for any reason are shackled and flanked by two guards wielding truncheons. Except for the sound of a door slamming or a voice on a speaker, the SHU is silent. Prison officials, not the courts, "sentence" prisoners to SHU terms.[38] Often, confidential tips from other prisoners serve as the basis for a disciplinary hearing to determine whether to send the prisoner to the SHU, and these hearings have few safeguards of due process. Many prisoners are sent there for filing grievances or lawsuits or for otherwise opposing prison injustices.[39] SHU prisoners report the use of "hog-tying" (the intertwining of handcuffs and ankle-cuffs on a prisoner), "cock-fights" in which guards double-cell enemies or otherwise allow them to attack each other, and forced cell moves using Taser stunguns, thirty-eight millimeter gas guns and batons.[40]

Conditions such as those at the SHU and Marion are replicated in state control units throughout the country. Many of these prisons feature their own innovations in controlling and dehumanizing prisoners. At a second California control unit prison at Corcoran, armed guards patrol the Plexiglas ceilings over the cells and peer in at prisoners through Plexiglas cell walls.[41] At Colorado's Centennial Prison in Cañon City, the administrative segregation unit is being expanded to include the whole prison.[42] A priest hired by the prison delivers communion through a small, knee-high food slot in a solid steel door. "If you ain't wrapped too tight, 23-hour lockdown can be enough to make you explode," says the priest. Guards are armed with "nut-guns," wide-bore guns that fire wildly caroming, acorn-sized "nuts" at prisoners from close range. "It's a miniature cannon," the priest explains. "The recommended technique is to fire at the floor so that the acorn ricochets." Prisoners hit by the nuts can be maimed. "One guy lost his eye, and since I arrived here three years ago, an acorn took off a guy's nose and plastered it to his cheek."[43]

At Lebanon, Ohio, prisoners under administrative control are held in eight by six foot isolation cells. Each cell has a second door so that prisoners can be locked in the extreme back, darkened portion of the cell. A prisoner describes being leg-shackled, having his arms cuffed to a belt about his waist and being escorted by three guards whenever he is moved from his cell. Other prisoners are forbidden to speak to him.[44] In Missouri, the state prison at Potosi is run by Warden Paul K. Delo, a Vietnam War veteran who, by Missouri law, doubles as the state's executioner since Death Row is at Potosi. Says Delo of his secondary duties, "One of our officers had an analogy. He said it's just like at your own house. Nobody likes to take out the garbage, but somebody has to."[45] Perhaps inspired by Delo's army experience, prison officials apply the "double-litter restraint" to recalcitrant prisoners. The prisoner's hands are cuffed behind his back, his ankles are cuffed and he is forced to lie face-down on an Army-type cot, his head turned to the side. A second cot is then tightly strapped upside-down over the prisoner and the ends are strapped shut, totally enclosing and immobilizing him. Carl Swope, a 21 year-old sentenced to seven years for credit card fraud, filed suit after being held in the restraint for three hours.[46]

Other state control unit prisons are at Ionia, Michigan;[47] Southport, New York; McAlester, Oklahoma; and Baltimore, Maryland.[48] A survey by the Federal Bureau of Prisons found that thirty-six states now operate some form of super-maximum security prison or unit within a prison.[49] The list will apparently continue to grow. A Pennsylvania Senate Judiciary Committee report studying the causes and proposing responses to the 1989 uprising at the state's Camp Hill prison had as a key proposal the construction of a Marion-style control unit.[50] Control unit technology is even trickling down to the local level. The Jefferson County Detention Center in Colorado holds each prisoner in an eighty square foot cell equipped with a concrete bed with a mattress on top, sink, toilet and concrete table. Everything from the lights to the locks on the doors is operated electronically by guards in control booths. The jail was designed to allow for a range of control measures, including nearly round-the-clock cell confinement.[51]

The Function of Control Units

The reasons for this proliferation of control units are multi-leveled. In the most superficial analysis it is seen to be a response to the prison population explosion. The U.S. incarceration rate (the number of people in prison per 100,000 of the population) is the highest in the world at 426 per 100,000.[52] This is well above rates in the Soviet Union (268 per 100,000) and South Africa under apartheid (333 per 100,000), and dwarfs rates in the Netherlands (forty per 100,000) and Australia (72 per 100,000).[53] These figures are even more striking when analyzed in terms of race. The imprisonment rate for black people is more than seven times that for white people.[54] The U.S. incarcerates black men at a rate *four times* higher than South Africa does.[55] The number of people in prison in the U.S. has more than doubled over the last decade and George Bush has promised to double it again in the 1990s. This would bring the number of people behind bars to over *two million*. Even in 1981 the situation was so bad that New York State Correction Commissioner Thomas Coughlin admitted that "the department is no longer engaged in rehabilitive and programming efforts, but is rather forced to warehouse people and concentrate on finding the next cell."[56] It is clear that to keep the prison population subdued in the face of more and more overcrowded and frustrating conditions will take substantial force. That force is provided by control unit prisons.

When the controlling role of these isolation units within the prison system is examined more closely, it is found to be a mirror of the effect of prisons in society as a whole. Let us first look at the claims made about control units and compare these to what is known. Prison officials claim that Marion, Pelican Bay and the other control units contain the most violent prisoners and reduce violence in the rest of the prison system. It is certainly true that prisoners in control units are so incapacitated that physical violence by these prisoners will be reduced while they are there. Most of them will, however, be released at some stage either back into the general prison population or into society. It is known that control unit conditions produce feelings of resentment and rage and mental deterioration.[57] Prisoners will have been so deprived of human contact that it will be hard for them to cope with social situations again. The inhumanity of control units cannot reduce violence, it can only increase it. Evidence includes the high level of violence at Marion during the period before the lockdown, when controls were being tightened but not yet to the extent of completely physically incapacitating the prisoners. The tighter controls certainly did not have a calming effect on the prison. In addition, the guard deaths of 1983 occurred in the Control Unit itself.

The BoP claims that since they concentrate the most violent prisoners in the federal system at Marion, they are able to reduce controls at other institutions. There has been no indication of this happening. In fact, aspects of Marion's super-maximum-security format are cropping up throughout the federal system. USP Lewisburg, for example, has a control unit with 180 isolation cells with solid, remote controlled doors. The only ventilation comes through tiny openings, called "wickets," in the doors, which are opened or closed at the guard's whim.[58] The BoP plans to construct a prison complex similar to the one under construction at Florence at the Lewisburg site.[59] It seems likely that this complex will include a control unit prison.[60] More dramatically, it is Marion that has invariable been cited as the inspiration for the numerous state control units.[61] Indeed, a delegation of the U.S. House Subcommittee on Courts, Intellectual Property and the Administration of Justice, which visited Marion in May, 1990, cited the need to "develop a more humane approach to the incarceration of the maximum-security prison population. This is particularly true because the Federal Bureau of Prisons serves as a model for state prisons and for other countries in the world."[62] The existence of Marion has not improved conditions at other prisons; its example has dragged them down toward greater brutality.

The other claim is that it is only violent prisoners who are put in control units. The facts of Marion disprove this. The BoP's own rules state that Marion should be for prisoners who have proved too violent for other prisons. A 1985 report by consultants hired by a Congressional oversight committee stated that *eighty percent of prisoners at Marion did not deserve that level of security.*[63] In fact, prisoners are sent to Marion for a variety of reasons and sometimes for no reason at all. For example, the U.S. District Court ordered a cap on prison population. As a result, so many prisoners convicted on felonies in the District of Columbia have been moved to Marion to relieve overcrowding that they constituted seventeen percent of Marion's population in 1990.[64] Virtually all of these prisoners are black.

There is, however, a trend to be seen. Prisoners have been transferred to Marion for writing "too many" lawsuits, for protesting the brutality of the prison system, or for angering prison officials in some other way.[65] In addition, among the many political prisoners who have been in Marion, American Indian Movement leader Leonard Peltier, Sekou Odinga, member of the Black Liberation Army, Alan Berkman, Tim Blunk and Ray Levasseuer were sent directly to Marion from court,[66] thereby disproving the claim that prisoners at Marion have been violent at other prisons. According to Ralph Arons, former warden at Marion: "The purpose of the Marion Control Unit is to control revolutionary attitudes in the prison system and in the society at large."[67] Notice that what is considered objectionable and threatening in Arons' statement is the display of "revolutionary *attitudes*," not actions of any sort.

The Prison Discipline Study initiated in 1989 by the Prisoner Rights Union of Sacramento, California, shows that the group of prisoners most frequently abused is jailhouse lawyers.[68] The most common form of discipline is solitary confinement. Included in this report are testimonies by prisoners that those of them exhibiting personal integrity are singled out for brutal treatment. Respondents to the survey described this group as "those with principles or intelligence"; "those with dignity and self-respect"; "authors of truthful articles"; "motivated self-improvers"; those "verbally expressing . . . [their] opinion"; "wanting to be treated as a human being" and/or "reporting conditions to people on the outside." The study shows, therefore, that a practice such as sending prisoners to control units, which is based on arbitrary and subjective judgments by guards and other officials, will target prisoners who are most likely to be challenging the prison system. A final indication as to the true purpose of control units is the timing of the institution of the initial Control Unit at Marion in 1972. Less than a year before, prisoners at the state prison at Attica in upstate New York rebelled against the inhuman and racist regime there, declaring their solidarity with all oppressed people and demanding their rights. The rebellion, and the consequent brutal murder of thirty-nine prisoners and hostages by New York State Troopers, under the orders of Governor Nelson Rockefeller, rocked the nation. The whole prison system was at boiling point. The BoP's response was to open the Control Unit.

Imprisonment as Socio-Political Control

Just as control units suppress the prison population, so prisons act in our poor, African-American and Latino communities. It is not exaggeration to say that hardly anyone in these communities escapes the shadow of the "criminal justice system." The devastation can be expressed in many ways. Black people are twelve percent of the U.S. population, but forty-three percent of the prison population.[69] Using data based on a single day in mid-1989, a study by Marc Mauer for the Sentencing Project in Washington, D.C., found that about one in four black men in their twenties was under some kind of control by the criminal justice system, and about one in twelve was actually behind bars.[70] In 1985, the U.S. Bureau of Justice Statistics published the results of a 1979 survey that sought to determine the probability that a person in the U.S. would go to prison in his/her lifetime.[71] Using the data in this report, it can be calculated that in 1979, the probability that a black man would go to prison sometime in his life was twenty-two percent. In 1991, it is probable that *one in four black men will go to prison in his lifetime*. What does that mean for the Afroamerican community? Families suffer financially and emotionally. Whatever few jobs are available to African-American men are further out of reach for an "ex-con." Prisoners rejoin their communities from prisons which don't even pretend to rehabilitate, and where conditions encourage violence and criminality.

The question, "Why do Afroamerican people go to prison at a rate seven times higher than white people?" can be answered in three different ways. One is that black people commit seven times as much crime as other people because they are genetically disposed to do so. The second is that black people commit seven times as much crime, and something about their disadvantaged social situation is responsible for this. The third is that black people do *not* commit that much crime, but the racism of the criminal justice system ensures that they end up in prison that often. With the first alternative rejected, the truth must lie somewhere between the last two answers, although it is impossible to determine how much weight to give to each. Notice that the belief that the imprisonment rate accurately reflects the crime rate leads to a radical (at least in the political climate of the 1990s) conclusion: in order to effectively combat crime, poverty and racism must be eliminated (even if one is not interested in eliminating them for any other reason).

The third alternative, that in fact African-American people do not commit such a disproportionate amount of crime, is indicated by much evidence, although it is impossible to calculate the degree of the disparity between the rates of crimes committed by black people and the percentage of black people imprisoned. The total number of crimes committed is so huge that only a small fraction of the people who perpetrate them are actually imprisoned. (The crime rate is difficult to determine, and the two major national sources of crime data disagree significantly on both quantity and trends. They do, however, both show that the amount of crime is very large: in 1986, between thirteen[72] and thirty-four[73] million crimes were committed.) Thus, from a huge pool of potential prisoners, i.e., people who have committed crimes, the criminal justice system singles out those who will go to prison. This is done mainly via policing policy. One example of how racist this can be is that in the "War on Drugs," police target poor, African-American neighborhoods for surveillance even though the great majority of drug users are white. For example, a front page story in the *Los Angeles Times* reported that while about eighty percent of the nation's drug users are white, the majority of those arrested for "drug crimes" are black.[74]

Crime is a problem that must be tackled. However, there is no evidence that high imprisonment rates are the answer to the problem of crime. Indeed, study after study shows that prisons do not deter crime, and, remarkably, we know of *no* research that indicates that they do.[75] The only slight reduction in the crime rate which is due to incarceration results from the incapacitation of those imprisoned. However, the studies referenced above conclude that massive increases in the imprisonment rate have only a tiny effect on the crime rate. Imprisoning large numbers of people in order to stop crime has been a spectacular and massively expensive failure. Academic research shows this and even prison officials sometimes admit to the reality of the situation. According to the Director of Corrections of Alabama, "We're on a train that has to be turned around. It doesn't make any sense to pump millions and millions into corrections and have no effect on the crime rate."[76]

If imprisonment does not reduce crime, what does it do? It causes direct suffering to prisoners and their families. More subtly but more relevant to our discussion here, it is a major cause of the deterioration of communities of poor people and especially of people of color. If one decides that the purpose of prisons cannot be to stop crime, because it has been known for years that they do not do so, then one can conclude that this devastation is the real intention. The consequent suppression of active protest amongst people of color against the injustices of a society based on the maximization of profit is obviously a gain for those with a vested interest in such a society.

What Can We Do?

Control units seriously violate prisoners' rights. The truth about Marion shows that control units serve to suppress dissent among the prison population just as prisons in general incapacitate and demoralize black people and other people of color, rendering them less able to organize and struggle for their liberation. These truths never appear on our televisions or in our newspapers, even though crime and prisons are practically a media obsession. The present system of mass incarceration, with the accompanying specter of more and more control units, can only be maintained with at least the tacit approval of society as a whole. So it is not surprising that those of us least likely to experience the brutality of prison are also subjected to appropriate control procedures. We face a constant barrage of anti-crime and anti-drug hysteria from the establishment. Prisoners are portrayed as incorrigible and dangerous, undeserving of even the most basic human rights. Politicians and the mainstream media never mention, let alone intelligently discuss, underlying problems of poverty, inequality and racism. Debate is thus limited to how to manage the ever-increasing flood of prisoners, the necessity of creating such a flood being taken as a given.

The reality of the role of control units is carefully hidden from public view. Most control units and other newly constructed prisons are located in isolated, economically depressed, rural areas. This serves several purposes. The ardent support of local people, who rely on the prisons for desperately needed jobs, is secured. Prisoners are isolated from their families and friends. Major media attention is reduced, effectively keeping control units "out of sight and out of mind." Political figures support increased imprisonment since most of them thrive on "tough-on-crime" platforms. The courts cannot be relied upon. In *Bruscino v. Carlson*, Marion prisoners sought compensation for the attacks which occurred during the October 1983 shakedown and relief from the ongoing conditions of the lockdown. A 1985 Magistrate's Report for this case was approved by the full U.S. District Court for Southern Illinois in 1987. The decision found that fifty prisoners who testified to beatings and other brutalities were not credible witnesses, and that only the single prisoner who testified that there were no beatings was believable.[77] When the prisoners appealed the decision, the ruling of the Fifth Circuit Court of Appeals described conditions at Marion as "ghastly . . . sordid and horrible . . . [and] depressing in the extreme," but maintained that they were necessary for security reasons and did not violate prisoners' constitutional rights.[78]

The Committee to End the Marion Lockdown (CEML) was formed from a group of people who, in July 1985, got together to talk about conditions at Marion. The Committee is working to end the lockdown at Marion, stop the building of the Florence control unit prison, and abolish all control units. Politicians and the legal system cannot be looked to—only ordinary people, people concerned for justice, can effect change. CEML tries to bring its concerns to such people. In August 1988, after two years of campaigning and protests led by the Puerto Rican independence movement, the BoP was forced to close the infamous Lexington

High Security Prison for women.[79] More recently, CEML protested the use of toxic water for prisoners at Marion, holding a demonstration at the prison and in the town of Marion, and exacting a promise from the BoP that the water source will be changed. Wells have already been dug and pipes are being fitted. So we can change things.

Since debate is stifled, we must reopen the discussion and challenge prevailing notions about the role of control units and prisons in our society. Even within the progressive community, there is little awareness of the scale and brutality of U.S. imprisonment and its devastating impact on communities of color. CEML tries to share what we learn with as many people as we can by sending out newsletters, holding conferences and forging contacts with groups already campaigning for peace and justice in other areas. CEML has developed a wide range of educational tools, literature and videos. We must challenge society's notions of what constitutes crime and who is to be considered a criminal. The black drug addict who sells drugs to keep up his habit, the poor man who robs a drug store at gunpoint, the woman who kills her abusive husband: they are all sent to prison and considered dangerous. However, the violation of safety codes by slum landlords and mine owners, embezzlement and fraud by savings and loan executives, and pollution of land, seas and atmosphere by oil and chemical company directors cause death, injury and impoverishment, yet are rarely punished by imprisonment. Many destructive acts are not even illegal.

Since the BoP tries to hide its activities from the public, we must work to uncover and disseminate the truth about prisons and control units. The more we know, the more effectively we can campaign. Since prisons seek to isolate prisoners from society, we must work to develop links with prisoners and use the resulting understanding to speak more persuasively on their behalf. CEML has established a list of prisoners at Marion with whom we and others correspond. Marion and the other control units are the center of the prison system, "the end of the line" in cruelty and repression. We must oppose them if we are truly to be able to say we wish for a new and just society.

Notes

1. Jessica Mitford, *Kind and Usual Punishment: The Prison Business* (New York: Vintage Books, 1973), p. 199.
2. Allen F. Breed and David A. Ward, *The United States Penitentiary, Marion, Illinois: Consultant's Report Submitted to the Committee on the Judiciary, U.S. House of Representatives*, December 1984, p. 10, in *Marion Penitentiary, 1985: Oversight Hearing before the Subcommittee on Courts, Civil Liberties, and the Administration of Justice* (Washington, D.C.: U.S.

Government Printing Office, 1985). The latter document is cited below as *Marion Penitentiary, 1985*, and all page references to documents printed in it refer to the page numbers from this document.

3. Mitford, *op. cit.*, pp. 134-35.

4. Speech by Rafael Cancel Miranda, Chicago, Illinois, November 7, 1990.

5. Decision in *Adams v. Carlson*, 1973, pp. 621-22, in *Marion Penitentiary, 1985*; Affidavit by Bobby Anderson in *Adams v. Carlson*, in *Behavior Modification: New Method of Prison Repression* (Eugene, OR: Coalition Press, 1975), p. 19; Robert Gruenberg, "GAO Assails Use of Isolation," *Chicago Daily News*, August 6, 1975.

6. Breed and Ward, *loc. cit.*

7. American Correctional Association, *Manual of Standards, 1959*, cited in *Adams v. Carlson*, *op. cit.*, p. 606, note 15.

8. *Ibid.*

9. Gruenberg, *loc. cit.*

10. Breed and Ward, *op. cit.*, pp. 11 and 22.

11. Jan Susler, *et al.*, "An Updated Public Report about the Continuing Lockdown and Torture of the Prisoners at U.S. Penitentiary, Marion," 1984, unpublished, p. 8.

12. Cisco Lassiter, "RoboPrison," *Mother Jones*, September-October 1990, p. 76; Breed and Ward, *op. cit.*, p. 12.

13. Letter from BoP Director Norman Carlson to Amnesty International Secretary General Jose Zalaquett, April 3, 1984.

14. Lassiter, *op. cit.*, p. 76.

15. Dennis Cunnigham and Jan Susler, "A Public Report About a Violent Mass Assault against Prisoners and Continuing Illegal Punishment and Torture of the Prison Population at the U.S. Penitentiary at Marion, Illinois," 1984, unpublished. The following account is based on this source.

16. Magistrate's Report in *Bruscino v. Carlson*, August 15, 1985, pp. 491-92, in *Marion Penitentiary, 1985*.

17. Christopher Dickey, "A New Home for Noriega?" *Newsweek*, January 15, 1990, p. 69.

18. The following sources were used in compiling this description: Magistrate's Report in *Bruscino v. Carlson*, 1985; William Hart, "The 'New Alcatraz,'" *National Centurion*, June 1984; William Gonzales, "The New Alcatraz," *Chicago*, February 1986 (all in *Marion Penitentiary, 1985*); Jackie Leyden, reports on National Public Radio's *All Things Considered*, October 28 and November 1, 1986, transcribed as "Marion Prison: Inside the Lockdown!" by the Committee to End the Marion Lockdown; Michael Satchell, "The Toughest Prison in America," *U.S. News and World Report*, July 27, 1987; "Where the Worst Go—Marion Federal Penitentiary," *The Economist*, June 30, 1990; Dickey, *op. cit.*; Lassiter, *op. cit.*; Michael Isikoff, "Hard Time: The Mission at Marion," *Washington Post*, May 28, 1991, Section A. pp. 1, 6; Susan Lehman, "Lockdown," *Wigwag*, September, 1990.

19. Leyden, *op. cit.*, p. 1.

20. For example, mail sent by the Committee to End the Marion Lockdown has been returned or "lost." In one case, then Warden Gary Henman, when challenged about a lost mailing, implied that the twenty-seven prison addressees had lied about not receiving it. Henman wrote, "You may want to look at their criminal/institutional records prior to putting

your faith completely on their statements." (Letter from Gary Henman to Steven Whitman, Committee to End the Marion Lockdown, January 27, 1989.) Another mailing was returned because it contained a general distribution leaflet for a demonstration with the phrase "Join Us."

21. Among the "Findings of Fact" in Magistrate's Report in *Bruscino v. Carlson, op. cit.*, p. 493.

22. Leyden, *op. cit.*, pp. 2-3.

23. Isikoff, *op. cit.*, Section A, p. 6.

24. Lassiter, *op. cit.*, p. 78.

25. Isikoff, *loc. cit.*

26. Lehman, *op. cit.*, p. 30.

27. Leyden, *op. cit*, p. 2.

28. *Ibid.*

29. Lehman, *op. cit.*, pp. 36-37.

30. Letter from Wallace H. Cheney, General Counsel for the Federal Bureau of Prisons, to Jan Susler, Attorney for People's Law Office, December 31, 1990. The entire text of the letter read: "This is in response to your request for information related to the Florence, Colorado project. The issues you inquired about have not yet been decided. Therefore, no records exist at this time pertaining to your request. I trust you you [sic] will find this information useful."

31. Kit Miniclier, "Florence Pins Hopes on Prisons," *Denver Post,* April 4, 1991, Section A, p. 1; Steve Henson, "Bad Dudes," *Pueblo (Colorado) Chieftain,* July 15, 1990, Section B, p. 1; Mike O'Keeffe, "Big House on the Prairie," *Westword,* April 24-30, 1991; Peter G. Chronis, "'Baddest of the Bad' Coming to New Federal Prison," *Denver Post,* May 11, 1990, Section B, p. 1; Tom Harmon, "Prison Construction Work Swells Florence Area Population," *Pueblo Chieftain,* March 24, 1991, Section B, p. 2; Associated Press, "Scientist Recommends Health-Risk Study of Lincoln Park Area," *Pueblo Chieftain,* December 8, 1990, Section A, p. 10; Jim Ritter, "Colorado Suit Accuses Edison of Radiation Pollution," *Chicago Sun-Times,* February 18, 1991, p.13.

32. This assumes that this aspect of the model for Florence, the Pelican Bay State Prison Security Housing Unit, is copied. See below, notes 36 and 38.

33. O'Keeffe, *op. cit.*, p. 10.

34. *Ibid.*, p. 10.

35. Miniclier, *op. cit.*, Section A, p. 1.

36. Moel K. Wilson, "Hard-Core Prisoners Controlled in Nation's High-Tech Prisons," *Chicago Daily Law Bulletin,* April 25, 1991, p. 2.

37. Wes Smith, "State puts Low Priority on High-Security Prison, " *Chicago Tribune,* April 1, 1991, Section 1, p. 1.

38. Miles Corwin, "High-Tech Facility Ushers in New Era of State Prisons," *Los Angeles Times,* May 1, 1990, Section A, p. 1.

39. Cory Weinstein, "Supermax Blues at Pelican Bay SHU," *California Prisoner,* August 1990.

40. *Ibid.*; letter from Pelican Bay SHU prisoner Thomas Fetters, June 30, 1991. Fetters writes that he was transferred to the SHU for filing a lawsuit after being injured by a guard who assaulted him while he was in physical restraints. Letter from SHU prisoner Robert Lee Davenport,

September 28, 1990. Davenport reports being hog-tied and left on his cell floor for ten hours, and witnessing other prisoners left like that for twenty hours.

41. Wilson, *loc. cit.*

42. Dick Foster, "Maximum Security to Live Up to its Name," *Rocky Mountain News*, May 5, 1990.

43. Richard Johnson, "Parish Behind Bars," *Denver Post*, November 11, 1990, Contemporary, p. 12.

44. John Perotti, *Prison News Service*, March-April, 1991.

45. Tom Uhlenbrock, "Soft-Spoken Executioner to Run New Prison," *St. Louis Post-Dispatch*, January 1, 1989, p. 1.

46. Tom Bryant, "Encased: Prison's Use of 'Cocoon' is Challenged in Suit Here," *St. Louis Post-Dispatch*, January 26, 1991, Section A, p. 3; David Aguillard, "Official Defends Inmate Restraint," *St. Louis Post-Dispatch*, January 31, 1991, Section A, p. 5.

47. "Prison Crackdown," *Detroit News*, February 3, 1989, section B, p. 3.

48. "Trying to Economize, New York Makes its Own Alcatraz," *New York Times*, February 20, 1991, Section B, p. 1; Jim Pfiffer and Garth Wade, "To the Max—Special Report," *Elmira (New York) Star Gazette*, April 7-9, 1991; Wade, Garth, "Prisons Reporting Success in Converting to Maxi-Maxi," *Elmira Star-Gazette*, April 8, 1991, Section A, p. 6.

49. Lassiter, *op. cit.*, p. 80.

50. "Pennsylvania Senate Committee Calls for 'Super-Maximum' Prison," *Criminal Justice Newsletter*, December 17, 1990, p. 4.

51. Pat McGraw, "Safety for Both Guards, Prisoners Designed into Jeffco's High-Tech Jail," *Denver Post*, September 7, 1986.

52. Marc Mauer, "Americans Behind Bars: A Comparison of International Rates of Incarceration," (Washington, D.C.: The Sentencing Project, January 1990). See pp. 22-37 above.

53. *Ibid.*, p. 5.

54. Steven Whitman, "The Crime of Black Imprisonment," *Prison News Service*, July 1991.

55. Mauer, *op. cit.*, p. 4.

56. Barbara Day, "Prison Revolt Squashed but Crisis Continues," *Guardian*, August 1988, p. 8.

57. Dr. Richard Korn, "The Effects of Confinement in the High Security Unit at Lexington," *Social Justice*, vol. 15, no. 1, pp. 8-19. See pp. 123-27 above.

58. Alan and Susan Raymond, "Life Inside the Big House," Home Box Office documentary, 1991.

59. O'Keeffe, *op. cit.*, p. 17; Chronis, *op. cit.*, Section B, p. 5.

60. This is speculation based on the following: Lewisburg is already the site of a maximum security prison and a minimum security prison camp, so that construction of a medium security prison and a control unit would make the complex mirror Florence's "Western Correctional Complex," which an early report specifically stated was intended to serve the western region of the United States (Associated Press, "New Fremont Prison Clears Senate Hurdle," *Denver Post*, September 14, 1989); also, the Federal prison population is projected to more than double to 125,000 during the 1990's (O'Keeffe, *loc. cit.*), so that it is likely that the BoP wants a second control

unit prison.

61. See, for example, "Pennsylvania Senate Committee Calls for 'Super-Maximum' Prison," *loc. cit.*, and Smith, *op. cit.*, a full-page plea, masquerading as a news report, for the Illinois prison system to build its own version of Marion.

62. Lassiter, *op. cit.*, p. 80.

63. *Marion Penitentiary, 1985*, p. 35.

64. Lassiter, *op. cit.*, p. 77.

65. *Marion Penitentiary, 1985, ibid.*

66. *Can't Jail the Spirit*, 1st Edition (Chicago: Editions El Coqui, 1989), pp. 37, 71, 145; Mike O'Keeffe, "America's Least Wanted," *Westword*, April 24-40, 1991, p. 12.

67. Steven Whitman, "The Marion Penitentiary—It Should be Opened Up, Not Locked Down," *Southern Ilinoisian*, August 7, 1988, p. 25.

68. Prison Discipline Study, Prisoners Rights Union, Sacramento, California, 1991.

69. Tom Wicker, "The Iron Medal," *New York Times*, January 9, 1991, op-ed page.

70. Marc Mauer, "Young Black Men and the Criminal Justice System: A Growing National Problem," (Washington, D.C.: The Sentencing Project, February 1990).

71. Patrick Langan, and Lawrence Greenfield, "Prevalence of Imprisonment," (Washington, D.C.: U.S. Department of Justice, 1985).

72. "Uniform Crime Reports" in *Sourcebook of Criminal Justice Statistics, 1987* (Washington, D.C.: U.S. Government Printing Office, 1989).

73. Bureau of Justice Statistics, "National Crime Survey" in *Households Touched by Crime 1988* (Washington, D.C.: U.S. Government Printing Office, 1989).

74. Ron Harris, *Los Angeles Times*, April 22, 1990, p. 1.

75. Alfred Blumenstein, Jacqueline Cohen, and Daniel Nagin (eds.), *Deterrence and Incapacitation: Estimating the Effects of Criminal Sanctions on Crime Rates* (Washington, D.C.: National Academy of Sciences, 1978); Christy A. Visher, "Incapacitation and Crime Control: Does a 'Lock 'em Up' Strategy Reduce Crime?" *Justice Quarterly* 4, (1987), pp. 513-543; Kevin Krajik and Steve Gettinger, *Overcrowded Time* (New York: The Edna McConnell Clark Foundation, 1982).

76. Scott Ticer, "The Search for Ways to Break Out of the Prison Crisis," *Business Week*, May 8, 1989, p. 80.

77. Magistrate's Report in *Bruscino v. Carlson*, *op. cit*, pp. 501-514; Leyden, *op. cit.*, p. 2.

78. Tim Landis, "Marion Warden Praises Decision," *Southern Illinoisian*, July 28, 1988, Section A, p. 1.

79. Associated Press, "Judge Bars U.S. from Isolating Prisoners for Political Beliefs," *New York Times*, July 17, 1988.

Mutulu Shakur, Marilyn Buck,
Geronimo Pratt, Albert Nuh Washington,
Sekou Odinga, Cecilio Chui Ferguson El,
Susan Rosenberg, and David Gilbert

Prisoners of War:
The Legal Standing of Members of
National Liberation Movements

The following essay is composed of excerpts from a defendants'
memorandum submitted to U.S. District Judge Charles S. Straight on
January 19, 1988, during the case of *U.S. v. Mutulu Shakur and Marilyn
Buck*. The accused were charged with conspiracy and other "crimes"
associated with their participation in the Revolutionary Armed Task
Force (RATF), an alliance composed of elements of the Black Liberation
Army (BLA), Weather Underground Organization (WUO) and the May
19th Communist Organization. The RATF was allegedly responsible
for the freeing of Assata Shakur (s/n: Joanne Chesimard) from New
Jersey's Clinton Correctional Institution on November 2, 1978, as well
as a lengthy series of expropriations from banks and armored cars in
New York state.

Dr. Shakur (s/n: Jeral Wayne Williams) directed the highly successful
Lincoln Detox Program in South Bronx, until the City of New York
withdrew funding—destroying this community-based effort—in November
1978. After that, he founded the Black Acupuncture Advisory Association
of North America (BAAANA), based in Harlem, through which he continued to successfully treat heroin addiction. Marilyn Jean Buck, a former
member of Students for a Democratic Society (SDS), has long been an
active and trusted supporter of the Black Liberation Movement. Both
defendants were sentenced to serve fifty years at the end of the trial
in which this motion was entered. Buck was already serving a twenty
year sentence as a result of a 1985 conviction related to a 1981 armored
car expropriation in Nyack, New York; Judge Straight ordered the
sentences be carried out consecutively, making Buck's total sentence
seventy years. She has also been named as a defendant in the upcoming

"Resistance Conspiracy Case" in Washington, D.C., meaning she faces a further fifty year sentence.

Proceeding from the basis of understanding that the United States holds colonies, both internal and external to its own claimed national territoriality, the memorandum utilizes the standards of international law to establish that those apprehended by the colonizing power while engaged in bona fide efforts to liberate the colonies are entitled to status as Prisoners of War (POWs) rather than "criminals." This is an extremely important distinction, because it clarifies the actual relationship between the U.S. and the peoples it oppresses, as well as many of the individuals it has imprisoned. Additionally, under international law, POWs are entitled to a range of rights not typically accorded "common criminals," or even recognized political prisoners. The insurance of these rights automatically becomes a matter of international concern rather than simply an "internal issue" of the United States. Opening up any dimension of the U.S. prison system to genuine international scrutiny is, of course, of benefit to all prisoners held therein. Such external pressures as can be brought to bear through an international monitoring process stands to improve U.S. prison conditions for everyone. Several expert witnesses, also POWs or political prisoners, called in the Shakur/Buck case joined in the drafting of the motion.

* * *

First, it is important to place this case in the broader context of the 400-year struggle for human rights and self-determination that Africans and their descendants have been waging in this country. The scope and character of this history, culminating in the emergence in the 1960s and 1970s of a strong Black Liberation Movement and "new left" movement, is inseparable from the charges against the two defendants. These movements that gave rise to the political and armed conflict continue up to the present day. The two defendants' consciousness and commitments were formed during the high tide of these movements. It is beyond dispute that they, for their entire adult lives, have dedicated themselves to fighting against the racist evils of this society and for the New African/Black Liberation Movement. Moreover, the government's targeting of these movements for repression and long-term surveillance of these individual defendants, which preceded the current indictment by over a decade, was entirely due to the defendants' political associations and commitments.

The prosecution's own witnesses have testified to the completely political goals the participants in the alleged offenses held. Further, the fact that Judge Abraham D. Sofaer, legal advisor to the Department of State, as well as attorneys for the Department of the Army and the Department of Defense, answered Judge Charles Straight's questions, rather than the criminal division of the United States Attorney's office indicates that the United States executive recognizes the intensely political context of this case. In the interest of justice, and as a matter of common sense, unless the political character of these acts that led to the indictment is acknowledged and is adequately addressed, there can be no objective determinations of the case at bar.

The government's response to the questions posed in the court's order of January 19, 1988, raised a host of issues about whether the 1977 Protocols to the 1949 Geneva Convention on Prisoners of War (6 U.S.T. 3316, T.I.A.S. No. 3364), are applicable and whether it would be appropriate for the court to evaluate the acts charged as part of an armed conflict. The government summarily dismissed the "political offense exception" as relevant solely to extradition hearings and thus irrelevant to the instant case.

Admittedly, the use of a political offense defense to a domestic criminal proceeding is unprecedented. However, the penal law makes no provision for a political exception as a defense to criminal charges, thus no test exists to make the distinction between political acts and ordinary crimes. This lack of a legal classification for political acts obscures the profound challenges the civil rights movement for black freedom raised, and criminalizes the historical developments that stimulated the eruption of the Black Liberation Movement.

This lack of distinction between common crimes and political actions means that thousands of black people arrested and tried in the course of the struggle for liberation were subjected to criminal prosecutions that deprived them of fair trials. We raise the political offense exception to extradition in this case because it offers the closest analogy in federal law to characterizing the charges that arose from a conflict between the American government and the New Afrikan/Black Liberation Movement upon which the indictment was based.

The government's indictment criminalizes the defendants and thereby denies the conflict itself and the participants therein from rightfully receiving the protection of international law and policies designed for such disputes. This concurrently allows the United States to escape its international responsibility to the world community to acknowledge freedom fighters. It is the judiciary's responsibility to prevent the unjust characterization of political offenses as criminal behavior.

On the first page of the government's memorandum in response to the January 19 order, it claims that defendants "are seeking to have the indictment dismissed on the basis that international law provides them an immunity from prosecution." This is *not* the sum total of the requested relief, and specifically within the application of the political offense exception we have requested varying levels of relief. This case is currently in trial, and we have not requested that it be stayed pending this court's determination on the issue of immunity. A hearing would enable this court to examine various international tests and decide whether the facts justify the application of international law in this case. Further, on the basis of such a hearing, the court could develop an instruction for the jury so it could adequately evaluate the facts.

The Prisoner of War Petition

We set before the court in our present petition two interrelated but distinct arguments: 1) the prisoner of war petition applied to Dr. Shakur, and 2) the applicability to the present indictment against both defendants of the political offense exception. We request the court to address the proposed relief for each argument separately.

We believe that the entire prisoner of war petition should be granted in full. However, we recognize that among the international community of nations, various standards of establishing the existence of a conflict, an insurgency or a war are used. The New Afrikan Liberation struggle is acknowledged and respected in many parts of the world, especially in nations that were former colonies of European powers, but the American government has never afforded this movement the international rights and protections it so justly deserves.

We believe that the struggle waged by New Afrikan/Black people against racial oppression in America incorporates all the elements of warfare, that the petitioner has demonstrated his resistance to that oppression in the war, and that he should be accorded prisoner of war status while held in the custody of the United States government. The fact that Protocol I has not been accepted by this administration and not ratified by the senate does not diminish the strength of the international community's intent to recognize conflicts that qualify for international protections.

The government answered the court's question on the history of the United States' position on the 1977 protocols by remarking that the initial negotiations were viewed with misgivings because the 1974 diplomatic conference was dominated by developing nations who held grudges against the United States.[1] We should analyze why so many poor nations are resentful towards the United States. Many were former colonies of nations that are allies of the United States. They may have fought for their independence against a colonial government which received military and economic support from the United States. These victims of colonial domination have fought to gain world recognition for the fundamental right of peoples to self-determination. Their experience of being branded as criminals and terrorists when fighting for their independence informed the spirit of the protocols.

The United States' rejection of Protocol I takes on a more sinister character in the light of policies like COINTELPRO and the government's position towards the Commonwealth of Puerto Rico. A major reason why the United States refused to ratify this protocol was because the spirit and intent of the protocol conflicts with the government's repressive approach that uses law to criminalize participants in liberation struggles. The provisions of Protocol I which defined any national liberation war as an international conflict caused the government to call it "irreconcilably flawed."[2] President Reagan refused to submit Protocol I to the senate because he stated its provisions would grant "a special status to 'wars of national liberation'. . . and . . . combatant status to irregular forces even if they do not satisfy the traditional requirements to distinguish themselves for the civilian population and otherwise comply with the laws of war."[3] The president insisted that Protocol I must be rejected in order to deny the recognition and protection of international law to "terrorist groups."[4]

History shows us one of the reasons the United States took so long to ratify the Convention on the Prevention and Punishment of the Crime of Genocide (78 U.N.T.S. 277) was because that treaty provided the means for charges of genocide to be pressed against a nation, and the United States feared that its history of racial discrimination could become the basis for a case against it. Indeed, in 1951, the Civil Rights Congress brought a petition to the United Nations charging the United States with genocide against the descendants of Afrikan slaves.[5] During hearings before the Senate Foreign Relations Committee on the ratification of several international human rights treaties in 1979, the late Charles Yost, an American diplomat who served as President Nixon's ambassador to the United Nations, testified in support of senate ratification of the genocide treaty. He stated that the United States' refusal to join in the international implementation of the principles we so loudly and frequently proclaim cannot help but give the impression that we do not practice what we preach, that we have something to hide, that we are afraid to allow outsiders even to inquire whether we practice racial discrimination or violate other basic human rights."[6] The rejection of Protocol I, like the four decades-long foot dragging on the genocide treaty is *not* the universal norm. The United States became the 97th nation to adopt the Genocide Convention when the Senate finally ratified it in 1986.

The International Convention on the Elimination of Racial Discrimination (60 U.N.T.S. 195) has been adopted by over 115 nations, but the United States Senate has not ratified it yet. As Charles Yost stated before the Foreign Relations Committee, the United States is lagging far behind the international community on human rights treaties, and "few failures or omissions . . . have done more to undermine American credibility internationally than this."[7]

The third question the court posed to the government was whether the 1977 protocols reflect the current state of international law on the issue of when prisoner of war status must be given to accused prisoners. *Our answer is yes.* The 1977 Protocols have been recognized by the majority of nations as prevailing international law, despite the fact that the senate has not ratified the protocol for the United States. It represents the height of arrogance for a handful of nations to assume that their refusal to sign a document invalidates its underlaying principles. The civilized world has condemned apartheid, yet South Africa still perpetuates its racist rule.

The government admits that Article 44 of the Geneva Convention, when combined with Protocol I, expands the categories of individuals who can be defined as prisoners of war under the 1949 Geneva Convention. The United States took forty years to ratify the Genocide Convention because it feared that charges might be brought against it, and given the government's reasons for rejecting Protocol I and Article 44 combined, we can surmise it was because such combatants as defined by the protocol have been captured within the United States, but the government refuses to treat them as prisoners of war.

President Reagan's statement, cited in the government's memorandum, makes the profound point that Article I(4) [of Protocol I] politicizes humanitarian law and makes the distinction between international and non-international conflicts depend upon whether the purpose of the conflict is to gain national liberation.[8] Before the adoption of the protocols, such irregular forces were always characterized as criminals and terrorists, the typical attitude an oppressor nation adopts towards the struggles of the oppressed for their freedom. Secretary of State George Shultz, in his letter of transmittal of Protocol II to the senate, condemned Article 1(4) of Protocol I for injecting "subjective and politically controversial standards into the issue of the applicability of humanitarian law" because the provision elevates to international legal status "self-described 'national liberation' groups that make a practice of terrorism."[9] The provision at issue gives a special status to those "armed conflicts in which peoples are fighting against colonial domination and alien occupation and against racist regimes in the exercise of their right of self-determination.[10]

Thus, the non-recognition of Protocol I allows the United States to brand groups such as the African National Congress in South Africa as terrorist, and do nothing while a national leader such as Nelson Mandela remains imprisoned as a criminal and subjected to inhuman treatment for years. This is the true politicization of humanitarian law. The protocol challenges the excesses repressive governments bent on denying oppressed peoples their human rights and disregarding international law have committed and that is why the United States rejected it.

Language distorts reality—New Afrikan freedom fighters and their allies are called terrorists, while the government monitors them and subjects them to the vicious whims of repressive policies. All the while war against the Black Liberation/New Afrikan Movement continues. Although the United States has not ratified Protocol I, the accused prisoners in this case should be acknowledged as prisoners of war by the international criteria therein set forth. Torture is against international law, and yet many nations practice it. The non-recognition of the law does not invalidate it.[11]

Responsibility to Apply International Law

The government acknowledges that "International law is part of our law, and must be ascertained and administered by the courts of justice of appropriate jurisdiction, as often as questions of right *depending upon it* are duly present for their determination."[12]

The government makes two arguments against the court's authority to entertain considerations under the 1977 protocols. The first is that other controlling executive and legislative acts, judicial decisions, and treaties preclude the applicability of international law. The second is that it is reserved to the political branches to decide whether a state of belligerency that would activate the POW provisions of the protocols in fact exists. Both of these positions seriously misread the law. While the figurative symbol of justice is blindfolded, the judge is not required to remain blind to the facts we present. The government argues that laws against murder, and bank robbery are other controlling legislative acts which prevent the court from applying customary international law. Obviously, every signatory to the protocols has such laws. The existence of such criminal law does not resolve whether the acts with which defendants are evaluated correspond to POW provisions of the protocols. Similarly, the pre-existing 1949 convention does not negate the application of the 1977 amendments. The government has simply begged the question by asserting that the protocols do not apply.

The real issue, assuming that the protocols do reflect current international law, is whether there are controlling executive or legislative acts that preclude the court from recognizing the international law applicable to this case. In this regard, the government cites President Reagan's recommendation against senate ratification of Protocol I. We question whether a mere recommendation constitutes a controlling executive act under the rule of *The Paquete Habana*.[13] The law requires a formal executive act such as an executive order or a signature on a treaty. A mere recommendation does not meet this standard. President Carter's signing of the protocols, however, does.

Fundamentally, the government's entire discussion of other controlling acts is misleading. Its argument collapses two aspects of the court's language in *Habana* to project a meaning opposite from that holding. The statement that "international law is part of our law" stands in a separate sentence from "where there is no treaty, and no controlling executive or legislative act. . . ." Clearly, the court did not juxtapose these two sentences to indicate, as the prosecution implies, that such acts would negate international law. Rather the court is saying such acts are the first place to look on how to implement and apply international law, but where such acts do not exist, then the court must resort to customary international usage among civilized nations.[14] This decision in fact affirms, rather than eliminates, the federal courts' jurisdiction in issues of international law and provides guidance on where to look for authoritative sources of customary international law.

We assert that reference to such acts does not prevent the court's application of international law, a principle established when Chief Justice Marshall in *Murray v. Schooner Charming Betsy* (6 U.S. (2 Cranch) 64, 118) stated that "an act of Congress ought never be construed to violate the law of nations, if any other possible construction remains. . . ." The senate's failure to ratify the protocols means that these amendments do not have the status of a United States treaty. But, if the protocols do indeed express contemporary international law, the senate's nonratification merely means that no codification on how such international law may or may not apply in the United States has been established. Chief Justice Marshall stated in *The Nereide* (13 U.S. (9 Cranch) 388, 423) that in the absence of an act of congress United States courts are "bound by the law of nations, which is part of the law of the land."

One way in which the government distorts *Habana* is by collapsing the clear distinction in law between a *ratified treaty* and other parts of the *law of nations*. The former, like the constitution, is the "supreme law of the land"; the latter must be considered as a "part of the law of the land." The *Habana* decision affirms the courts' jurisdiction in such issues of international law as part of United States common law.

Thus, while the lack of ratification does mean that the protocols are not a United States treaty, we are still left with the jurisdictional issue of a part of international law in the absence of any legislative enactment. The Second Circuit Court of Appeals addressed this issue squarely in *Filartiga v. Pena-Irala*,[15] stating that "appellees . . . advance the proposition that the law of nations forms a part of the laws of the United States only to the extent the Congress has acted to define it. This extravagant claim is amply refuted by the numerous decisions applying rules of international law uncodified in any act of Congress."

In short, the prosecution attempts to use the phrase about controlling acts in *Habana* to negate the court's jurisdiction to apply international law. In fact, both *Habana* and *Filartiga* affirm the court's jurisdiction with regard to international law not ratified as an United States treaty. Where there is no congressional or other codification, as with the 1977 protocols, these decisions instruct the court to look to international usage—*which is precisely the standard we have asked the court to adopt in adjudicating this issue.*

The government says that the right to define international and internal conflicts is reserved to the political branches. Members of the United States senate in the Church Committee concluded in their final report that the United States government was at war with the New Afrikan and Black Liberation Movement as well as with their allies in the new left.[16] The body of factual data in the defendants' affidavit about the war against New Afrikans and the Black Liberation Movement and the massive documentation the Church Committee revealed that the government's "secret war," involving the army, the CIA, the FBI, the IRS and the state and local police against the Black Liberation Movement, was such that if taken against any foreign nation would clearly constitute overt "acts of war" in international law. Any person captured would be considered a prisoner of war. Protocol I would accord such individuals involved in internal conflicts the status of prisoners of war. BLA communiques issued at the time stated there was a war, and the government treated the situation as a war, and the United States senate's failure to ratify the protocols does not preclude this court from investigating the issue of the true nature of the accused prisoner's status. The government insists that the judiciary must defer to the political branch because the president and congress alone can exercise the power to declare war. But the massive actions directed against the New Afrikan Movement and people demonstrate that the executive has already declared war.

Further, the government asserts that since the civilian police are not part of the United States' regular force, the legal requirements for an internationally recognized armed conflict have not been met. This self-serving statement defies historical facts. Four New York City policemen were shot within two days in 1971 by the Black Liberation Army. Afterwards, President Richard Nixon called a White House meeting of internationally renowned experts on urban guerrilla warfare. As a consequence of that meeting, a Pentagon desk on urban guerrilla warfare was established. The president was kept informed on developments in the case, and three BLA soldiers were sentenced as Prisoners of War by a New York State judge.[17]

In the majority of colonial situations, the civilian police are used first, and the dominated population sees them as occupying troops. These police use military weapons and, in many cases, are trained on military bases, and belong to paramilitary organizations. The United States Army and the local New Jersey police operated jointly in the search of the East Orange house and the raid in Mississippi, both pursuant to this case. Further, the National Guard operated jointly with local police forces on numerous occasions in the bloody suppression of the New Afrikan urban uprisings during the 1960s, 1970s, and 1980s.

The government knows that a secret war has been going on for years that every so often hits the headlines. The conduct of the victims has been criminalized while the government's has been concealed. The torture of prisoners Ruben Scott and Harold Taylor and others in New Orleans in 1973, the torture of Assata Shakur in New Jersey in 1973, and of Sekou Odinga and of Samuel Brown in New York in 1981, and the deliberate murders of Frank Fields in Florida in 1972, of Twyman Myers in New York in 1973, of Mtyari Sundiata, in New York in 1981, and many others are the very type of heinous acts that the protocols were drafted to prevent by creating an international status for freedom fighters.

COINTELPRO essentially federalized the local police for its politically repressive purposes, and military intelligence played a major role in the successful implementation of the program.[18] The subsequent creation of the Joint Terrorist Task Force centralized the command to bring the actual day-to-day operations of the war under federal executive control. The court should bear in mind that only one party to the conflict is required to acknowledge it. The New Afrikan Movement does so openly, while the United States government does so tacitly.

The prosecution cites many cases on how the state of belligerency in the context of armed conflicts within one country or between different countries is defined. This argument evades the precise issue of law at bar—the adjudication of a POW claim. The history of law in this arena shows a clear and consistent recognition that one party cannot be allowed to negate its provisions by an unilateral declaration that no state of war exists. This point is quite explicit in Article 2 of the 1949 Geneva Convention, a treaty ratified by the United States.

Thus, regardless of who determines belligerency in other situations, the 1949 Geneva Convention precludes the political branches from doing so to rule out a POW claim against them. Otherwise, it would allow the government to violate a ratified treaty. While it is true that the 1949 convention does not account for modern national liberation struggles as a form of international conflict, it did establish a legal basis that precluded unilateral determinations on a state of war as a basis for dismissing POW claims. *Whether* a POW claim can be ruled out by the political branches is determined by the 1949 convention. *When* the POW claim is finally adjudicated, it must be done according to the international standards that have evolved subsequent to the 1949 convention, including the widely accepted 1977 protocols that amended the convention.

The government makes other specific statements about why the standards for recognition as a prisoner of war have not been met in this case. We presented the grounds for such recognition in our initial brief. Rather than re-argue this issue at length in our reply, we urge the court to hold a hearing on the question. Here we simply want to reiterate that the long and determined history of the black struggle for national liberation and the now exposed documented war waged against it by the United States government lies at the heart of our claim. The very purpose and spirit of the 1977 protocols was to update international law to include modern wars of national liberation.

Even if the court does not recognize Dr. Shakur's claim to POW status, it still can consider granting relief under the provisions for internal armed conflict. These are stated in common Article 3 of the 1949 convention and in the 1977 Protocol II. Both these conventions are recognized as prevailing law by the United States. These provisions provide some protection for individuals engaged in political resistance and national liberation movements. Further, common Article 3 does not preclude consideration of the protections afforded to POW's in the other articles for it explicitly states that "The parties to conflict should further endeavor to bring into force, by means of special agreements, all of the other provisions of the present convention."[19] In addition to common Article 3 and Protocol II, there are other binding treaties, such as the American Convention of Human Rights, that afford even wider protections to those captured pursuant to an armed conflict.

The government's reply to the court's fifth question, asking whether the criminal enterprise charged in the indictment should be regarded as an insurgency as analyzed under the 1977 protocols, evaded the central issue: whether the conspiracy charged is a part of the ongoing conflict between black people in America and the United States government. Does this criminal indictment actually refer to a series of politico-military offenses taken in furtherance of this conflict, which the FBI, operating as the political police for the government, has distorted?[20] The RICO statute has become a tool for criminalizing political movements that has enabled the government to define the New Afrikan Independence Movement as a criminal enterprise. Criminalizing the essentially political acts which are undeniably involved in the conflict between the New Afrikan Independence Movement/Black Liberation Struggle and the United States government such as riots, civil disorders, and rebellion, places the United States in violation of international law. Resolution 3103 (XXVIII), U.N. General Assembly, reads in relevant part that:

> The following basic principles of the legal status of combatants struggling against colonial and alien domination and racist regimes without prejudice to their elaboration in future within the framework of the development of international law applying to the protection of human rights in armed conflicts.
> 1. The struggle of people under colonial and alien domination and racist regimes for the implementation of these rights to self-determination and independence is legitimate and in full accordance with the principles of international law.
> 2. Any attempt to suppress the struggle against colonial and alien domination and racist regimes is incompatible with the Charter of the United Nations, the Declaration of Principles of International Law concerning Friendly Relations and Cooperation Among States in Accordance with the Charter of the United Nations, the Universal Declaration of Human Rights and the Declaration of Granting of Independence to Colonial Countries and Peoples and constitutes a threat to international peace and security.[21]

The United States and South Africa both voted against this resolution. Both are racist.[22] The United Sates government's assertion that no conflict exists which meets the criteria of the protocols is not true.[23] Article 43 of Protocol I states that

> ... the armed forces of a party to a conflict consists of organized armed forces, groups and units which are under a command responsible to that party for the conduct of its subordinates, even if that party is represented by a government or authority not recognized by an adverse party. Such armed forces shall be subject to an internal disciplinary system which, inter alia, shall enforce compliance with the rules of international law applicable in armed conflict.

Article 44-1 of Protocol I, states that "any combatant as defined in Article 43 who falls into the power of an adverse party shall be a prisoner of war."
The government maintained throughout its response memorandum

that no conflict exists, and cited the fact that the civilian police do not constitute part of the military forces as evidence for their claim. The police fall under Protocol I, Article 43-3, which states that "whenever a party to a conflict incorporates a paramilitary or armed law enforcement agency into its armed forces it shall so notify the other parties to the conflict."

We see two things at work here: on the one hand, the political branch defines the terms of the conflict, and on the other, the political branch asserts that the police are civilians.[24] While the police in the white community may play the role of civil servants, in the black community they operate as a colonial occupying army. They express a racist attitude of belligerence, hostility, and intimidation towards New Afrikan people. Atrocious incidents have been widely reported in various parts of the country concerning how police have abused or killed blacks in their custody. A few years ago a congressional committee here in New York City commented on the police killings of blacks.

The FBI/police attacks against the Black Liberation Movement have been widely documented. These attacks were fatal in many cases, such as when the Chicago Police killed Black Panther Party officers Fred Hampton and Mark Clark in 1969 as well as scores of other militants and combatants. The use of military helicopters with tracer bullets against Mark Essex in New Orleans in 1972 demonstrated that the police hardly act like civilians. The militarization of the police forces combined with the high technology computers and the close working relationship with the political police (the FBI) add up to a national police force/internal army. Further, the National Guard, as well as regular army troops, have acted in concert with local police to suppress urban rebellions.

Criminal laws such as RICO which are geared to suppress national liberation movements within the United States thoroughly politicize law enforcement and thereby violate international human rights law. The RICO indictment in the instant case is calculated to conceal the insurgency upon which the events preceding and including the October 20, 1981, incident was based. While the term insurgency may not be used in the protocols, conflict is, and accordingly there are international laws to cover such a conflict regardless of whether the other party has acknowledged it.

In the instant case a factual hearing is essential to determine whether this insurgency was a criminal enterprise. Given the amount of evidence to the contrary, and given the United States policy towards oppressed people fighting for the right to determine their own destiny, this court should employ the above-outlined concepts of international law to clarify the true nature of the acts upon which the indictment was based.

The Political Offense Exception in Domestic Prosecution

The government summarily dismissed the political offense exception, stating that it was irrelevant. Thus, it avoided the truly relevant, indeed defining, questions in this case: how the existing political conflict is related to the acts charged in the indictment. The government vehemently denies this reality—even while its own targeting of and attack against these defendants preceded this indictment by over a decade—because the government wants to conceal its own grave violations of human rights and international law. Specifically, the issue at stake in this political conflict is the right of people to struggle for self-determination against racist regimes.[25] The political offense exception recognized both in national and international law to apply to a wide range of political conflicts must certainly be relevant to one that revolves around the most fundamental issues of human rights.

The first issue that we raise before this court is how it may use the political offense exception developed within the extradition context as a standard for evaluating the acts charged in this indictment. The political offense exception is an internationally recognized defense to extradition incorporated in the law of virtually every modern state. The international tests that establish the political offense exception are used to distinguish common from political crimes. We believe this court has the full authority to make a similar determination in the instant case and that it would be in the interest of justice for it to do so.

There are two types of political offense exceptions—the "pure" political offense that involves acts directed solely against the state, such as treason, espionage, and sedition, and the "relative" political offense, in which the act is "a common crime so connected with a political act that the entire offense is regarded as political."[26] The concept of the "relative" political offense in American law has been taken from the English extradition case In re Castioni (1 Q.B. 149) which interpreted the British Extradition Act of 1870 authorizing the refusal to surrender a fugitive if his offense was of a political character, or involved a common crime so connected to a political act to make the entire offense political.

The court may exercise its judicial discretion and examine the political context of the defendants' conduct. The law is not fashioned from unyielding iron that remains unaffected by the changing social conditions. Rather, the law must reflect the life and hopes of the people who shape it. The body of international and domestic law concerning extradition has developed to cope with international alliances and their relationship to conflicts among nations and their peoples.

The "political offense exception" to extradition arose in Europe and

American because democratic governments supported the right of individuals "to resort to political activism to foster political change."[27]
The underlying tenets of domestic extradition law arise from (1) the
desire to insulate executive involvement in the extradition determination, which is made by the court, and (2) the political decision that
the executive should not help another country suppress its own internal
political dissent.[28] These concerns have governed American extradition
policies for 150 years.[29]

Fundamental to the American legal order is the Lockean concept
that as there is a basic legal right to achieve self-government through
political revolution. Thus, courts in democratic states must remain
neutral towards all sides in foreign rebellions. The court should shield
political fugitives from being returned to the very same regimes which
they have fought to change, because surrendering such a fugitive signals
support for the challenged authority.

Nonetheless, for the past 400 years of American history there has
been a blind refusal to recognize that the national hopes and aspirations
of black people are not only legitimate, but essential to their obtaining
justice and peace in this world. The court cannot fail to analyze the case
at bar in the context of the bloodstained history from which it directly
flows.

We ask that this court apply the concept of the "relative" political
offense to the instant case, and recognize that it is not exclusively
relevant to extradition or deportation proceedings. We also ask the court
to use the "political offense exception" to analyze the defendants' conduct,
using the same guidelines that the prevailing international tests (i.e.,
the Anglo-American, the French, or the Swiss) have established.

United States courts vary as to stringency of the criteria applied
to determine whether an offense is political. In the recent decision of
Quinn v. Robinson,[30] the determining criteria were "(a) the existence
of an uprising; (b) that the charged offense be in furtherance of that
uprising; and (c) that the accused be a member of the uprising group."
In *re Castioni*[31] is the authority on which most subsequent definitions
of political offense are premised. Drawing on it, American courts have
"uniformly construed a 'political offense' to mean those [acts] . . .
incidental to severe political disturbances," such as war, revolution and
rebellion.[32] In recent United States extradition cases the courts have
differed over what factors are appropriate to consider in making the
determination of whether to apply a political offense exception. In *re
Doherty* (599 F.Supp. 270, 275 (S.D.N.Y. 1984)) elaborated a more flexible
standard for applying the political offense exception. It stated:

> The Court rejects the notion that the political offense exception
> is limited to actual armed insurrections or more traditional and

overt military hostilities. The lessons of recent history demonstrate that political struggles have been commenced and effectively carried out by armed guerillas long before they were able to mount armies in the field. It is not for the courts, in defining the parameters of the political offense exception, to regard as dispositive factors such as the likelihood that a politically dissident group will succeed, or the ability of that group to effect changes in the government by means other than violence, although concededly such factors may at times be relevant in distinguishing between the common criminal and the political offender. . . . Nor is the fact that violence is used in itself dispositive. Instead the Court must assess the nature of the act, the context in which it is committed, the status of the party committing the act, the nature of the organization on whose behalf it is committed, and the particularized circumstances of the place where the act takes place.

In the use of the political offense exception to extradition, a court need not determine whether the violence of a political disturbance has reached a specific intensity, but rather it "need consider whether some incidents of violence have occurred."[33]

The political offense exception is not merely a narrowly specialized concept used in extradition and deportation proceedings, but rather incorporates a fundamental principle of law: a person should not face a criminal trial for offenses that are essentially political. This consideration is especially compelling when the political posture of the prosecuting government makes a fair trial unlikely. In addition to extradition law, the general tenets of international law require nations to take account of the distinction between criminal and political offenses.[34]

This underlying principle of justice has been most developed in the extradition context because there it is widely recognized that many situations exist in which a foreign government may engage in a political prosecution and/or cannot provide a fair trial. If the principle around political offense exception has not been developed in criminal law, it is because of the presumption that there would not be a problem of political prosecutions within the United States. However, we have made an overwhelming historical and factual showing that the political elements are totally integral to this case.[35] We also contend that a fair trial cannot be held when prosecuted by a politically hostile and—to New Afrikans—alien government.

There is a very important aspect of domestic law that allows, even mandates, that the court use its discretion to take account of fundamental underlying principles of law in a situation where there is no specified procedure. It is called acting "in the interest of justice." For example, on occasion judges have acted to dismiss or modify charges or reduce sentences because of paramount considerations of justice that were not adequately provided for by the routine legal procedures. The interest of justice application calls on the judge to perform his or her highest and most fundamental duty—to see that justice is done.

Indeed, far from the political offense exception to extradition being a remote analogy, it is essentially applying the same principle and standard in this particular setting. In extradition hearings the court's role is not to decide on guilt or innocence. Rather, the courts operate on two objective bases to determine if said acts are political or criminal. We believe that in applying these standards to the case at bar, this court would be acting in the interest of justice, and taking a proper, judicially honest approach which would lead to a truly fair determination. The court would be acting upon the authority of the "interest of justice." The political offense exception decides nothing more than whether an offense is essentially political in character. The court cannot pass judgment on the wisdom or necessity of the acts themselves.[36]

In applying the political offense exception in the instant matter, the court would be extending the protection of law now afforded aliens facing an unfair prosecution to those the government asserts are subject to its laws and afforded the full panoply of rights. The court would thus be implementing a fundamental principle of law in a setting that cries out for such application. What is more, the court is in a much stronger and more specific footing than in many *interest of justice* applications because there is a considerable body of international law and United States precedent that establish standards for granting political offense exception. These long-established standards are judicial means for evaluating the distinctions between political acts and common crimes.

The fundamental concept of due process fully supports the application of the political offense exception to this domestic conflict. It has long been established that fundamental due process imposes upon the court "an exercise of judgement . . . in order to ascertain whether [the proceedings] offered those canons of decency and fairness which express the notions of justice of English-speaking peoples, even toward those charged with the most heinous offenses."[37] Further, the requirement for fundamental fairness is more stringent where, as in the political offense circumstances, a deprivation of physical liberty is at stake.[38] The right to a fair trial in a criminal case "is a fundamental liberty."[39] An impartial and disinterested tribunal is a central concern of due process.[40] These authorities expressed the recognition in the domestic context of the fundamental concepts of due process and justice that form the basis for applying the political offense exception in the extradition and deportation context. Thus, its suggested application for a legal analysis is not "irrelevant," as the government maintains, but rather is consistent with basic concepts of fairness.

In the instant case, the court has a considerably greater body of factual material than available in most extradition hearings. This court should utilize any of the international standards to determine whether the petitioners themselves, the overall "conspiracy," and the acts charged are a result of and in furtherance of political objectives. Factors to consider here are: "the circumstances attendant upon the commission of the 'crime.'"[41] In this case the court would determine that there is a political conflict/uprising of New Afrikan people for self-determination and human rights. The very definition of the "conspiracy" as defined by the testimony of the government's witness states the self-conscious objectives that the indictment flows from. The use of a RICO statue is clearly an attempt by the hostile prosecuting government to distort the character of a political conflict. The coerced confession of Sam Brown as dictated by the Federal Bureau of Investigation's head case agent included the phrase "the overthrow of the government."[42] Further, in the original wiretap applications for BAAANA and Barrow Street, FBI Case Agent Maxwell submitted an affidavit in support of the application which stated clearly it sought the "government analysis of the political objectives of the alleged conspiracy."[43]

The government's own language and investigation reveals the political nature of the case at bar. Another factor courts examine to establish whether the political offense exception applies is "the respondent's past participation in and involvement with a political movement."[44] To demonstrate that the defendants have been politically involved in that conflict for their entire adult lives, we point to the documentation from the counterintelligence files obtained under the Freedom of Information Act for Dr. Shakur. The first FBI memo on Dr. Shakur dates from 1969. Dr. Shakur was nineteen years old at the time. In 1975, in an FOIA file, Dr. Shakur is listed under "investigation involving activities constituting possible violations of Title 18 (U.S.C. § 2385), Rebellion, Advocating the overthrow of the U.S. government." Further, the trial testimony on his state of mind, the bail hearing, and the prosecution's witnesses all acknowledge Dr. Shakur's long-standing participation in the New Afrikan Independence Movement.

In relation to Ms. Buck, she has long been characterized by the government and federal enforcement personnel as the only white member of the Black Liberation Army. The government sentencing memo (85 Cr. 1086 (RLC), at 4) states that in 1973 "Ms. Buck was closely associated with members of the Black Panther Party. . . ." Assuming the government believes what it says about Ms. Buck, her role in the political conflict of the Black Liberation Movement both as a participant and as an ally is clear.[45]

Finally the acts and the overall conspiracy charged in the current indictment arise from the commitment to and furtherance of the liberation struggle. In the instant matter, Dr. Shakur is accused of membership in an underground New Afrikan unit, which functioned apparently as a Black Liberation Army unit. Ms. Buck is accused of membership in a related unit composed of white people who supported and engaged in joint activities. This unit engaged in armed struggle to further the political objectives of the Black Liberation Movement. The acts alleged stem from the BLA's attack on federally insured banks. These actions were designed to raise money for the New Afrikan Independence Movement. The liberation of a soldier of the BLA, Assata Shakur,[46] was also included in the indictment.

Tyrone Rison, a government witness, was an alleged member of this same unit. His testimony confirmed the self-conscious political and military objectives. His statements speak directly to the acts charged.[47] Rison also testified that the money taken from the federally insured banks was in a part for the purpose of freeing Assata Shakur from prison.

Peter Middleton, another government witness, testified in his alleged capacity as a supporter that the funds expropriated were used for the Republic of New Afrika and other groups, for the combatants and their families, and for legal fees for imprisoned BLA members.[48] In Eain v. Wilkes, the Court stated that "an accomplice's accusations are not automatically incompetent to support a determination of probable cause."[49] Clearly, the petitioners meet all the requirements and fulfill allied criteria for an application of the political offense exception. Further, the argument that these questions are "political questions" that are beyond the jurisdiction of the court is simply wrong. In Eain v. Wilkes,[50] the court states "the government's argument that the political branches should decide the question of whether the crime charged is a 'political offense' under the treaty has no basis in United States case precedent." And when there is no controlling authority, international law and standards become customary law. Further, the court in Eain v. Wilkes,[51] stated "we have not found any case where an American court declined to consider the applicability of the political offense exception when it was squarely presented. If anything, one of the major criticisms leveled at American extradition law is that federal courts have intended to invoke the political acts exception in situations of common crimes mixed with political overtones upon a showing of any connection, however weak, to an uprising or rebellion or condition of domestic violence."[52]

Therefore, we request the court to hold a fact-finding hearing on this matter utilizing the political offense exception test. Unless the court makes a clear distinction between criminal conduct and political objectives, the interests of justice will not be served. We further request that a determination be made at this hearing on whether the indictment or parts of the indictment should be dismissed. In the alternative, we request that the court charge the jury on the distinction between criminal and political conduct based upon the results of this hearing, thereby empowering the jury to make a proper determination.

Notes

1. Government's Response Memorandum, Exhibit A, (Gov't. R. Mem., Exh. A), p. 4.
2. Message from the President Transmitting the Protocol II Additional to the Geneva Conventions of August 12, 1949, and Relating to the Protection of Victims of Non-International Armed Conflicts, Concluded at Geneva on June 10, 1977, Treaty Doc. 100-2, 100th Congress, 1st Sess. at III (January 29, 1987).
3. *Ibid.* at IV.
4. *Ibid.*
5. See *We Charge Genocide: The Historic Petition to the United Nations for Relief from a Crime of the United States Government Against the Negro People* (New Ed. 1970).
6. *International Human Rights Treaties: Hearings before the Committee on Foreign Relations of the United States Senate*, 96th Congress, 1st Sess., at 4. (November 14, 1979) (testimony of Charles Yost).
7. *Ibid.*
8. See Message from the President (January 29, 1987), *supra* at IV; Govt's R. Mem., Exh. A at 10.
9. Treaty Doc. 100-2, *supra* at IX.
10. *Ibid.*
11. See *Filartiga v. Pena-Irala*, 630 F. 2d 876, 884 (2d Cir. 1980).
12. Gov't R. Memo., Exh. A., at 13, citing *The Paquete Habana*, 175 U.S. 677, 700 (1900).
13. *Supra.*
14. *Ibid*, p. 700.
15. *Supra*, p. 886.
16. See *Final Report of the Select Committee To Study Governmental Operations with Respect to Intelligence Activities*, 94th Congress, 2nd Sess., Book III, April 23, 1976.
17. See *People v. Bottom*, Ind. No. 5694-74, (N.Y. Co.) 1971 Sentencing Memorandum, May 12, 1975.
18. See the *Select Committee Report*, *supra* at 785-835.
19. Geneva Convention of August 12, 1949, *supra*, Article 3.
20. See e.g., Section 8, Executive Order 10450, "Security Requirements for Government Employment," April 27, 1953, as amended.
21. See Resolution 3103 (XXVIII) of the United Nations General Assembly (adopted on December 12, 1972 by a vote of 83 in favor, 13 against and 19 abstentions).
22. See *We Charge Genocide, supra.*
23. See POW brief.

24. "A murder of a police officer is related to an uprising whether the reason for the act is to avoid discovery of munitions or to avoid reduction of 'forces' by capture." *Quinn v. Robinson*, 783 F. 2d 776, 811 (9th Cir. 1986).

25. See U.N. General Assembly Res. 3103.

26. *In re Mackin*, 80 Cr. Misc.1, slip op. (S.D.N.Y., Aug. 13, 1981) [available on Lexis]. See also *Quinn v. Robinson*, 783 F.2d 776, 793-94 (9th Cr. 1986).

27. "American Courts and Modern Terrorism: The Politics of Extradition," 13 *New York University Journal of International Law and Policy* (1981), pp. 617 and 622.

28. See *San Diego Law Review* (1987), p. 549.

29. It should be noted that while this law has been applied in international relations for the past 150 years, the United States Supreme Court has never applied it to New Afrikans who were forcibly enslaved in America. See POW Petition at 24 for discussion of *U.S. v. The Libellants— Amistad*, 15 Peters 518, 10 L.Ed. 826 (1841). Nor did the United States recognize runaway slaves with any legal rights, and would return them without ever considering their rights to political asylum.

30. *Supra*, p. 810.

31. *Supra*.

32. *Sindona v. Grant*, 619 F.2d 167, 173 (2nd Cir. 1980).

33. *Eain v. Wilkes*, 641 F.2d 504, 514, n.14.

34. See Article 14 of the Universal Declaration of Human Rights.

35. See the affidavit accompanying the POW motion.

36. See *In re Mackin, supra*, p. 42.

37. *Rochin v. California*, 342 U.S. 165, 169.

38. See *Lassiter v. Dept. of Social Services*, 452 U.S. 18, 26-27 (1981).

39. *Estelle v. Williams*, 425 U.S. 501, 503 (1976).

40. See *Marshal v. Jerrico, Inc.*, 446 U.S. 238, 242 (1980).

41. See *Garcia-Guillerin v. U.S.*, 450 F.2d 1189, 1192 (5th Cir. 1971), cert. denied, 405 U.S. 989 (1972).

42. See FBI Case Agent Cordier's Notes of Dec. 3, 1981 as reported in Transcript of *Franks* Hearing, May 6-7, 1987, *U.S. v. Shakur*, 82 Cr. 312.

43. See Maxwell Affidavit for original wiretap application, Transcript of *Franks* Hearing, April 27-29, May 4-5, 1987, *U.S. v. Shakur, supra*.

44. See *In re Mackin, supra*, p. 84-91.

45. At this time it is impossible to offer any kind of evidence from the government's own documentation as Ms. Buck has been repeatedly denied access to her FBI, CIA, and other agency files under the FOIA. See *Eain v. Wilkins, supra*, p. 515. In extradition proceedings the Judge can view *in-camera* evidence (i.e., FOIA materials) not available to the defendants. See *Eain v. Wilkins, supra*, p. 515.

46. We note for the Court's consideration in this matter the recent disclosure of Assata Shakur's location. The Cuban government has granted her political asylum from the United States government, and defined her current status in Cuban society as a political refugee. A. Shakur, *Assata: An Autobiography* (1987); also, "The Soul Survivor," *The Washington Post*, February 29, 1988, p. B6.

47. See Trial Testimony, Dec. 1, 1987, p. 2122-23.

48. FBI Interview 4/7/82 No. 3505-UUW.

49. *Supra*, p. 515.
50. *Supra*, p. 513.
51. *Ibid.*
52. Finally, Ms. Buck is not petitioning this court to hold a hearing on her status as a prisoner of war. She has joined in the section of the petition which deals with the question of political offenses and status. We believe Ms. Buck meets the established guidelines within the definitions of the political offense exception. Ms. Buck is viewed by the Black Liberation Movement itself as a long-standing genuine ally.

Contrary to appearances, this is not a scene from nazi Germany. The location is Columbus, Ohio. The year is 1989. These special police units have proliferated to more than 50,000 since 1970. This action is part of the "war on drugs" which in reality is the wholesale suspension of civil rights in black and ladino communities. By all accounts the scope of this war against the poor and potentially rebellious people will escalate in the coming years. (photo: *New York Times*)

Karen Wald with Ward Churchill

Remembering the Real Dragon—
An Interview with George Jackson
May 16 and June 29, 1971

The following is a previously unpublished interview conducted in San Quentin Prison with George Jackson, shortly before his assassination on August 21, 1971. The interview was conducted—and the raw tapes provided to Ward Churchill—by Karen Wald, a long-time North American anti-imperialist activist (SDS, Bay Area Radical Union, and the Soledad Brothers Defense Committee during the late '60s and early '70s) and former Liberation News Service reporter. Author of, among many other things, *Children of Ché* (Ramparts Press, 1978), Wald has lived and worked in Cuba since 1973. In editing the interview, Churchill has deleted only such material as appeared to be purely topical or which was redundant. Because the interview was conducted on two different days, more than a month apart, the sequence of questions and answers has also been altered somewhat for purposes of continuity.

For those who don't already know, George Jackson was perhaps the primary figure of the black and prison liberation movements twenty years ago. In 1960, at the age of 18, he was arrested for participation in a $70 gas station hold-up, convinced to plead guilty by a "public defender" who convinced him he'd get off light as a result, and promptly sentenced to one-year-to-life by a California judge. Outraged at what had been done to him and refusing to "kiss the ass of a bunch of white guards and bureaucrats," Jackson proved to be a "recalcitrant," spending an active period as a gang member in Soledad Prison. His refusal to bend to the will of prison officials led directly to his being repeatedly denied parole, continuing to serve hard time long after the normal period of two years incarceration for the kind of petty offense by which his imprisonment had been justified in the first place.

By the mid-60s, Jackson had met and attached himself to an older and quite politically developed prisoner, W. L. Nolen. Essentially uneducated, Jackson proved an avid student under Nolen's guidance, immersing himself in the study of Afro-American history and nationalism, as well as the revolutionary theories of Marx, Lenin and Fanon; by the time of his death, several hundred volumes of difficult material—all well used—were to be stacked beneath the bunk in his cell. He also began a well-disciplined regimen of martial arts training which earned him the sobriquet "Karate Jackson" among at least some prison guards. He was known to perform 1,000 fingertip pushups each day in his cell, and to sleep less than four hours per night as he alternately read and wrote out his thoughts, longhand, in lengthy letters to family and friends. The young prisoner's anger and rebelliousness rapidly congealed into consciousness, purpose and ability, a matter which made him even less likely to see parole than mere membership in a prison gang.

On January 13, 1970, W. L. Nolen, along with two other black prisoners—Cleveland Edwards and Alvin "Jug" Miller—were executed by Opie G. Miller, an expert marksman armed with a .30 calibre carbine, placed in a tower above Soledad's O-Wing courtyard for this purpose. Nolen had been successfully organizing a response to the arbitrary killings of two other black prisoners—Clarence Causey and William A. Powell—by Soledad guards in recent months. The sharpshooter's carefully placed shots put a stop to this, as all three wounded men were left lying where they fell until they bled to death. The assassinations were so blatant that even Billie D. "Buzzard" Harris, a self-proclaimed racist and head of the prison's "Aryan Brotherhood," condemned them as "cold-blooded murder." Nonetheless, an official Board of Inquiry exonerated Opie Miller approximately two days after the event.

In apparent retaliation for the murders of Nolen, Edwards and Jug Miller, guard John V. Mills was beaten and tossed from a third-story tier on January 16. Accused in the death of Mills were George Jackson, Fleeta Drumgo and John Cluchette, the so-called Soledad Brothers. Jackson, who was already serving a life sentence, was faced with a mandatory death penalty under California law. All three prisoners were shortly transferred from Soledad to San Quentin, the state's hardest-core penal facility. It was at about this time that Jackson's first book, *Soledad Brother*, was released, calling for a physical response to the systemic violence of the state. Introduced by Jean Genet and containing profound analyses of U.S. colonialism and the role of prisons in society, the volume immediately propelled Jackson to the forefront of international progressive attention. It also moved the Soledad Brothers Defense Committee, headed by Angela Y. Davis, to the center of the North American anti-imperialist movement.

In short order, George Jackson—who was already at work on a second book (this became *Blood In My Eye*, published posthumously)—had been appointed a Field Marshal of the Black Panther Party by Minister of

Defense Huey P. Newton. Through this medium, he was able to actually begin to organize what he called the People's Army, a force through which he hoped to bring about a positive transformation of the social order he saw as having deformed not only his own life, but those of most people. The very success of his endeavor made him a marked man: not only were the "wheels of justice" grinding along with the objective of putting him in the gas chamber, but there is much evidence that an official conspiracy was hatched to bring about his assassination within San Quentin. Considerations of the latter were not lost on the target or his supporters.

As a result, on the morning of August 7, 1970, Jackson's 17-year-old brother, Jonathan, walked into a courtroom in the Marin County Civic Center (near the prison), pulled a weapon from beneath his raincoat, and freed three San Quentin prisoners—William Christmas, Ruchell Magee and James McClain—in court for a hearing. The younger Jackson also took several prisoners of his own, including Judge Harold J. Haley, Assistant District Attorney Gary Thomas and three jurors. Having armed Christmas, Magee and McClain, Jonathan then led the way to a van parked outside. The plan appears to have been to take the official prisoners to San Francisco International Airport, where they could be bartered for the Soledad Brothers and a jet aircraft capable of taking the entire party to join exiled Panther leader Eldridge Cleaver's International Section in Algeria. The prisoners would then have been released unharmed.

Unbeknownst to Jonathan Jackson, however, was the fact that the plan was well-known to the police. On hand when the group emerged from the civic center were a pair of anti-Panther specialists—Ray Callahan and Daniel P. Mahoney—from the Los Angeles Police Department's Criminal Conspiracy Section (CCS), as well as representatives of the LA-FBI office's notorious COINTELPRO section (with which CCS was tightly interlocked) and an entire company of San Quentin riflemen (who "just happened" to be in the area, rifles in hand). The police simply shot the van to pieces, killing young Jackson, Christmas and McClain, as well as Judge Haley. Magee and a juror were badly wounded, while Assistant DA Thomas was paralyzed for life. Exactly what the southern California Red Squad and FBI personnel were doing in this northern California location—especially without informing local authorities—has never been explained, but the whole affair carries the unmistakable aroma of a set-up.

There is considerable evidence—never officially rebutted—that the FBI and CCS had utilized an infiltrator/provocateur named Melvin "Cotton" Smith to set the whole thing in motion in hopes that an appreciable number of LA Panthers would participate, and could be "legitimately" gunned down as a consequence. There is also indication that CCS expected George Jackson to have been called at the hearing. To the extent that this is true, what happened in Marin County amounted to—not to the "misguided act" of a black teenager—but a carefully planned ambush by the police entities involved, a line of "counter-intelligence" action which caused the murders not only of three black revolutionaries, but of a county judge as well. In fact, as former CCS/FBI operative Louis E. Tackwood has observed, Callahan and Mahoney seemed genuinely disappointed that the "body count" wasn't far higher. They had, after all, fully expected George Jackson and a substantial Panther contingent to be caught in their trap.

In any event, in the wake of the civic center bloodshed, the police diverted attention from their own conduct by charging that Angela Davis had masterminded the whole affair. Under such conditions, she not unnaturally harbored certain doubts as to the quality of justice she was likely to receive, and went promptly underground. There ensued a sensational manhunt, with both J. Edgar Hoover and President Richard M. Nixon proclaiming Davis to be the country's "number one terrorist," before she was captured in New York on October 13, 1970. She was then held in an isolation cell before being whisked back to California in direct contravention of extradition laws. After that, she was held without bond—again in isolation—for nearly a year, until being acquitted of any complicity whatsoever in the "Marin County Shoot-Out."

By then, George Jackson himself was dead, executed by a bullet fired into the top of his skull while he was kneeling in a courtyard at San Quentin, one leg already having been shot out from under him. The official story was that he'd been smuggled a huge Astra 9 mm pistol—an Astra is more than 8 inches long and 5 inches wide, and weighs some two-and-a-half pounds when unloaded—inside a tape recorder by a legal consultant, Stephen Bingham. After receiving the weapon, so the story went, Jackson placed it atop his head, covered it with an Afro wig, underwent a strip search, and then drew the gun on guards upon reaching his cell block. He then supposedly organized several other prisoners to cut the throats of four guards and shoot another, before running out into the prison courtyard with a vial of "explosives" with which he intended to blow a hole in the prison wall and escape. It was there that he was shot to death. Jackson was buried next to Jonathan in the family plot in Mt. Vernon, Illinois.

In the aftermath, even so staid and conservative a newspaper as the *San Francisco Chronicle* found the official story of how the Astra was allegedly smuggled into the prison to be impossible. Then it came out that the weapon in question had been impounded by police in Denver more than a year previously. The supposed explosives turned out to be a mild sulfuric acid solution. Drumgo and Cluchette went to trial for the murder of Mills, and were acquitted. Cluchette was subsequently paroled. Drumgo was charged—as one of the "San Quentin Six"—with direct participation in the deaths of the four guards on the day of George Jackson's assassination. He was acquitted of this as well, and was paroled in 1976. In November of 1979, he was mysteriously shotgunned to death on an Oakland street corner. Stephen Bingham went underground, remaining in hiding in the U.S. and Canada for 15 years, until he surfaced during the spring of 1986. He then went to trial on charges of conspiracy and complicity in the deaths of the San Quentin guards. A jury found him innocent on all counts. In 1988, newly disclosed evidence of a police plan to secretly precipitate the bloody events of August 21, 1971 caused the release from prison of Johnny Spain, another member of the San Quentin Six, who had received a double-life sentence as a result. The final resolution of Spain's case has not yet been made.

Given the circumstances of the last two years of his life, and the nature of his death, George Jackson has become a pre-eminent symbol—for both those in struggle, and those they struggle against—of resistance, commitment and the will to liberation.

Karen Wald: George, could you comment on your conception of revolution?

George Jackson: The principal contradiction between the oppressor and oppressed can be reduced to the fact that the only way the oppressor can maintain his position is by fostering, nurturing, building, contempt for the oppressed. That thing gets out of hand after a while. It leads to excesses that we see and the excesses are growing within the totalitarian state here. The excesses breed resistance; resistance is growing. The thing grows in a spiral. It can only end one way. The excesses lead to resistance, resistance leads to brutality, the brutality leads to more resistance, and finally the whole question will be resolved with either the uneconomic destruction of the oppressed, or the end of oppression. These are the workings of revolution. It grows in spirals, confrontations, and I mean on all levels. The institutions of society have buttressed the establishment, so I mean all levels have to be assaulted.

Wald: How does the prison liberation movement fit into this? Is its importance over-exaggerated or contrived?

Jackson: We don't have to contrive any. . . . Look, the particular thing I'm involved in right now, the prison movement was started by Huey P. Newton and the Black Panther Party. Huey and the rest of the comrades around the country. We're working with Ericka [Huggins] and Bobby [Seale, Chairman of the BPP; at the time they were co-defendants in a murder trial in New Haven, Connecticut, on charges which were subsequently dismissed], the prison movement in general, the movement to prove to the establishment that the concentration camp technique won't work on us. We don't have to contrive any importance to our particular movement. It's a very real, very-very real issue and I'm of the opinion that, right along with the student movement, right along with the old, familiar workers' movement, the prison movement is central to the process of revolution as a whole.

Wald: Many of the cadres of the revolutionary forces on the outside have been captured and imprisoned. Are you saying that even though they're in prison, these cadres can still function in a meaningful way for the revolution?

Jackson: Well, we're all familiar with the function of the prison as an institution serving the needs of the totalitarian state. We've got to destroy that function; the function has to be no longer viable, in the end. It's one of the strongest institutions supporting the totalitarian state. We have to destroy its effectiveness, and that's what the prison movement is all about. What I'm saying is that they put us in these concentration camps here the same as they put people in tiger cages or "strategic hamlets" in Vietnam. The idea is to isolate, eliminate, liquidate the dynamic sections of the overall movement, the protagonists of the movement. What we've got to do is prove this won't work. We've got to organize our resistance once we're inside, give them no peace, turn the prison into just another front of the struggle, tear it down from the inside. Understand?

Wald: But can such a battle be won?

Jackson: A good deal of this has to do with our ability to communicate to the people on the street. The nature of the function of the prison within the police state has to be continuously explained, elucidated to the people on the street because we can't fight alone in here. Oh yeah, we can fight, but if we're isolated, if the state is successful in accomplishing that, the results are usually not constructive in terms of proving our point. We fight and we die, but that's not the point, although it may be admirable from some sort of purely moral point of view. The point is, however, in the face of what we confront, to fight and *win*. That's the real objective: not just to make statements, no matter how noble, but to destroy the system that oppresses us. By any means available to us. And to do this, we must be connected, in contact and communication with those in struggle on the outside. We must be mutually supporting because we're all in this together. It's all one struggle at base.

Wald: Is the form of struggle you're talking about here different from those with which we may be more familiar with, those which are occurring in the Third World, for example?

Jackson: Not really. Of course, all struggles are different, depending upon the whole range of particular factors involved. But many of them have fundamental commonalities which are more important than the differences. We *are* talking about a guerrilla war in this country. The guerrilla, the new type of warrior who's developed out of conflicts in the Third World countries, doesn't fight for glory necessarily. The guerrilla fights to *win*. The guerrilla fights the same kind of fight we do, what's sometimes called a "poor man's war." It's not a form of war fought with high-tech weaponry, or state-of-the-art gadgets. It's fought with whatever can be had—captured weapons when they can be had, but often antiquated firearms, homemade ordnance, knives, bows and arrows, even slingshots—but mostly through the sheer *will* of the guerrilla to fight and win, no matter what. Huey [P. Newton] says "the power of the people will overcome the power of the man's technology," and we've seen this proven true time after time in recent history.

You know, guerrilla war is not simply a matter of tactics and technique. It's not just questions of hit-and-run or terrorism. It's a matter of proving to the established order that it simply can't sustain itself, that there's no possible way for them to win by utilizing the means of force available to them. We have to prove that wars are won by human beings, and not by mechanical devices. We've got to show that in the end they can't resist us. And we will! we're going to do it! There's never going to ever be a moment's peace for anyone associated with the establishment any place where I'm at, or where any of my comrades are at. But we're going to need coordination, we're going to need help. And right now, that help should come in the form of education. It's critical to teach the people out there just how important it is to destroy the function of the prison within this society. That, and to show them in concrete terms that the war is on—right now!—and that in that sense we really aren't any different than the Vietnamese, or the Cubans, or the Algerians, or any of the other revolutionary peoples of the world.

Wald: In an interview with some imprisoned *Tupamaros*, urban guerrillas in Uruguay, the question was raised about the decimation of the ranks of *Tupamaros*; comrades killed or imprisoned by the state. Those interviewed assured me that there were far more people joining the ranks than were being lost to state repression, and that the movement was continuing to grow. Do you feel the same confidence about the Black Panther Party, about the revolutionary movement as a whole in this country?

Jackson: We're structured in such a way as to allow us to exist and continue to resist despite the losses we absorb. It was set up that way. We know the enemy operates under the concept of "kill the head and the body will die." They target those they see as key leaders. We know this, and we've set up safeguards to prevent the strategy from working against us. I know I could be killed tomorrow, but the struggle would continue, there would be 200 or 300 people to take my place. As Fred Hampton put it, "You can kill the revolutionary, but you can't kill the revolution." Hampton, as you know, was head of the Party in Chicago, and was murdered in his sleep by the police in Chicago, along with Mark Clark, the Party leader from Peoria, Illinois. Their loss is tremendous, but the struggle goes on. Right?

It's not just a military thing. It's also an educational thing. The two go hand-in-hand. And it's also a cyclical thing. Right now, we are in a peak cycle. There's tremendous energy out there, directed against the state. It's not all focused, but it's there, and it's building. Maybe this will be sufficient to accomplish what we must accomplish over the fairly short run. We'll see, and we can certainly hope that this is the case. But perhaps not. We must be prepared to wage a long struggle. If this is the case, then we'll probably see a different cycle, one in which the revolutionary energy of the people seems to have dispersed, run out of steam. But—and this is important—such cycles are deceptive. Things appear to be at low ebb, but actually what's happening is a period of regroupment, a period in which we step back and learn from the mistakes made during the preceding cycle. We educate ourselves from our experience, and we educate those around us. And all the while, we develop and perfect our core organization. Then the next time a peak cycle comes around, we are far readier than we were during the last time. It's a combination of military and education, always. Ultimately, we will win. You see?

Wald: Do you see signs of progress on the inside, in prison?

Jackson: Yes, I do. Progress has certainly been made in terms of raising the consciousness of at least some sectors of the prison population. In part, that's due to the limited victories we've achieved over the past few years. They're token victories perhaps, but things we can and must take advantage of. For example, we've struggled hard around the idea of being able to communicate directly with people on the outside. At this point, any person on the street can correspond with any individual inside prison. My suggestion is, now that we have the channels for education secured, at least temporarily, is that people on the outside should begin to bombard the prisons with newspapers, books, journals, clippings, anything of educational value to help politicize the comrades who are not yet relating. And we, of course, must reciprocate by consistently sending out information concerning what's really going on in here. Incidentally, interviews like this go a long way in that direction. There should be much more of this sort of thing.

Wald: You disclosed a few months ago that you had been for some time a member of the Black Panther Party. Certainly, the work of the Party in this state and elsewhere, the work to free political prisoners, and of course the Party's work within the black community have been factors which influenced your decision. But has the internationalism of the Black Panther Party been one of the key aspects which attracted you to it? And, if this is so, is internationalism meaningful for people in prison, and is it therefore one reason why they'd relate to the Party?

Jackson: Well, let's take it a step at a time. Huey came to the joint about a year ago because he'd heard stories about the little thing we had going on already. He talked with us, and checked it out, and he decided to absorb us. Afterwards, he sent me a message and told me that. He just told me that I was part of the Party now, and that our little group was part of the Party as well. And he told me that my present job is to build, or help build, the prison movement. Just like that. Like I said, the objective of our movement is to prove the state can't seal us off in a concentration camp, so I accepted. What else could I do? It was the correct thing.

Now, as to your second point, the people inside the joint, the convict class, have related to the ideology of the Party 100 percent. And we've moved from . . . well, not we, I've always been an internationalist. And a materialist. I guess I was a materialist before I was born. I'm presently studying Swahili so that I will be able to converse with the comrades in Africa on their own terms, without having to rely on a colonial language. And I've been working on Spanish, which is of course a colonial language, but which is spoken by millions upon millions of comrades in Latin America and elsewhere. I plan to study Chinese after that, and possibly Arabic. When I complete this task, I will be able to speak to something like seventy-five percent of the world's people in their own tongue, or something akin to their own tongue. I think that's important.

The other brothers here are picking up on it. And there are some, especially those who were already politicized before they came inside, who are on top of it. But like I said, it's of utmost importance that people outside bombard this place with material which will help prisoners understand the importance of internationalism to their struggle. It's coming, but it's still got a way to go before the educational process is complete. Ignorance is a terrible thing and being cut off from the flow of the movement is really detrimental. We must correct the situation as a first priority.

Wald: Can you receive mail and publications from other countries?

Jackson: Mail can be received from anywhere on the globe. I get stuff right now from Germany and England and France as a result of the book being published in these countries. And a few copies of *Tricontinental* [a Cuban revolutionary journal] have gotten in. They've helped broaden the scope, and explained a few things to comrades that they didn't understand. This is something that really upsets the goons. In years past, every time a black prisoner would achieve an intellectual breakthrough and begin to relate our situation to the situation of the Cubans, say, or the Vietnamese or the Chinese—or anywhere else in the Third World—well these prisoners would be quickly assassinated. Now that's become a little harder to do. So, I believe the people on the street should just start to flood the prisons with things like *Tricontinental.*

Wald: Despite a few peaceful victories in Latin America, such as that of Salvador Allendé in Chilé, many people still believe that armed struggle is the only way most Latin American countries are going to be free. Also, there've been some recent victories in the courts for members of the Black Panther Party, *Los Siete de la Raza* [seven Chicano activists from San Francisco charged with murder in 1969; they were acquitted], and so on. Do you believe the victories in Chilé and in the courts. . . .

Jackson: They were appeasement. Allendé . . . the thing that happened with Allendé . . . look, it was *not* a "peaceful revolution." That's deception. Allendé is a good man, but what's going on in Chilé is just a reflection of the national aspirations of the ruling class. You will never find a peaceful revolution. Nobody surrenders their power without resistance. And until the upper class in Chilé is crushed, Allendé could at any time be defeated. No revolution can be consolidated under the conditions that prevail in Chilé. Blood will flow down there. Either Allendé will shed it in liquidating the ruling class, or the ruling class will shed his whenever it decides the time is right. Either way, there's no peaceful revolution.[1]

Much the same can be said for the court cases you're talking about. They're an illusion. Every once in a while the establishment cuts loose of a case—usually one which was so outrageous to begin with that they couldn't possibly win it without exposing their whole system of injustice anyway—and then they trot around babbling about "proof that the system works," how just and fair it is. They never mention the fact that the people who were supposed to have received the justice of the system have often already spent months and months in lockup, and have been

184 • Karen Wald and Ward Churchill

forced to spend thousands of thousands of dollars, keeping themselves from spending years and years in prison, *before* being found innocent. All this to defend themselves against charges for which there was no basis to begin with, and the state knew there was no *basis*. Some system. You get your punishment before your trial in this country if you happen to be black or brown or political. But they use these things to say the system works—which I guess it does, from their perspective—and to build their credibility for the cases that really count, when they really want to railroad someone into a prison cell. The solution isn't to learn how to play the system for occasional "victories" of this order, although I'll admit these sometimes have a tactical advantage. Winning comes only in destroying the system itself. We should never be confused on this point.

Wald: But the alternatives sometimes bear dire consequences. This raises the difficult question of the death of your brother, Jonathan, and whether his life may to a certain extent have been wasted.

Jackson: Well, that's obviously a tough question for me because, emotionally, I very much wish my little brother was alive and well. But as to whether I think Jonathan's life may have been wasted? No, I don't. I think the only mistake he made was thinking that all of the 200 pigs who were there would have, you know, some sort of concern for the life of the judge. Of course, they chose to kill the judge, and to risk killing the DA and the jurors, in order to get at Jonathan and the others. It may have been a technical error. But I doubt it, because I know Jonathan was very conversant with military ideas, and I'm sure it occurred to him that there was a possibility that at least one pig would shoot, and that if one shot, they'd all shoot, and it'd be a massacre. Judge or no judge. It was all a gigantic bluff, you know? Jonathan took a calculated risk. Some people say that makes him a fool. *I* say his was the sort of courage that cause young men of his age to be awarded the Congressional Medal of Honor in somewhat different settings. The difference is that Jonathan understood very clearly who his real enemy was; the guy who gets the congressional medal usually doesn't. Now, who's the fool?

Personally, I bear his loss very badly. It's a great burden upon my soul. But I think it's imperative—we owe it to him—never to forget why he did what he did. And that was to stand as a symbol in front of the people—in front of *me*—and say in effect that we have both the capacity and the obligation to stand up, regardless of the consequences. He was saying that if we all stand up, our collective power will destroy the forces that oppose us. Jonathan lived by these principles, he was true to them, he died by them. This is the most honorable thing imaginable. He achieved a certain deserved immortality insofar as he truly had the courage to die on his feet rather than live one moment on his knees. He stood as an example, a beacon to all of us, and I am in awe of him, even though he was my younger brother.

Wald: The news today said that Tom Hayden[2] declared in front of the National Student Association Congress that there will be more actions like the one Jonathan attempted. Do you agree?

Jackson: I've been thinking a lot about the situation. I'm not saying that these particular tactics—even when successfully executed—constitute the only valid revolutionary form at this time. Obviously, they don't. There must also be mass organizing activities, including large-scale nonviolent demonstrations, education of the least developed social sectors, and so on. These things are essential. The revolution must proceed at *all* levels. But this is *precisely* what makes the tactics necessary, and far too many self-proclaimed revolutionaries have missed the point on this score. Such tactics as Jonathan employed represent a whole level—an entire *dimension*—of struggle which has almost always been missing from the so-called American scene. And while it is true that armed struggle in-and-of-itself can never achieve revolution, neither can the various other forms of activity. The covert, armed, guerrilla dimension of the movement fits hand-in-glove with the overt dimension; the two dimensions can and must be seen as inseparable aspects of the same phenomenon; neither dimension can succeed without the other.

Viewing things objectively, we can readily determine that the overt dimension of the movement is relatively well-developed at this time. Over the past dozen years, we've seen the creation of a vast mass movement in opposition to the establishment in this country. I won't go into this in any depth because I'm sure that everyone already knows what I'm talking about. It should be enough to observe that within the past two years, the movement has repeatedly shown itself able to put as many as a million people in the streets at any one time to express their opposition to the imperialist war in Indochina [this seems to be a reference to the November 1969 Moratorium to End the War in Vietnam, staged in Washington, D.C.]. The covert dimension of the movement is, by comparison, very much retarded at the present time. In part, this may be due to the very nature of the activity at issue: guerrillas always begin in terms of very small numbers of people. But, more to the point, I think the situation is due to there having been a strong resistance to the whole idea of armed struggle on the part of much of the movement's supposed leadership—particularly the white leadership—up to this point. I hear them arguing—contrary to history, logic, just plain common sense, and everything else—that armed struggle is unnecessary, even "counterproductive." I hear them arguing in the most stupidly misleading fashion imaginable that the overt dimension of the movement can bring off revolution on its own. This is the sheerest nonsense, and "leaders" who engage in such babble should be discarded without hesitation.

We may advance a simple rule here: the likelihood of significant social change in the United States may be gauged by the extent to which the covert, armed, guerrilla aspect of the struggle is developed and consolidated. If the counterrevolutionaries and fools who parade themselves as leaders while resisting the development of the movement's armed capacity are overcome—and the struggle is therefore able to proceed in a proper direction—I think we will see revolutionary change in this country rather shortly. If, on the other hand, this leadership is able to successfully do what amounts to the work of the state—that is to say, to convince most people to shy away from armed struggle, and to isolate those who do undertake to act as guerrillas from the mass of support which should rightly be theirs—then the revolution will be forestalled. We will have a situation here much the same as that in Chilé, where the establishment allows a certain quantity of apparent social gains to be achieved, but stands ready to strip these "gains" away whenever it's convenient. You can mark my words on this: unless a real revolution is attained, all that's been gained during the struggles of the past decade will be lost during the next ten years. It might not even take that long.[3]

At the present time, I see a number of very hopeful signs—very positive indications—that a true revolutionary force is emerging. Most notably, of course, the direction taken by the Black Panther Party is correct. But there are many other examples I could name. Even in the white community, we have seen the development, or at least the beginnings of the development, of what is necessary with the establishment of the Weatherman organization. We clearly have a long way to go, but it's happening, and that's what's important at the moment. The very fact that Tom Hayden, who is of course a white radical himself, was willing to make the statement he made, and before the audience to which he made it, indicates the truth of this. So, yes, I tend to agree with him and hope we are both correct. Clear enough?

Wald: Yes. Do you see a relationship between what happened at the Marin County Civic Center, between what Jonathan and the other brothers did, and the kinds of things that happen in the Third World, say, in Latin America?

Jackson: Well, of course. Jonathan was a student of . . . he was a military-minded brother. He was a student of Ché Guevarra and Ho, and Giap and Mao, and many others. Tupamaros, Carlos Marighella. He paid close attention to other established guerrillas, other established revolutionary societies, revolutionary cultures around the world. He was very conscious of what was going on in South America and, well, let's just say that about ninety-nine percent of our conversation was centered on military things. I knew him well. He understood.

Wald: I was going to ask if the Cuban revolution had significance for you and Jonathan in any concrete ways.

Jackson: Hmmmm . . . I don't think it did for Jonathan. But it did for me, because I was in prison. I was just starting my time on this beat right here when Castro, Ché and the rest carried the revolution there to a successful conclusion. And the alarm that spread throughout the nation, especially, you know, within the establishment and the police . . . well, let's just say that as a newly-made prisoner I enjoyed that a lot. Someone else's liberation at the establishment's expense, it was a vicarious boost at a time when I most needed it. And I've always felt very tenderly toward the Cuban revolution as a result.

Wald: Then you weren't an anti-communist when you came into prison?

Jackson: Oh, I've never been an anti-communist. I suppose you could say I didn't have much understanding of communism when I came in, and so I wasn't pro-communist in any meaningful way. But I was never "anti."

Wald: But didn't you initially find it terrible that Cuba had "gone communist"?

Jackson: *No-no-no!* That's what I'm trying to tell you. I'm trying to get across that I've always been fundamentally anti-authoritarian. Communism came later. And when the Cuban revolution happened, the very fact that it upset the authorities here so bad made me favor it right off and made me want to investigate it much further. The idea was that if they don't like it, it must be good. You see? And that's what led me to seriously study socialism. I owe much of my own consciousness to the Cuban revolution. But that's *me*. It doesn't necessarily pertain to Jonathan. Okay?

Wald: Did the fact that such a tiny country so close to Florida pulled off a successful revolution give you a sense that, "If they can do it, we can do it"?

Jackson: Yes, both then and now. It caused me to consider the myth of invincibility. You know, the idea of U.S. military invincibility was just completely destroyed by the Cuban revolution. The U.S. supported Batista with rockets and planes, everything he needed, and he still lost. He was destroyed by guerrilla warfare, the same thing that's taking place in Vietnam right now. And the U.S. is losing again. The Viet Cong, I mean they take these gadgets—the best things the best military minds in the western world can produce—they take them and they ball them up and they throw them right back in the face of these imperialist fools. Cuba and now Vietnam; these things catch my attention. I try to learn the lessons from other peoples' success. Now, in that sense I'm sure the Cuban revolution had significance for Jonathan, too.

Wald: I see our time is almost up. Do you have any last remarks you'd like to make?

Jackson: Yes. I'd like to say POWER TO THE PEOPLE! And I'd like to say that by that I mean all power, not just the token sort of power the establishment is prepared to give us for its own purposes. I'd like to say that the only way we're ever going to have change is to have the real power necessary to bring the changes we want into being. I'd like to say that the establishment is never going to be persuaded into giving us real power, it's never going to be tricked into, it's never going to feel guilty and change its ways. The only way we're ever going to get the power we need to change things is by taking it, over the open, brutal, physical opposition of the establishment. I'd like to say we must use, as Malcolm X put it, *any means necessary* to take power. I'd like to say that we really have no alternatives in the matter, and that it's ridiculous or worse to think that we do. That's what I'd like to say.

Notes

1. *Editor's note:* True to Jackson's prediction, the Chiléan military—in combination with the CIA, Kissinger's State Department, and transnational corporations (notably ITT and Anaconda)—brought down the Allendé government in September of 1973. More than 30,000 progressives and Allendé himself were killed during the coup and the following three years. Many thousands more were driven into permanent exile. The Chiléan people have been saddled with the neo-fascistic regime of Colonel Augusto Pinochet ever since. Although demonstration elections did take place in 1989, Pinochet still remains in charge of the military.

2. *Editor's note:* This was the period before he totally sold out.

3. *Editor's note:* Actually, it took a bit longer; the Reagan administration of the 80s was required to validate Jackson's prediction.

The ghost of Nat Turner cries out to me

Brother, how can it be
    In da twenty-first centree
    We's still ain't free!

Could it be
    We don't 'memba what hit means
    Ta hang from trees
    Or be on our knees?!

Nigga, don't call me brutha
    If you won't 'fend my mutha

Nigga, don't call me sista
    When you care mo fa mista
    Than you do for self.

I cuss the day
    When night turned to light
    An' fightin' gave way ta prayin'!

—Daoud Ahmed

Note: Down through our history in this Kountry, many slave rebellions have taken place during the month of August. Ever since the death of young Jonathan, man-child, on 7 August 1970, and the death of George one year and fourteen days later, on 21 August 1971, many men in these Kamps honor them on those days. It just so happens i was in the hole & had been since early August. So i went on a fast (only drinking water) starting on August 7 & ending on the morning of August 22nd. On the morning of August 21st, i had a dream/vision in which Nat Turner, Denmark Vesey, Sojourner Truth, Cinque, Maceo, Harriet Tubman, Jane Pittman, Rosa Parks, Granny (Grandma's Mama), Grandma, Malcolm, Bunchy Carter, Jon Huggins, Li'l Bobby Hutton, Jonathan & George Jackson, and a host of other freedom fighters were all gathered in a big meadow flanked on three sides by the foothills of a mountain range. Nat Turner was the only one who spoke. He had a tongue of fire—as did all the others. i "woke" with a unquenchable thirst, covered with sweat, & immediately recorded his words. Us fighters are all of the same seed & it runs through the generations. They are all my relations.

(Written in the hole, Lompoc, on August 21, 1982; eleven years ADG— After Death of George Jackson. Comrade George was murdered on August 21, 1971.)

Alan Berkman and Tim Blunk

Thoughts on Class, Race, and Prison

Having been locked up as political prisoners for the past five years, we have found a lot in several recent articles which was familiar and thought provoking. Certain descriptions of ping-ponging from jail to jail could be a log of some of our own trips conducted by the Bureau of Prisons (BoP), and we can verify accounts of how prisoners typically support one another. Perhaps most importantly, we strongly agree with the view—best expressed in an article by Sam Day published in the October 13, 1989 issue of *Isthmus*—that the threat of prison should not deter political activists from acting. We are concerned, though, that in so vividly portraying his own experience and utilizing it to demystify prison life, he may have played into some common misrepresentations of life in U.S. prisons.

First, a word about our own experiences. We've each spent time in prison for a variety of politically motivated acts. One of us (Alan Berkman) spent two years in a number of county jails in the Philadelphia area. The other (Tim Blunk) spent a year in New York's Riker's Island. We've both been in a number of federal prisons, including the BoP's most repressive facility at Marion, Illinois. For the past eighteen months, we've been together in the equivalent of a county jail in Washington, D.C. where we and four women activists face federal charges of resisting U.S. war crimes through "violent and illegal means" (we call this the Resistance Conspiracy Case). Tim is presently serving a fifty-eight year sentence; Alan, twelve years. Having spent considerable time in the whole range of penal institutions, from county jails where most prisoners are pre-trial to Marion, where the average sentence is forty years, we've been struck by how directly prisons reflect the social and economic realities of society as a whole.

We live in a country where large numbers of people, particularly young Afro-American, Latino and Native American women and men, have been written off by society. Government leaders look at the human devastation caused by their policies and declare war on the victims (the "war on drugs"). The racism and malignant neglect that permeate the schools, the labor market, the welfare system and social services of the Third World and poor white neighborhoods of our cities bear their inevitable fruit in the prisons. In prison, though, even the usual facade of "fairness" and "justice" by which such inequity is usually accompanied is dropped.

There are almost a million people in U.S. jails, state and federal prisons. More than ninety percent of these prisoners are in county jails and state prisons. D.C. jail, for example, is filled to capacity with poor, mis-educated, profoundly alienated young Afroamerican men and women. It's a warehouse. There are no programs, no contact visiting, no privacy, and most importantly, no justice.

Particularly for political activists who are white and middle class, prison can be one of the few places where we look at America from the bottom up. We can understand poverty differently when we live with young people who've never had $20 in their pocket and who are constantly bombarded with the Gucci ads, the BMWs on *Miami Vice*, and the idea of free trips to Rio on *The Price is Right*. In a consumer society, if you've got nothing, you're considered to be nothing, and the frustration of this reality leads people into crime and drugs. You can see the deadness and despair in the eyes of too many of the people around you as they realize the American Dream is not for them now, and probably wasn't from the day they were born into the ghetto, the barrio or the reservation. And you'll get a feeling in your gut about the rage racism and poverty generate in the hearts of the oppressed. In fact, if you allow yourself, you'll learn quite a lot about the feelings that accompany that word, "oppressed."

What we've come to understand ever more deeply from our experience as prisoners is that the essence of oppression lies in dehumanization and disrespect. Being oppressed isn't just being a bit poorer or having a rougher life than your oppressor; it means being treated as if you're less of a human being than they are. For instance, we've consistently experienced the fact that you can be getting along okay with the guards and prison officials when they suddenly do something which is not only totally outrageous, but often a complete violation of their own supposed rule structure. You call them on it, and their response is to look at you— *through* you would be more accurate—as if you just weren't there. It doesn't matter a bit whether you're right or wrong. They deny that you have the right even to hold an opinion on the matter. It cuts at the very core of your sense of humanity and self-worth. It is infuriating and degrading.

Self-worth. Dignity. Self-respect. These are the feelings prison consciously or unconsciously is designed to destroy. These are the same feelings that racism and economic inequality in society work to destroy in the poor and people of color. This is why we believe Sam and others err when they reduce prison life to "three hots [meals] and a cot" and other minor indignities. It's like reducing chattel slavery to hard work, bad pay and poor living conditions. It leaves out the truth of the human dimension of oppression. And it leaves out the human reaction to prison conditions: rebellion. Prison "riots' are fundamentally slave rebellions.

Over the past few weeks, there have been one major and two minor prison uprisings in the Pennsylvania prison system. At Camp Hill, where prisoners destroyed much of the prison, the precipitating event seems trivial: the prison cancelled the semi-annual family day picnics where prisoners' relatives can bring home-cooked food and eat with their loved ones out on the yard. What's the big deal about two afternoons per year? Well, at one level, when you don't have much, even a *little* more deprivation hurts rather badly, especially when that deprivation concerns those precious bits of time you can spend with those closest to you and when you manage to feel most fully human. At a deeper level, the arbitrariness of the prison officials' decision in Pennsylvania gave the prisoners a clear message that they had nothing at all coming to them: *everything* is a "privilege," *nothing* is a right. The oppressor giveth, the oppressor taketh away. The oppressed have nothing to say in the matter, one way or the other. The oppressed—the prisoner in this instance—is a cipher, a statistic, nothing more than an animal whose basic needs of calories, shelter and waste disposal must (usually) be met. No more.

The "senseless violence" of burning buildings and smashing equipment which marked the Camp Hill rebellion—and which has marked prison uprisings from Attica to Atlanta, New Mexico, Los Angeles, and elsewhere—is, perhaps paradoxically, the most basic assertion of human dignity and self-respect. "We do have a say," the prisoners are insisting. "We will exercise our rights as human beings one way or another, either as reasonable human beings in a reasonable situation, or this way if you insist the situation remain unreasonable. But either way you can ultimately do nothing to provide our demonstration of the fact that *we are people*." It is a very human response to a very inhuman situation, the same impulse which led to the great ghetto uprisings of Watts, Detroit and Newark during the '60s, and which has led to similar phenomena in places like Miami during the '80s.

Political activists who come to jail and are able to keep their eyes and hearts open will learn an enormous amount, both about themselves and about the world they live in. How do we deal with our own race/class biases to build principled relationships with those we live with? If we're white, how do we respond when the Aryan Brotherhood tells us they'll kick our ass if we eat with Afro-American, Latino or American Indian prisoners in the *de facto* segregated mess hall? How do we struggle against the pervasive and intense sexism in men's prisons? How do we remain caring and giving people without allowing ourselves to be taken advantage of and disrespected? How do we decide when to directly confront the power of the officials, and when not to? When do we get involved in other people's beefs, whether among prisoners or between prisoners and guards?

There's a lot to learn in prison, although it's certainly not the only, or even necessarily the best, place to learn it. Whatever else may be said, time spent behind bars—no more or less than any other sort of time—need never be "wasted." We agree with Sam and others when they say that fear of prison should never be paralyzing. While locked up, you'll more than likely get in shape, have the opportunity to read many of the books you always meant to plow through but never managed to get around to, learn to write letters which say more than just "howdy-do." Most importantly, you'll finally have the chance to identify with the oppressed on a gut level which is typically absent from the life experiences of most Euroamericans. You'll come to understand power relationships in a new and far more meaningful way. And we're willing to bet that you'll come out more committed than ever to the need for fundamental social change.

Note

Tim Blunk, along with co-editor Ray Luc Levasseur, has published a truly excellent collection of writings and art by political prisoners and POWs in the United States. Entitled *Hauling Up the Morning*, the book is available from Red Sea Press, 15 Industry Court, Trenton, NJ 08638.

Standing Deer

Prisons, Poverty, and Power

As the state of Texas was murdering Charles Brooke by "humane" lethal injection, a Marion prisoner wrote the poem that follows. For obvious reasons his identity cannot be revealed, but I can say that he was due to be released in 1983. I have known this man for over a year and find him to be intelligent, rational, and an altogether likeable person. On the other hand, I realize that he is totally deranged. His insanity is the product of too long living in the bowels of this monster called *Marion*. I can vouch for the seriousness of the sentiments he expresses in his poem. That he will do what he can of what he threatens I haven't the slightest doubt. Big bucks spent on ever more sophisticated mind-control techniques which are administrated by moral imbeciles with high I.Q.s at behavior modification legal, torture chambers like Marion have brought you this man who is a living example that unsuccessful mind torture creates monsters.

That was the good news. The bad news is that I know of seven more of these raging children of your right-handed selves who are due to be released from your maximum security american prisons within the next three years. These monsters, whom society created in its mirror image, are waiting to consume america's chest, lungs, liver and spleen . . . and at last its decaying, bleeding, incongruously virgin heart. Virgin because america has had so little experience with concentrated purposeful violence that some news analysts naively dubbed the Washington Monument incident a "terrorist act." Spectacular, it was. Exciting, perhaps. Mass entertainment, without a doubt. Terrorist? No.

The poor non-violent man who "terrorized" Washington, D.C., was no part of a terrorist. I am going to give you a glimpse into the mind of what a terrorist is and let you be the judge of what would have happened at the Washington Monument if the man who wrote the poem "When I Get Out" had been in charge. I am living out my existence at the Marion federal prison and I have witnessed what the poet has suffered—having suffered similar atrocities myself—and due to these factors, although I condemn his views as extreme, I must say his response seems not an unreasonable reaction. Don't blame this man for *your* insanity. It's too late for lamentations, laws or longer sentences.

Remember, that is the sickness that got you in the fix you're in. So listen carefully; you're about to step into the nightmare that your prisoncrats & police have created for you in your name. I pray this man harms no one. But I know he will.

When I Get Out

When I get out
the first thing I'm gonna do
is get me a gun to protect myself from the police.
Probably more than one gun because
there's so many different kinds of police.
Maybe a .460 Weatherby with a twelve power scope
for kings, dictators, presidents and popes.
A .357 magnum for law enforcement officials in general,
and a nice nine millimeter Browning High Power
for just plain folks like you.

When I get out
I want to kill as many people as I can
before they get me.
I'd like to get the Queen Mother and the Pope
and the president if I have the time.
But for sure I'll come back and kill the Warden.
I'll probably kidnap him
and chain him spread-eagled
to an old-fashioned pot-bellied stove.
Before I light it, I'll cut off his eyelids
and make him watch a pornographic movie because
he can't stand S-E-X.
I'll give him a shot of extremely dangerous drugs
so he won't suffer
while I chop off his legs a piece at a time
with a McCullough chain saw.
I mustn't forget to use green wood in the stove
so he won't fry fast.

It was you who cut off my eyelids by putting me in a
sensory deprivation chamber in total darkness because I
wanted to go to my Mother's funeral.
It was you who chained me to a bed in Springfield and
beat on my feet with wooden paddles

until they turned to blood
and swelled up like basketballs.

When I get out
I'm going to spend the hatred you've taught me
by becoming a mass murderer.
And all you judges, jurypersons, cops, jailers
and executioners can't stop me
because it was you who murdered Charles Brooke
and taught me that it's cool to kill.

It was you who told me I lived in a free country
as you ground your heel in my humanity,
and laughed at my pleas for dignity
and spat on my manhood.

It was you who charged me with shields and ax handles
and beat me to the floor and drugged me with Prolixin
because I couldn't stop calling my baby daughter's name
when she left this world.

So, in return for the lessons you have given me
I'm going to teach you two things:
First that these sealed-tomb,
tiger-cage prisons belong to you
Mr. & Mrs. America,
and it is you who must accept the responsibility
for what you and your hirelings have done to me.

The second thing I'm going to teach you is something
you should already know
but don't act like you do, namely
the Christians say "Do Unto Others, etc."
the Buddhists say something about
"what goes around comes around."

In prison we simply say:
"Payback is a motherfuckin' motherfucker,
Motherfucker."

It won't be much longer.
I'm counting the days.
So, you better pray I don't find you, gentle reader,

'cause when I've paid my debt to society
society must pay its debt to me.
When I get out. . .

Prison is a control device designed to make poor people want to do what the rich want them to do. We were just sitting around yesterday talking about what the establishment would do if they woke up some morning and found their scientists had invented a pill that people with "criminal tendencies" could eat and lo and behold all their spirit of resistance would be neutralized. Instead they would all be pleading for a job in a mine or factory or some other work place. Some of the naive fellows said they would beat us over the head with a hammer and administer it to us immediately. But most of us knew, that never in life would they give out that pill and furthermore, the invention of it would be totally non-publicized.

Prisons in this country have become such big business that they have made power moguls out of ordinary people. All the judges, prosecutors, lawyers, police, and prison guards would have to go out and get a job if us crooks were suddenly no longer crooks. We spent a whole morning on this with one man listing prison connected parasites as the others would name them and explain how they were connected with the prison business. Before too long, we had a list so long we couldn't believe it. The economy would fall if they didn't have us—the fodder—to occupy their prisons. Prisons are a hustle for millions of people. They pay guards about fifteen thousand a year here at Marion and many of them don't have walking around sense. Their claim to a paycheck is knowing how to insert a key in the lock and how to cock their feet up on a desk in front of a fan and blow whistles at prisoners. Where would these automatons fit in if there was all of a sudden a free society and they had to do something constructive? I wouldn't want them jailed because I don't believe in any kind of jail for any reason. But how the hell would you rehabilitate some of these oafs and make productive citizens out of them. Not productive in the economic sense, but productive in their contribution to humanity.

There is an illumination with me—a spark of life like a dream that tells me that human beings were meant for something better than knocking their brains out in somebody's mine or factory. I think this system is insane to expect anybody to do that. They have stolen just about all the land and resources from my people. They have taken the lumber from the forests and now the game and fish are almost gone since they have poisoned the lakes, rivers and streams. Our Mother Earth Suffers. Oh, how she cries out but the pitiless have no pity. Now that they've stolen all our shit, they make us volunteer to become their slaves without even putting chains on our hands and feet. They steal our labor. They issue us pieces of green paper to buy food, clothes and things we just have to have and then they tell us we are free. And while we work until we wear out like used up automobiles, they become richer and richer and more powerful.

How can some of them be so rich and pass through squalor, unbelievable poverty, suffering and despair without feeling the least bit of desire to want to help alleviate these conditions? Some people say these capitalists are this way because they are evil and have bad thoughts in their heads. But that's bullshit. The reason they compete in building and destroying personal empires is because they are driven by the real material forces at work within the social system of production which they direct. And while some of them are good "god-fearing" christians they will mash your guts in the street before they will concede one iota of the riches that they have stolen from the children of the poor. Somebody once said, "No amount of moralizing, of philosophizing, of preaching, of clean living, of eating natural foods, or praying will change any of this." Only when the people who suffer the immediate deprivations and punishments of this insane form of social organization are organized into a force that can physically wrest control of this society from the tiny minority of criminals who today "own" all the mass technology and the means of production, only then will freedom become a possibility. And in the happy event that that should ever happen and somebody jumps up and says he is the new general, king, dictator or pope that is the man I'm going to strangle with my bare hands before he has a chance to gather about him some more sickos who want to run something to do with my life.

With soup lines in all the major cities, and unemployment ranging from ten to eighty percent (depending on whose numbers you want to believe) politicians are selling the political snake oil of longer sentences to get at least part of the work force off of the streets and into the prisons. Admittedly, this approach is a tremendous vote-getter because ever since John Wayne showed the world how a real man is supposed to act (before his stomach rejected him) people have admired the get tough approach to everything. The off the cuff remark by Sturdley Quane: "The total destruction of the planet is a small price to pay to keep America number one" is a case in point. Now judges blithely hand out 200 year sentences and the public loves it. But when it comes time for legislators to appropriate money to run all these packed prisons the people don't want to have anything to do with it. Apparently, they imagine we prisoners who have forever sentences are just supposed to disappear, but unfortunately, it doesn't work that way.

They create self-fulfilling prophecies like Marion. They claim that here they cage the meanest, most dangerous creatures on the face of the planet. So they bring a prisoner here and beat him, torture him, gas him, deny him access to his loved ones, deny him medical treatment and starve him and lo and behold, when he gets out, instead of being rehabilitated, he writes a poem like *When I Get Out*. What manner of madness is this? Most of the guys in here grew up in special sections of the country with savage neighborhoods, abandoned housing, wretched schooling and massive unemployment, all of it sustained for so long that a proportion of these children of the underclass, white and non-white, have a culture that is at odds with the affluent segment of society.

They can increase their machinery of so-called "justice" by increasing the number of police. They can appoint more prosecutors and judges and hire more administrators and prison guards, build more jails and prisons and murder more prisoners by "humane lethal injection." But until the problem of the masses who are without any way to make a dollar to feed themselves is alleviated there will be courageous people who will get a gun and do what the violence oriented TV teaches them in order to get what they have been conditioned to believe they are supposed to have to be a worthwhile member in the great society of Ronald Reagan. They have my greatest respect and admiration. I'll save my umbrage for the cowards who will let their little ones starve to death in the midst of plenty. Expropriations by compulsion must come from the oppressor and not the oppressed; a good way to tell the difference is to look for a four letter sign that says "B-A-N-K." You can't go wrong.

New Afrikan Prisoner of War—
Albert "Nuh" Washington Speaks

My name is Albert Washington. I am called Nuh (Noah) and am among the longest-held political prisoners in the country. As a member of the Black Panther Party during the 1960s, I worked to raise the political consciousness of the African American people, and to teach them the methods self-defense. The government's COINTELPRO operations against us left many Panthers dead or falsely imprisoned, and created situations which led to splits in the BPP. This forced many of us to go underground to survive while continuing our work. Underground, we became the Black Liberation Army (BLA) and moved forward with our efforts to end police aggression against our community. In defending the community in San Francisco, I was shot and captured along with Jalil Abdul Muntaquin (s/n: Anthony Bottom). Later, I was charged with killing two New York City cops, along with Jalil and BLA member Herman Bell. Together, we became known as the "New York Three," were convicted in 1975 during a second trial (the jury refused to convict us in the state's first try), and sentenced to life imprisonment.

Just recently, I was moved to Wende Prison in Alden, New York, over 400 miles from New York City, a measure taken to isolate me from my family, friends, and prisoners with whom I'd built up close and trusting relationships. Orders were issued to place me in a unit with forty-two other prisoners. It is called the "White House," because almost all the others are Caucasians. The place has a triple fence, sensors, and cameras which monitor us 24-hours-a-day. All movement is controlled, mine more than the others. I am kept in my cell—where I can take two and a half steps in any direction—much of the time. The lights are permanently on in the corridor outside, so my cell is never dark.

Wende is the only prison operated by the state of New York where your family and friends cannot bring you clothing, food, or anything else to ease your circumstances. I am not allowed family reunion visits because, it is said, I am an "extreme escape risk." I have never escaped from prison, nor is there tangible evidence that I have attempted to escape. Meanwhile, prisoners who *have* escaped on one or more occasions are allowed the sorts of visitation rights I am denied. It is now much harder for my mother to visit me than at any point since I was imprisoned. I have not been allowed to embrace my wife for a long, long time. The situation speaks for itself.

The state has conceded that I committed none of the acts for which I am incarcerated. However, it is argued that, as an "admitted" member of the BLA, I taught political education classes and that it is therefore "appropriate" that I remain in prison under the tightest possible security. I have imprisoned, not because I killed police officers, or even because any government official seriously believes I did, but because I spoke out against racism and oppression in the United States, and because I was a member of organizations which were effective in combatting that racism and oppression. That makes me a political prisoner, pure and simple. I am also a prisoner of war, because of the war-like nature of the aggression carried out against New Africans by the government and other entities which believe in white supremacy.

In the end, I can say this about myself with neither hesitancy nor equivocation. My parents gave me love and I, in turn, tried to give love to those around me. My family instilled in me values and a sense of pride in myself, my community, my heritage, and my people. They were always there for me, and I have tried my best to be as steadfast for others who were not so fortunate as I in this regard. Twenty-one years as a prisoner, and the memory of being with the people still brings a smile to my face. This is something I have always tried to share with other prisoners, especially those who never had the opportunity to develop their political consciousness. The Black Panther Party was physically destroyed, but its spirit lives on in a lot of us. Just recently, a brother asked me for the goals and rules of the party, and more than a few wish to be part of it again. This is not simply a desire for militancy on our part, but a desire to once again (or still) experience realization of the concepts of unity, movement and love that the party embodied. That the spirit of the party remains alive, and appears to be growing stronger once again, after all this time and all this pain, can only be because the things it—and we who comprised it—were and are still correct.

There is little of me here, in these words, yet in a way it is all of me. I would like to take a walk at night and hug my baby. I'd like to sit down and eat in a restaurant and have a quiet night's sleep. I'd like to be able to turn out the lights when I want, to look at the trees, drive a car, do all the things people take for granted in their so-called "freedom." Not being able to touch and share special moments with another makes one generalize. I tell myself I am all right, but who can be all right after all these years under conditions which grow steadily worse, never better? Still, I am in command of my politics, my understanding of the process which has done this to me and so many others who were and are the best of my generation, and the generations before and after my own. I understand the reality and the necessity of the struggle in which I have engaged, am engaged, and will continue to engage until my last breath. I can still laugh, and I continue to love, so the damage is not so great as one might expect (or my enemies might hope). All power to the people.

Black Panthers in New Haven, CT, call the public attention to the imprisonment of their members. (photo: Library of Congress)

Ward Churchill

A Person Who Struggles for Liberation—
An Interview with Geronimo Pratt

Geronimo ji Jaga Pratt (s/n: Elmer Gerard Pratt) is one of the longest-held prisoners of war in the United States today, having been been incarcerated in California's maximum security facilities for more than 18 years. On July 28, 1972, Pratt—a much-decorated Vietnam veteran and then head of the Los Angeles chapter of the Black Panther Party (BPP)—was convicted of the "Tennis Court Murder" of white school teacher Caroline Olsen in Santa Monica on the evening of December 18, 1968. He was sentenced to a seven-year-to-life term under then-prevailing California sentencing guidelines. At the time of his conviction, he had already spent nearly two years in maximum security lockup awaiting trial on a variety of charges (most of which resulted in his acquittal). Since being imprisoned, he has served more time in solitary confinement than any other prisoner of the U.S., a total of eight years. The average time served in California on a murder conviction is four years. At Pratt's last parole hearing, in November 1987, LA Deputy District Attorney Dianne Visanni made clear that he was being kept in prison, not because he is thought by the state to be a "murderer," but because he is "still a revolutionary man."

Through it all Pratt has consistently maintained he was some 350 miles north of Santa Monica—in Oakland, attending a national leadership meeting of the BPP—on the night of the Olsen murder. He also maintains the FBI has always been aware of his innocence, given that the Bureau electronically surveilled the meeting in question. At trial, the FBI denied the existence of such taps and bugs. It was later forced to admit that it had indeed electronically monitored the meeting, but then claimed to have "lost" the logs which would have served to exonerate the defendant. The Bureau also initially denied having infiltrated Pratt's defense team or having placed undercover operatives on the stand to testify against him; in fact, the FBI was later forced to reveal that it had done both. Finally, the FBI denied at trial that it had a "particular interest" in Pratt, but it was later established that he had been listed in the Bureau's "National Security Index" and his picture included in its "Black Nationalist Photo Album" of individuals the FBI considered prime targets for what it termed "neutralization."

Since Geronimo Pratt's trial, more than 100,000 pages of FBI documents released under provision of the Freedom of Information Act with regard to his case prove beyond doubt that he was a principle focus of the illegal COINTELPRO (Counterintelligence Program) campaign conducted by the Bureau against the Panthers during the late 1960s and early '70s. The documented scope of FBI operations during this exercise in political repression included the massive infiltration of agents provocateurs into the BPP and the use of these provocateurs to systematically spread rumors within the party and the black community, a tactic designed to sow discord in both quarters. Cartoons and other bogus "literature" were also produced and distributed by agents in the party's name, another ploy aimed to drive wedges between the Panthers and their base of community support. This placed the FBI in a perfect position to foster "shooting wars" between the Panthers and other organizations such as the Black P. Stone Nation in Chicago and Ron Karenga's United Slaves in southern California, a strategy which resulted in numerous fatalities. In the midst of all this, the Bureau's COINTELPRO operatives excelled at forging letters and other internal BPP documents in order to disrupt BPP communications and foment factional fighting within the group. This in turn caused the isolation of what the FBI termed "key party leaders," a situation that allowed the successful fabrication of cases through which to bring about the lengthy imprisonment of targets or, in some instances, their selective assassination by police. All of this was covered by a mantle of official secrecy as well as a wholesale anti-BPP disinformation surfaced through the mass media in order to misrepresent and "justify" what was being done to the Panthers before the public.

By the mid-70s at the latest it was clear that the BPP and other progressive organizations in the U.S.—as well as scores of the individuals who had participated in them—had been destroyed by a pattern of FBI activity which a senate investigating committee described as being "lawless" and "little more than a sophisticated vigilante operation" violating "even the most minimal standards of official conduct within a democratic society." Still, no FBI agent was ever punished for what had happened, and the courts have consistently demonstrated a willingness to leave COINTELPRO victims languishing in prison for "crimes" invented by the Bureau solely to bring about their elimination from the political movements of which they were a part. Pratt's appeals have been repeatedly denied over the past two decades, often on the narrowest of technical grounds, while former Los Angeles FBI office COINTELPRO specialists such as Richard Wallace Held (currently

Special Agent in Charge of the Bureau's San Francisco office) have been allowed to take the stand and profess not to recall even the rudiments of the operations they directed against him.

At present, the only real hope for justice ever being done in the case of Geronimo Pratt appears to lie in a dramatic increase in public consciousness and concern regarding his circumstances, and in pursuit of remedies outside the U.S. legal system. Much the same can be said for many others—several of whom are represented in this volume—currently residing in the country's penal institutions, who have been victimized by COINTELPRO and its successor forms of political persecution. Toward the end of generating some portion of the necessary awareness, the following text derives from a series of conversations with Pratt undertaken in San Quentin over a period of two years, most recently in July 1989. It is bolstered by excerpts from material contained in an interview conducted by the John Brown Anti-Klan Committee and published under the title "I can't see myself being anything but a person who struggles for liberation."

Churchill: Let's begin with your trial. How is it you came to be convicted of the so-called Tennis Court Murder?

Pratt: I was convicted on the testimony of a man named Julio [Julius C.] Butler, who was secretly an undercover operative of the FBI. We didn't know this at the time he was on the stand, but he was on the FBI payroll. At trial, we asked whether he'd ever worked for the FBI or any other police agency, and he got all rocks in his jaw, saying: "I resent that question. I've never worked with any police organization," and all that sort of thing. It was very convincing to the jury, and it wasn't until six or seven years later that we got the documents proving he worked for the FBI. Now that's perjury, and the FBI officials who testified that the Bureau had no informers among the witnesses committed perjury, but nothing happened to them. What's more, given that Butler—who was, after all, the key witness—was shown to have perjured himself, my case should have been automatically dismissed. I should have had a retrial right then and there, but, as you can see, it didn't happen.

Churchill: What exactly was the nature of Julio Butler's testimony against you?

Pratt: Well, for starters, he stated that I had confessed the killing of Mrs. Olsen to him. He also solved the ballistics problem in the state's case. You see, they claimed I'd killed the woman with a .45 automatic. And they had a .45 they had taken from the Panther pad in a roust at Ericka Huggins' house the night her husband, Jon, and Bunchy

[Alprentice] Carter were assassinated.[1] The problem for the prosecution was that slugs from the .45 attributed to me didn't match the slugs recovered from the Olsen murder scene. Butler fixed this right up by testifying he'd seen me change the barrel of the gun or some such nonsense. It wasn't particularly plausible, but the jury believed it.

Churchill: Was there other evidence against you?

Pratt: Yes. Kenneth Olsen, husband of the dead woman, who was with her the night she was murdered and who was wounded in the attack, testified that I was the man who'd shot both of them. This was reinforced by the testimony of a shopkeeper named Barbara Redd, whose business was near the tennis court, who also claimed to be able to identify me as the man. What the prosecutors forgot to mention during the trial was that Mr. Olsen had positively identified another man, who doesn't look a thing like me, during a line-up very shortly after the murder. When he identified me over a year later, he was emphatic about it. It took LAPD detectives months of coaching, using photo spreads with my picture in them, to bring the witness around to being "sure" I was the guy who'd pulled the trigger. And both Mr. Olsen and Mrs. Redd originally insisted the killer had been cleanshaven. Everybody knows I've always worn this goatee and mustache, ever since I got out of the army.

Churchill: What happened to the guy who was originally identified as the killer? Did you know him?

Pratt: No, I never knew the man. And as far as I know nothing ever happened to him. They just let him slide. I'm not saying this particular guy did the crime, it might have been somebody else entirely. But I *am* sure it wasn't me. Somewhere along the line the decision was made to let the real murderer walk in order to be able to hang it on me. It's funny in a way, but I've heard they were a little confused as to exactly what they wanted to charge me with. I mean, they seem to have actually held a little strategy meeting and tried to figure out which murder, out of a bunch of unsolved homicides, would be the best one to stick me with. And they settled on the murder of Mrs. Olsen. Kind of like eenie-meanie-minie-mo. But that's "law enforcement" for you.

Churchill: When you say "they" held a meeting to decide which murder would be best to charge you with, do you mean the FBI?

Pratt: Oh yeah, the FBI. But not just the FBI. In those days, the LAPD had something they called CCS, the Criminal Conspiracy Section, which was really the cover name of the local red squad, and it was very tightly interlocked with the FBI's COINTELPRO section. There were three FBI agents named Richard Held, Brendan Cleary and Richard Bloeser, and a couple of CCS detectives named Ray Callahan and Daniel P. Mahoney. There were others, of course, but these guys seem to have been the core of the anti-Panther action in LA. Callahan was the one who eventually brought my murder case forward. We had them all on the stand in a hearing in 1985, and they all pretended not to remember much of anything about what they did for a living back in the early '70s. But we know pretty much how it went down; a couple of their infiltrators later spilled the beans, and at least one former FBI agent—a guy named [M. Wesley] Swearingen—has corroborated a good deal of it.

Churchill: What did the witnesses get out of mis-identifying you?

Pratt: Well, with Mr. Olsen, I think you have to look at it as a matter of grief. I mean, the man's wife had been brutally murdered right before his eyes. He himself had been shot. From his point of view, it's natural that *somebody* had to pay for what had happened. Right? And the police used this honest emotion of his to just really do a number on him, to convince him that not only was I the somebody who should pay, but that I was the *right* somebody. It's all pretty akin to brainwashing. Same with Mrs. Redd. She was trying to be helpful to the police, and the police

Geronimo Pratt in San Quentin, 1987. (photo: Kathy Raddatz)

were making it pretty clear what they wanted. And you have to remember that this was all happening toward the end of a sustained national campaign on the part of the government to convince people that the Black Panther Party was an extremely violent bunch of hoodlums, a "hate group" out to get white people and all of that nonsense. The whole propaganda effort was designed to bring people around to the point of view that Panthers were something to be destroyed by any possible means, regardless of whether they'd personally done anything at all which could be called criminal. Being a Panther, or thinking like a Panther, or identifying with the Panthers were matters treated as being criminal acts. And here I was, projected as this big, bad Black Panther. You can see how the racism works. At some level or another, I think a lot of people—including some witnesses—*knew I'd had nothing to do with this murder of a white woman by a black man, but they still* held me responsible for it, simply because of who I was projected to be. So when I was sent up, I suppose they derived a certain satisfaction from it.

Churchill: How about Julio Butler?

Pratt: Butler's a different story. They took real good care of him. They let him walk on several felony convictions, and they paid his way through law school, and I understand he eventually got a job with municipal government in the LA area. They've also protected him from ever having to go back on the stand with regard to my case. Julio definitely benefited from what he did.

Churchill: Let's go back a little bit. Before you joined the Black Panther Party, you were a paratrooper in Vietnam. Could you talk about your military experience and how it affected your political consciousness?

Pratt: First things first, here. I'm from the South, from rural Louisiana. I grew up in a very segregated situation, and within a long tradition of armed struggle, armed self-defense. This is, you know, the area of the Maroons—people, like me, of mixed black and American Indian heritage—the area which produced the Deacons [for Defense], and so on. As I was growing up, as I was absorbing the tradition of my people's struggle, Emmett Til got killed. Four little black children were blown up in a church in Birmingham. You know the history.

So, yeah, I went airborne in the army, became a paratrooper, learned light weapons and small unit tactics and volunteered for training in long range reconnaissance operations. Contrary to some false information that's been put out there, I was never in Special Forces, I was never a Green Beret. I was in the brigade of the 82nd Airborne [Division] they sent to Vietnam. Spent my whole year doing recon, mostly in the highland region in the central and northern parts of the country, but also across the border into Laos and Cambodia sometimes. I got wounded, was awarded a bunch of combat medals, made sergeant and came back to the States. I barely got adjusted to being here when the Tet Offensive happened [January-February of 1968], and they shipped me right back. I did my last six months in the military on a mandatory second tour in Nam, doing the same ugly shit I'd done the first time. More long range patrols, more killing, more wounds, more medals.[2] I got out and came home as soon as my time was up.

So I come back and the war is on here, too. I was in Chicago during the summer of '68, and the police had pulled some brothers over and had them lying on the ground. Guns drawn all over the place. One cop had his foot on top of this guy. And there was a helicopter hovering overhead with a searchlight shining down. This is going on and I'm flashing back, thinking this shit is identical to what's going on in, say, Cheo Reo or Dalat. A whole lot of our people were being killed, gunned down. And the police were pulling people in, calling them "detainees" instead of prisoners because they weren't even bothering to go through the motions of arresting them. And I'm flashing on Nam; same terminology, same situation. Guys are getting killed in shootouts staged by the police, they're getting shot with handcuffs on. The police are just blowing them away. So here I am with the knowledge to teach them to adequately defend themselves. This is my role, I'm going to do this, you see. This was one of the things I consciously saw I could help with, teaching the brothers how to defend themselves against physical attack, helping them learn the things a nation should know.

Churchill: Do you ever feel guilty about what you did in Vietnam?

Pratt: Do *you*? We had pretty much the same experience, as near as I can tell.[3] I think you already know the answer. But let me say this: I'm not proud of having been part of an army used to try and colonize another people. That's a fact. But I *am* proud of the skills I developed, the knowledge I gained, the level of attainment I achieved. I wasn't involved in the My Lai sort of thing; I fought other soldiers, out in the bush, a long way from civilians. I find no shame in combat. And that's also a fact, even if I was on the side that was in the wrong. I think most combat veterans understand what I'm saying because there's a unity among combat veterans on this even when we can't agree on other things. Our loyalty is to each other, not to the government that sent us to fight. It's an irony. You can ask the most self-conscious right-wing, racist combat vet and he'll say exactly the same thing I just said. There are some *non*-combat vets, of course—a lot of 'em making careers off being veterans these days—who sing a different tune, but that's another story and I don't want to get into it just now.

Anyway, I inherited no burden of guilt from my experience in Vietnam. Instead, I inherited a burden of responsibility to use what I'd learned there to respond to the Nixon-Mitchell regime that was continuing the genocidal war both abroad and at home. That's a different thing entirely, and the government certainly knows it. A lot of combat vets felt this way. That's why so many of us either are or have been in prisons since the war. The government used us for its own purposes while we were there, and then set out to kill us or lock us up so we couldn't bring what we'd learned to bear against them when we came back. In my own case, the Assistant DA from Los Angeles [Dianne Visanni] said at my 1987 parole hearing—she actually just came right out and said it!—that a major reason I shouldn't be released from prison is the effect Vietnam is supposed to have had on me. And the parole board treated her statement as if it were the most reasonable sentiment in the world. So, what does that say? The pay-off for all those medals is a life stretch in the joint. It seems to me this adds up to a very eloquent statement about how the U.S. government *really* feels about its combat veterans.

Churchill: After you got out of the army in '68, you enrolled at UCLA and hooked up with the Black Panther Party. In fact, you became head of the LA chapter of the party. Could you tell us something of how that came to be, the sorts of programs you were into developing, that sort of thing?

Pratt: Actually, I went to Louisiana first, visited with my family. Then I went to UCLA and enrolled through the EOP [Educational Opportunity Program], signed up for the GI Bill and everything. I more or less immediately became involved in the black student organization on campus, and through that I came in contact with Bunchy Carter, one of the most beautiful brothers I ever met in my life. Bunchy was head of the LA Panthers, and he sort of took me under his wing, brought me along politically. Once I became involved with the party, they cut off my GI Bill, which was totally illegal, but they did it anyway. When Bunchy was assassinated, we found he'd left a tape behind stating that if anything happened to him, I was to succeed him as head of the chapter. I was still a UCLA student. The sorts of programs we developed are fairly well known: the Free Breakfast for Children Program, the Free Clothing Giveaway Program, medical clinics in the black community, legal education and assistance, teaching the people what to do if the police stopped them on the street or arrested them. We were developing a comprehensive political education program and did a lot of legal defense work, not only for party members who got busted, but for community people as well. Our overall objective was to gradually develop a base of self-reliance and self-sufficiency within the black community which would eventually result in the exercise of the right to self-determination by that community.

Churchill: Wasn't there a solid military dimension to all this? Wasn't that what put the status quo most uptight about the Panthers in general, and perhaps you in particular? Were the Panthers unique in this?

Pratt: Let's take these questions one at a time. First, no, the Panthers were *not* unique in terms of advocating armed self-defense. I've already mentioned that my own Louisiana heritage is rich in that tradition, which dates back to the slave revolts. I'd also refer students of the issue to the period running from roughly 1918 to 1921, the rise of the Garvey movement and the African Blood Brotherhood. In the early '60s, years before the Black Panther Party—which was, incidentally, originally called the Black Panther Party for *Self-Defense*—Robert Williams, an NAACP leader in North Carolina, had a lot to do with raising black consciousness around picking up the gun. And there was Malcolm X, who was such a model for militant black pride and who was absolutely unequivocal about the need for and right to engage in armed self-defense. He formed the Organization of Afro-American Unity on this principle. During the mid-60s, there was RAM, the Revolutionary Action Movement, and there was Ahmed Evans' organization in Ohio. Even SNCC, the Student Nonviolent Coordinating Committee, changed its name to Student *National* Coordinating Committee and adopted a hard line on the necessity of armed self-defense before the Panthers appeared in Oakland. In fact, Kwame Turé [Stokely Carmichael] had already founded a Black Panther Party in Lowndes County, Alabama—a party based in the right to armed self-defense—more than a year before Huey Newton and Bobby Seale started the party of the same name here in California. So the BPP was absolutely not unique in this. In fact, it wasn't necessarily ever even the most important part of the question.

But, yes, there *was* a military dimension to the party, and to my role in the party. I've already said that I saw—still see—myself as a soldier in the struggle for black liberation, and that I felt my role—or one of my roles—should be to share my own training and experience in military matters with others in the movement. And it's fairly clear that this really did put the powers that be in a frenzy. Here I had had the training and I'd tempered that training with actual combat experience, not once, but twice, and now I'm no longer in their service. Instead, I'm out there passing it all along to a bunch of crazy niggers who are actually trying to take direct control over their own lives and their own communities. Well, you can sort of see how this was driving people in certain circles a little further off their nut than they already were. You could say it drove a few of them just plain batshit, and, yeah, they came after me very hard as a result. Not because of what I did, but because of what they *thought* I was doing. And it wasn't just me; they went after a *lot* of people in the party the same way. Maybe a hundred Panthers went up on heavy time between, say, the beginning of 1969 and the end of 1971. You don't have to be Sherlock Holmes to figure out that with the sort of heat we were drawing in those days, we weren't exactly running around committing the sorts of criminal offenses we were getting convicted for. They just had themselves a railroad—a sort of "Panther Express"—running straight into the nearest maximum security prison. And they put as many of us on it as they could, for purely political reasons. They may have convinced the public and maybe even some regular beat cops that we were criminals, but the police officials themselves always knew better. That's *why* they went to such lengths to get us off the street.

Now, let's see, the other question was whether it was the matter of our advocating armed self-defense—whether that scared them—that this made them come at us the way they did. And the answer is no, it wasn't. In spite of what they fed the public, the police officials knew we weren't violent. We weren't cop killers or anything like that. If we were, there would never have been a situation where the police killed 30 or 40 Panthers in barely a two year period, with no cops killed in response. It would just never have gone down that way if we were in any way what they portrayed us to be. The point is, we'd always had that capability, and we didn't choose to use it. So, what I'm saying is that what really put them uptight wasn't so much this thing about guns as it was the other things we were doing. It wasn't the question of armed self-defense which was at issue, but the question of what we were defending. That, and the success that was being achieved in these other areas of activity. All you have to do is examine the extreme lengths they went to to destroy the Breakfast for Children Program. Look what they did to our clinics and our legal education program. That'll tell you all you need to know.

One last point on this. In any movement, you have the political elements, and the political elements have their security forces. This is the role organizations like the Panthers sought to take on, because of their youth, vitality and strength. What we were saying to the people was, "take control of your own destiny and we'll defend you with our lives in the process." And the people were responding, you see. So the state set out to destroy the Black Panther Party. It had to, in order to destroy what it was the party was seeking to protect.

Churchill: Does any of this relate to the famous shootout with police at LA Panther headquarters, in which you were involved?

Pratt: Yes, very much so. That happened on the 8th of December, 1969, during a period when police across the country, operating under coordination of the FBI, were in a frenzy to assassinate those they considered to be the party leadership. It was just four days after a similar police action in Chicago had resulted in Fred Hampton and Mark Clark, a brother from Peoria, being murdered in their sleep. In fact, it turns out Hampton had been drugged into unconsciousness by an FBI infiltrator named William O'Neal prior to the cops kicking in his door and blowing his brains out. That was on December 4 at about four in the morning. So, on December 8, they tried to run the same drill in LA, but it didn't work. We were on alert and had sentries posted when they came to hit us at about 5 a.m. We managed to hold off the raiders and their reinforcements—which eventually amounted to about a hundred men, SWAT teams, an armored car, helicopters and every-thing—until it was broad daylight, the neighborhood had turned out to see what was going on and the media was on the scene. At that point, we knew they couldn't just gun us down, so we came out. We didn't kill any cops. We weren't trying to. The point is, we didn't let them kill us either, and that's what they'd come there to do.

Churchill: How do you know that was their purpose in conducting the raid?

Pratt: Well, none of the police officials ever just came right out and admitted it, if that's what you mean. But look at it this way, it was a hand-picked group of raiders commanded, not by a regular SWAT team leader or other police commander, but by Callahan and Mahoney of CCS. The charges they later said they were there about were a joke; there was no reason for a SWAT-type raid, certainly not at the crack of dawn. This was not your normal police operation that was being run. Or, look at it another way. Thirteen of us were arrested when we came out. We were charged with all *kinds* of shit, like conspiring to assault and murder police officers, attempted murder, you name it. I spent more than two months in jail behind $125,000 bail on that. But when it came to trial in 1971, we were all acquitted on every main charge. Every one. With all the evidence presented, the jury believed that we acted reasonably under the circumstances in firing at the police, that we had acted in self-defense. So they acquitted us. That's just another way of saying it was proven that the police had come to kill us.

Churchill: You mentioned William O'Neal, the FBI infiltrator in Chicago who set up the assassinations of Fred Hampton and Mark Clark. Was the LA chapter also infiltrated, and did that play into the December 8 shootout? This is aside from Julio Butler, who we've already discussed.

Pratt: Yes, on both counts. In Chicago it was O'Neal, who'd worked himself into a position as head of Panther security in that city. He provided a detailed floor plan of Fred Hampton's apartment to the FBI agent who was his contact, and that agent passed it along to the police unit which ran the raid, during the planning. The floor plan pinpointed exactly where Hampton would be sleeping, things like that. And, as I said, O'Neal also slipped Hampton a dose of seconal in a glass of kool-aid shortly before the raid. In LA, the infiltrator was Cotton [Melvin] Smith, who had also worked his way into being head of local security. He provided a cardboard mock-up of our headquarters layout that was used in planning the raid. Just like Chicago, it had information like where people were supposed to be sleeping. But he never managed to slip anybody a mickey. The cops put a couple of bursts directly into my bed, but I wasn't in it.

There's a couple of other interesting things about Cotton. First, he's doing a life sentence of his own now—in Kentucky, I think—for a murder he's supposed to have done there. Second, he's one of those who's come forth and detailed parts of the FBI/CCS plan to railroad me into prison, including the meeting where they sat around trying to figure out which murder would be best to frame me with. He's said straight out that the agent who was his contact—George Aiken—laid the whole thing out to him, and pumped him for any sort of information which could be used to make the Olsen murder charge seem more plausible to a jury. Now, again, you'd think this might be grounds for my case being taken back to trial. Well, guess again. The courts have shown absolutely no interest.

Churchill: Let's return for a moment to the party's military dimension, and your role in it. Did this involve establishing a facility in the Santa Cruz Mountains and using it to train "troops"?

Pratt: That's absurd. I've never set foot in the Santa Cruz Mountains, for *any* reason. And, to the best of my knowledge, no such facility ever existed. But I know where you got the idea. It comes from an infiltrator named Louis Tackwood. He worked for both the FBI and CCS among other police agencies. Tackwood became something of a celebrity in 1973 by peddling the story of what he'd done to a bunch of white radicals—people like Bob Duggan and Marilyn Katz—in LA. They published the stuff in a book called *The Glass House Tapes*, which had its problems but, to be fair about it, sort of blew the whistle on the sort of political repression operations that had been going on. Along comes this liberal Englishman, Jo Durden-Smith, a couple of years later wanting to do a book on the subject. He goes to Tackwood for what he figured would be the inside scoope. Tackwood's beginning to fade from the limelight, he needs something really spectacular to keep up his image, so he feeds the guy a real line, all full of secret Panther training bases and other crazy shit. Durden-Smith buys the whole nine yards, writes it up and publishes it under the title *Who Killed George Jackson?*

Now, I should be very clear about something here. Louis Tackwood was never in the BPP. He was never allowed in our policy or strategy meetings, or anything else of consequence. So, he was never in any position to know what he claimed to know about the inner workings of *our* organization. What Tackwood *did* know was the inside stuff on the sort of police methods used against us, and what the police thought we were doing. So, what he was really laying out to Jo Durden-Smith was police speculation—and outright lies—about what was going on, and how certain things had happened. Almost all of which was totally inaccurate, just fantasy-land sorts of stuff. Maybe the police actually believed some of this. Maybe Tackwood did too. It's hard to tell when you're dealing with psychopaths. You know, it's like I said, a lot of things were done to the Panthers because of what the cops *thought* we were doing, *not* what we actually did.

What really pisses me off about Durden-Smith is that he *could* have written a tremendously useful book. Instead, he produced a piece of garbage which ends up perpetuating even the wildest sorts of police propaganda. Just about me, he repeated as fact at least twenty major inaccuracies that Tackwood fed him. And here I was the whole time he was writing the thing, sitting only a few minutes away, across the bay in San Quentin. Never once did he try to contact me and ask whether these assertions were true. It's not that I should have had control over the book necessarily, but the guy should have used a few reality checks— actually, he was morally and ethically obligated to use them—rather than just going forward on the word of an admitted police agent who was also a well known psychotic. A visit could have been arranged. He could have gotten at least the pertinent portions of the manuscript to me. He could have asked for comments, criticisms, suggestions. And I would gladly have given them. But it either never occurred to him, even though it's standard practice, or he deliberately avoided it. Either way, it's inexcusable. And he produced a very damaging pack of lies as a result. It just proves you don't have to be a cop to do a cop's work.

Churchill: Durden-Smith *never* contacted you?

Pratt: No, he didn't. In fact, even though my name is splattered throughout the text, I never even knew the book existed until a friend happened to mention it to me three or four *years* after it came out. Of course, I asked for a copy to be sent in to me. After I read it, I contacted *him*. That proves communication wasn't impossible. At that point, he went all gee-whiz, shucks, I'm sorry, I didn't mean it; promised to do all sorts of things to correct the problems he'd created, but never came through on any of it. Now he seems to be actively dodging me again, which obviously isn't too difficult, given my accommodations. The man clearly has some serious character flaws. There's an incredibly arrogant dishonesty in using someone else's pain and struggle for your own purposes—to further your own fame and fortune, literary stature, or whatever—and at their direct expense. That's true regardless of other factors. When it's a white liberal doing it to a black liberation movement, you can toss in a heavy dose of racist presumption, to boot. That's about all I have to say on the matter of Jo Durden-Smith, other than that people should treat him and his book for what they really are.

Churchill: Just one other thing. Durden-Smith runs down a whole account of how you were involved in the action at Marin County Civic Center on August 7, 1970 which resulted in a firefight which killed George Jackson's younger brother, Jonathan, Judge Harold Haley, and a pair of San Quentin inmates, William Christmas and James McClain. What's the story on this?

Pratt: Here we go again. This comes from Tackwood. Look, I was nowhere around during any of the things leading up to the Marin County action, was completely out of the loop on the whole thing, and I can prove that beyond question. I wasn't even in California during the whole period. Believe me, if the cops thought it could be made to appear any other way, I'd have been on trial for it years ago. This clearly establishes my non-involvement for anyone who wants to look at the situation. But it made a good story, I guess: so that's probably why Tackwood told it and why Durden-Smith wrote it up as being "the truth." Tackwood also claimed that Cotton Smith, who was still part of the LA Panther organization at that time, was involved in the planning and logistics of the action, providing weapons and so on. This may or may not be true; I really don't know, although it should be treated skeptically for obvious reasons. Whatever the truth is on this score, people would do well to remember that Cotton was functioning as a police agent during this whole period. So, instead of the Panthers setting up the Marin County action, you have a situation where the *police* set it up. Follow? It would be a COINTELPRO kind of thing where four people—including William Christmas, James McClain and Jonathan Jackson—got killed. A couple of others were badly wounded, including a Marin County DA [Assistant District Attorney Gary Thomas] who was paralyzed for life.

This takes us to a couple of important points on police activities—which, as I said, Tackwood *did* know about—concerning what happened at the civic center. For example, the police on the scene were not commanded by local cops. Instead, our old friends Callahan and Mahoney from CCS were in command. Now, reasonable people have to ask themselves what a pair of red squad detectives from LA were doing 400 miles north of their jurisdiction, commanding an action in Marin County. And they didn't just fly up in response to the news that an action was occurring; they were already there. And their colleagues from the COINTELPRO section of the Los Angeles FBI had already established a base of operations up north. Now, if you think about it, all of this says they knew in advance what was coming down. But they didn't follow normal procedure and mobilize the local police to prevent it from happening. Not at all. There were very few local police on the scene during the action. Instead, they used prison guards from here at San Quentin to provide the firepower. They later said the guards just "happened" to be in the area, armed with rifles because they'd been engaged in target practice at a nearby rifle range. All I can say is that if you're willing to believe *that*, you'll believe anything, and maybe you'll buy a bridge in Brooklyn.

A final point. You mentioned a "firefight" in which all these people were killed. There was no firefight. It was a firing squad. There's no evidence at all that Jonathan Jackson or anyone else fired on the police or guards. What appears to have happened is that one of the cops—probably Mahoney or Callahan, but maybe someone else—fired first, and then the whole mass of guards opened up. They just shot the van in which the Jackson group was sitting to pieces. I think everyone in it was hit. But no cops were hit. The guards may have thought the first shot or two came from the van—I'm not saying they didn't, and it would be just like CCS to use 'em that way, without their knowledge—but it wasn't true. Jonathan Jackson and the others were executed as part of a deliberate police counterintelligence strategy. I don't see any other explanation of what happened that makes any sense.

Churchill: As you've pointed out, so many Panthers were killed and so many more were imprisoned during such a short period. Could you talk about the impact of the repression on the party's ability to continue organizing, or even to survive?

Pratt: It's not easy to talk about because there was a lot of foul play involved. And the victims were often close personal friends—and always brothers and sisters—who shared a common purpose and a unity of struggle. We were just talking about George and Jonathan Jackson, and about Mark Clark and Fred Hampton. And I've mentioned that Bunchy Carter was an extremely important figure in my life; his assassination was an incredible blow. I was also close with Jon Huggins, who was murdered along with Bunchy. Then there was Sylvester Bell, down in San Diego the following summer, another casualty of the

COINTELPRO which pitted Karenga's US organization against the party, and Li'l Bobby Hutton, murdered by the police in Oakland in 1968. And Captain Franco [Frank Diggs], whose murder remains "unsolved." There was Carl Hampton, murdered by the police in Houston in 1969. And there was Fred Bennett, whose body was never even found. The list just goes on and on; many of the names are people you've never heard of, but they were murdered for political reasons.

And, of course, there was my first wife, Red [Sandra Lane Pratt]. She was one of the party's major success stories, proof that what we were trying to do could in fact be accomplished. Red was a prostitute and a heroin addict at the time we brought her into the BPP. Within months, she was clean, off junk, not hustling anymore. Instead, she'd become one of the strongest, most consistent and hardest working members of the LA chapter. She was an example of what could be achieved through the BPP program. While I was in jail without bond [November 11, 1971], waiting for my trial for the murder of Mrs. Olsen, Red turned up alongside a freeway, five bullets in her, stuffed into an old sleeping bag. She was eight months pregnant. They couldn't allow for any success stories, you see. Hers is another one of those "unsolved" murders that keep popping up in any study of COINTELPRO.

Under such conditions, effective organizing eventually became impossible. People naturally became increasingly preoccupied with trying to stay alive and out of prison. The party itself, of course, didn't survive. It *couldn't* survive under those circumstances. And so it had to change form, become something else. What you have to understand is that when you're attacked by a psychological enemy—as we were—you're involved in a war, an actual war, not just a shoot-out or a few stand-offs, but an actual war. The government secretly spent millions and millions of dollars attacking the BPP. Not just on surveillance and bullets and trials—although plenty of resources went into those areas—but on a massive campaign of propaganda and psychological operations. I've been told they utilized more force and deception to destroy the Black Panther Party than was used in Chilé to bring about the overthrow of Allendé. Think about *that.*

Churchill: Does this relate to why you view yourself as a Prisoner of War?

Pratt: Absolutely. Even the U.S. senate, in its so-called Church Committee Report, acknowledged that what amounted to a counter-insurgency war had been waged against us by the FBI, approved by the highest officials in the country. I am a victim of that war, taken prisoner two decades ago and still held in captivity, quite illegally under international law. I'm not alone in this. There are many others like

Sundiata Acoli [s/n: Clark Squire], Sekou Odinga [s/n: Nathaniel Burns], Dhoruba Al-Mujahid Bin Wahadi [s/n: Richard Moore], Nuh Washington, Mutulu Shakur [s/n: Jaral Wayne Williams], Abdul Jajid [s/n: Anthony LaBorde], Ed Poindexter, and on and on. These are all POWs, and it's not something restricted to fighters from the black liberation movement. Counterinsurgency warfare has been directed at the liberation movements of all the colonized populations in North America. Leonard Peltier, a warrior in the American Indian Movement, is one of the better known examples. But there are many, many *Puertorriqueño independentistas* incarcerated as POWs at the present time: Alejandrina Torres, Carmen Valentín, Ida Luz Rodríguez, Haydeé Torres, Oscar López Rivera, Filberto Ojeda Ríos and Dora Garcia, just to name a few. For that matter, there are a number of white brothers and sisters, people who materially aided the liberation struggles, who are held as political prisoners. I'm talking about Marilyn Buck, Susan Rosenburg, Judy Clark, David Gilbert, Tim Blunk, Dr. Alan Berkman, Linda Evans and others. And, of course, there's the Ohio Seven group. This is far from an exhaustive accounting.

Churchill: Have the conditions of your confinement been more-or-less humane?

Pratt: If by humane you mean being held for eight solid years in solitary confinement—in total isolation from other prisoners, never mind the world outside—then I guess so. If you consider being held in a concrete cell without proper exercise or light or ventilation, with no sink or toilet— just a hole in the floor, and the stench that comes with it—for eight consecutive years to be humane, then I guess it's been humane. If you mean humane is being kept in a cage without a chair or stool or bunk— so that you have to sit and sleep on a concrete floor—for eight solid years, then I've been treated humanely. From 1970-75, I never heard a radio or saw a t.v. My reading material was extremely restricted, as was my right to receive mail and visitors. And my situation is not unique. At Marion, Illinois, they have an entire federal prison devoted to dispensing this sort of treatment. At Lexington, Kentucky, they had, until very recently, an experimental women's facility—where most of the population was selected on the basis of its politics—buried completely underground. It specialized in sensory deprivation. I understand they've established a much larger unit for women, based on the Lexington model, at Marianna, Florida. And they're cloning versions of the Marion/Marianna model into facilities throughout the U.S. prison system. All of this is contrary to international law concerning the *minimum* standards for treatment of prisoners. I think that fairly well sums it up.

Churchill: Geronimo, what do you think it's going to take to finally get you out of here?

Pratt: Well, I could be out tomorrow. All I'd have to do would be confess to a crime I didn't commit: the murder of Mrs. Olsen. This would serve to prove the cops were right all along, provide a non-political justification for all the years I've spent behind bars, and help validate the government's pretense that the Black Panther Party was really just a bunch of criminals that deserved what was done to it. It would fit into the present effort to absolve COINTELPRO of its real meaning. They have their rewards for rendering such services, you see. But I'll never play that game. Don't hang me with a murder I didn't do. Hell, if murder was what I was in for, I'd have been on the street 15 years ago.

Ultimately, I intend to bring a big case before the United Nations. By definition, it will involve far more than my own situation; it will encompass the cases of all the people I mentioned earlier, and many more. And it will present a brief which will demystify the nature of the official repression within which all of these cases arose: the infiltration and setups, the disinformation and assassinations. All of it. This is a major undertaking, but it's the only way I see of ever coming to grips with the problem. In a real sense, my own liberation is directly tied to that of others in the same circumstance. That's how I see it. An international legal effort of the sort I'm talking about will require a lot of support, financial and otherwise. But it can be done. Some of the foundation has already been laid through the research people like yourself have done, and through the various reports of Amnesty International investigations of places like Marion and Lexington, and my and Peltier's cases. There's even official U.S. government stuff like the Church Committee Report which will be useful. And there's literally hundreds of legal briefs and trial transcripts to go along with all the previously secret FBI documents we've obtained over the years. The documentary base plainly exists by which we can do what I'm talking about. We just have to organize ourselves to get it done.

Churchill: But, even if the international hearing you're talking about occurs, and the results are favorable to you, isn't it likely the U.S. will just ignore the whole thing?

Pratt: It is true that the U.S. government has a track record of defying any element of international law which it finds inconvenient. The thing about the CIA's mining of harbors in Nicaragua, which was condemned by the World Court, illustrates the point. Ronald Reagan simply announced that the World Court had no jurisdiction over U.S. actions in this regard. That's true. But the government has been able to do this by convincing the great bulk of the U.S. population that it was in its own interest to allow such defiance. In the Nicaragua case, enough people couldn't be convinced, so—even while he was posturing itself as flaunting the court—Reagan was having the CIA quietly remove the mines. That was a victory for Nicaragua—a limited victory, but a victory nonetheless—and a defeat for the U.S.

The case I'm talking about presenting in the international arena is even better. The government is caught in a contradiction here from which there is really no escape. The U.S. already has the highest percentage of its population imprisoned of any major industrialized nation. And what is the government planning to do? It's going to double the number of prison beds available over the next few years. That, and it's experimenting with all kinds of electronic gadgetry with which it can sentence people to do time in their own homes, using the gadgets to monitor them twenty-four hours a day. So, let's figure they're planning to imprison as many people in their own homes as they plan to have locked away in real prisons by about 1995. That's *four times* the number of people doing some sort of time then, as are doing time now. I don't know off the top of my head what percentage of the overall population this represents, but it's obviously extremely high. And its completely unprecedented.

Now, who do you figure it is that's going to volunteer to fill all those new prison beds? Who's gonna offer to go on house arrest? The government has, over the past few years, been able to sell the people a heavy bill of goods on the need to fight a "war on crime." More lately, they've called it the "war on drugs." They've manipulated statistics to show that "crime" in society has increased to such an extent that drastic measures are needed to combat it: vastly increased expenditures on police, involvement of the military in anti-smuggling operations, increasing suspensions of basic rights and liberties, beefing up the prison system and creating new technologies of incarceration. All of it. An amazing proportion of the population is buying into it at the moment, because government propaganda has them scared of the "criminal element." But the dynamic of the situation is such that as the thing progresses, more and more people are going to be forced to discover that they are the ones considered criminal by the government, that it's them and their friends and relatives who are being arbitrarily stopped and searched on the street, who are getting beat up by the cops at curbside, whose doors are getting kicked in for unwarranted searches in the middle of the night, who are being held in preventive detention and who are being whisked off to prison or placed under a few years worth of house confinement.

What's being missed here is that all this so-called increase in crime is just the natural response of people to Ronald Reagan's bold-faced policies of taking from the poor to concentrate more wealth in the hands of the rich that have prevailed throughout this whole decade. For almost twenty years, ever since the war against the Black Panther Party, the government has been peddling the idea that things were getting better for blacks in particular, but also for ladinos and American Indians in this society. There was, according to the official line, really no need for organizations like the Panthers because everything was working out on its own. All the while, things have been getting steadily worse. The signs have been there all along: the decrease in the numbers of blue collar jobs available in the U.S., increased unemployment among black youth, the slicing of social welfare programs, the visibly expanding numbers of homeless in the cities. Now, even the government is publicly admitting that the material situation of blacks has deteriorated dramatically since 1970. The same holds true for Indians and Chicanos and *Puertorriqueños*. Even poor whites. Things are not just worse, they are *far* worse than they were twenty years ago, just like the party said they would be unless revolutionary changes occurred *then*.

Okay. It's the people who've suffered most from the government's social and economic policies so far who are now being called criminals and slated to be warehoused in prisons. But the policies, the social structure that's generating the situation will continue, and as it continues, it can only broaden the sectors of the population that are criminalized and targeted for warehousing. As it broadens, it means less and less people can buy into the government's game plan. You see? The establishment has no option but to keep increasing the level of social repression so long as it holds to the policies that define its character. It's in a trap. Ultimately, the government can no longer convince enough people that its strategy of flaunting the basic international standards of human decency—inside as well as outside the U.S.—is in the interest of the people. At that point, only two outcomes are possible. Either the establishment sees the writing on the wall and voluntarily undertakes the sorts of fundamental changes necessary to address the real needs of the people, or the people force that kind of change on the establishment. History shows the latter as being by far the more probable. In fact, the former has never happened. But, either way, we win.

So, to sum up on this, the way we see of addressing the problem of prisons and the treatment of prisoners in this society is part of a much broader vision of social change. You can separate the two tactically from time to time, but they can never be separated strategically. The plan for seeking an international forum I was talking about earlier fits into this just fine. It's part of the process of politically educating the people to the realities that confront them. And no, the government can't really ignore it, not in the long run, not in the context at hand. You've got to look at things over the longer term, take the broader view, not just on an immediate, momentary basis. It's very important to hold a long range perspective, in which things can be see from all angles. The issue is not one of reform, it's one of liberation. Period. That's my understanding of it. And that's what I've dedicated my life to. I can't see myself ever being anything but a person who struggles for liberation.

Notes

1. *Editor's note:* Carter and Huggins were shot to death by gunmen from the United Slaves organization on January 17, 1969 as a by-product of a COINTELPRO campaign aimed at sparking war between it and the BPP; the FBI took credit for their deaths in internal memoranda.

2. Pratt was awarded eighteen combat decorations, including the Silver Star, two Bronze Stars with "V" device for valor, Purple Heart, and the Vietnamese Cross of Gallantry.

3. Churchill was airborne-qualified and in a 4th Infantry Division LRRP team in the highlands region in 1968.

New Afrikan Prisoner of War—
Sekou Odinga Speaks

My name is Sekou Mgobogi Abdullah Odinga. I am a Muslim and a POW. I was born in Queens, New York, on June 17, 1944, and raised in a family of nine: father, mother, three sisters, three brothers, and me. I was kicked out of school in the tenth grade for defending myself against an attack by a teacher. At age sixteen, I was busted for robbery as a "youthful offender" and spent thirty-two months at Great Meadows Correctional Institution (Comstock) in upstate New York, where I finished my high school education. During the period 1961-63, while I was there, Comstock was very racist. One of the sergeants commanding other guards was known to be head of the area ku klux klan klavern. You can figure out the rest of the environment from that single fact. In 1963, there was a serious race riot at the facility.

My first political education came at Comstock. The teachings of Malcolm X, who was with the Nation of Islam at that time, were a big influence on me. After my release, I became heavily involved in political activity in New York City, especially activity that led in a revolutionary nationalist direction. In 1964, I also became involved in the cultural nationalist movement. By 1965, I had joined the Organization for Afro-American Unity (OAAU), founded by El Haij Malik Shabazz (Malcolm X) after he left the Nation. My political consciousness grew daily. I was reading and listening to many African nationalists, both from the continent and from the U.S., and became convinced that only after an armed struggle would my people gain freedom and self-determination, emerging from the cauldron of our "New World experience" as *New* Africans. I also became convinced that integration would never solve the problems faced by New Africans.

After Malcolm's assassination, the OAAU never seemed to me to be going in the direction I desired. By late 1965, or early '66, I hooked up with other young revolutionary nationalists to organize ourselves for purposes of implementing what we felt was Malcolm's program. We founded the Grassroots Advisory Council in South Jamaica, New York. We were all very young and inexperienced, and got caught up in a local, liberal, anti-poverty program. By late 1967, I was thoroughly disillusioned with that, and, when I heard about the Black Panther Party in Oakland, California, I—along with some of my closest comrades—decided this was the type of organization we wished to be part of. We decided to go to California, investigate, and—if it was what it claimed to be—join the BPP. As it turned out, during the spring of 1968, we heard that party representatives were coming to New York to explore the possibility of establishing a chapter there. I attended the meeting, and decided to join and help build the BPP in New York. I became section leader for the Bronx, sharing an office with the Harlem Section, in Harlem.

On January 17, 1969, the day LA Panther leaders Bunchy Carter and Jon Huggins were assassinated at UCLA, I went underground. I was told that Joan Bird, a sister in the party, had been busted and severely brutalized by the police, and that the cops were looking for me in connection with a police shooting. I was subsequently indicted in the so-called "Panther 21" case, but stayed underground. On April 22, 1969, I awoke around 5:30 a.m. to the sound of wood splintering around my door. When I investigated, I found that my house was completely surrounded by pigs. They were on my roof, fire escape, in the halls, on the street, etc. I was fortunate enough to evade them by jumping from an unguarded window—they apparently thought it was too high off the ground for me to use it in such fashion—and go into deeper hiding. In early 1970, I was asked to go to Algeria to help set up the International Section of the BPP.

After a split in the party caused by the FBI's COINTELPRO operations against us, and my acquittal *in absentia* on the Panther 21 conspiracy charges, I decided to return to the U.S. to continue the struggle. Remaining underground, I continued to work until my capture in October of 1981. I was charged with six counts of attempted murder of police, for shooting over my shoulder at a whole horde of pigs who were chasing and shooting at *me*, as well as nine predicate acts in a RICO indictment. Convicted of the attempted murders—although a clearer case of self-defense is hard to conceive—I was sentenced to 25-years-to-life imprisonment. I was also convicted of two counts on the RICO indictment—the liberation of Assata Shakur from her New Jersey prison cell, and the expropriation of an armored truck—and sentenced to twenty years and a $25,000 fine on each count (forty years and $50,000 in total). All sentences were set to run consecutively, meaning I was sentenced to serve a minimum of sixty-five years. The maximum, of course, is life, and the pig judge recommended strongly that I *never* be paroled.

Although the facility is allegedly reserved for those, already incarcerated within the federal system, who have proven themselves

"incorrigibly violent" or otherwise "uncontrollable" in regular prisons
—a profile I patently did not meet—I was sent directly to the "super-
max" prison at Marion, Illinois. After three years in that hellhole, I
was transferred to the maximum security prison at Leavenworth,
Kansas, where I was held until being returned—without explanation—
a year later to Marion, where I am now being held "indefinitely."

The storefront office of the Black Panther Party in New Haven, CT, shows the
impact of the FBI's repressive COINTELPRO. The criminalization of dissent
was a nationwide FBI strategy. (photo: Library of Congress)

Dan Debo

The Struggle Continues—
An Interview with Dhoruba al-Mujahid Bin Wahad

In 1969, as a member of the New York chapter of the Black Panther
Part (BPP), Richard Dhoruba Moore was targeted as a "key activist"
subject to priority "neutralization" through the FBI's anti-BPP counterintelligence program (COINTELPRO). His name was placed in the
Bureau's "Security Index," his picture in its "Black Nationalist Photo
Album." In April of that year, he and twenty other members of the
chapter were arrested by the New York Police Department's (NYPD's)
"Black Desk"—a subsection of the Red Squad which worked closely with
the FBI's COINTELPRO specialists—and charged with conspiracy to
bomb the New York Botanical Gardens and other sites within the city.
Although the police produced no evidence other than the statements
of several undercover agents that any such conspiracy existed, the
"Panther 21" were publicly branded as "terrorists" and bound over for
trial on twenty-three separate charges apiece. Despite the fact that no
tangible violence was even alleged to have occurred in the case, each
defendant was described as being too "dangerous" to be released from
custody. Consequently, their bail was set at a prohibitively high $100,000
each, causing most to remain in jail under maximum security conditions
for the duration of their trial.

The state dragged the whole spectacle on for as long as possible.
On May 13, 1971, however, an almost all-white jury found the Panthers
"not guilty" of each of the 483 aggregate charges lodged against them.
The experience of more than two years incarceration prior to this mass
acquittal caused several of the 21 to deactivate politically, but not
Dhoruba Moore. Bailed out shortly before the end of the trial, he'd gone
underground, and had made it abundantly clear he intended to continue
the full range of his activities as a Panther. Hence, the priority attached
to his targeting was raised by the FBI.

On June 5, 1971, less than a month after the Panther 21 trial ended
in utter defeat for the state, Dhoruba and two other party members
were arrested during a supposed "hold-up" of an after-hours club which
was a notorious hangout for South Bronx drug merchants. Their con-

tention was that no robbery had been occurring and that they were instead participating in a BPP effort to dry up the flow of heroin and other narcotics into the black community. Statements of certain of the alleged victims, and police surveillance records themselves, tended to corroborate the Panther account. Dhoruba was nonetheless held in the matter for several days, until "investigators" could charge him with entirely different and much more serious "offenses."

On the night of May 19, 1971, two NYPD guards at the home of Panther 21 prosecutor Frank Hogan had been shot and wounded in what the police termed "an assault carried out with military precision." Two evenings later, another pair of cops were shot to death in a similar attack in Harlem. The Black Liberation Army (BLA) issued communiques taking responsibility for both actions. Responding to a demand by President Richard M. Nixon to use "any and all means available" to destroy the BLA and BPP, the FBI initiated a COINTELPRO operation dubbed NEWKILL (for New York Police Killings). Although there was no evidence that Dhoruba had been involved in either of the shootings, or that he was a BLA member, he was charged with two counts of attempted murder of a police officer with regard to the "ambush" at Hogan's home, as well as sundry conspiracy charges. Again he was denied bond; again he remained in jail while having never been convicted of a crime.

To say the state's case was weak would be to misinterpret the facts. The case was actually nonexistent. The prosecution's bald manipulations in attempting to overcome this "deficiency in its evidence" resulted in a mistrial. The district attorney immediately announced his intention of going back to court, however, and Dhoruba continued to be held without bond. A second trial produced the same result, and again the defendant was taken back to jail. The third time, as they say, is a charm, and the accused was finally convicted in 1973. He was sentenced to life imprisonment, the customary penalty visited upon those who try and kill New York's finest. The verdict had accomplished what was desired by NEWKILL operatives. Whoever actually wounded the two cops in May of 1971, no serious attempt was ever made to apprehend them or bring them to trial. The FBI's major purpose—and probably the Red Squad's as well—had been fulfilled. Dhoruba Moore had been permanently neutralized.

For several years, there was little motion in the case. Various appeals were attempted and invariably denied. As is all too typical of the American left, even supposedly progressive people began to forget about him and the blatant injustice of his circumstance, moving on to "other agendas." Generally, the Church Committee revelations during the mid-70s concerning the FBI's historical record of politically repressive misconduct, confirming much which had already been suspected about COINTELPRO, set in motion what appears to have been a decisive break for the victim. In late 1975, his attorneys filed a suit under the Freedom of Information Act (FOIA) demanding release of all FBI documents pertaining to their client. The Bureau adamantly refused to make any such disclosure, variously contending that no such documents existed, that they existed but were "irrelevant," that they existed and were possibly relevant but exempt from disclosure on unexplained "national security" grounds, and so on. Ultimately, the FBI was able to stall for twelve years, avoiding having to produce its files other than in the most piecemeal fashion. Finally, by 1986, a sufficient quantity of data had been compiled on the basis of the reluctantly divulged sprinkling of documents for a court to order a more comprehensive release.

As a result, by the end of the latter year, what the Bureau had been hiding under the mantle of "state secrets" had begun to come out. It is now known definitively that one of the prosecutors during Dhoruba's final trial—a man who currently sits as a Reagan-appointed federal judge—deliberately suppressed exculpatory evidence. More importantly, the FBI's COINTELPRO documents show that the prosecution's chief witness, a woman named Pauline Joseph, had initially contacted police to enter substantial evidence that Dhoruba was not guilty of the charges against him. She was quickly whisked away to a hotel where she was held incommunicado for two years while being "convinced" by both FBI agents and NYPD detectives that her initial information was "erroneous." Eventually, she went on the stand to testify to the exact opposite of what she originally contended.

Pauline Joseph's testimony was probably the most critical single component of the entirely circumstantial case through which Dhoruba was convicted. At trial, the prosecution made no mention of her having made prior and contradictory statements concerning his alleged involvement in the shootings. To the contrary, in response to defense motions for disclosure on such matters, the prosecution insisted that no such statements had ever been made. The FBI, the internal files of which reveal its agents were well aware of the facts, and thus that Dhoruba's civil rights were being blatantly denied—a violation of federal laws the Bureau is pledged to uphold—not only did nothing to intervene, but instead facilitated the plot through allocation of its personnel and other resources. Afterwards, the Bureau engaged in a twenty year cover-up to insure the victim remained in prison without ever having received anything remotely resembling a fair trial.

In April 1988, defense attorneys filed a motion with the New York State Supreme Court arguing that on the basis of the belatedly obtained FBI documents, their client's conviction should be overturned and his case reopened. In August of the same year, the New York high court agreed to hear oral arguments in the matter. On March 17, 1989, New York Supreme Court Justice Peter McQuillan issued a five-page opinion reflecting the court's conclusion that, contrary to the law, the prosecution had withheld evidence, especially with regard to Pauline Joseph, which could have led to an acquittal. McQuillan specifically acknowledged that Joseph's testimony could "very possibly" have been successfully challenged, had the exculpatory evidence been disclosed during the trial, and that this might have had a major impact upon the jury. The justice also admitted that, had the illegally withheld evidence been available during the defendant's direct appeals, a reversal of his conviction would have been required.

Despite these findings, however, McQuillan announced that the high court declined to reverse Dhoruba's conviction. The "reasoning" advanced to support this absurd and outrageous position was purely technical, having nothing whatsoever to do with concepts of justice or even common decency: since Dhoruba's direct appeals had long since been exhausted, a reversal—while still entirely possible if the court wished to grant it— was no longer *required*. It was not until defense lawyers were able to cite a precedent leading to an exact opposite conclusion, made by the same court as recently as 1987, that McQuillan decided to rethink the matter. Finally, during the spring of 1990, having spent a total of 21 years behind bars with no bona fide conviction against him, Dhoruba al-Mujahid Bin Wahad, the name Dhoruba had adopted while imprisoned, was released. As of this writing, New York prosecutors insist they are still holding open the option of retrying him. If history is any indicator, whether they do or not will have far more to do with the nature of his political activities than upon the merits of their case.

Debo: Can you start out by talking a little about your early days in the Panthers?

Dhoruba: Well, maybe ironically, I joined the Panthers in 1968, at the outset of the FBI counterintelligence program—COINTELPRO as they called it in those days—against the party. It was at that time that I began seriously dealing with issues effecting the black community and black liberation movement in the United States. My early activities in the Black Panther Party included organizing in the breakfast for children program, developing programs of community control around police and education, the anti-heroin program, that sort of thing. As a consequence I was targeted as a security index subject. "Security index" was a classification the FBI had to identify those individuals it felt represented a threat to the stability of the U.S. government, or the U.S. system more generally. Usually, what qualified one for this particular index was merely their vocal, articulate opposition to U.S. domestic and foreign policy. Those individuals who were classified as security index subjects were targeted by the federal and local law enforcement agencies for what they called "neutralization."

Debo: And this was previous to the Panther 21 trial?

Dhoruba: The part about the FBI was actually subsequent to the Panther 21 trial. I was just giving sort of a capsulated history. Being a defendant in the Panther 21 case brought about an increased focus on me as an individual and it was as a result that I was placed in the FBI's agitator index as well as on the security index. Prior to that, I was field secretary to the New York Black Panther Party and I traveled around on the eastern seaboard primarily dealing with organizing new chapters and developing programs. Actually, the Panther 21 conspiracy case was one of the first major efforts to neutralize me. Well, not just me, of course; me, along with twenty other members of the New York chapter of the party. We were accused of plotting to blow up department stores and all kinds of crazy stuff which the police knew was false. But, merely by charging us with conspiring to commit such acts, they were able to lock us up under $100,000 bond apiece, knowing full well we couldn't raise that kind of money. So we sat in our cells, month after month, without ever having been convicted of a thing. Pretty slick, don't you think? That's the way counterintelligence operations work.

In the end, I, along with my co-defendants, was acquitted of all charges. This came to about twelve dozen different counts, all told. It took the jury about forty-five minutes to reach the not guilty verdicts on nearly 150 charges, after a trial that lasted almost a year. That's how much of a case the government really had against us. Most of the others weren't released until the very moment of the acquittal, having by that point spent nearly a year and half in lockup over nothing. But I'd gotten out a little earlier. A couple of months before the end of the trial, enough funds had finally been raised to allow a few of us to be bailed out. The defendants felt as a group that I should be one of those in order that I be able to do public organizing around the case, and also resume my party functions. That's when the FBI and police "red squads" *really* began to come after me. As it turned out, I had to jump bail and flee underground as a result of the COINTELPRO attempts to take my life. By then, they had sown dissension within the Black Panther Party, carrying out operations designed to vilify certain people within the party who they felt could provide principled and correct leadership, while promoting others who were fools and agents provocateurs.

As a consequence of these types of activities my life came into danger at a crucial point in the trial. The government apparently thought that by forcing me to jump bail they would effect the outcome of the trial. The idea was that the jury would think that my co-defendant Michael Tabor, who was also out on bond, and I were guilty and therefore afraid of the verdict. This, they thought, would prejudice the jury against the whole bunch of us. But the plan backfired on them. You see, the judge refused to sever my case from the rest of the defendants, the rest of the Panthers on trial. This was such a transparent collaboration with the prosecution, at the end of a trial riddled with such collaborations between the judge and the prosecutors that as a consequence we were all acquitted. That's not the only reason for the verdict, but it was a big part of it. So, the blatant racism of the judge and his obvious hatred for the Panther 21 actually afforded me the unique opportunity of being acquitted *in absentia*. Strange how things work out sometimes.

Debo: Did you surface again after the verdict? What happened next?

Dhoruba: No, the verdict didn't change the reasons I'd gone underground in the first place. Besides, I was engaged in important work in an underground capacity. At that time the black underground in the United States was conducting an anti-drug campaign in the black community, carrying out a campaign of search and destroy against the various drug dealers and their hang outs. This was coupled to above ground efforts like anti-drug propaganda, developing community controlled drug clinics, rehab programs and what have you. It was a good plan, and was working pretty well until it was derailed by the FBI and cooperating police agencies. Now, that's something people should think about very seriously, especially in the midst of all this current ballyhoo about a government "war on drugs" in which the FBI plays a prominent role. If they were serious about fighting drugs all they had to do was stand aside and let us do what needed doing twenty years ago. Instead, they actually backed the drug dealers against us. There's a lot more to this than meets the eye, and you can bet it's not about what they're saying it's about.

So anyway, I was captured during an operation against an after-hours club frequented by drug dealers and their associates. This was shortly after the Panther 21 verdict. At the time of my arrest some weapons were seized and, according to the police, one of them was identified as having been used to shoot two policemen a week earlier. I was then indicted for the attempted murder of the two policemen. It's important to note that this indictment was consistent with the policy of the New York DA's office after the 21 acquittal. After we were acquitted, New York District Attorney Frank Hogan said that he would no longer bring conspiracy indictments against militants, against radicals, that from that point on the radicals and militants would be dealt with within the confines of "straight" criminal proceedings. In other words, his policy was to tie us to specific acts, whether we'd committed them or not. That way he could avoid the public *impression* that his office, and the police, and the FBI were persecuting us for "thought crimes," even though that's exactly what they intended to do. You follow?

Debo: And you were convicted?

Dhoruba: Right. But it took them two warm-up trials—the first one ending in a hung jury and the second in a mistrial—to get the job done. After the mistrial I was finally convicted and sent to prison on a 25-year-to-life sentence. This was in 1973. They'd been working non-stop on getting some sort of conviction against me since 1968, so you can tell they meant business. Anyway, in 1975, after the existence of COINTELPRO became public information, I filed a suit in federal district court in New York City contending I'd been a target of COINTELPRO and had been framed as a consequence of this targeting. My argument was that my civil and constitutional rights had been violated by various officials intelligence organizations and law enforcement agencies, including the President of the United Sates, Richard Nixon, the FBI, CIA, local police intelligence units, etc. This suit continues today, largely because the feds keep stonewalling. It took approximately six years before they admitted having documents about me and turning those documents over. They spent about four years denying that any such material existed, and then ended up turning over 300,000 pages of FBI files.

Debo: That's pretty normal FBI procedure, as I understand it. They're habitual liars, a character trait that seems to go with the job. But this mass of "nonexistent" file material is what ultimately broke your case, right?

Dhoruba: Yeah, that's pretty much correct. In these files were, among many other things, the reports of key witnesses against me in my trial. These reports indicated that a key witness had made statements during her testimony at trial which contradicted the information she'd provided police investigators in the first place. The documents indicated that this witness had given testimony at trial which was either erroneous or false. They also show that her story had changed according to the scenario scripted by the prosecutor. So it looks like she was saying whatever the government needed her to say in order to get a conviction. Further, the government was obliged under the law to provide me with copies of these reports during my trial so that the witness could've been properly cross-examined by the defense. Remember, their case was very weak against me. One jury had already failed to convict me, even without my having complete information with which to engage in cross-examination. I'm certain that, had I been provided with my legal entitlement to the material with which to mount a thorough cross-examination of the government's "star" witness, the last jury would have voted for a complete acquittal. But the FBI withheld this exculpatory evidence, not only during the trial, but for about ten years thereafter. They deliberately denied me the right to any kind of fair trial, and then had the audacity to babble about "justice being served."

But, to return to your question, with this information finally in hand, I filed for a reversal of my conviction. After a two year struggle, in which the courts seem to have done everything possible to avoid such an outcome, my conviction was overturned on March 22, 1990. Not counting the brief period when I was out on bond toward the end of the Panther 21 trial, and a couple of weeks after the verdict on that, I've been in one or another lockup since the beginning of 1969. That's more than twenty-one years when you add it all up, and I've yet to be legitimately convicted of any crime. I was in prison because I was a member of a political organization, the Black Panther Party, and because the government of the United States objected to the philosophy of that party. I was put in prison for more than twenty years for holding and expressing a political viewpoint that the U.S. government didn't like. There is simply no other rational explanation for what happened to me. I mean, you can't exactly look at the record of my case and conclude that this was all just a series of "honest mistakes" on the part of the authorities, can you? So, I was a political prisoner, pure and simple. And my situation was hardly unique. There's at least a hundred other people doing time in this country right this minute, for exactly the same kinds of reasons I did mine. People really need to think about these facts.

Debo: What is the status of your case now?

Dhoruba: Well, I have been released on my own recognizance. Technically, I still have an indictment pending for the same shooting of two police officers. However, my lawyers have made motions to have the indictment thrown out, because the case is insufficient on its face given the fact that the testimony of the key witness was subject to disbelief at best. The prosecution claims it wants another trial and I would desire another trial because I think it would serve to galvanize the progressive community in New York around the issue of prisoners. But, I don't really think they're going to go back to trial, because this would allow me to put a number of individuals associated with my original conviction on the stand. One of them is now a federal judge, and several now have Wall Street positions. That sort of thing. And there are serious questions of perjury, etc., involved with their past performance. So you can expect them to let this die, once they've made a few gestures to save face.

Debo: Since you experienced all this from inside the process, so to speak, you have a rather unique perspective on an important question. How do you think the effects of COINTELPRO, such as the splitting of the Black Panther Party into "Newton" and "Cleaver" factions figured into the emergence of the Black Liberation Army during the early 70s? In other words, do you feel the FBI's campaign of political repression more or less forced elements of the party into reliance upon clandestine armed struggle rather than above-ground community organizing?

Dhoruba: Well, I think we need an accurate historical perspective here. In order to achieve this, we must understand the Black Panther Party's heritage. The party represented a significant change in the way African Americans related to racist conditions of exploitation in this country. This representation was embodied in the Black Panther Party's Ten Point Program, which is still relevant today. This program synthesized the needs and aspirations of black people into something anyone—black, white, or polka dot—could understand, and the justice of which could not be denied. Consequently, the Ten Point Program had a wide appeal among broad segments of the African American community. The powers that be understood the very popularity of the program as a threat to their position of dominance over black people insofar as implementation of the program could only result in African American community self-control, self-sufficiency and self-determination. That's why J. Edgar Hoover called the party "the greatest threat to the internal security of the United States." So, the police were dispatched to block the program's being fully developed. When the party made it clear that it was prepared to physically defend its right to pursue its political agenda within the black community, the repression was escalated through the massive application of COINTELPRO tactics. The purpose of this was to destroy the 10 Point Program by way of destroying the party.

You have to understand that COINTELPRO repression was lethal. Something like forty Panthers were murdered by police during a three year period running from 1968 through 1971. Scores of others were wounded. Hundreds were badly beaten. Hundreds of others suffered variations of my own experience with the judicial system, while our offices were ransacked, mailing lists and equipment destroyed. It just goes on and on. An outright war was waged against us. Under these conditions, many party members reached the logical conclusion that we were being presented with a clear choice: either abandon our politics altogether and thereby surrender, or develop ways and means of fighting fire with fire. We weren't ready to surrender, and so you see the creation of the Black Liberation Army as a result of that fact. It's very important to remember the cause and effect here: BLA actions did not begin until a long time after massive police violence was imposed on us. So, the BLA came into being as a direct result of COINTELPRO, not the other way around.

Debo: What about in prison? Did COINTELPRO extend into the prisons?

Dhoruba: Not exactly. At least not under that heading. What they had was a program called PRISAC. Not too many people have even heard of this one. But PRISAC was the vehicle used to attempt to destroy the political consciousness which was developing among prisoners during the early 70s, to block the emergence of a strong, unified, national movement among prisoners and their supporters on the outside. Part of it was to assassinate key leaders like George Jackson on the inside. Another part was to neutralize key activists like Angela Davis on the outside. Other parts included formulating and implementing new rules and guidelines within the prison system designed to prevent political education and organizing, and to train prison personnel in the ways and means of dealing with politically conscious prisoners. PRISAC, or comparable programs coming under other titles, are still very much in effect. The idea has been incorporated directly into standard operating procedure in every prison system in the country by this point.

Debo: Given the range of your experiences over the past 25 years, what do you see as being necessary at this moment? How do we move forward? What sorts of politics and programs do you see as viable?

Dhoruba: There are a number of things, mostly involving clarity. To begin with, we must understand how absolutely important and correct the 10 point program of the Black Panther Party was. The state certainly understood this. It was absolutely terrified at the prospect of large numbers of people accepting the program, moving on it and actualizing it at a community by community level. That's why the police and FBI assigned such a high priority to destroying the party. It follows that any movement seriously seeking to bring about political change in Amerika must be equally serious about pushing the program and seeing to it that it becomes a reality. A lot of clarity on this has been lost since 1970. Too many people have allowed themselves to be diverted away from this real agenda, taking up "causes," either because they are afraid of the state's response to their forcefully addressing the real issues, or because they're confused, or because of some combination of these two ingredients. We have much work to do of an educational nature, re-creating an adequate political consciousness even within the more politically active social sectors. This may in fact be our foremost task at this point.

But by this, I don't mean we should just launch a series of political education classes. These are, of course, important and must be organized, but I'm talking about a much more concrete educational agenda, one based in real activities. We need to raise consciousness through actual political processes registering real political victories. For one thing, we need to reconstitute the Rainbow Alliance. Now I'm talking about the Black Panther Party's version of the Alliance, not this sorry excuse for a political movement brought into being by Jesse Jackson later on. You see, the original Rainbow Alliance created by the party was composed of the Panthers, a Chicano organization known as the Brown Berets, the *Puertorriqueño* Young Lords Party, and anti-imperialist elements of North American groups like SDS. Once it got rolling, the American Indian Movement also linked up. We need to recreate this sort of structure in order to pursue strength through unity, forge a common strategy against our common oppressor, that sort of thing. All the ingredients exist. We just need to get it together.

On this basis, we can begin to do a number of things much more effectively than is now the case. We can, for instance, put out collectively produced information, completely separate and independent from the establishment press, which will make sense to a far greater range of people than can the material disseminated by any one of our scattered organizations at this point. We can start to recreate grassroots level community self-sufficiency efforts like the old Breakfast for Children Program. And we can deal much more effectively with things like the POW/Political Prisoner issue through coalition than we can through the channels which have been used over the past fifteen years or so. I can't over-emphasize the importance of this. You see, every time we obtain the release of a POW—say Geronimo Pratt or Leonard Peltier, as examples—we not only regain the services of one of our best and most committed and experienced activists, but we demonstrate in the most tangible possible terms that through unity, struggle and persistence we can actually force the state to do things it absolutely doesn't want to do. In other words, we can win. It's extremely important that large numbers of people come to understand this, not in the abstract, but through witnessing it actually happening. You follow? That's why I've personally made this a central area of my own work through Freedom Now!

Debo: I understand. But what about the other things that emerged as the focus of political attention since 1970? In other words, what about things like feminism, environmentalism and gay rights? Aren't they important?

Dhoruba: Of course they are! There can be no question but that these and a number of other things represent valid and pressing concerns. The question is not whether there are matters to be addressed in these areas, but how do we get to the point of actually doing something about them. You can recognize the environmental holocaust which is going on, and you can be outraged by it, and you can complain about it forever. The point, however, is to acquire the power necessary to effect change, to bring into being a new ecological order. Yes? The same may be said with regard to the abuse suffered by women and gays, not simply as individuals, but as entire classes of people. The point is not simply to understand the problem and to criticize the social arrangement which is responsible, but to gain the power necessary to change the structure of society. Okay?

The key to how the present status quo—and that's maybe three percent of the population—does what it does is the way it controls and manipulates, exploits and dominates everyone else. It does it in somewhat different ways and to different extents to different groups. The thing we have to ask is what it does most commonly to the greatest overall number of of people in order to maintain and continue to develop itself. This is inherently where we will discover our greatest area of our common ground, our common oppression, and thus our greatest area of unity in opposition to the status quo. And I will submit that this area is to be found in the exploitation of people by race. All black, brown, red and yellow people are exploited by the present system regardless of gender or sexual preference. It follows that poor white people are exploited by virtue of being into a false racial division from their natural allies: the poor people of other races. So the sort of program I've already outlined is the logical sort of political initiative we need to undertake.

As the program reaches fruition, and the primary problems it is designed to address are diminished, then we will be in a position to really do something about these other issues. I mean, then we will be able to accept leadership from women as women in a truly meaningful way, to actually solve the matter of sexism. We will be able to accept real leadership from Native Americans, who know this land better than anyone, in solving our mutual ecological crisis. And so on, straight on down the line. I'm framing the matter more cleanly than it's going to work in practice. It's not that we wait to address things like sexism and the environment until "after the revolution." Addressing these problems must be an integral part of the whole process all along. But it's a matter of priorities, of assigning emphasis to our scarce political resources, to putting first things first in order to get the job done.

Debo: So, after all these years of repression, you've never abandoned your political principles.

Dhoruba: Ah, to the contrary, my friend! To the contrary! The repression has only reinforced my knowledge of the correctness of my analysis, my positions. My experience has strengthened my belief in my principles, strengthened my resolve to see the struggle through to its finish. And that is true of so many of the brothers and sisters who are now POWs and political prisoners. You see, our existence proves something very important. This is that while we may suffer greatly under repression, we have demonstrated that we're able to take the best shots the state has to offer. And we're still here. We're still here, and now we've learned their tricks. Now we know how COINTELPRO works, how the prison system is used and all the rest. Before, we were to a certain extent naive about such things. This is no longer the case. Now, we are prepared to win.

M. Annette Jaimes

Self-Portrait of a Black Liberationist—
An Appraisal of Assata Shakur's Autobiography

> Assata's story is my story. Assata's story is the story of oppressed
> black Afrikans here in North America. Assata's story is the story
> of progressive New Afrikans here in North America struggling
> to break the chains of U.S. fascism. Assata's story is continuous
> because our oppression is continuous. *Assata: An Autobiography*
> (Lawrence Hill Publishers, 1987) should be read by all oppressed
> Afrikans here in North America.
> —Ojore N. Lutalo, February 1988

Obviously, this is an important book. On its face, it deserves to be
read as a major political statement by a woman who stands as perhaps
the crucial female figure of her generation in the North American black
liberation struggle. Yet it will undoubtedly surprise readers who come
to it in anticipation of the sort of stilted prose of Bobby Seale's *Seize
the Time* or the icy polemics marking Huey P. Newton's *To Die for the
People* and *Revolutionary Suicide*, to choose prominent examples from
the genre.[1] More, it avoids the natural but regrettable undercurrent
of ruthlessness evident in Jimmy Carr's *Bad*, Eldridge Cleaver's *Soul
on Ice* and *Post-Prison Writings and Speeches*, or George Jackson's *Blood
In My Eye*.[2] In the main, Assata Shakur's recounting of her life, and
her assignment of meaning to it, offers much more than is to be found
in most volumes with which it shares a common heritage.

Assata is a political chronicle, to be sure, reflecting as it does its
author's odyssey through the black revolution of the second half of the
1960s, and on into the early '70s. It articulates the temper and setting
of those times quite lucidly, explaining in terms of pride, self-concept
and dignity the writer's discarding of her given ("slave") name, Joanne
Chesimard, in favor of the Afrikan sobriquet by which she is more
generally known. Also described are her early interactions with cultural
nationalism, subsequent joining of the revolutionary nationalist Black
Panther Party (BPP) in New York, and the forces which caused the
evolution of the BPP organization in that city into one of the strongest
and most effective sections of the Black Liberation Army (BLA) by 1971.

Shakur is candid—without going so far as to compromise those with whom she worked—about the nature of her clandestine existence in the BLA, the sorts of operations in which the organization engaged, and the extent to which she herself was involved in given actions and leadership of the group. In the latter connection, she softly ridicules the media campaign which projected her as "Mother of the BLA."

She spends sufficient time on the famous May 2, 1973 firefight on the New Jersey Turnpike in which she was badly wounded and captured, along with Sundiata Acoli (s/n: Clark Squire)—and in which BLA leader Zayd Malik Shakur (s/n: James Costan; Assata's brother in law) as well as state trooper Werner Forster were killed—to confirm what was already known: the police stopped the car in which the BLA members were riding for no other reason than to engage in the sort of random harassment of blacks for which they are deservedly notorious. Realizing that this time they had bitten off more than they expected, Forster and another officer, James Harper (who was himself seriously wounded in the resulting exchange of shots), opened fire. Assata Shakur was hit immediately, receiving a wound which completely incapacitated her. She was nonetheless charged with murder in the first degree. It is with regard to this event that the author extends the sole apology of her book: for she and her colleagues having been so "sloppy" as to allow themselves to be trapped in the open along a highway on which they knew there was an active possibility something of the sort might happen. Her own political activities are, as one consequence of this "lack of professionalism," constrained by exile; Sundiata Acoli remains in prison to this day; Zayd Shakur, of course, is dead. It is clear that she considers the whole thing to have been an inexcusable waste of resources valuable to the black liberation movement.

Far more space is expended in delineating the series of trials, mostly for alleged participation in New York bank robberies, to which she was subjected after her arrest and recovery from her wounds. With considerable precision, she points out the flimsiness of the state's various cases against her and the ways in which assorted prosecutors attempted to make the sheer fact of her BLA affiliation rather than any concrete evidence of criminal activity sufficient basis to establish her "guilt" in that of which she was accused. In the end, she calmly dismisses the record of the state's having failed to gain a conviction in any of the bank robbery cases as being in any way indicative that "the system worked" in her behalf, observing instead that all through the years the trials were going on she was being held without bond and under extreme security conditions in a collection of jail cells, usually in men's facilities, often underground, without anything resembling proper light, ventilation or heat, her mail and visitation prerogatives were effectively negated.

The punishment inflicted upon her was systematic, both physically and psychologically. All this occurred without the hint of a conviction. Her argument that even her most fundamental human rights were deliberately and consistently violated by the state in this process is both plainly posed and compelling.

Turning next to her murder trial, Shakur explains how she was convicted by an all-white jury on March 25, 1977, despite testimony by medical experts that the nature of her injuries had made it physically impossible for her to have delivered the fatal wound to Forster. Sentenced to life, she was bounced around several New Jersey facilities before being sent to a federal prison for women in West Virginia. When the federal institution was closed, she was returned to New Jersey and lodged in the maximum security building of the Clinton Prison for Women. It was from there that members of the Revolutionary Armed Task Force, an offshoot of the BLA, managed to free her on the night of November 2, 1979. Arriving in Cuba not long thereafter, she has spent the ensuing years attending the university in Havana, working in education and penning her memoirs as a long-term project. Within the United States, the very fact of her freedom has, because of the way in which it was obtained, come to symbolize a significant victory and cause for hope among those who stand in opposition to the status quo.

This constitutes the book's political dimension. Not only is it a highly readable chronicle of events, but a firm reassertion of the principles which have made Assata Shakur who she is. There is harshness in this, however. It is as if the author wishes not to expend the time and energy of belaboring the obvious, choosing instead to simply define circumstances and situations as she has experienced them, allowing readers to determine the character of a state which would conduct itself as she describes. Rather than devoting herself to rage, Shakur expends her emotions in expressing an open tenderness toward those who were formative in her life—here an aunt, there her grandmother, elsewhere friends and cousins—and to those who later shared her struggle. Such concentration upon childhood and family, in both the literal and extended senses, is perhaps closest to *The Autobiography of Malcolm X* in its ability to render the writer comprehensible to a broad range of readers.

She emerges as a remarkably whole individual, warm and utterly human, who embarked upon her revolutionary trajectory not on the basis of hatred or dogma, but through compassion for the suffering of those around her and because the system she confronted allowed her no practical alternative in pursuing positive social change. Ultimately, it is squarely within this element of vulnerable but essential humanity that *Assata* provides the most profound insights, both into the motivations of its author and into the nature of the revolutionary dynamic itself. In sum, this is far and away the best book of its type to come along since the publication of George Jackson's *Prison Letters*. It should stand as an inspiration to all of us.

Notes

1. Bobby Seale, *Seize the Time: The True Story of the Black Panther Party and Huey P. Newton* (New York: Vintage Books, 1970); Huey P. Newton, *To Die for the People* (New York: Vintage Books, 1972) and *Revolutionary Suicide* (New York: Harcourt Brace Jovanovich, 1973).

2. Jimmy Carr, *Bad: The Autobiography of Jimmy Carr* (New York: Herman Graf Associates, 1975); Eldridge Cleaver, *Soul on Ice* (New York: Delta Books, 1968) and *Post-Prison Writings and Speeches* (New York: Ramparts/Vintage Books, 1969); George Jackson, *Blood In My Eye* (New York: Random House, 1972).

Jim Vander Wall

A Warrior Caged—
The Continuing Struggle of Leonard Peltier

> how many have come before?
> and I wonder how many more
> must be lost to the Indian wars. . . .
> —Jim Page,
> *Leonard Peltier*

Leonard Peltier is a prisoner of war, one of the many victims of a covert war waged by the United States government against the American Indian Movement (AIM) and its supporters. This operation, conducted by America's secret political police—the Federal Bureau of Investigation (FBI)—during the mid-1970s, left scores of activists dead, hundreds injured, and many of the survivors imprisoned. Peltier, an AIM activist, is now serving two consecutive life sentences in Leavenworth federal prison, allegedly for the murder of two FBI agents. The two were killed in a June 26, 1975 firefight on the Pine Ridge Sioux Reservation in the state of South Dakota. Both the charges on which he had been incarcerated and the evidence on which his conviction was obtained are complete fabrications of the FBI.

Peltier, an Anishinabé-Lakota, was born in 1944 in North Dakota and grew up on the Turtle Mountain Reservation there. In 1958, during a period when the U.S. was attempting to "terminate" reservations and relocate Indians to urban ghettos, he joined his relatives in the Pacific Northwest, living in Seattle and Portland. Peltier first became involved with AIM-style politics when he participated in the 1970 occupation of Ft. Lawton, an abandoned military base which was legally Indian land. It was at Ft. Lawton that Peltier first became acquainted with AIM organizers.[1]

After the occupation ended, Peltier became increasingly involved in AIM activities. In 1972, he was a Milwaukee organizer for the Trail of Broken Treaties, a march from reservations across the country to the U.S. government's Bureau of Indian Affairs (BIA) Building in

Washington, D.C. intended to focus public attention on the oppression of Indian people. When the caravan reached Washington on November 3, Peltier was one of those chosen to direct security. While Trail leaders were attempting to negotiate with BIA officials on a twenty-point program of reforms, supporters waiting in the lobby of the BIA Building were attacked by club-wielding police. The police were overpowered and thrown out. What started as an attempt to evict the Indians turned into an occupation as the doors were barricaded to prevent the police from re-entering and BIA employees left via the windows. Indians held the building until November 9, when the government agreed to an amnesty for the occupiers and to respond to the twenty points. The occupiers returned to their homes taking with them, in some cases, BIA records documenting its program of systematic expropriation of Indian lands and resources.[2]

It was apparently following The Trail of Broken Treaties that Leonard Peltier was targeted for "neutralization" by the FBI. On November 22, 1972 Peltier was attacked in a Milwaukee diner by two off-duty policemen. He was beaten severely and then charged with attempted murder of one of the policemen. Peltier spent five months in jail before he could make bail, and went underground soon after he was released. He was eventually tried and acquitted on the charges. During the trial one of the policemen's former girl friends testified that around the time of the incident he had shown her a picture of Peltier and boasted of "catching a big one for the FBI."[3]

A Reign of Terror on Pine Ridge

In 1972, as the Trail of Broken Treaties marched on Washington, Richard "Dick" Wilson was elected as Pine Ridge's Tribal President, becoming head of a colonial regime created by the U.S. to administer the reservation for the benefit of non-Indian ranchers and corporations. Pine Ridge was the scene of a growing activism on the part of traditional Oglalas (i.e., those who attempt to follow the spiritual and cultural ways of their ancestors) to regain control of the lands and resources—much of it thought to be resource rich by federal authorities—guaranteed them by the 1868 Fort Laramie Treaty. It was Dick Wilson's primary objective to suppress this movement. To this he created a private army, called the GOONs (Guardians of the Oglala Nation), equipped and funded by the U.S. government. As the GOONs began a campaign of terrorism directed against traditionals and activists returning home from the Trail of Broken Treaties, the FBI—responsible for the investigation of serious crimes on Indian reservations—consistently ignored complaints of civil rights violations, harassment of activists and assaults. The FBI's inaction, in light of the increasingly serious nature of the charges, gave rise to the suspicion that the GOONs were acting with the collusion, if not the direction, of federal authorities. Complaints filed with the Bureau of Indian Affairs (BIA) police bore even less fruit. This was hardly surprising, since there was considerable overlap in personnel between the GOONs and the BIA police who, in any case, acted under Wilson's direction.[4]

In February 1973, traditional Oglalas asked the American Indian Movement for assistance in dealing with GOON violence. On the 28th of the month, following a meeting near Pine Ridge village, a caravan of several hundred traditionals, AIM members and supporters drove to Wounded Knee and occupied the tiny village as a symbolic gesture of protest. They awoke the next morning to find themselves surrounded by scores of heavily armed FBI agents, U.S. marshals, GOONs and vigilantes. The occupiers issued a statement demanding hearings on treaties and an investigation of the BIA and gave the government the choice of negotiating their demands or removing them by force. The besiegers soon reinforced their positions with additional personnel and weaponry. Thus began the 71-day siege of Wounded Knee which focused world attention on the Pine Ridge Reservation.

U.S. military "advisors" were directly and illegally involved in the siege, almost from its inception, and military weaponry poured onto the reservation. Tank-like vehicles called armored personnel carriers, Bell "Huey" helicopters, .50 calibre heavy machineguns, M-79 grenade launchers and M-16 assault rifles were brought to bear on the occupiers. The hundreds of thousands of rounds of ammunition fired into the hamlet claimed the lives of two warriors—Frank Clearwater and Buddy Lamont—and wounded dozens more. A number of supporters who were backpacking supplies into the village at night through the federal siege lines simply disappeared. It is generally believed that they were murdered by GOON patrols and were buried somewhere on the reservation. The siege ended in May of 1973 with an agreement by the U.S. government to negotiate on treaty issues.[5]

The siege led to the arrest of 562 people of whom 185 were indicted for the most part on charges which were completely groundless and eventually dismissed. Only 15 people were ever convicted on charges stemming from Wounded Knee, most on minor offenses such as interfering with a federal officer or on "collateral" charges such as "contempt" resulting from the trials themselves.[6] The judicial proceedings in the cases which went to trial were riddled with government misconduct. The "Wounded Knee Leadership Trial" of Russell Means and Dennis Banks is a classic example of such use of the courts to pursue political ends. Charges in this case were dismissed by Judge Fred Nichol after the government was found to have knowingly presented false evidence, infiltrated the defense team with an FBI informant and lied to the judge about both of these issues. In dismissing the case, an angry Judge Nichol wrote:

> I am forced to conclude that the prosecution acted in bad faith at various times throughout the trial and was seeking convictions at the expense of justice. . . . The fact that incidents of misconduct formed a pattern throughout the course of the trial leads me to the belief that this case was not prosecuted in good faith or in the spirit of justice. The waters of justice have been polluted, and dismissal, I believe, is the appropriate cure for the pollution.[7]

Nichol later stated that he believed "that the FBI were determined to get the AIM movement and completely destroy it." A similar pattern of misconduct would emerge in the trials of many AIM activists over the next four years, but, unfortunately, few federal judges had the integrity of Judge Nichol.[8]

While Wounded Knee cases dragged on in the courts, violence escalated on Pine Ridge. In the two years following the beginning of the occupation, more than sixty AIM members and supporters died at the hands of the GOONs and hundreds were victims of assaults and harassment. Dick Wilson was returned to office in 1974 in an election described by the U.S. Commission on Civil Rights as being "permeated with fraud."[9] Government inaction on Wilson's abuses was taken by Wilson as license to physically destroy AIM. In the first five months of 1975, the Commission on Civil Rights recorded eighteen homicides on Pine Ridge and the situation had become so tense that few dared to leave their homes without carrying guns. The rate of political murders on the reservation for the period 1972-1976 was 170 per 100,000, almost exactly the rate for Chile in the three years following the U.S.-supported coup of Augusto Pinochet.[10]

Throughout this entire period the FBI failed to obtain a single conviction for the murder of an AIM activist and complaints of assault and harassment went uninvestigated. Confronted with this singular absence of success in carrying out their legally mandated mission, the FBI asserted that "lack of manpower" prevented them from investigating complaints. Yet a brief look at FBI force levels during the same period shows that, between mid-1972 and mid-1973, the personnel assigned to the Rapid City resident agency—whose attention at that time focused almost exclusively on Pine Ridge—increased from three to eleven. In 1973 a ten-member Special Weapons and Tactics (SWAT) team was assigned to the village of Pine Ridge, giving the reservation the highest ratio of agents to citizens of any area of the U.S.[11] Clearly, it was not a lack of manpower which impaired investigation of crimes against AIM members and supporters, but a conscious policy of selective prosecution. While the FBI compiled massive files on AIM members and jailed them for even minor offenses, the most serious crimes committed by the GOONs—murder, rapes, and felony assaults—were not so much as investigated. In effect, open season was declared on AIM and its supporters.

During 1973 and 1974, Peltier and the Northwest AIM group to which he belonged had become increasingly involved in providing security support for local people from an AIM encampment on the land of the Jumping Bull family near the Pine Ridge village of Oglala. They came at the request of local organizers and traditional elders to protect the community from GOON attacks which had been particularly intense in the Oglala area, regarded as a bastion of traditionalism. During the late spring GOON activity decreased around Oglala due to the AIM presence. The camp became a center of spiritual activities, attracting local youth who were preparing for the sun dance.[12] During the same period, however, there were increasingly numerous indications of FBI interest in the AIM camp. During the first week of June, an FBI memo noted "there are pockets of Indian population which consist almost exclusively of American Indian Movement . . . members and their supporters on the Reservation."[13] The memo went on to state, falsely, that fortified enclaves had been built which would require armored vehicles to successfully assault. No such fortifications actually existed, but such disinformation had the effect of "psyching-up" agents for an armed confrontation with AIM.

The Oglala Firefight

On June 25, 1975, FBI Special Agents (SAs) Ronald Williams and Jack Coler entered the Jumping Bull Compound, ostensibly searching for a young Oglala, Jimmy Eagle, on the charges of "kidnapping, aggravated assault and aggravated robbery." The charges stemmed from a brawl involving Eagle and some other teenagers who had been drinking together. During the altercation, Eagle and his friends had taken a pair of cowboy boots from one of the other boys who later filed a complaint. The only warrant issued for Eagle, dated two weeks later, was for robbery. So, with dozens of murders of AIM members and supporters uninvestigated due to "lack of manpower," two FBI agents were assigned to look for a teenager, suspected, at most, of the theft of a pair of used cowboy boots. Later the same day, three youths from the AIM camp were detained and questioned by the FBI on suspicion of being Jimmy Eagle. Interestingly, they were questioned not about Eagle but about who was at the camp.[14]

By the next morning, June 26, it was clear that something ominous was in the offing. Oglala residents noted that large numbers of para-military troops—GOONs, BIA police, state troopers, U.S. marshals and FBI SWAT teams—were massing in the area. Around 11:30 a.m., two AIM members drove into the Jumping Bull Compound in a red pickup truck on their way to a meeting of the Northwest AIM group. They stopped at the Little residence (at the north end of the compound) to talk to Wallace "June" Little, Jr. Shortly thereafter, they observed two cars turn off Highway 18 and head towards them. The vehicles were driven by SAs Coler and Williams, who the FBI would later claim had come to "carry out an arrest under warrant" of Jimmy Eagle. As the cars approached, the AIM members got back into their pickup and headed south across a meadow toward the AIM camp. When SAs Coler and Williams followed them, they got out of the truck carrying their weapons. According to one of the truck's occupants, the agents stopped and got out of their vehicles, guns drawn, and one of the agents—believed to be Coler—fired on them with a rifle. The AIM members returned fire and, as the agents took cover behind their cars, got back in their pickup and drove east to the compound. The agents continued to fire on them as they went.[15]

Hearing gunfire from the direction of the compound, occupants of the AIM camp believed themselves to be under attack from GOONs or vigilantes. They ran toward the sound of the firing, weapons in hand, and, observing two white men in civilian clothes shooting at the houses, joined in the return fire. Almost immediately, federal reinforcements began to enter the Jumping Bull property. Radio transmissions from SA Williams indicate the agents expected just such rapid support. Unfortunately for them, one of the teenagers from the camp had managed to position himself to cover the approach to the compound, and shot out the tires of the first two cars to arrive, driven by SA J. Gary Adams and Fred Two Bulls, a BIA police officer and known GOON. Pinned down by gunfire, they were unable to help SAs Coler and Williams, who were subsequently seriously wounded.[16]

When it became clear they were surrounded by a large number of heavily armed police, Northwest AIM members Bob Robideau, Darelle "Dino" Butler and Leonard Peltier decided to take the wounded agents hostage as a bargaining chip with the besieging forces. To this purpose, they circled around to the west, in the trees along White Clay Creek, and approached the agents from behind. When they were about fifty yards from the agents' cars, they observed the red pickup approach the cars and stop. They heard heard several shots from the vicinity of the agents, after which the red pickup drove off. When Robideau, Butler and Peltier reached the agents, they found both of them were dead. In the cars, they found equipment marked "FBI DENVER." It was not until that point that the Northwest AIM members knew their attackers were FBI.[17]

It was later revealed that the two AIM members in the red pickup had approached Coler and Williams, also hoping to capture them. The driver stopped the truck near the agents and his companion got out with an AR-15 rifle and approached them. According to this man, SA Williams raised his revolver and fired at him, missing at very close range. The AIM member then opened fire, killing both agents. He then got back into the pickup, and was driven off the Jumping Bull property, past Adams and Two Bulls, who were still pinned down by rifle fire.[18] FBI radio logs indicate the pickup left the area at 12:18 p.m.[19]

By early afternoon, police forces involved in the firefight had increased to nearly 200. They faced a group of eight or so adults and teenagers from the AIM camp.[20] By 4:30 p.m. the FBI, further reinforced by SWAT teams flown in from Minneapolis and Chicago, decided they had sufficient personnel to assault the compound. At this time, Edgar Bear Runner, a local AIM supporter, was sent into the compound to try and negotiate a surrender. When Bear Runner returned and reported that agents Coler and Williams were dead and that the defenders had disappeared, the FBI began their assault, gassing Jumping Bull's houses and shooting everything in sight.[21]

Also killed in the firefight was AIM member Joe Stuntz Killsright, who, according to official reports, died from a bullet, fired at long range by an FBI sniper, which struck him in the forehead. Conflicting reports of the nature of Killsright's wounds have given rise to the suspicion that he may have been wounded during the firefight and then executed by the FBI. In contrast to the intensive investigation which followed the deaths of SAs Coler and Williams, the death of Joe Stuntz Killsright was never investigated.[22]

The Invasion of Pine Ridge

Although the deaths of Agents Coler and Williams were probably an unintended consequence, the provocation of the firefight achieved its intended objective: the justification of a massive paramilitary assault on AIM. By the following day, there were more than 180 FBI agents on Pine Ridge, headed by one of the Bureau's foremost experts in political repression, Richard G. Held.[23] Held brought with him a number of other specialists and technicians in such matters, including his son, Richard W. Held, who had recently coordinated the Bureau's lethal counterintelligence operations against the Black Panther Party in Los Angeles,

SA Thomas Greene, leader of the Chicago SWAT team and specialist in "anti-terrorist" operations, and Norman Zigrossi, assigned to take operational control of the Rapid City FBI office.[24]

Along with U.S. marshals, BIA police and GOONs, FBI personnel carried out military-style sweeps for the next three months, both on Pine Ridge and the adjacent Rosebud Reservation, which were clearly designed to terrorize AIM members and supporters. Assault teams were equipped with the full panoply of counter-insurgency weaponry—M-16 assault rifles, M-79 grenade launchers, Bell UH-1B "Huey" helicopters, armored personnel carriers, fixed-wing aircraft and tracking dogs. With the excuse of searching for participants in the firefight, they broke into homes, conducted warrantless searches and illegal seizures, destroyed private property, harassed and threatened residents and arrested people on illegal "John Doe" warrants. A report of the U.S. Commission of Civil Rights noted "numerous reports and complaints of threats, harassment, and search procedures conducted without due process of law." The chairman of the Civil Rights Commission, Arthur J. Flemming, characterized the operation as "an over-reaction which takes on aspects of a vendetta . . . a full-scale military type invasion." He went on to say:

> [The presence of such a massive force] has created a deep resentment on the part of many reservation residents who feel that such a procedure would not be tolerated in any non-Indian community in the United States. They point out that little has been done to solve numerous murders on the reservation but when two white men are killed, "troops" are brought in from all over the country at a cost of hundreds of millions of dollars.[25]

The Bureau's sweeping operations resulted in the death of at least one Oglala, an elderly man named James Brings Yellow, who was frightened into a fatal heart attack when a team of raiders headed by SA J. Gary Adams sneaked up to his home and abruptly kicked in his door.[26] Such tactics were also coupled to another method of intimidation, an open-ended "grand jury probe" of AIM, used as a means to jail selected organizational members and supporters—arbitrarily and for indefinite periods—who expressed the "contempt" of failing to cooperate with the Bureau's agenda. One victim of this process, Joanna LeDeaux, pregnant at the time of her incarceration, spent eight months behind bars without being charged with any crime. Her child, of course, was resultantly borne in prison.[27] Another, Angie Long Visitor, was sent to lock-up for "refusing to respond to questions" an extended period while her husband was driven into hiding in order to avoid the same fate. The situation left their several small children effectively parentless for an extended period. In the end, it became plain that neither Long Visitor nor LeDeaux had known anything which might have been of value to the FBI.[28]

252 • Jim Vander Wall

To assure public acquiescence to such massive violations of constitutional rights, the FBI conducted an extensive disinformation
campaign. Banner headlines across the U.S. proclaimed the FBI's story
of how the helpless agents, carrying out their lawfully appointed duties,
had been "ambushed" at "Wounded Knee" by AIM "guerillas" from
sophisticated "bunkers." Newspapers which had shown no interest whatsoever in the systematic murder of dozens of AIM members on Pine Ridge,
now printed detailed descriptions of how the agents were executed while
pleading for their lives, their bodies riddled with machinegun bullets.
At least one publication announced the agents had been scalped.
Retractions of these claims a few days later by FBI Director Clarence
Kelley were run on the back pages. The technique was so effective that
even the "liberal media" denounced the victims, rather than the
perpetrators, of this large-scale terrorist operation.[29]

The Arrests, Cedar Rapids Trial, and Extradition of Leonard Peltier

From an original list of some thirty known or suspected participants
in the firefight, the FBI targeted four for prosecution as the slayers of
SAs Coler and Williams. One of these, Jimmy Eagle, was apparently
included simply to justify the presence of the agents on the Jumping
Bull property. There was no demonstrable connection between Eagle
and the agents' deaths and eventually the charges against him were
simply dropped. Not surprisingly, the other three indictments—on two
counts of first-degree murder and "aiding and abetting"—were against
what the FBI had decided was the leadership of the Northwest AIM
Group: Robideau, Butler and Peltier.[30] Butler was arrested in a
September 5 pre-dawn air assault on "Crow Dog's Paradise," the home
of Brûlé spiritual leader Leonard Crow Dog. More than 100 heavily-
armed FBI SWAT personnel descended on the medicine man's home
in Huey helicopters, ostensibly to "investigate a fist fight" between
teenagers. Robideau was arrested in Wichita, Kansas on September 10
when his car caught fire and exploded on the Kansas Turnpike. Peltier,
in the meantime, had fled to Canada. He was arrested on February 6,
1976 by the Royal Canadian Mounted Police at the camp of traditional
Cree chief Robert Smallboy near Hinton, Alberta.[31]

Butler and Robideau were tried in Cedar Rapids, Iowa on June 1976
before Judge Edward McManus. McManus was certainly no friend of
AIM, having earned the nickname "Speedie Eddie" for convicting and
sentencing three AIM members on Wounded Knee charges in one week.
Nevertheless, he allowed the defendants to argue that they had acted
in self-defense in the shootout. Although the prosecution resorted to

use of doctored testimony, defense witnesses established that the atmosphere of terror which existed on the reservation contributed directly to the firefight, a situation for which the FBI was, at least in part, responsible.[32] Presented with a picture of wholesale violence on Pine Ridge and FBI duplicity, the jury acquitted the defendants concluding:

> that an atmosphere of fear and violence exists on the reservation, and that the defendants arguably could have been shooting in self-defense. While it was shown that the defendants were firing guns in the direction of the agents, it was held that this was not excessive in the heat of passion.[33]

Jury foreman Robert Bolen that later observed that, placed in context, much of the government's case had simply not been believable to him and his colleagues.[34] Faced with this bitter defeat, the FBI and federal prosecutors now vowed to convict the remaining AIM defendant, Leonard Peltier, by any means, legal or otherwise. Charges against Eagle were dropped "so that the full prosecutive weight of the Government [could] be directed against Leonard Peltier."[35] Showing as little regard for the sovereignty of Canada as for that of indigenous nations, the U.S. violated the extradition treaty between the two countries by fraudulently extraditing Peltier. At the extradition proceedings the U.S. presented an affidavit signed by a woman named Myrtle Poor Bear—one of three mutually contradictory accounts of the matter signed by her—which falsely stated she had personally seen Peltier murder agents Coler and Williams. Based upon this fraud, Canada ordered Peltier to be extradited and he was returned to the U.S. on December 16, 1976.[36]

Poor Bear, it is worth noting, had a long history of treatment for psychological disorder. Her statements concerning Peltier's "guilt" were obtained by SAs David Price and William Wood during a period when they had essentially kidnapped her and were holding her incommunicado at the Hacienda Motel, in Gordon, Nebraska. She was apparently threatened with death unless she "cooperated " with the FBI by signing a series of documents, prepared by the agents, incriminating Peltier. Tellingly, the first two Poor Bear affidavits—the existence of which were concealed from the Canadian court during extradition proceedings—contend that Poor Bear was not an eyewitness to the deaths of Coler and Williams. Instead, they state that Poor Bear was Peltier's "girl friend" and that he confessed he was "a murderer" to her in a bar.[37] This was precisely the content of the testimony—that she was the girl friend of the accused, and that he'd confessed his guilt to her in a bar—Poor Bear was simultaneously presenting evidence against a completely different AIM member, Richard Marshall, in an unrelated murder case. This testimony was, according to the jury, a primary factor in Marshall's subsequent conviction and life sentence.[38] Poor Bear later recanted, admitting under oath that she'd never so much as met either Peltier or Marshall, and stating that the only reason she'd entered false evidence against the two men was that she'd been terrified as to what SAs Price and Wood might do to her if she failed to do and say exactly what they told her to.[39]

While the Peltier extradition was in progress in Canada, the FBI was making a careful analysis of what went wrong in the Cedar Rapids trial, the results of which were outlined in a memorandum of July 20, 1976. It noted that: 1) ". . . the defense was allowed freedom of questioning witnesses"; 2) the court allowed testimony concerning the FBI's illegal counterintelligence operations against other dissidents; 3) the government was forced to turn over agents' reports concerning the incident and the defense was allowed to cross-examine agents on discrepancies between their testimony and written reports; 4) the defense was allowed to present evidence that the ". . . FBI had created a climate of fear on the reservation which precipitated the murders"; 5) the defense was uncontrolled in its dealings with the media; 6) the jury was not sequestered; 7) the jury was "confused" by "irrelevant" information presented by the defense, i.e., testimony concerning massive FBI misconduct on Pine Ridge.[40]

The Trial of Leonard Peltier

Their analysis completed, the FBI then went shopping for a judge who was likely to be more cooperative with the prosecution than Judge McManus. They found one in Judge Paul Benson, a Nixon appointee. Peltier's trial began on March 21, 1977 in Fargo, North Dakota. It can hardly be a coincidence that Benson ruled: 1) since Peltier would be tried as the principal—i.e., the person responsible for shooting the agents at close range—the self-defense argument would not be allowed; 2) as a consequence, the defense's ability to question witnesses would be restricted: evidence concerning the atmosphere of terror on Pine Ridge and the FBI's role in creating it was irrelevant and 3) no testimony concerning the FBI's other similar illegal operations would be permitted; 4) defense attorneys would not be allowed to question agents on discrepancies between their written reports and their testimony; 5) there would be a media blackout on the trial; 6) the jury would be sequestered; 7) when the defense attempted to call Myrtle Poor Bear as a witness to describe how she had been coerced by the FBI into signing false affidavits implicating Peltier, Judge Benson would not allow it. He ruled that "to allow her testimony to go to the jury would be confusing the issues, may misled the jury, and could be highly prejudicial." These rulings sealed Leonard Peltier's legal fate before the trial even began. Prevented from presenting a reasonable defense, his conviction was inevitable and successful appeal rendered unlikely.[41]

In the end, the government's case rested on a weak chain of circumstantial evidence:

> • The prosecutor's claim that the slain agents had reported they were following a red and white van, not a red pickup, when the firefight began. Peltier was known to drive a red and white van, a matter which appeared to "place" him in the midst of the shooting from the moment the first round was fired.[42]

> • Mutually contradictory coroner's reports on the autopsies of the slain agents were presented. These indicated only that both men had been hit by bullets fired at close range from a small-caliber, high-velocity weapon of an unspecified type. No slugs were recovered, either from the dead agents' bodies or from the ground beneath them.[43]

> • A spent .223 (5.56 mm) caliber cartridge casing—a small caliber, high velocity bullet—was allegedly recovered from the trunk of SA Coler's automobile. Its pedigree, however, was greatly suspect, since conflicting FBI documents and testimony indicated that it was found by two different agents on two different days. Further, the Bureau could not verify to whom this "most critical piece of evidence" had been given, or how it arrived at the FBI Crime Lab in Washington, D.C., regardless of who supposedly found it.[44]

> • A Colt AR-15 rifle—which fires a .223 caliber round—was recovered from Bob Robideau's exploded car near Wichita, and linked by the prosecution, in an extremely questionable manner, to the firefight.[45]

> • The cartridge was then linked to the Wichita AR-15 by FBI Firearms and Toolmarks expert Evan Hodge. Hodge testified that based on extractor markings, the .223 caliber cartridge casing had been loaded into and extracted from the Wichita AR-15. He said that a more definitive firing-pin test had been performed but that it was "inconclusive." Since an AR-15 cannot eject cartridges more than about five meters, it was inferred that the cartridge had been fired near the agents' cars, i.e., near where the agents' bodies had been found.[46]

> • Hodge also testified that ballistics evidence revealed that only one AR-15 had been used by AIM during the firefight. *Ipso facto*, whoever could be shown to have carried an AR-15 rifle on the fatal day would appear as "the murderer."[47]

> • All that was left was to have eyewitnesses testify that Peltier was seen carrying an AR-15 rifle on the day of the firefight. This eyewitness testimony was suspect, to say the least. For example, one of the witnesses, FBI agent Fred Coward, testified that he identified Peltier (whom he had never seen before) through a 2x7 power rifle scope at a distance of more that 800 meters, and while Peltier was allegedly running away at an angle oblique to the observer (making identification in profile necessary) and carrying an AR-15. Such an

256 · Jim Vander Wall

256 • Jim Vander Wall

identification was shown to be impossible under even ideal circumstances, never mind the conditions of severe atmospheric distortion known to have prevailed during the firefight. Other eyewitnesses later testified they had entered false testimony, having been threatened and coerced to do so by prosecutors and the FBI.[48]

The government then argued that the agents had been killed with an AR-15 fired at close range; that such a weapon linked to Peltier, had been fired close to the location of the agents' bodies; and since that weapon was the only AR-15 used in the firefight Leonard Peltier must have used it to slay SAs Coler and Williams. As prosecutor Lynn Crooks put it in his closing argument to the jury:

Apparently Special Agent Williams was killed first. He was struck in the face and hand by a bullet . . . probably begging for his life, and he was shot. The back of his head was blown off by a high powered rifle. . . . Leonard Peltier then turned, as the evidence indicates, to Jack Coler lying on the ground, helpless. He shoots him in the top of the head. Apparently feeling he hasn't done a good enough job, he shoots him again through the jaw, and his face explodes. No shell comes out, just explodes. The whole bottom of his chin is blown out by the force of the concussion. He dies. Blood splattered against the side of the car.[49]

There was little the defense could do to counter this argument, since Judge Benson would not allow agents to be cross-examined concerning discrepancies between their testimony and either their prior sworn statements or written communications. Based upon this flimsy chain of circumstantial evidence and Crooks' inflammatory closing statements, the all-white jury found Peltier guilty of two counts of first-degree murder on April 18, 1977. Peltier was sentenced by Judge Benson to serve two consecutive life terms. Despite the fact that he had no prior felony convictions, he was sent to the infamous "super-maximum security" prison at Marion, Illinois. This prison, ostensibly the final stop for the most dangerous criminals in the federal penal system, had been increasingly used to intern political prisoners under the most severe conditions.[50]

The Appeals

Somehow, I now think, in the back of my mind there was a lingering belief that, with fearless and bright lawyers, it would be possible to use the contradictions of the law to defeat them even in their own courts. . . . In my mind, in a recess, there must have lingered a phantom of a group of dispassionate appeals

judges—white United Statesers, to be sure, but nonetheless fair
and distant—cooly weighing the facts of the crystal clear law.
—Imari Obadele
RNA 11 Defendant

An appeal of Peltier's conviction based on documented FBI misconduct, such as the Myrtle Poor Bear fraud, was rejected by the U.S.
Eighth Circuit Court of Appeals. One of the members of the three-judge
panel, Judge Donald Ross, commented in reference to the Poor Bear
affidavits:

> But can't you see . . . that what happened happened in such a
> way that it gives some credence to the claim of the . . . Indian
> people that the United States is willing to resort to any tactic
> in order to bring somebody back to the United States from
> Canada. And if they are willing to do that, they must be willing
> to fabricate other evidence as well.[51]

The court, however, while expressing "discomfort" with its own
reasoning, opted to ignore evidence of FBI crimes and, citing the particular importance of the ballistics evidence, upheld Peltier's conviction.
At about the same time, the Eighth Circuit Court's Chief Judge, William
Webster—who had headed the Peltier appeal panel through most of its
deliberations—left the bench to assume a new position as *Director of
the FBI*. An appeal was filed with the U.S. Supreme Court which, on
February 11, 1979, refused without comment to hear the case.

In 1981, as a result of a Freedom of Information Act (FOIA) suit,
12,000 pages of FBI documents pertaining to Leonard Peltier were
released to his appeal team. Another 6,000 pages were withheld on the
grounds of "national security."[52] The documents directly contradicted,
on several points, testimony given by FBI agents and other prosecution
witnesses during the Peltier trial. The most serious contradiction was
a Bureau teletype dated October 2, 1975, indicating that Evan Hodge
had performed a firing-pin test on the Wichita AR-15 immediately after
he received it and compared it to the cartridges found at the scene. Contrary to his trial testimony that the test was inconclusive, this memo
conclusively stated that the rifle contained *"a different firing-pin"* from
the weapon used in the firefight.[53] In other words, the memo called into
question the validity of what the prosecutor deemed—and the courts
agreed—was the most important piece of evidence in the case. Based
upon precedents that the withholding of exculpatory evidence by the
prosecution was grounds for a retrial, the appeal team filed a motion
for a new trial with Judge Paul Benson in April, 1982. Since the FOIA
documents also revealed what were arguably improper pretrial meetings
between the prosecution, the FBI and Judge Benson, the latter was asked
to remove himself from the case. Given his previous record in the Peltier

258 • Jim Vander Wall

case, few were surprised when Benson rejected both of these motions on December 30, 1982.

Upon dismissal of the motions, an appeal was again filed with the U.S. Eighth Circuit Court of Appeals. In April 1984, the appeals court reversed Judge Benson's decision. Citing the apparent contradiction implied by the October 2 teletype and the critical nature of the .223 cartridge casing to the government's case, the court ordered Judge Benson to hold an evidentiary hearing on the ballistics evidence. The hearing was held in Bismarck, North Dakota at the end of October, 1984. A very nervous Evan Hodge explained that the conflict between his testimony and the October 2, 1975 teletype arose from a misinterpretation. The teletype, he asserted, referred to comparison of the Wichita rifle to cartridge casings from *other* AR-15s found at the scene of the firefight, not to the .223 casing from SA Coler's trunk.[54]

When questioned as to why he had not tested that cartridge against the Wichita AR-15 immediately, Hodge claimed he was not aware of the urgent need to do so. This proved to be, as the Eighth Circuit Court was later to put it, "inconsistent with . . . several teletypes from FBI officials, agents requesting [Hodge] to compare submitted AR-15 rifle with .223 casing found at the scene, and [Hodge's] response to these teletypes."[55] Hodge also committed perjury by testifying that only he had handled the ballistics evidence, statements which proved to be false. When confronted with handwriting on the lab notes which was plainly not his own, he changed his testimony to admit that one lab assistant, Joseph Twardowski, had also been involved. Threatened with a handwriting analysis of the material, Hodge was forced to admit that he "misspoke" when he made even this "revised" assertion, and that the handwriting of at least one other person—the identity of whom Hodge professed not to know—appeared on the critical lab notes.[56]

Hodge's testimony created a host of problems for the government's case against Peltier. His claim that he failed to compare the Wichita AR-15 to the critical casing until late December or early January is literally incredible. Worse yet, if Hodge is to be believed, the FBI had numerous .223 caliber cartridges from the firefight scene fired by *AR-15s which have never been identified.* Either Hodge lied in his trial testimony that the .223 caliber cartridge had been matched to the Wichita AR-15 or the prosecutor lied when he asserted that only one AR-15 had been used in the firefight. Moreover, the fact that Hodge was willing to commit perjury to conceal the fact that persons other than himself and his assistant had possession of the critical evidence, cast doubt on the chain of custody of the .223 cartridge, and raised the possibility that the cartridge could have been inadvertently or deliberately switched in the lab. Faced with contradictions of this magnitude, the court deliberated for almost a year before holding oral arguments on October 15, 1985.

In a tacit admission that their circumstantial case based on the ballistics evidence was falling apart, the federal prosecutors now put forth the argument that Peltier had been convicted of aiding and abetting in the deaths of the agents, not of murdering them. "We can't prove who shot those agents,"[57] prosecutor Lynn Crooks admitted before the circuit court. When a confused judge asked Crooks if he meant that Peltier had been aiding and abetting Butler and Robideau (who had been determined by a jury to have acted in self-defense), the flustered prosecutor replied:

> Aiding and abetting whoever did the final shooting. Perhaps aiding and abetting himself. And hopefully the jury would believe that in effect he did it all. But aiding and abetting, nevertheless.[58]

The appeals court, after deliberating for nearly another year, finally handed down their decision on September 22, 1986. They rejected the government's argument that Peltier had been convicted of aiding and abetting, noting he had clearly been tried and committed to the jury as the principal. They also noted that the prosecution's assertion that a single AR-15 had been used in the firefight was untrue, citing evidence of several such weapons. Despite the contradictions exhibited by the prosecution's arguments, the court upheld Peltier's conviction. In defense of this dubious decision, the court argued:

> There are only two alternatives... to the government's contention that the .223 casing was ejected into the trunk of Coler's car when the Wichita AR-15 was fired at the agents. One alternative is that the .223 casing was planted in the trunk of Coler's car either before its discovery by the investigating agents or by the agents who reported its discovery. The other alternative is that a non-matching casing was originally found in the trunk and sent to the FBI laboratory, only to be replaced by a matching casing when the importance of a match to the Wichita AR-15 became evident. ... *We recognize that there is evidence in this record of improper conduct on the part of some FBI agents, but we are reluctant to impute even further improprieties to them* [emphasis added].[59]

It is clear, however, that it is not a matter of "improper conduct by some FBI agents," but of an illegal program of political repression coordinated at high levels within the Bureau. The probability of such a pattern of abuse resulting from the random actions of over-enthusiastic individual agents is vanishingly small. In a similar fashion, the court's other line of reasoning—that the suppressed evidence, had it been presented at trial, might "possibly" have led to Peltier's acquittal, while a distinct "probability" of this outcome was required before a retrial might be ordered—is thin to the point nonexistence. Indeed, the Ninth Circuit Court of Appeals had already established the precedent of ordering a conviction overturned because new evidence might possibly have altered the original verdict, and it did so on the basis of exactly the same 1985 Supreme Court opinion the Eighth Circuit claimed supported its denial of Peltier.[60]

The decision of the appeals court is the logical outcome of judicial collusion with the FBI's plan—enunciated in their July 20, 1976 report—to prevent Peltier from establishing the political context of the firefight. Looked at in the narrow context prescribed by Judge Benson's rulings, it is possible to conclude that the new evidence would not have changed the jury's verdict. Viewed in the context of FBI counter-insurgency operations on Pine Ridge, it is not only probable, but—as the Cedar Rapids trial demonstrated—certain that the outcome of the trial would have been different. The Eighth Circuit Court rejected motions by the defense team for an *en banc* rehearing of the case. Leonard Peltier's "legal remedies" were exhausted on October 5, 1987 when the U.S. Supreme Court again refused without comment to hear the case.[61]

On December 3, 1990, Peltier began a new round of legal battles with the filing of a writ of *habeas corpus* in the U.S. Court for the Eastern District of Kansas.[62] The writ asserts that Peltier's constitutional right to be informed of the charges on which he was tried and to defend himself on these charges were violated by the government. While the prosecution maintained at trial that Peltier was the "principal" in the killing of SAs Coler and Williams—i.e., that he had actually fired the fatal shots at close range—they have since admitted they cannot prove this. The government now claims that Peltier was not tried as the principal but as an "aider and abettor," charges he was never given the opportunity to defend himself against.

The prosecution claims this is an irrelevant distinction since the burden of proof is less stringent for aiding and abetting and the penalties are similar. However, the nature of the allowable arguments and evidence presented by the defense are different for aiding and abetting than for murder *per se*. It was the fact that Peltier was tried as the principal which permitted Judge Benson's disallowal of the self-defense argument and the exclusion of evidence of FBI misconduct contributing to the firefight—evidence which led to the acquittal of his codefendants at Cedar Rapids—to go unchallenged. The *habeas* writ further claims that Peltier's constitutional right to a fair and impartial trial was violated by the atmosphere of intimidation created by the government's unwarranted "security arrangements" which pervaded the trial proceedings and other "enormous and continuing" federal misconduct.

The writ was remanded to the U.S. Court for the District of North Dakota (and Judge Benson) for consideration. As Benson was to be called as a witness on the issue of intimidation, the writ was reviewed by Federal Magistrate Karen Klein. She excluded the issues of intimidation and government misconduct by retroactively applying a recent egregious Supreme Court decision, *McClesky v. Zant,* which prevents a petitioner from raising an issue in a *habeas* writ which could theoretically have been raised in an earlier writ.

On April 18, 1991, in an extraordinary action for a federal judge, Gerald Heaney—senior judge of the Eighth Circuit panel which heard Peltier's appeal—wrote a letter to Senator Daniel Inouye supporting his efforts to obtain executive clemency for Leonard Peltier. While continuing to defend the court's decision to reject Peltier's 1986 appeal, Heaney cites a number of "mitigating circumstances" which must be considered when reviewing the case. These include: 1) "the United States government over-reacted at Wounded Knee. Instead of carefully considering legitimate grievances of the Native Americans, the response was essentially a military one which culminated in a deadly firefight on June 26, 1975 between the Native Americans and FBI agents." 2) "the United States government must share in the responsibility for the June 26 firefight," because of their role in "escalating the conflict." 3) "more than one person was involved in shooting the FBI agents." 4) "the FBI used improper tactics in securing Peltier's extradition from Canada and in otherwise investigating and trying the *Peltier* case."[63] Judge Heaney had previously expressed his "discomfort" with the court's decision because, "It appeared . . . that the FBI was equally to blame for the shootout and that the entire responsibility can't be placed on Peltier."[64]

Conclusion

Today, the case of Leonard Peltier serves as a symbol—in both a positive and a negative sense—to indigenous people everywhere who are struggling against illegal expropriation of their lands and destruction of their cultures. Peltier's uncompromising resistance fueled the growth of an international movement which had focused attention not only on his case, but on broader issues of indigenous land rights and political imprisonment in the United States. Literally millions of individuals worldwide have written letters and signed petitions demanding a new trial for Leonard Peltier. They have been joined by fifty members of the U.S. House of Representatives, fifty-one members of the Canadian Parliament (including the Solicitor General at the time of Peltier's extra-

dition), the Archbishop of Canterbury, Nobel Peace Prize winner Bishop
Desmond Tutu, and many other political and religious leaders. In 1986,
Peltier was awarded the International Human Rights Prize by the
Human Rights Commission of Spain.[65]

In the negative sense, the U.S. government has made Leonard Peltier
an example of how far it is willing to go to destroy a movement which
is committed to defending the rights of indigenous peoples. The case
provides a clear message-that the ostensible protections under U.S. law
of civil and human rights are fictional where matters of "state security"
are concerned. The systematic program of political repression of dissidents demonstrated in the Peltier case belied the U.S. government's
publicly articulated advocacy of human rights. Until Leonard Peltier
is freed, it is a fundamental disservice to political prisoners in other
countries for the U.S. to advocate their cause. Their struggles are
cheapened and potentially discredited by their cynical use as instruments
of propaganda.

Leonard Peltier continues his work as an activist from his prison
cell. He has used the publicity surrounding his case to focus attention
on wider issues such as the denial of religious rights to indigenous
prisoners, denial of critical medical treatment to prisoners and other
violations of international human rights conventions. Meanwhile, his
supporters are calling for a Congressional investigation into the FBI's
criminal activity and misconduct which led to his imprisonment. In light
of recent revelations concerning similar FBI attacks on the Committee
in Solidarity with the People of El Salvador (CISPES) and other such
groups working in the U.S. for human rights, public sentiment may
be more favorable to such a proposal. Leonard Peltier may yet be proven
innocent and returned to freedom. Until that time, his name remains
a rallying cry for the struggle of all indigenous people and a condemnation of the U.S. government's blatant disregard for human rights
within its own borders.

Notes

1. For the best account of Peltier's early history and involvement in
AIM, see Peter Matthiessen, *In the Spirit of Crazy Horse* (New York: Viking
Press, 1983), pp. 33-58.
2. The Trail of Broken Treaties is the subject of two books: see Vine
Deloria, Jr., *Behind the Trail of Broken Treaties: An Indian Declaration
of Independence* (New York: Delta Books, 1974) and Editors, *BIA, I'm Not
Your Indian Anymore, Akwesasne Notes,* Mohawk Nation via Rooseveltown,
NY, 1974. For a description of Peltier's participation in the Trail, see
Matthiessen, *op. cit.,* pp. 51-56.

3. See Matthiessen, *op. cit.*, pp. 56-58, for a description of the police attack on Peltier and the ultimate disposition of charges. As was later pointed out by Peltier's attorneys, Milwaukee "was the only trial Mr. Peltier has ever had where the government did not suppress material evidence and where he was able to present a full defense." See "Submission of Detailed Facts in Pre-Sentence Investigation Report," *U.S. v. Leonard Peltier*, CR 77-3003-1, United States Court for the District of North Dakota, November 1990, p. 12.

4. See Ward Churchill and Jim Vander Wall, *Agents of Repression: The FBI's Secret Wars Against the Black Panther Party and American Indian Movement* (Boston: South End Press, 1988), pp. 182-97, for an account of the creation of the GOONs and their connection to domestic counter-intelligence operations. Concerning resources within the Lakota treaty area: the Black Hills alone contain what is estimated as being perhaps the most mineral-rich 100 square miles in the world. The 1973-76 conflict on Pine Ridge was, however, centered in efforts by federal authorities and their surrogates in the Wilson regime to block traditional Lakotas from recovering the Sheep Mountain Gunnery Range, the northwestern one-eighth of the reservation which had been "borrowed" by the U.S. in 1942, at the outset of its involvement in World War II. Although Washington had pledged to return the gunnery range at the end of hostilities, it never did. Instead, in 1970—at just the same time the matter was coming to a head among the Pine Ridge residents—a collaborative effort between the National Aeronautics and Space Administration (NASA) and the National Uranium Research and Evaluation (NURE) institute, using specialized satellite photography, secretly discovered considerable uranium and molybdenum deposits in the area (see J. P. Greis, *Status of Mineral Resource Information on the Pine Ridge Indian Reservation* (Washington, D.C.: S.D., BIA Report No. 12, U.S. Department of Interior, 1976). From there on, the federal government appears to have become committed to retaining permanent control over the land in question, a matter which necessitated outright repression of the Oglala traditionals who sought its return. The land was finally and officially taken from the Indians through passage of P.L 90-468 in 1976, at the very end of the FBI's anti-AIM campaign in that area.

5. The Wounded Knee siege and the events leading up to it are described in *ibid.*, pp. 59-83. Also see Editors, "Voices from Wounded Knee, 1973," *Akwesasne Notes*, Mohawk Nation via Rooseveltown, NY, 1974.

6. Should there be any doubt about the purpose of such massive judicial harassment, Colonel Volney Warner (commander of the illegal 82nd Airborne Division presence at Wounded Knee) explained, "AIM's most militant leaders are under indictment, in jail or warrants are out for their arrest. But the government can win, even if no one goes to jail."

7. Quoted in *New York Times*, September 17, 1974. For more on the Wounded Knee Trials, see Matthiessen, *op. cit.*, pp. 84-103; Churchill and Vander Wall, *op. cit.*, pp. 287-94; and Rex Weyler, *Blood of the Land: The Government and Corporate War Against the American Indian Movement* (New York: Vintage Books, 1984), pp. 111-21.

8. On the continuing pattern of judicial harassment of AIM activists and prosecutorial misconduct, see Churchill and Vander Wall, *op. cit.*, pp. 329-42.

9. U.S. Commission on Civil Rights, *Report of Investigation: Oglala Sioux Tribe, General Election, 1974* (Washington, D.C.: U.S. Commission on Civil Rights, October, 1974).

10. See Bruce Johansen and Roberto Maestas, *Wasi'chu: The Continuing Indian Wars* (New York: Monthly Review Press, 1979), pp. 83-84.

11. United States Department of Justice, *Report of the Task Force on Indian Matters* (Washington, D.C.: U.S. Government Printing Office, 1975), pp 42-43.

12. Matthiessen, *op. cit.*, pp. 146-51. This interpretation is reinforced by discussions and interviews conducted by Jim Vander Wall and Ward Churchill with several camp residents, including Dino Butler, Bob Robideau and Nilak Butler.

13. Memorandum, SAC Minneapolis (Joseph Trimbach) to Director, FBI, dated June 3, 1975 and titled, "Law Enforcement on the Pine Ridge Indian Reservation." The documentary film *Anna Mae: A Brave Hearted Woman* (Los Angeles: Brown Bird Productions, 1979), produced and directed by Lan Brookes Ritz, features this document and accompanies it with the maps issued to Bureau personnel on Pine Ridge, falsely reporting the locations of "AIM bunkers" and other alleged fortifications.

14. Churchill and Vander Wall, *op. cit.*, pp. 236-38.

15. This account of the actions of the occupants of the red pickup regarding the initiation of the firefight and the eventual deaths of SAs Williams and Coler derives from an interview of the individual who actually fired the fatal shots (hereinafter referred to as *Interview*). The interview was conducted in Seattle by Peter Matthiessen and Bob Robideau in December 1989. Every precaution was taken to protect the identity of the person being interviewed. He wore a hood, gloves and dark glasses, so that no part of his body was visible. His voice was electronically altered. The interview was undertaken, and the results made public, at the request of the interviewee. As to why he came forward, he stated, "My friend Leonard Peltier is in prison for the rest of his life for something he didn't do." He had heretofore hoped the appeals process would free Peltier. That having failed, he felt he had no alternative but to take the risk of going on record. However, he has no intention of turning himself in. He points out that if Leonard Peltier has found no justice in U.S. courts, there is no reason to assume his own experience might be different. He also stated that, in thirteen years of imprisonment, Peltier has never pressured him to come forward and confess. Peltier's position has always been that it is irrelevant who fired the fatal shots; the AIM members were acting in self-defense, and no one should be imprisoned on this basis. It is rather the FBI which bears full responsibility for the deaths of Coler and Williams.

16. Churchill and Vander Wall, *op. cit.*, pp. 238-43.

17. This account derives from a conversation between the author and Bob Robideau on September 28, 1990. A close variation also appears in Matthiessen, *op. cit.*, pp. 560-61. As to the impact of discovering the identities of the attackers, Robideau commented, "We considered ourselves dead, from that moment on."

18. *Interview, op. cit.*

19. See Jim Messerschmidt, *The Trial of Leonard Peltier* (Boston: South End Press), p. 101.

20. The AIM personnel were Leonard Peltier, Dino Butler, Bob Robideau, Joe Stuntz Killsright, Wilfred "Wish" Draper, Norman Brown, Mike "Baby AIM" Anderson and Norman Charles. According to Robideau, at no time did the defending force exceed ten people, the aforementioned eight, plus the two people in the red pickup truck. The FBI would later claim that "at least 30" AIM members and supporters took part in the firefight.

21. Matthiessen, *op. cit.*, pp. 190-91.

22. Churchill and Vander Wall, *op. cit.*, pp. 244-45.

23. For a profile on Richard G. Held and his son, Richard W., see Ward Churchill, "COINTELPRO as a Family Business: The Case of the Two Richard Helds," *Z Magazine*, March 1988.

24. Zigrossi publicly defined his role as being the heading up of a "colonial police force" overseeing a "conquered people." See David Weir and Lowell Bergman, "The Killing of Anna Mae Aquash," *Rolling Stone*, April 7, 1977, p. 55.

25. Letter from the Chairman of the U.S. Commission on Civil Rights, Arthur J. Flemming, to U.S. Attorney General Edward S. Levi dated July 22, 1975.

26. On James Brings Yellow, see Matthiessen, *op. cit.*, p. 211.

27. Concerning LeDeaux, see *ibid.*, p. 217.

28. On the Long Visitors, see Churchill and Vander Wall, *op. cit.*, pp. 255-60.

29. The Bureau had imported a "Public Relations" (read: propaganda) specialist named Tom Coll to Pine Ridge, apparently for the express purpose of handling the dissemination of such disinformation during the days immediately following the firefight, when public impressions were of utmost importance. See Joel D. Weisman, "About that 'Ambush' at Wounded Knee," *Columbia Journalism Review*, September/October 1975, pp. 28-31.

30. The "aiding and abetting" charge is routinely added to federal indictments. Should the prosecutor have a weak case, the defendant can always be tried on such an "offense of general applicability," which carries the same penalty as the principle charge but carries a much lesser burden of proof.

31. See Matthiessen, *op. cit.*, pp. 223-83 for the best account of the events leading up to the capture of the various fugitives.

32. A classic example of the government's use of bogus witnesses at Cedar Rapids is that of James Harper, who admitted under cross-examination that he habitually lied under oath in order to obtain favors from or gain advantage against the police. At the point of his testimony at Cedar Rapids, he was awaiting sentencing on a burglary conviction. Clear indication that a false testimony deal had been struck lies in the fact that Harper later sued the government for "breach of contract" in having sent him to prison despite his having testified "as requested" against Butler and Robideau. See Churchill and Vander Wall, *op. cit.*, pp. 301-02.

33. Quoted in Matthiessen, *op. cit.*, p. 318.

34. Quoted in Churchill and Vander Wall, *op. cit.*, p. 302.

35. FBI teletype from Gallegher to B. H. Cooke, dated 8/20/76, titled "RESMURS—Contemplated Dismissal of Prosecution Against James Theodore Eagle; Continuing Prosecution of Leonard Peltier." The document is reproduced in Ward Churchill and Jim Vander Wall, *The COINTELPRO*

266 • Jim Vander Wall

Papers: Documents from the FBI's Secret Wars Against Dissent in the United
States (Boston: South End Press, 1990), p. 287.

36. During an interview on the CBS news program *West 57th Street*
aired September 14, 1989, federal prosecutor Lynn Crooks explained the
use of the false Poor Bear affidavit to extradite Peltier:

> *Crooks:* I don't know why they shipped up [to Canada] what they
> did because I wasn't involved in it, but I can assure you that if
> I would have been, I would have shipped up her affidavits.
> *CBS:* Even though you believed her not to be a credible witness?
> *Crooks:* Yeah! During a probable cause stage, it wouldn't have
> bothered me at all. I'd have said, "Judge, here's what we've got.
> . . ."
> *CBS:* No matter how you cut it, you can't get away from the fact
> that it was her testimony that got Leonard Peltier extradited
> from Canada to stand trial. . . .
> *Crooks:* I guess I don't ultimately know, and ultimately I don't
> really care. Doesn't bother my conscience. If everything they say
> on that is right, it doesn't bother my conscience one bit.

37. The three Poor Bear affidavits are reproduced in *The COINTELPRO
Papers, op. cit.*, pp. 288-91. According to Poor Bear's subsequent testimony,
one of the techniques of intimidation used by SAs Price and Wood was to
show her morgue photos of the body of AIM member Anna Mae Aquash,
reported to have been earlier threatened with death by Price, and found
murdered on Pine Ridge on February 24, 1976. SA Wood seems to have
explained to Poor Bear that he and Price could get away with such killings
"because they were agents." Peltier trial transcript at 3790, quoted in *Agents
of Repression, op. cit.*, pp. 314-15. For additional information on the bizarre
case of Aquash, see Johanna Brand, *The Life and Death of Anna Mae Aquash*
(Toronto: Lorimer, 1978).

38. On the Marshall case, see *Agents of Repression, op. cit.*, pp. 335-42.

39. Poor Bear's complete recantation was made before the Minnesota
Review Commission to Investigate the FBI in Minneapolis in February 1977.
The testimony was videotaped, but not transcribed. Videotape copies were
reposited with the law office of Kenneth Tilsen in Minneapolis.

40. Teletype to Director, FBI, from ASAC, Rapid City, dated July 20,
1976, reproduced in *The COINTELPRO Papers, op. cit.*, pp. 283-86.

41. See Messerschmidt, *op. cit.*, pp. 40-41, for a point by point comparison
between the FBI's analysis of the Cedar Rapids trial and Benson's
evidentiary rulings in the Peltier case.

42. The prosecution went to great lengths to insure that their carefully
coached and coerced witnesses stuck to their story on this point. For instance,
at one point in the testimony of Mike Anderson, the following exchange
occurred:

> *Prosecutor Evan Hultman:* And what, if anything happened?
> *Anderson:* Well, I guess they [Coler and Williams] seen the orange
> pickup going down that way and they followed.
> *Hultman:* Now, when you say "orange pickup," is that the red
> and white van to which. . . .

Defense counsel objected, but Anderson quickly corrected his statements to reflect the story that the slain agents were following Peltier's van rather than a pickup. Further, agents such as J. Gary Adams, who had testified at Cedar Rapids that they'd heard radio transmissions suggesting that Coler and Williams had followed a red pickup onto the Jumping Bull property reversed their testimony against Peltier, swearing they'd heard their dead colleagues state they were following a red and white van. Judge Benson ruled any reference to these witnesses' Cedar Rapids testimony by the defense "inadmissable."

43. See *U.S. v. Leonard Peltier*, CR C77-3003, "Motion to Vacate Judgement and for a New Trial," pp. 40-45, for a summary of the pathologists' testimony and the inconsistencies therein.

44. Besides the Poor Bear affidavit, the government submitted, as part of the documentation supporting Peltier's extradition from Canada, an affidavit signed by SA Courtland Cunningham stating that he had personally found the cartridge casing in the trunk of Coler's car. At trial, Cunningham admitted under cross-examination that he himself hadn't "actually" found the casing. Instead, on the stand Cunningham contended that a fingerprint expert named Winthrop Lodge had found it on a completely different date than that previously sworn to in the affidavit, and that Lodge had then turned it over to him. Cunningham professed to be "unable to recall" to whom he'd turned over the cartridge casing. Nor could he (or anyone else) say where the cartridge casing went or who had handled it from that point until it turned up in the FBI ballistics lab halfway across the country. Consequently, no one could really attest to the fact that the item tested by Hodge was really even the same item supposedly found by Lodge or Cunningham, on one or another day—depending on which version you wish to accept—in Coler's trunk. In a normal trial, such hopelessly tainted "evidence" would simply have been disallowed. The trial of Leonard Peltier was, however, decidedly other than normal.

45. A witness testified at trial that he observed an AR-15 being placed in Robideau's car at Crow Dog's Paradise which he "believed" had been used in the firefight. Peltier was not present at the time.

46. See "Motion to Vacate Judgement and for a New Trial," *op. cit.*, pp, 6-12, for a summary of Hodge's testimony. Also see Messerschmidt, *op. cit.*, pp. 89-93.

47. *Ibid.*

48. See Messerschmidt, *op. cit.*, pp. 50-54, 66.

49. Peltier trial transcript at 5011, quoted in *Agents of Repression, op. cit.*, p. 322.

50. See Bill Dunne, "The U.S. Penitentiary at Marion, Illinois: An Instrument of Oppression," *New Studies on the Left*, vol. IV, nos. 1-2, 1989, pp. 20-28. See also above, pp. 38-82.

51. Transcript of the proceedings (oral arguments) in *U.S. v. Leonard Peltier*, Criminal No. C77-3003, "Motion to Vacate Judgement and for a New Trial," at 7326-7.

52. It has never been explained how this classification, which applies to U.S. interests *vis à vis* foreign powers, is in any way applicable to what the government insists is a "purely domestic matter."

53. FBI teletype, Director to SAC, Rapid City (Norman Zigrossi), dated October 2, 1975 and captioned "RESMURS—PHYSICAL EVIDENCE—[deleted]." The teletype and associated lab notes concerning the firing pin test at issue are reproduced in *The COINTELPRO Papers, op. cit.*, pp. 296-97. When this withholding of plainly crucial exculpatory evidence became public knowledge, the government used a ruse suggesting the defense had been in possession of the key document all along. As prosecutor Lynn Crooks asserted in his earlier-mention *West 57th Street* interview:

> *Crooks:* As we sat at trial, we're saying to ourselves, "When are they going to hit us with that October 31 [sic] teletype? We're waiting to get impeached. They don't do it! They never mentioned the stupid thing! They didn't use their best evidence!
> *CBS:* Well, they claim they never had it.
> *Crooks:* Aurgh! They're lying!

Crooks' attempt was to confuse the October 2 teletype with another, dated October 31, which the defense did indeed have at trial. However, far from impeaching the government's position, the October 31 document simply states that the key cartridge casing could not be matched to the Wichita AR-15, a finding consistent with trial testimony that firing pin tests had been "inconclusive." The defense thus had no reason to make an issue of its contents. The conclusively negative results indicated in the October 2 document—which was in fact withheld from the defense—are a far different consideration. Crooks' unintended acknowledgement that the withheld information would have represented the "best evidence" of the the defense goes directly to what is at issue.

54. "Motion to Vacate Judgment and for a New Trial," *op. cit.*

55. United States Court of Appeals for the Eighth District, "Appeal from the United States District Court for the District of North Dakota," *U.S. v. Leonard Peltier* (written by Judge Gerald Heaney), Sept. 11, 1986, p. 9.

56. As it turned out, the mysterious third party handwriting belonged to William Albrecht, an FBI laboratory trainee.

57. Transcript of Oral Arguments before the United States Court of appeals for the Eighth Circuit, in *U.S. v. Peltier*, October 22, 1985, p. 18.

58. *Ibid.*

59. "Appeal from the United States District Court for the District of North Dakota," *op. cit.*, p. 16.

60. *U.S. v. Bagley*, U.S. 105 S. Ct. 3375 (1985).

61. The high court declined to review the case despite the fact that it had a compelling need to do so: the "probability" standard adopted by the Eighth Circuit was/is in direct conflict with the "possibility" standard already employed by the Ninth Circuit. Absent clarification of Supreme Court intent in Bagley, both standards remain in effect, an obvious contravention of the "equal justice" provision of the U.S. Constitution. The high court's refusal to hear Peltier's second appeal was therefore a glaring default on more than one level.

62. *Leonard Peltier v. G. L. Henman, Warden, United States Penitentiary, Leavenworth, Kansas*, "Verified Petition for Writ of *Habeas Corpus* and Other Appropriate Relief," U.S. District Court for the Eastern District of Kansas, filed December 3, 1990.

63. Letter from Gerald W. Heaney, U.S. Senior Circuit Judge, to Senator Daniel K. Inouye, dated April 18, 1992.

64 Interview on the CBS news program *West 57th Street*, aired September 14, 1989.

65. On Canada, see *House of Commons Debate*, vol. 128, no. 129, 1st Session, 33rd Parliament, Official Report, Thursday, April 17, 1986. Concerning the human rights award, see "Peltier back in Penitentiary, wins prize in Spain," *Rapid City Journal*, December 12, 1986.

Members of AIM occupy the office of the Bureau of Indian Affairs (BIA) in Washington, DC. (photo: Library of Congress)

Leonard Peltier

Statement to the Canadian Court
May 13, 1976

This is only a continuation of past North American governmental policy of oppressing Indians by using the court systems against our people. At present, there exists a dual system of justice: one for the white society and one for Indian people. Indian people are being attacked and murdered on our reservations and on the streets of the U.S. and Canada, and yet no one is being called a criminal in the courts for the commission of these crimes.

When colonial white society invades and occupies our territories, these are not called criminal acts. But when Native people stand up and resist, these acts are considered criminal. But these are not crimes. They are political acts in which our people stand for their rights of self-determination, self-dignity, and self-respect against the cruel and oppressive might of another nation. My ancestors signed what are called treaties with the governments of the U.S. and Canada. These treaties recognized the existence of independent sovereign nations. And Indians continue to recognize their sovereignty today. . . . We may have been happy with the land that was originally reserved to us. But continually over the years, more and more of our land has been stolen from us by the Canadian and U.S. governments.

In the nineteenth century, our land was stolen for economic reasons because the land was lush and fertile and abounded with food that the greedy white settlers wished to have for their own. We were left with what white society thought was worthless land. Still we managed to live, and we defied white society's wish to exterminate us. Today, what was once called worthless land suddenly becomes valuable as the technology of white society advances. White society would like to push us off our reservations because beneath the barren land lies valuable mineral and oil resources.

It is not a new development for white society to steal from non-white peoples. When white society succeeds, it is called colonialism. When white society's efforts to colonize other peoples are met with resistance, it is called war. But when the colonized Indians of North America meet this theft with resistance, we are called criminals. . . . We are Indian Nations, and the governments of Canada and the U.S. and the dominant white society they represent have made war against our people, our culture, our spiritual ways, and our sacred Mother Earth for over four hundred years. For over four hundred years, we have struggled against colonial rule, and to reassert our rights as members of independent sovereign nations within those territories established by treaties. These treaties are sacred documents binding signatory nations to an inviolate international relationship. Yet you force us into your courts, courts that have never been just with Indian people. The high ratio of Native people in North American prisons attests to this fact.

The general political persecution directed at Indian people is specifically focused on representatives of the American Indian Movement. These political persecutions, started in the U.S., are aimed at the American Indian Movement as an organization to crush this Movement and its struggle for the liberation of all Indian people in Canada and the U.S., as well as the colonized Indian Peoples of Central and South America. . . . It is a struggle to remove the yoke of colonial rule if we are to survive as a people.

Robert E. Robideau

Leonard Peltier

Bob Robideau

Refuge

Looking around the little green steel cage that I had once again been locked into, I stood wondering how long I would be forced to remain pent up in it this time. It was a thought, nothing more, for I had been here many times before. I had long ago learned the way to live in or escape from the agonizing solitude of a prison cell.

It all began when I was eleven years old. A friend and I had run away from a juvenile detention center in Washington, but I was caught and brought back after three days of freedom, tramping around in the midst of winter half starved, with a thin tee shirt, Levi pants and light tennis shoes on. Yes, you can imagine how very cold, wet and sick I was of it all by the time they caught up with me. Even though I was relieved to get back to a nice warm building, I was at the same time frightened of my situation, not knowing the consequence of my act. I wanted to ask, "What will become of me now?" but I was afraid, because their faces seemed so strange and unfriendly. A feeling of unreality began to creep into my mind and being. I kept quiet and waited for what the future had in store for my young soul.

I was not long in waiting when a blank faced man turned towards me and said, "Come along." I was quickly taken to the upper floor of the building and told to enter a small room with a steel door and no windows. The only view of outside the cell would be a tiny opening cut out of the steel door. But that too, I was to find out shortly, would be closed and used only for the purpose of passing my food trays through and for the man to look through when checking on me from time to time during my stay there. After my being ushered into the cell, the custodian had me remove all my clothing, which I did not mind getting out of since they were wet and as cold as ice is against the skin. He gathered them up and left without another word, locking the heavy steel door behind him. Then he peeked through the small opening once, looking through it with blank staring eyes to affirm in his mind that I was still in the cell and hadn't slipped out by him. Satisfied, he closed the small door to the peek hole with a bang and then I heard his footsteps quickly receding. I was not to see another set of clothing until my release from the hole.

I stood inside the cement room next to the locked steel door for a long moment and gave my cell a quick survey. I had a metal sink, metal toilet, a thin badly soiled mattress, which was on the floor, and a ragged soiled old army blanket. After another moment more of standing there freezing, I went quickly to the mattress and blanket that were the only things offering warmth and laid down; grabbing the blanket, I pulled it over my aching, weather racked body and tried to sleep, but I could not, my body was still too cold, so I laid awake shivering for some time and stared at a small light which glowed softly back at me high in the ceiling. The friendly light was just beginning to soothe my racked nerves and cold tired naked body when all of a sudden it died—leaving me in complete darkness. I knew then what it meant to be alone, and the lonesomeness made me shiver anew with a sudden chill.

I rolled over on my side, drawing my cold and weak limbs up and around my body to help drive the chill away and closed my eyes and thought about yesterday's freedom. I began to feel that what I had been standing on had broken down, and that I had nothing left under my feet. What I had lived on no longer existed, and I had nothing left to live on.

Motivated by the dire necessity of having something to do after seven days and nights of naked solitude, I tried, in my darkness, to recall all I knew. I devoted what seemed to be endless days and nights in recalling past experiences, reliving them, and changing the scenes to what I would instead have liked them to be, rather than what in reality they were. Being a very young boy, I . . . after a short period of time exhausted my small store house of experiences and so, in the end I had to revert to creating scenes of life, which for the most part consisted of daring exploits, avenging deeds that helped make my heart warm with joy. Time was no more, my mind flowed over space and time at will . . . there was no limit to my mental adventures.

Fifteen years have slowly passed me by since that, my first encounter with the hole, and yet I am still experiencing its tormenting solitude. "Reality has been drowned in steel and cement!"

Ward Churchill

Wages of COINTELPRO—
The Case of Mumia Abu-Jamal

In the solitary confinement of death row in Pennsylvania's Huntington State Prison sits a man awaiting an appointment with the electric chair. Foreclosed upon in the media as a "cop killer" since well before he ever went to trial or was convicted of any crime, Mumia Abu-Jamal is one more in an ever-lengthening list of New Afrikan activists "neutralized" as a legacy of the notorious COINTELPRO operations aimed by the FBI at the Black Panther Party and other black liberation formations during the late 1960s and early '70s. It has been a long and tortuous route from those days to these, for Mumia and hundreds of others sharing his political experience. His story is in many ways indicative of them all.

The Black Panther Party

It was in 1968, at the age of fourteen, that Mumia first joined the Panthers in his home town of Philadelphia. Over the next two years, he worked a considerable proportion of the time in the Bronx-based East Coast Information Ministry of the party, understudying to BPP Minister of Culture Emory Douglass and his wife Judy, as well as Deputy Minister of Culture Brad Brewer. He received a thorough grounding in "graphic arts, newspaper layout and related propaganda skills," and in 1970, at the age of sixteen, he was appointed communications director for the Philadelphia Panther chapter. As such, he became a prime target for political repression by both city and federal police.

This was a period when, as thousands of FBI documents eventually released under provision of the Freedom of Information Act (FOIA) amply demonstrate, the Bureau was engaged in what amounted to a secret war against the BPP. At least thirty-eight Panthers were gunned down by various police agencies between 1968 and '72, while another dozen died in "shooting wars" deliberately provoked through an assortment of disinformation ruses employed by FBI COINTELPRO specialists.

Scores of party members were railroaded into prison on what has since been revealed to have been highly suspicious—and sometimes plainly false—information provided to local police by Bureau counterintelligence operatives. Other hundreds of the party's members and supporters experienced serious beatings or gunshot wounds, a systematic pattern of arrests on charges which never went to trial (but which consumed astronomical amounts of bail and legal defense money), repeated warrantless searches and corresponding vandalization of their homes and offices, gratuitous firing from jobs and subsequent blacklisting with other potential employers. All of this, as it turned out, was orchestrated by the FBI on a nation-wide basis. In Philadelphia, FOIA documents reveal, COINTELPRO-BPP was particularly well developed, following only the anti-Panther campaigns undertaken in Chicago, New York, Los Angeles and the San Francisco bay area in intensity.

For its part, the Philadelphia COINTELPRO's "cooperating local police agency," the Philadelphia Police Department (PDP), was headed by Frank Rizzo, an individual whose personal philosophy was perhaps best described in a slogan he coined for a later (successful) bid to become mayor of the "City of Brotherly Love." If elected, Rizzo promised voters, he would foment policies "so far to the right, I'll make Attila the Hun look like a faggot!" In conjunction with the FBI, the Philadelphia police approached the Panthers with a special brutality. This was capstoned in August of 1970, when Rizzo personally led a large strike force—complete with an ample SWAT component—on a nocturnal raid of the city's BPP headquarters, rousting the dozen or so people inside. The prisoners were dragged into the street, forced to strip at gunpoint, and lined up naked against a wall for an extended period before being carted off to jail. No meaningful charges were ever filed against the arrestees, and they were shortly released, but Rizzo's major purpose in staging the spectacle had been largely fulfilled. The August raid marked the point after which the Black Panther Party in Philadelphia began to crumble beneath the weight of such extra-legal but officially sanctioned repression.[1]

With the dissolution of the BPP during the early '70s, Mumia moved into other, more independent forms of politics. He developed a career as a free-lance writer on community issues and events, becoming president of the Association of Black Journalists in 1979. He also gravitated toward electronic media, doing a series of local origination television interviews, and creating community programming for several Philadelphia radio channels. Ultimately, he achieved the position of presenting his own talk radio program on station WUHY for several years during the late '70s and early '80s. Not content simply to perfect his own skills, he consistently devoted time and energy to sharing what he'd learned about communications with young people "off the block." Eventually, the quality of his work seems to have earned a degree of grudging respect from even the mainstream journalistic institutions his own well-honed political consciousness led him to spurn. One solid indication of this is that in December of 1981 he was profiled in the *Philadelphia Inquirer* under the headline, "Jamal: An eloquent activist not afraid to raise his voice." It was this sort of unstinting commitment to the cause of black liberation, and the attention he was able to focus upon its meanings and motivations, which caused him to retain the attention of the same forces which had once stalked him as a Panther.

"The Voice of the Voiceless"

All this undoubtedly began to come to a head on August 8, 1978, when Philadelphia police decided to lay siege to the headquarters of MOVE, a highly self-determining (and therefore objectionable, from the official perspective) black community organization. As was the case after a massive 1969 police attack upon the Los Angeles BPP headquarters, authorities in Philadelphia immediately set out to construct a public justification for their aggression by charging MOVE members with having "precipitated the incident." And, as in Los Angeles, official investigators quickly picked up the cue, concluding that the PDP had acted "reasonably," and that the victims rather than their victimizers were guilty of the crimes which had been committed.[2] As the police were exonerated for having provoked the lethal firefight, MOVE members were bound over for trial on capital charges. Predictably, Mumia Abu-Jamal stepped into the breach.

During the immediate aftermath of the siege, and throughout the 1979 mass trial of MOVE members concerning the death of a cop during the standoff, Mumia was highly active. Using his press credentials to gain access to the prisoners, he conducted a lengthy series of interviews which provided the only real public exposure of MOVE's side of what had happened. More, he allowed the accused to present themselves as intelligent, caring and well-motivated human beings rather than as the grotesque and strikingly animalistic caricatures portrayed in the mass media. Even worse—from the viewpoint of the police, mayor and prosecutors—he used his radio show and his various newspaper columns to pick apart the official version of events, acquainting a large portion of the Philadelphia population with the fact that this account failed to hold up under even minimal scrutiny, in court or out. As city hall and the PDP were increasingly faced with the the necessity of reconciling the blatant contradictions imbedded within their story, being repeatedly embarrassed when the falsity of their "facts" was revealed, their resentment grew. By 1980, Mumia was marked for elimination.

Hence, when on May 13, 1985, the PDP—acting under orders from Mayor Wilson Goode—launched its major assault on MOVE, dropping an incendiary bomb on the organization's residence facility, the "voice of the voiceless" had himself been stilled. There was no one to provide a comprehensive alternative account of the causes of the resulting conflagration, which burned eleven people alive (six adults and five children) and incinerated an entire block of low income housing in the black Powelton Village area of Philadelphia. Nor was there an effective media challenge to the bizarre official explanation—following the pattern established in Chicago in the wake of the assassinations of Illinois Panther leaders Mark Clark and Fred Hampton on December 4, 1969—that, all evidence to the contrary notwithstanding, the atrocity was "justified" because MOVE had attacked the police rather than the other way around. In such an informational vacuum, government investigators were able to follow the Chicago model to the letter, finding that police had acted correctly, "defending themselves" against a never-quite-defined MOVE "threat."[3] It follows that there was no one to point up the similarities to the Chicago example—which was eventually proven to have been part of the FBI's anti-BPP COINTELPRO in that city— when the MOVE survivors were charged with major felonies while the police received applause and commendations.

The "Crime"

On the night of December 9, 1981, Mumia was driving a cab—an occupation he had adopted in order to retain his autonomy as a reporter rather than tempering the content of his often unwelcome news to conform with the demands of a paycheck—when he saw a black man, stopped for a minor traffic violation, being beaten by a policeman. He pulled over to the curb, planning to intervene. Moments later, an unarmed Mumia Abu-Jamal was sitting on the curb, a serious bullet wound from a police service revolver in his stomach. Nearby, the patrolman who had been engaged in the beating lay dead, killed by a weapon which was never recovered. Large numbers of police arrived; the wounded man was left bleeding at curbside until after the morgue wagon had removed their dead colleague. At the hospital, Mumia was placed under round-the-clock armed guard and handcuffed to his bed, despite his critical condition. By the morning of December 10, Philadelphia's mainstream newspapers were trumpeting the notion that a radical black "cop killer" had been wounded in a "shoot-out" and apprehended.

Witnesses to the event did not describe Mumia as being the man who shot the cop. Instead, they described a "short" individual of approximately "200 pounds" and wearing "an Afro hair-do" as having pulled the trigger. Mumia is 6'1" tall and weighed less than 170 pounds on the night of the shooting. Further, far from wearing his hair in Afro style, it was arranged in a distinctive dreadlock, as it had been for several years prior to 1981. Yet, in an eerie parallel to the 1967 killing of patrolman John Frey in a rather similar Oakland incident, a matter which resulted in Black Panther founder Huey P. Newton's subsequently overturned conviction for "manslaughter," Mumia was charged with the first degree (premeditated) murder of a police officer. He was bound over for trial on the charge and held without bond. There is no evidence that the PDP ever conducted any sort of investigation into the identity of the individual described by witnesses as having been the killer.

The "Trial"

At trial, the prosecution faced obvious evidentiary difficulties in demonstrating that Mumia had killed anyone at all, despite the defendant's having been denied the right to be represented by the counsel of his choice (MOVE founder John Africa). Hence, much emphasis was placed upon distortion of his political philosophy in order to cast him as an intrinsically "violent black nationalist." Thus, *ipso facto*, he would be perceived as guilty of whatever the state wished to claim in the eyes of the 11 white members of his jury. The following exchange between Mumia and the prosecutor during the proceeding is indicative of the whole:

> *Question:* (To Mumia) Do you recall saying "All power to the people"?
> *Answer:* Yes.
> *Question:* Do you believe your actions as well as your philosophy are consistent with the quote, "Political power grows out of the barrel of a gun"?
> *Answer:* I believe America has proven that quote to be true.[4]
> *Question:* Do you recall saying that "the Black Panther Party is an uncompromising party, it faces reality"?
> *Answer:* (Mumia nodding affirmatively) Yes.

The defense called a number of character witnesses to testify that the defendant could hardly be accurately described as the sort of violence-crazed gunman the prosecution was attempting to paint him. To this, the district attorney responded with smears of the witnesses themselves, often based in perfectly circular reasoning. The "credibility" of renowned poet and Temple University professor Sonia Sanchez, to cite a prominent instance of this, was challenged on the basis that she was a known "friend of cop killers," such as Mumia himself. Having indulged in comparable plays to the grandstand throughout the proceedings, the prosecution capped its performance in its summation by arguing that the defendant must be guilty simply on the basis of his having believed in the Panther ideology of black liberation and armed self-defense for nearly twwenty years. Such a menace, it was implied, had to be "removed from society" at all costs, regardless of whether he had committed the specific act with which he was charged. The jury quickly returned a guilty verdict and, during the sentencing hearing held on July 3, 1982, the prosecution was able to successfully argue for imposition of the death penalty. It would be a useful "deterrent to other cop killers," the district attorney contended. Besides, the whole thing would be a largely "symbolic" gesture; Mumia would have "appeal after appeal" during which to escape execution.

On Death Row

On March 6, 1989, the Pennsylvania Supreme Court denied Mumia's last possible appeal to the state judicial process. Attorney Marilyn Gelb, who handled the appellate work, and who had managed to obtain submission of an *amicus curiae* brief on behalf of her client from both the National Conference of Black Lawyers and the ACLU, immediately petitioned for rehearing and reconsideration by the state high court, but the prospects of success appear increasingly dismal in the quarter.

By the same token, recourse to the U.S. Supreme Court does not look especially propitious on its face, insofar as Chief Justice Rehnquist has made it abundantly clear that he considers death row appeals an outrageous waste of time, despite the fact that two condemned men—Randall Dale Adams and Clarence Brandley—were able to establish their innocence shortly prior to their scheduled executions in 1988. Apparently, in Rehnquist's view, "due process" should more properly follow the pattern exhibited in the case of Robert Streetman, executed last year by lethal injection even as his lawyer was calling the governor's office to inform it that the the Supreme Court had grudgingly agreed to review lower court decisions in the matter. Better, perhaps, is the example of Willie Jasper Darden, executed just hours after appearing on ABC's *Nightline* program. Darden's death occurred three weeks before the normal thirty-day limit on filing appeals had elapsed, and there is substantial indication he was not guilty.[5]

Despite condemnation by Amnesty International and other human rights organizations as lately as 1987, the U.S. appears bound and determined to remain one of the very few industrial countries clinging to the barbarity of the death penalty, a situation unlikely to change without massive citizen protest. Such has not been forthcoming lately.

As it stands, Mumia Abu-Jamal is the only overtly political prisoner on death row in the United States. The signs are that unless something truly dramatic happens, he will die for an act he was never proven to have committed. His situation is likely due in significant part to the fact that, by and large, there has been very little protest or even commentary on the matter in progressive circles. Accordingly, the state has been able to pursue its agenda against him unhampered even by public awareness of what is transpiring. Any individual with Mumia's record of service and commitment deserves far better treatment than this. It is possible that something as simple as a mass mail and/or petition campaign could serve to cause his sentence to be commuted to life, allowing time for the legal maneuvering which could ultimately set him free. Such things have happened in the past. Beyond this, one thing seems quite certain: while Mumia Abu-Jamal may be the first political prisoner slated for execution in recent years, he will not—if the state is successful in killing him—be the last. That, if nothing else, should be ample motivation for all of us to take up his cause. And time is running out.

Notes

1. For a general study of the FBI/police war on the Panthers, including what happened in Philadelphia, see Robert Justin Goldstein, *Political Repression in Modern America* (Cambridge and New York: Schenkman Publishing Company, 1978), pp. 523-29.

2. On the LA "shoot-out," see Ward Churchill and Jim Vander Wall, *Agents of Repression: The FBI's Secret Wars Against the Black Panther Party and the American Indian Movement* (Boston: South End Press, 1988), pp. 82-85.

3. Details of the Chicago assassinations may be found in Roy Wilkins and Ramsey Clark, *Search and Destroy: A Report by the Commission of Inquiry into the Black Panthers and the Police* (New York: Metropolitan Applied Research Center, 1973).

4. At trial, Mumia explained his understanding of the quote as follows: "It's very clear that political power grows out of the barrel of a gun or else America wouldn't be here today. It is America who has seized political power from the Indian race, not by God, not by Christianity, not by goodness, but by the barrel of a gun." His position was thus that the power of the state, not political activists like himself, is realized in this fashion.

5. For more on the death penalty in the U.S., see Amnesty International, *United States of America: The Death Penalty* (London, 1987).

Ray Luc Levasseur

The RICO Act and Political Targets: Statement to the Jury, January 10, 1989

My name is Raymond Luc Levasseur. Luc is my grandfather's name. I grew up in a small mill town in Maine. My father was born in Québec, a French nation in Canada. He and his father came to this country to look for work in the woolen mills and shoe factories of Maine. That's how I trace my roots back to Québec. When I say I'm French-Canadian, I'm French on both sides of my family. I have grandparents that went to work in those mills when they were thirteen and fourteen years old. My mother and father went into those mills when they were sixteen. And my turn came when I was seventeen. I grew up in the shadow of those mills really, because not only did they leave an impression on me, an imprint on my life and my thinking, but I literally lived within those shadows; we used to have a little apartment across the street from a shoe shop.

I worked in a mill when I was seventeen where we made heels for shoes. I worked with primarily French-Canadian people, people who didn't have much education. I didn't have much good education myself at the time. It was non-unionized labor. All the unions had been broken years earlier by runaway shops. It was low pay. It was the kind of money that was difficult to support a family on. We were subjected to speed-up on those machines. They would crank those machines up to however much they wanted, so that you would have to produce a certain number of heels in a specified period of time. I saw what the future was going to look like for me to work in those mills. And that future became very clear and very glaring when a school chum of mine by the name of Albert Glaude, who worked in the mill across the road, got his arm caught in the machine one day and he was choked to death. Just six months earlier he had been in school with us and the next thing you know he was dead, and those machines killed him. They can kill you very quickly or take a long time to do it.

And I say this because I was very close to my grandparents. My *mémère*, my grandmother, she was like a second mother to me. And my grandfather worked in those mills year after year after year. This was a man I had a great deal of respect for. I used to stand up to his knee, and what I saw happen was that I saw his life begin to be devastated by the kind of work that he was subjected to, to the point where his health was broken down. What happened was a man to whom I once stood only up to his knees, I ended up holding in my arms. I remember one time being called out to the chicken coop where he lived to pick him up off the floor because he couldn't stand up after he had fallen down. Working in those woolen mills and shoe shops has that type of eroding effect on a person year after year. We brought him to the VA Hospital because he was a World War I vet. But I found out something else: if you don't have health care from a good union or something, then you are not going to get it from the VA, because they just warehoused him. So we brought him back home to die. And that's what happened to him. He died. And I always thought that those mills had a big part in killing him.

I wanted to escape that destiny. What I saw was a dead end. So at seventeen years old I went to Boston. I started working on the loading docks. And over the years, all my life really, I've done that type of work. I've worked as a farm laborer and logger, I've worked in factories and mills. You heard about overt acts from the judge during the instruction. An overt act. That you have to take a step in a conspiracy, you actually have to do something for it to happen. My first overt act in this alleged conspiracy is I was born into a particular class of workers that was severely exploited and subjected to certain kinds of conditions. And that left an imprint on my mind that I was going to have to do something about it, when a factory owner puts more value on his profits than your health and life. I think those are priorities that need to be changed.

While I was in Boston all I used to read was the sports page when I rode the subway on the way to work. So I didn't know anything about what was going on over in Southeast Asia. There was a war going on at the time called Vietnam. And the way I grew up was to love my country. Even though I felt like I was being totally exploited in the work that I was doing at the time. I felt I had an obligation to serve my country like my father and my uncles and my grandfather.

I enlisted in the Army in 1967. I went to Vietnam and I served a full tour of duty, twelve months. And what I saw there was another side of war. Not some Hollywood production, not some Rambo type of thing that they feed young guys so they can manipulate them into the military and use them. I saw another side of U.S. foreign policy. Bombings, killings, search and destroy, devastation, poverty, hunger. I was part of a foreign occupation Army. I saw human rights violations when I was there, and I saw violations of international law. And I've been to Bien Hoa, I've been to Long Binh, I've been to Xuan Loc, I've been to Bear Cat. I've been around areas around the Iron Triangle. I've been to Saigon. I've been to base camps like Black Horse. While I was there I did flying in helicopters, so I got a view of a land that should have been supporting villages and farms and human life that was totally being destroyed. A wasteland. Bomb craters. Nothing but a couple of bushes or a downed helicopter here and there. And I saw the human suffering of the Vietnamese people, and in particular, women and children.

You are going to hear about weapons in this case. I come from an area in Maine where it was natural to grow up with a .22 or .410 shot gun, as I did. The first pistol I ever fired was in Vietnam. There will be a piece of evidence in here, because the FBI seized it, that shows a picture of me when I was twenty years old with automatic weapons. I'm standing there with an M-16 and an M-60 machine gun in front of a helicopter that says "Gang Busters" on it. Not gangsters, gang busters. And that's the sort of role that I was asked to fulfill for this government. I was trained to kill. And I was fully armed and sent to Vietnam. You know, there's a lot of vets who came back with post-Vietnam stress disorder. I've worked with those veterans. I didn't suffer any mental illness or syndrome when I came back. I came back enraged by what I saw. To see open and blatant racism by white American soldiers towards Vietnamese people because of the color of their skin or their religion or their culture, their language, was shocking to me. I had never seen anything that devastating. And the Vietnamese are really beautiful people. To see young mothers forced to sell their thirteen and fourteen year old daughters into prostitution, so that American GIs could prey on them, that was a shock to me. That was a shock to me, the way I was brought up, the values that I had and supposedly what my function was to be there.

One of the functions I had there was to do security work. I had to guard Vietnamese who hadn't had a security clearance. Mostly it was children, women and older folks, because the men were out there somewhere else. I was to make sure that they didn't go over towards the tents and leave a hand grenade or do some reconnaissance. But every time I saw them move off, what they were looking to do was get near a trash can or garbage can, so they could take something to bring home to their families. I saw American soldiers die that I didn't even know because I was on the same convoy with them when we got hit. And I lost a good friend, Brins Griffen. He was nineteen years old. He was killed near the end of my tour of duty. I came back on leave and I went to his funeral. This is a kid I used to drink wine with on the corners of Boston. I wore my uniform out of respect for his family to his funeral. But I never wore my uniform with any pride again after that. Not after

what I saw in Vietnam. I never saw so many missing arms and legs
before. We used to say that's the walking wounded. They're more
valuable to us than dead Vietnamese because they can be seen every
day by the other people as a warning of what happens if you oppose
the United States government.

After Vietnam I asked the most seditious question of all: WHY? Why
is this government committing crimes in our name? Why were so many
of us from poor and working class backgrounds; why so many black and
latino GIs over there told to do the killing and the fighting while the
kids who have the money are going to the good schools in the United
States? I wasn't coming back to a university. I was going to come back
and face the prospect of going back and making some more heels for
those shoes. The blood of innocent people stirred my conscience and I'm
going to ask it to move your conscience during this trial. I came back
and I saw that the Vietnamese had a will to win, a will to fight. I wanted
to do whatever I could to help bring that war to an end. It didn't take
any great educated mind to figure out that children are innocent, whether
they're Vietnamese or young black children, or children of workers. But
the United States government has never figured that into its policies.

I received an honorable discharge from the army when I came back
and I became politically active with the Southern Student Organizing
Committee in Tennessee. Educating people, mobilizing people to oppose
the war in Vietnam. We supported the unionization of non-unionized
workers. We were involved with organizing support for attempts to
unionize workers in meatpacking plants throughout the South. If you've
ever been in a meatpacking plant, you'll understand you work under
very unhealthy and unsafe conditions. This is not a union looking for
higher wages. This is to get unionized and have the basic minimum
protection that a worker should have. I've been in those plants, though
I have not worked in them. But I have worked in a tannery and it's
very similar. I've had to unload hides off pallets that had maggots eating
on the flesh on one side of them. That's what they look like before they're
turned into a pair of shoes or a leather jacket.

We made a connection between what was happening in Vietnam
and some of the things that were happening in this country. And in
particular, the black liberation struggle at that time. The civil rights
struggle. The fight of black people to have decent housing and decent
medical care. Jobs. The right to live life to its fullest potential. The right
to be free from the fear of being attacked by the ku klux klan or killer
cops. We're going to hear a lot about cops who kill unarmed black and
latino people in this trial. I felt as a white working class person having
seen some of the racism in the United States that I saw, that it was
not my responsibility to go to black people and tell them what their

agenda is. They were making it clear what they wanted. They wanted freedom. They made it clear in Watts, they made it clear in Detroit. Malcolm X was making it clear. My task was to organize white people to support that struggle. And the union struggle was a multinational struggle of black and white workers together, so that was part of our agenda.

In 1969 I was in Atlanta at the Ebeneezer Baptist Church on the first anniversary of the death of Martin Luther King, Jr. where we marched in support of civil rights as part of this organization, SSOC, while white racists stood on the sidelines and spit on us. These I call early resistance activities. There's going to be a thread that runs through all of the political activity that I've been involved in over the years and that thread is that every single organization I have been associated with has come under police surveillance and some have come under police attack. When I talk about attack, I'm talking about physical attack. When I was in Tennessee I was set up by a police undercover agent, and, ultimately, convicted for selling seven dollars worth of marijuana. I don't condone drug use, and I worked later as a counselor in drug programs. But this was 1969. I had come back from Vietnam. Seven dollars worth of marijuana was nothing in Vietnam. It was openly used. I was a product of the times. I was a product of Vietnam. Seven dollars worth of marijuana was used to get me a five year maximum sentence. I had never been in prison before. No felony convictions. But because of my political activity, because I'm a person who doesn't have money to pay for a high-priced lawyer, because I can't influence the government, I was given that five year max. That's the price I had to pay for being a Vietnam veteran opposed to the war and opposed to racism.

Something I found out directly from my experience is that jails and prisons are nothing more than concentration camps for poor people. And people of color in particular. Black people in Tennessee, African-Americans. I saw that. The conditions in the Tennessee jails and prisons were horrible. They were brutalizing. You had to struggle just to keep your humanity from slipping though your fingers as you try and survive from one day to the other. And we were mistreated in jail. I was in a county jail. They were feeding us very poorly, very bad food, and we began to get sick. We got intestinal sicknesses. We had weight losses. We finally couldn't stand it anymore, and we went on a food strike to see if we could improve the conditions. I was asked to speak for the prisoners to present our grievances to the administration.

The way I was rewarded for that was I found myself in the Tennessee State Penitentiary in Nashville, classified as an "agitator," what I would call a political prisoner. It's a label that has stuck with me for the twwenty-one years that I've been politically active. I found that prison is nothing more than another kind of concrete and steel ghetto. The men I met in prison were there primarily for economic crimes. Taking because you haven't got a job. Taking because you don't have enough to provide for your family. Taking because you are part of a racist system that doesn't offer you any opportunity. The conditions were bad. I've seen prisoners cut themselves up. I wrote about this and the government seized these documents. I wrote about what it was like to sit in a cell and watch a 20 year old guy take a piece of glass six inches long and cut himself so he could go to the hospital and get something decent to eat. But he made a mistake and cut himself a little too deep. So he got hurt a lot more than he should have been. He miscalculated.

I write what it's like to read mail to another prisoner because he's illiterate and can't read letters that he's getting from his family. I have to write down for him, "I love you, wife," because he cannot write the words "I love you." He feels it but he can't write them because he's illiterate. In those Tennessee prisons we defied Jim Crow. I know some of you know who Jim Crow is. Jim Crow is: you eat racism, you sleep it, you walk it, they enforce it on you. Forced segregation by race. We fought that. Fought the ku klux klan and we fought the administration. Most of the time you couldn't tell the difference between the two. They profited from dividing black and white prisoners just like they profited in the union struggles from trying to divide black and white. They were afraid of that solidarity. Again, the reward for that was banishment. Banishment to isolation cells. Segregation cells, solitary confinement. Eventually, they put me in the ultimate solitary confinement, they put me on death row. At that time, they had made part of death row a segregation unit and that was the tightest place they could keep me so that's where they kept me, locked down 23 hours a day. I exercised one hour a day with people who were condemned to die. Most of them were black and all of them were poor. I never met one who wasn't from a background of poverty. I learned a great deal from these men—black men who had grown up in the urban and rural South at that time. That's when I was introduced to the ideas of Malcolm X. Malcolm said to accelerate and advance the struggle from civil rights to human rights.

There was no work. Very little exercise. Never enough to eat. This had a great impact on my thinking. I was continually kept in isolation cells. I was kept out of contact with other prisoners. But the influence continued. It came to me through the pages of books I was reading: Marx, Lenin, Mao, Ché Guevara, Frantz Fanon, Malcolm X, Rosa Luxemburg, Emma Goldman, the writings of the Black Panther Party. This is how the struggle for social justice has become my life. I've gone into those factories, those mills, those fields; I've sweat for the boss and know what it's like. I was in the Army. I've been in their jails and prisons. This is how I came to understand what I refer to as the class struggle and class conflict and this is how I became a revolutionary.

The banishment continued when I got out of prison. The only way I could leave prison was on the condition I leave the state of Tennessee. So I returned to my family in Maine where my mother and grandmother were living and I slept on a couch there. Started to work ten, twelve hour days. Making concrete blocks. Trying to save up some money to go to school, because I realized I had to get an education. Then I became a state organizer for Vietnam Veterans Against the War. This was a period of time when the air war in Vietnam was raging. When tens of thousands of Vietnamese civilians were being killed on the orders of people like Nixon and Kissinger. VVAW had documentation about what was going on in Vietnam. We held investigations and we had compiled information from ourselves, because we were there. Pilots, ground soldiers, support troops. We knew what was going on there. Vietnam Vets Against the War became a real thorn in the side of the government. I was trying to put into practice what it means to be a revolutionary. We were organizing marches and demonstrations, speaking, educating all over northern New England. And I went back to the Togus Veterans Administration Hospital where I had seen my grandfather so many years earlier, because I never forgot it. I went back on a hunch, and sure enough, we found a ward of young Vietnam veterans who were just warehoused there. VVAW came under police surveillance. And I'm going to return to this theme because it's important. Every political organization I have ever been associated with has come under police surveillance, and has ultimately been attacked.

When the war wound down, I began to work with other organizations that did work primarily with prisoners, ex-prisoners and their families. One of these organizations was called SCAR. With SCAR I was involved in putting together what we call survival programs: survival pending significant social changes, survival pending revolutionary changes that would meet the needs of the people who suffer most from class and racist oppression. It was an adaptation of what the Black Panther Party was doing at that time. Our motto was: Serve the People. And our programs were always free to the people who we served. SCAR is an organization that I worked with at the time this alleged conspiracy began. I was directly involved in setting up literacy programs in several county jails in southern Maine at the time, so we could teach prisoners how to read and write. And GED programs so they could get their high school diplomas. I was involved in drug counseling. And we set up a prisoners union at the state prison. We provided free transportation to prison for families and friends of prisoners because they didn't have much money. We were involved in getting jobs for people. We were involved in getting temporary housing for people. We were involved in daycare for children. We put out our own paper. We did support work for political prisoners. We monitored cases of police brutality in the community in which we lived.

There are two things about SCAR's work at that time that I think casts a different light on the organization than the government's witness is going to. We worked in a neighborhood coalition with other groups. We worked with people on welfare; we worked with tenants' rights people. I was involved in setting up two programs that came out of this coalition. We went to people and we said, what can we do for you, what do you need? One of the things they said was our kids and young people and sometimes older people are being imprisoned and they can't get out because they don't have the hundred dollars bail or two hundred dollars bail. So we organized what we called the Portland Community Bail Fund. Portland was the name of the community I lived in. That bail fund is still in existence today, fifteen years later.

The other thing that I was involved with was kids in the projects. The kids were drinking a lot, doing drugs, and there was a problem with the cops. Mothers said the kids were losing respect for them. Primarily women were raising these kids in the projects. They came to SCAR for help. At the time I was teaching free karate classes at the university to people in the community. So I went to the Bayside Projects and the Kennedy Park Projects and started a karate program for young kids, because I found out through my years of practice, that martial arts serve to instill a certain measure of self-respect and self-discipline in a person. And if you have respect for yourself, then you're going to respect your elders, you are going to respect the people in your neighborhood. That's what a revolutionary does if a revolutionary loves the people. I try to put that into practice.

In 1974, I became involved in opening up the Red Star North Bookstore which was loosely associated with SCAR. You are going to see evidence about this bookstore. You are going to see a photograph of the bookstore and myself. It isn't hard for the government to get photographs. The store was under police surveillance all the time. We sold books on labor history, black history, revolution, feminism. We had a free-books-for-prisoners program. We mailed books free to prisoners who requested it. We maintained correspondence with prisoners. As I said, the bookstore was under surveillance. If you're going to oppose this government at any level, you're going to have to live with the fact that the police are going to be breathing down your neck and listening to the telephone.

But it didn't stay at that level. It accelerated, it intensified. I became aware of the existence of a police death squad, a police assassination squad that had been formed in the Portland Police Department. I had several sources of information for that: 1) it was on the street that myself and my comrade, Tom Manning, were to be targeted, along with other ex-prisoners, by this assassination team; 2) I was told this by a guy named Stevie Poullen, who, it would be revealed at city council hearings, was also on that list. Stevie Poullen's not coming in to talk about it because he got a .357 in his head. Some people say he put it there. Other people speculated that cops put it there; 3) there were city-wide hearings held in city hall to investigate the allegations of a death squad. SCAR demonstrated at city hall to bring as much public attention as we could to what was happening. At that demonstration a woman named Linda Coleman came up to me and introduced herself. It was the first time in my life I had seen her. She's a government witness now.

We were looking to see if we could find justice. What we got was a whitewash and a cover-up. A lot of cops were implicated at those hearings and ultimately only one was indicted for solicitation to murder. Another one of the cops who was involved in this was named Bertrand Surphes. This becomes important in terms of the bookstore, because the bookstore came under attack. The bookstore became a focus for the cops to zero in on. Then there was an incident where one of the workers in the bookstore was attacked by two men who slipped in the door. She was brutally beaten and she was raped. She told me it was the police. It was hard for me to fathom it could be anybody else. Because they're parked across the street. They were always watching us.

There were other incidents. The bookstore was ransacked. Books were destroyed. Posters were ripped up. The little money that was there was taken. There were death threats, both on the phone at SCAR and through mailings that contained ku klux klan and nazi slogans. There were arrests. A squad of police officers came burrowing through the front door one day, and who should be in front of the squad and the arresting officer but Bertrand Surphes, who had been implicated in the death squad. Why was I arrested? Because after searching the bookstore, they say they found a can of beer that had its top open in the back room. Naturally, the judge threw that out. That was a bogus arrest to come in and hassle us and close the store and threaten us. I took this as a real serious threat, not only to our political work but to our lives. I started to carry a gun. Now I'm in a bad situation. I'm a convicted felon. I sold seven dollars worth of marijuana, so a gun is going to get me ten years in a federal penitentiary. But I got a choice between that, or getting one of these cop's bullets in my head. I didn't think it was a choice, so I started to carry a gun. I always thought it was a very wise move. Remember, this is the early 70s. There's a larger framework involved.

I became familiar with COINTELPRO, counterintelligence programs of the FBI The target of the COINTELPRO programs were primarily organizations and individuals that worked for social change and opposed government policy. Their tactics included everything from harassment, surveillance and wiretaps to assassinations. One of the earliest targets was Martin Luther King, Jr. The government has always targeted any leadership that's ever risen up either in the civil rights struggle involving black people or human rights struggle. Over forty members of the Black Panther Party were killed during this period of COINTELPRO activities. Dozens of Indian activists were murdered. Vietnam Veterans Against the War was a COINTELPRO target, as was the Puerto Rican Independence Movement. That was the climate of the time. I did not want to remain vulnerable to police attack, their agents, their provocateurs. So I made a decision that I was going to continue my work away from the eyes and ears of the government. I call that going underground. Some people call it clandestine. Of course I had to take those police attacks into consideration. But I will tell you, I'll be totally up front about it, it merely accelerated what I had wanted to do for a period of time. I ultimately would have gone underground.

The reason that I went under was because I wanted to contribute to building a revolutionary resistance movement in this country that has the capability to defend itself at any stage of its development, at any stage of history, regardless of what particular activity it's engaged in at the time. You cannot expose all the organizations of a political movement to the government. Some of them have to be away from its eyes and ears. I wanted to help build a movement that would grow and sustain itself. A movement is always subject to attack at any point in time. And I wanted to help build something that could sustain any attack. I freely admit to being part of a revolutionary movement. The government can't tolerate serious opposition to its own criminal policies, so they do what the prosecutors are trying to do here. They want to criminalize my life, my ideas, my values, and the organizations that they allege I've been a part of.

They begin to do this in the indictment by talking about "manner and means." Use of fictitious identification, renting houses with names other than your own, using public telephones to communicate, private mailboxes. The possession of weapons. Practicing with weapons. Monitoring police activities. If you look at the context in which things are done, I think that, in this case, you are going to find out this is not criminal activity. You know, when I went to Vietnam I was twenty years old. I couldn't vote and I could not have a legal drink. So I did what a lot of other GIs did. I had a fake I.D., so I could have a beer and celebrate the idea that I might get killed in another year to defend this system.

More to the point, if you want to stay alive and survive, you have to utilize these methods. In nazi Germany, if·they hadn't had secret meetings (I'm talking about Jews, labor leaders, communists, gay people, everybody who the nazis went after), if they hadn't used false passports or identification, if they didn't carry a gun now and then, do you think that more would have gotten killed? When the nazis spread their fascism into France and you had a French government that collaborated with the nazis, how far do you think the resistance would have got if they hadn't utilized these types of methods? It had a hard enough time as it was.

And the same could be said for South Africa today that murders and tortures its opponents. They want you to carry a pass in South Africa today. So you are going to have to find something else if you don't want to end up in one of those South African prisons. Or the sanctuary movement today, which utilizes churches to move refugees through the country from Central America, refugees from wars that the United States is responsible for creating. Think for a minute about a woman named Harriet Tubman, who used to come through Springfield up to Amherst

In the majority of colonial situations, the civilian police are used first, and the dominated population sees them as occupying troops. (photo: LNS)

and into Canada. She carried a gun and she used a name other than her own and she used so-called safe houses. That's what the underground railroad was. How many of those slaves do you think would have made it if she hadn't done that? Part of what they were fleeing from was the Fugitive Slave Act. It was the law at the time.

I would like to digress for a minute and tell you why I'm choosing to defend myself. I was underground for ten years. It's not easy for me to stand here before you now and speak in what is essentially a public forum. What I'm simply trying to do is to add my voice to that of millions of others who cry freedom from South Africa to Central America to the South Bronx in New York. They don't have much choice about it, and I don't have much choice. I would rather not be here. But since I am, I want to defend myself and I want to defend issues that I think are important. And the important issue here, is the issue of human rights. I see that as a central part of this trial. The prosecutor mentioned one of his snitch witnesses comes from Harvard University, and of course, the prosecutor himself went to the same school. I can tell you that I never went to any prestigious law school. He has indicated that he is going to bring a computer in here to put on his table. You won't see any computer over there on my table. And I don't have a squad of FBI agents running my paperwork around for me. I do all my preparation from a prison cell. I'm one of over a hundred political prisoners in the United States which the United States refuses to recognize.

The judge has said I don't have to ask questions. I don't have to testify. I don't have to cross-examine. But I do want to defend myself and I do want to participate in certain parts of this trial. What he didn't tell you is that he decides what it is I can do. I have a defense, but you are not necessarily going to hear or see it. He makes that decision. That's the power he has. But if you don't hear it, it's not that I haven't tried. You will see me angry in this trial. That anger will never be directed towards you. My anger is reserved for the government and some of the agents and witnesses who they're going to bring in here. Now, over the years, after Vietnam, I felt I needed to engage in a self-education project. You will see a lot of material that was seized by the FBI. They seized everything in the house, including my kids' report cards and a copy of the Bill of Rights. I monitored and collected a lot of data, research, fiscal data, articles documenting human rights violations in South Africa, Central America, human rights violations by this government. I collected information on military contractors; who they are selling their weapons to and how much they are getting for it.

I tried to document every incident I could find where black and latino people were murdered by the police. And, if I stood here now and started giving you each one of those names, I would still be standing here next week. I kept a file on the numbers of homeless and hungry and the numbers of unemployed. And there was a special notebook which I kept on prisons, documenting the guard murders of prisoners and, in particular, political prisoners. I documented civil rights violations and violations of international law. The judge has said that you are triers of facts and I think you should look at the facts. But I'm going to ask you to look for something else. I'm going to ask you to look for the truth.

Over the years, directly and indirectly, I have become aware that the United States government and some of the corporations headquartered in this country have engaged in serious violations of international law, what are referred to as crimes against humanity and war crimes. The government has referred to communiques that will come into evidence. The evidence is going to show that a lot of these bombings were done in support of freedom in South Africa. And that no other government in today's modern world is as close to being like nazi Germany as the government of racist South Africa.

South Africa has a system called apartheid. Apartheid means hate black people; segregate black people. The United Nations has condemned apartheid as a crime against humanity. The closest ally to racist South Africa in this world is the United States government. The United Nations has condemned the collaboration of the United States, including U.S. corporations, with racist South Africa. There's a saying I heard once: "The blood of oppression in South Africa runs as deep as the mines." Because we know who works in the mines in South Africa—who mines the gold and diamonds—black people. They do it for next to nothing. They do it for starvation wages. Because they've had their land stolen from them. Black people are eighty percent of the population and they don't even have the right to vote.

There was an action carried out by the Sam Melville-Jonathan Jackson Unit in 1976 against Union Carbide. It was right after the Soweto Uprising in South Africa in which 1,000 or more black people, mainly women and children, were gunned down by South African troops. It started as a student demonstration. People demanding to preserve their language and culture were shot in the back by South African troops. The very first to be killed was Hector Pieterson, a young African boy. He was fourteen years old. Why were they gunned down? Because they were in the streets of Soweto, a black township, with their fists in the air, shouting "Amandla, Amandla"—power that brings freedom. They want their country back. They want their land back. And they want their rights.

The Sam Melville-Jonathon Jackson Unit attacked the property of the Union Carbide Corporation while the U.S. government was collaborating with the South African police and military to kill 1,000 black people. I'm here to support the liberation struggle in South Africa; these prosecutors are here to defend the interests of the United States government in South Africa. The United Freedom Front also paid a visit to the South African Airways Office, a front for an office of the South African government in New York City. They did it after there was a massacre in Lesotho, next to South Africa, where South African troops had gone in and gunned down black activists. That's called massacre. We're going to learn in this trial what the word massacre means.

American corporations are the legs upon which the racist system in South Africa walks. Troops in South Africa ride in General Motors trucks that are fueled by Mobil Oil Corporation. So do the entire police and military system. In South Africa, those prisons, that pass system, all of that is computerized by corporations like IBM. The blood of innocent people must stir your conscience. I think that you ought to ask yourself a question throughout this trial, and that is: Who are the real criminals? Those who support that racist system in South Africa or those who are opposed to it?

I believe the evidence will show that there is a war in Central America and that it is a U.S. sponsored war. This trial's going to have a lot to do with bombings. The United Freedom Front took responsibility for bombings of U.S. military contractors and facilities. The evidence is going to show the UFF objected to the United States shipping bombs and armaments to the government of El Salvador which uses them to slaughter its own people. One of these particular bombs is a 750 pound fragmentation bomb. The prosecutor referred to 600 pounds of dynamite. This is one bomb that weighs 750 pounds. It's dropped by an A-37 Dragon Jet made by General Electric. That was also used in Vietnam. They're anti-personnel bombs. They explode before they hit the ground. That's not designed to destroy property as much as it's designed to kill people. And while we are standing here there is a corporation up in Burlington, Vermont, General Electric, that is making machine guns that's going on this aircraft. The guns that the peasants in El Salvador refer to as flying death squads. The issue of state terrorism is going to be a central issue that comes up during this trial.

A lot of SMJJ bombings were done in support of Puerto Rican independence and the release of Puerto Rican political prisoners. All national struggles in which people are trying to be free are close to my heart, but the struggle for Puerto Rico to be free is especially close to me. I have three young girls and I used to tell them bedtime stories about Puerto Rican patriots like Lolita Lebron and her *compañeros* who spent a quarter of a century in U.S. prisons because they dared to take the struggle for a free Puerto Rico to the heart of the beast, right here in the United States. Half of the Puerto Rican population have been forced by economic conditions to migrate to this country. The American flag flies over Puerto Rico. While you may think it represents freedom here, it does not represent freedom to the vast majority of Puerto Rican people.

The United States invaded Puerto Rico ninety years ago and it has been militarily occupied since then. There are bases all over the nation of Puerto Rico. The United Nations has ruled that Puerto Rico is a colony of the United States and that colonialism is illegal under international law. It is a crime under international law. I believe that it is inhumane by any standard to subject another country or another people to what you want to do. The United Nations has ruled that Puerto Rico is being held illegally, illegally occupied, therefore it has the right to resist that occupation. And I support that. You are going to see evidence in this trial about the police murders of unarmed Puerto Rican men right here in Springfield. That is something the Sam Melville-Jonathan Jackson Unit felt was necessary to respond to. You will see evidence of the abusive treatment of Puerto Rican political prisoners held in the United States.

Like me, you probably hold high value and respect for the principles on which the American Revolution was founded, the Declaration of Independence and the Constitution. But as I look back at those documents and what they represent, I ask myself, I don't remember anybody conferring on this government or its military and police apparatus the right to engage in violations of human rights in the name of the American people. In school as a kid I would do the pledge of allegiance all the time. But, based on my experience since then, I don't feel like I owe any blind allegiance to a system that perpetuates this kind of suffering of people throughout the world, including here within the United States.

I mentioned earlier that the question of killer cops is going to be an important issue in this trial. When officers of the New York City Police Department beat to death a young black community artist named Michael Stewart, the United Freedom Front responded by supporting the black communities in their struggle to stop killer cops. There's little difference between a lynching by the KKK and a police officer who puts a bullet in the head of a young black man, and it happens time and time again. And lest we think the klan is not active, I expect that we're going to have a close look at the New York City Police Department during this trial. I think what you are going to see is the largest ku klux klan chapter in the Northeast.

The sedition law and RICO law were addressed earlier and I now want to address them briefly. Sedition laws in general have always been designed to break what has been a tradition of resistance and political activity in this country, whether it was Native American people resisting the theft of their land or slaves trying to be free, or union leaders or anti-war activists. And this specific sedition law, seditious conspiracy,

296 • Ray Luc Levasseur

has been almost exclusively used against Puerto Rican *independentistas*, that is, advocates for a free and independent Puerto Rico. Now the government has expanded its use to try and target those who support Puerto Rican independence. You are going to see very clearly that I support Puerto Rican independence with all my heart. And I don't support it idly, I support it actively. I participate in the struggle. The government wants you to believe that three people are going to conspire to overthrow the most powerful government on the face of the earth. Or eight people as the original indictment says. Or eighty or 800 for that matter. That is a fabrication. That goes against my political thinking. Because I don't think there's going to be significant social change in this country unless a lot of people participate and make it happen. That's what self-determination is all about.

They're spending over ten million dollars on this trial to try to convince people that a 125 year old sedition statute is going to keep the United States from sinking. What they're really looking for with their ten million dollars is a government show trial. A propaganda trial. Sort of a version of what they used to have years ago where you take a dissident and you put him in a wooden stock and try to humiliate him, denigrate him, criminalize him. This is what they want to use the prosecution of myself and others for. As a warning to other political dissidents, to organizers, to revolutionaries. Against those who challenge a government conducting their bloody business as usual.

They want to see to it that I spend the rest of my life in prison. They want to make me bleed. One of the ways they do that is they go not just after me, but they go after everybody whom I'm associated with—friends, family, supporters. I've had friends subpoenaed before a grand jury that refused to testify; refused to give up information. They have been jailed. That's called political internment. Because you're jailed without a trial. I was arrested in November 1984. Since I've been arrested, I've been beaten and I've been stun gunned. A stun gun is like an electric cattle prod. I was arrested with my wife and our three children, who were four, six, and eight at the time. Government agents attempted to bribe my eight year old daughter at that time. She wouldn't take a bribe. So they put her in a room with FBI agents and state police and they threatened her. There was a time when these agents sitting here and their colleagues were hanging from trees in the cemetery when my grandma died, because they thought that they could pick up on my whereabouts, because they think my family is going to turn me in. I don't come from that kind of people. We don't turn each other in. We don't turn over for this government.

The treatment of the children at the time of our arrest, and particularly the children of Thomas and Carol Manning, who were grabbed and held for two months incommunicado, separate from their family members who pleaded to have them released, and ultimately they were released after widespread attention was brought on the case and after a hunger strike. What I'm getting at, is the abuses that the government is prepared to carry out in an attempt to not only convict me and keep me in prison, but also to take that pound of flesh and hurt everybody that I'm associated with.

In June of 1984 it became public knowledge of the existence of a task force called BosLuc. You remember I said my middle name is Luc. Bos, B-O-S, Boston; Luc, L-U-C, my middle name. I was the target. This task force existed before June of '84 but it became public knowledge in June of '84. It had to because they put a bullet in the head of a kid named Ralph Richards. I read about it in the newspaper. How this kid had his hands up and he got shot in the head by BosLuc agents. I felt that bullet had my name on it.

There's another reason for this prosecution and what the government is doing that sheds some light on their intent. Not only do they want to keep me in prison, but they want to put my wife in prison. If you listened to the prosecution earlier, you heard them characterize our marriage and our love for each other as if it was some kind of criminal enterprise. You know I'm separated from my three young daughters by prison walls and my wife brings them in to visit me, but the government isn't going to be satisfied until those three kids are orphans. That is the nature and extent of the punishment that they want to put out to anyone who even thinks of challenging this government's policies, particularly where I am so outspoken about it. It's hard to believe that those government prosecutors are going to build their careers on the backs of political prisoners and children who are left without their parents. But that's what they are doing.

I want to just briefly address the issue of the RICO charges. Racketeering Influenced Corrupt Organizations. I can't tell you how insulted I am these prosecutors charge me with being a racketeer. That law was passed in the '70s and it was specifically passed to be used against real gangsters and real racketeers. Racketeering Influenced and Corrupt Organizations I do not believe has the word revolutionary in it, or political dissident. They're trying to bend the law. You cannot be a revolutionary and be a racketeer. It's a contradiction. It's either one or the other. You cannot support freedom struggles in South Africa or Central America or the black nation within this country from the foundation of a criminal enterprise. It can't be done. History shows that.

I'm neither profit oriented nor drug oriented. In twenty-one years of political activity I've never done anything for personal gain or profit. Nothing. That has never been part of my motivation or intent. The

298 • Ray Luc Levasseur

government wants to charge that bombing the office of the South African government is an act of racketeering? A bombing that was done in response to a massacre in South Africa and to support the struggle for freedom there. This is an act of racketeering? No, it's an expression of support for freedom. It's that simple. If we could have Nelson Mandela here today, or Winnie Mandela, would they think attacking an office of the racist government of South Africa is an act of racketeering?

The government stood up for forty-five minutes essentially saying nothing more than that I'm a criminal and a racketeer and part of a criminal enterprise. That's not true. And I want to refute it and I want to put as much evidence in as I can to refute it. I want to participate in certain parts of this trial to refute it. If you want to see a corrupt and criminal enterprise let's take a good look at the highest levels of the United States government and what some of these military contractors are doing. Then we'll see what real corruption and criminality looks like.

These prosecutors do not represent the American people. They represent the government. And since Vietnam, I have always made an important distinction between the two. I hope that you will. They're here to present certain interests and I'm here to defend certain issues. I began this by talking about children. The children I began talking about were my own grandparents. They were merely children when they had to go to work in those mills and shoe factories. My grandfather was thirteen years old. That and my own experience I've outlined to you have left a deep imprint on me. And it does not leave me with any criminal intent or a criminal mind. It leaves me with the heart of a revolutionary, somebody who's committed to social justice. My wife and I have a marriage. We don't have a criminal enterprise. We have three daughters. My oldest daughter is going to be thirteen day after tomorrow. We named each of our kids after their grandmothers, one of whom is sitting here now, and one after their great-grandmother. Because we are proud of our working class roots and we're proud of our families.

I still remember the children of Vietnam, the suffering of those children who I saw there. But I also remember the beauty of their smiles. And I never have lost sight of what human potential there is in people. This is at the heart of what motivates me—my intent, my purpose, my goals, my values, this is where it's at. It's my commitment. This is what the government fears. That I didn't go back to that mill to make those shoe heels, that I took another course with my life. I have a commitment to a future that holds the human potential of poor and working class people as a great asset to be developed, a commitment to a future in which no child will ever suffer from racism, poverty, or war, a future where justice brings peace for our children and generations to come.

Jennie Vander Wall

The Death Penalty and the Supreme Court: A Case-Study in "American Democracy"

Somewhere between 10,000 and 16,000 human beings, the records on this being anything but clear, have met their deaths through execution during the history of the United States.[1] These numbers reflect only so-called "legal" executions. Lynchings, predominantly of black victims by white mobs—with a total which runs well into the thousands—are excluded. Also excluded are those many thousands whose lives have been arbitrarily terminated by police bullets, beatings and the like. In this last connection, it should be noted that "blacks far more often than whites are killed by police."[2] About those officially executed by the state, certain conclusions are inescapable: overwhelmingly they have been poor; disproportionately they have been men of color.

Racism has always been inextricably woven into the fabric of U.S. capital punishment. A 1988 publication by Amnesty International, *United States of America: The Death Penalty*, details some sordid history. Between 1900 and 1967, more than half of the executions in the U.S. took place in southern states. These included numerous implementations of the death penalty for the crime of rape. Almost all such executions took place in the south, and were mostly of black men, usually convicted of raping white women. From 1930 to 1967, about two-thirds of the people executed in the south for all crimes were black, although blacks formed a distinctly minority proportion of the population. Of those prisoners executed in the southern states for rape during that time period, 89 percent were black.[3] In 1977, the Supreme Court ruled (in *Coker v. Georgia*) that the death penalty was unconstitutional when imposed for the rape of an adult woman.

After 1967, executions in the U.S. temporarily ceased, and in 1972 (*Furman v. Georgia*), the Supreme Court ruled that the death penalty as it was then applied constituted "cruel and unusual punishment" and outlawed it. (In that year, at the national level, although black people made up only eleven percent of the total population, more than half of the prisoners on death row were black.)[4] However, in 1976 the Supreme Court reversed itself to a considerable extent, deciding in *Gregg v. Georgia* that the death penalty when applied to convicted murderers was constitutional under "guided discretion" in sentencing, requiring the use of "objective standards."[5] Despite the court's bow to the principle of objectivity—whatever that might mean in a given instance—the racial bias in imposition of the death penalty continued to be glaringly obvious. Statistics concerning the percentage of black people on death row as compared to the percentage of the U.S. population which is black have held fairly steady over the past decade. The true determinant of who dies at the state's decree, however, is not ultimately the color of the alleged perpetrator but the color of the victim. Between 1976 and 1986, of the fifty-six people executed, fifty-two were convicted of murdering a white victim. In no case was a white person convicted of murdering a black person executed.[6]

In 1990, despite the fact the rate at which black people died from homicide was almost six times that at which white people suffered the same fate, only five per cent of those executed were convicted of killing black people.[7] Says activist attorney Ron Kuby of the Center for Constitutional Rights, "We can prove through statistics that anyone accused of killing a white person is five times more likely to get the death penalty than someone accused of killing a Black person."[8] From a more conservative source, a 1990 General Accounting Office study, comes the conclusion, "Those who murdered whites were found to be more likely to be sentenced to death than those who murdered blacks."[9]

These statistics are destined to become even more appalling. In April of 1991, Attorney General Dick Thornburgh, acting on behalf of the Bush administration, made a special appearance before the Supreme Court. He asked that the court overturn two of its own recent precedents barring prosecutors from presenting "victim impact" evidence to juries considering imposition of a death sentence. (The specific case in question, *Payne v. Tennessee,* concerned a mentally handicapped black man, Pervis Payne, who was convicted of—in what the prosecution described as a "drug induced frenzy"—repeatedly stabbing a white woman and her two young children. The woman and one of the children died.) Thornburgh argued that the jury should be allowed to consider the character of the victim to "get the full picture of the harm that was done." The obvious question was raised by Supreme Court Justice David Souter. If the lives of different victims are to be given different value, Souter asked, "isn't the real problem one almost of equality before the law?"[10]

Given two months in which to reconsider, Souter was able to overcome any scruples he might have had about furthering inequality. On June 27, 1991, the last day of the Supreme Court's 1990-91 term, he joined with the majority in the six to three vote against Payne. In his concurring opinion Souter stated, "Any failure to take account of a victim's individuality and the effects of his death upon close survivors would thus more appropriately be called an act of lenity than their consideration an invitation to arbitrary sentencing."[11] The only direct reference as to what qualifies a given victim for a higher level of "individuality" advocates the theory that those with caring relatives, especially children, have a greater value. Other than that, we can be safe in assuming that the biases of the past concerning a murder victim's relative worth will be strengthened in the immediate future. Meanwhile, death row populations have skyrocketed. In 1987, the national roster of condemned prisoners was four times what it had been a decade earlier. As of April, 1991, the total stood at around 2,400.[12]

Predictably, attempts to use the courts to eliminate racist inequality and overall injustice in death penalty cases have, during the Reagan-Bush years, produced an almost unmitigated disaster. In 1985, Warren McCleskey, a black man sentenced to die for killing a white Atlanta police officer, appealed to the Eleventh Federal Circuit Court of Appeals. His appeal was based on a study by a Professor Baldus. Baldus examined homicide cases in Georgia between 1973 and 1979. He found that the race of the victim was a determining factor in whether or not the death penalty was imposed. Although blacks accounted for some sixty percent of Georgia homicide victims, killers of black victims were punished by death less than one-tenth as often as were killers of white victims.[13] When this appeal was denied, McCleskey turned to the Supreme Court. In April of 1987, that court held that the death penalty is not racially discriminatory. Writing for the majority, Justice Lewis Powell stated, "At most, the Baldus study indicates a discrepancy that appears to correlate with race."[14] The four dissenting justices saw things in a different light:

> Warren McCleskey's evidence confronts us with the subtle and persistent influence of the past. His message is a disturbing one to a society that has formally repudiated racism and a frustrating one to a nation accustomed to regarding its destiny as the product of its own will. Nonetheless, we ignore him at our peril, for we remain imprisoned by the past as long as we deny its influence in the present.[15]

A much more insightful statement was made by Shabaka Sundiata Waqlimi, a black man falsely convicted of robbery, rape and murder of a white woman in Florida in 1973. Sentenced to death, he spent fourteen years in prison before his conviction was overturned and the charges dismissed. When asked how he felt about finally being free, Waqlimi said:

> I, of African descent, am not a free person in this country and

never was. It is not my country. When they say that I am free,
I say it is because I am no longer restrained by bars, but that's
as far as it goes, because they are still killing a lot of my brothers
and sisters and they are doing it for the wrong reasons, and I
don't think I could be free until I control my own development.[16]

It should be noted that support for the death penalty also reflects
race/color. In a Media General-Associated Press poll conducted in 1987,
86 percent of Americans were reported to support the death penalty.
Forty-seven per cent wanted it expanded to be used for crimes other
than murder; of these, fifty-four percent favored execution for rape. Only
nine percent of whites said there should be no death penalty—but one-
third of the blacks polled wanted executions abolished. (Of all the
respondents, half did not think the death penalty was carried out
fairly.)[17] National support for the death penalty reflects the punitive
mood prevalent in the U.S. Says Henry Schwarzschild, head of ACLU's
Capital Punishment Project: "We live in a culture that is in a very bad
mood. People no longer want the death penalty as an answer to crime
and violence. They want it because they think the SOB should die."[18]

Warren McCleskey's attorneys continued the struggle to save their
client from execution. They filed a Freedom of Information Act (FOIA)
request, which produced evidence that the state had violated McCleskey's
Sixth Amendment right to counsel by placing an informer in the cell
next to his. (A 21-page statement from the informer, which was in the
possession of the state, was withheld from McCleskey's defense team
during his trial.) A month after receiving the FOIA material, McCleskey's
lawyers filed a second petition on his behalf, which was granted by the
Federal District Court. The Eleventh Circuit Court of Appeals overturned
this decision, on the grounds that McCleskey had not included (in the
appeals court's words, "deliberately abandoned") a Sixth Amendment
argument, made in an earlier state court appeal, within his first federal
habeas corpus petition. In true Kafkaesque fashion, the Eleventh Circuit
Court came to this decision *despite* the fact that the reason that
McCleskey did not have documentary proof of violation of his Sixth
Amendment rights was that said proof had been deliberately withheld
from his lawyers by the state.

On April 16, 1991, the Supreme Court ruled six to three to uphold
the decision of the Eleventh Circuit Court. Writing for the majority,
Supreme Court Justice Anthony M. Kennedy observed that "perpetual
disregard for the finality of convictions disparages the entire criminal
justice system," and redefined the judicial "abuse of the writ" doctrine
in such a way that second or subsequent *habeas corpus* petitions will
not be heard, except in cases of a "fundamental miscarriage of justice,"
which he said would occur only in "extraordinary instances."[19] One

might ask—if deliberate withholding of evidence from a defendant's attorneys does not constitute a "fundamental miscarriage of justice,"— what does? This, however, is the evolution of justice in the Reagan/Bush years. The three dissenting Justices, Thurgood Marshall, Harry A. Blackmun and John Paul Stevens, were described in a *Denver Post* editorial as "aging liberals."[20] (Marshall subsequently resigned.) In the early morning of September 25, 1991, Warren McCleskey was killed by the state of Georgia.

The most poignant comment on the second McClesky ruling was made by Florida prisoner Roy Allen Harich, executed on April 24, 1991, hours after the Supreme Court rejected his last appeal, the first prisoner to be executed following the court's April 16 decision. Said Harich, in what was described as a "barely audible voice," after he was strapped into the electric chair:

> I'm disappointed with the almost total lack of fairness in the American criminal justice system. This is truly a sad time in our country's history, when political concerns take on more importance than the fundamental rights of the individual.[21]

The second McClesky ruling, while it does not apply only to death penalty cases, is expected to have a particularly serious impact on them. About forty percent of all death sentences are overturned because federal courts determine that there was constitutional error in the conviction or in imposition of the sentence.[22] It is not known at present how many of these decisions came as a result of second or subsequent *habeas corpus* petitions. It is known that—despite the dedicated work of many fine lawyers working as public defenders or doing *pro bono* defense work— defendants who are poor/indigent often go to court without competent counsel, and defendants who are not white are, in addition to facing the special problems caused by racism, usually at the lower end of the economic scale. The situation is particularly serious in death penalty cases. Chief Judge James Oakes of the Court of Appeals for the Second Circuit, believes that "inadequate representation is, without a doubt, the most significant problem in capital litigation today."[23] According to Amnesty International, the majority of defendants facing execution cannot afford to retain their choice of attorneys and are therefore defended by court appointed lawyers, producing a quality of defense which is often abysmal.

On June 11, 1990, *The National Law Journal* published an in-depth study of attorney competence and performance in capital cases in the states of Mississippi, Texas, Georgia, Alabama, Louisiana, and Florida. (As of May, 1990, those six states had been responsible for nearly eighty percent of the executions performed since 1976.) The article is appropriately titled "Fatal Defense." Its key findings included these statistics:

• The trial lawyers who represented death row inmates had been disbarred, suspended, or otherwise disciplined at a rate three to forty-six times the average discipline rates for the six states.
• More than half the defense attorneys who were interviewed for the study said they were handling their first capital trial when their clients were convicted and sentenced to death.
• Capital trials often last only one to two days, and penalty phases, which usually start immediately following a guilty verdict, may last only several hours, and in one case took only *fifteen minutes.*
• Most significantly, "[T]he U.S. Supreme Court decision that lays out the test for ineffective assistance of counsel is itself ineffective, according to capital law experts and defense lawyers. The test has made it all but impossible for death-sentenced inmates to challenge the performance of their trial lawyers."[25]

Bluntly put, as an anonymous lawyer in Louisiana told *The National Law Journal,* "If you're poor or black, you don't stand a chance."[26] This situation has been found quite acceptable—indeed, perhaps, desirable, by the conservative-dominated Supreme Court. On June 24, 1991, in what *The New York Times* termed "the most sweeping of several decisions sharply constricting the ability of state prison inmates to pursue appeals in Federal courts," the court reversed a 1963 decision written by Justice Brennan which bound federal courts to hear habeas corpus petitions from state prisoners whose earlier appeals to state courts were in some way flawed, as long as such prisoners had not "deliberately bypassed" the state courts' processes. The new ruling, used to reject an appeal from a Virginia death row prisoner, permits the denial of the right of habeas corpus petition for any failure—whether deliberate or not—to comply with the state process. In the case in question, *Coleman v. Thompson,* the lawyer for Roger K. Coleman missed the deadline for filing his state habeas corpus petition to the Virginia Supreme Court by *three days.* Writing for the majority, Justice Sandra Day O'Connor stated that "attorney ignorance or inadvertence" are not adequate cause for error and that "the petitioner must bear the risk of attorney error." It should be noted that Coleman, who is white, had at trial two court-appointed lawyers who had never before handled a serious criminal case. Ineffective assistance of counsel was one of Coleman's grounds for appeal.[27] In spite of substantial new evidence of his innocence, Coleman died in the electric chair in May of 1992.

Less than twenty-four hours after the Supreme Court ruling on *Coleman v. Thompson* was announced, Florida death row prisoner Bobby Marion Francis died in the electric chair. A federal appeals court in Atlanta had granted him a stay of execution; the stay was lifted after the ruling, by an order from the Supreme Court itself that the appeals court reconsider his case in light of its decision against Coleman. It should also be here noted that the jury which convicted Francis recommended that he receive a sentence of life imprisonment, not death, but was overruled by the trial judge. Francis was the twenty-seventh Florida prisoner, and the 148th in the entire U.S. to be executed since the use of the death penalty was resumed in 1976.[28] It is beyond doubt that some of these victims of execution were totally innocent of the crimes for which they died. According to a 1987 study quoted by David C. Leven, Executive Director of the New York Prisoners' Legal Services:

> • More than 350 people have been erroneously convicted of crimes potentially punishable by death in this century; 116 of them were sentenced to death, and 22 were executed.
> • Certain legal 'experts' see these deaths as within acceptable limits. For example, Ernest van den Haag, a professor of jurisprudence at Fordham University, states, '[But] the state does not intend to execute an innocent person. These things happen. ... Most human activities involve killing people, indirectly. But we feel the desirable effects more than off-balance that.'[29]

For many other people, it is not so easy to dismiss these dead prisoners, particularly those whose wrongful convictions were probably the result of their color, socioeconomic status, or other factors unrelated to any question of guilt or innocence. William Jasper Darden, a black man convicted of killing a white man in Florida, was put to death on March 15, 1988, despite a massive wave of last-minute letters, telegrams and telephone calls desperately trying to convince Governor Bob Martinez to stay the execution. Considerable evidence suggests Willie Darden was innocent of the crime which precipitated his state-imposed death. Shortly before his electrocution, Darden wrote the following,

> If we executed all murderers, we would execute 20,000 per year; we face execution because we are the scapegoats. Like those stricken with a terminal illness, I feel I was chosen at random. And, while morally it is no worse to execute the innocent than to execute the guilty, I will proclaim until the electric chair's current silences me that I am innocent of the charge that sent me here. ... Our society executes as much *for the person as for the crime*. We execute for heresy—for being different, or for being at the wrong place at the wrong time. We execute for the traits of the person found guilty. If the person is black, uneducated, poor, outspoken, slightly retarded, eccentric, or odd, he stands a much higher chance of being executed than do those convicted of even worse crimes than he. Juries find it hard to convict one of their own, so middle class whites are rarely in our ranks. Like those stricken with a terminal illness, I feel a tremendous sense of injustice. Unlike others preparing to die, studies have been conducted by the best minds in America that show I am right.[30]

It cannot, of course, be proven that Willie Darden would be alive—
and shown to be innocent—today if he had been white. But David Bruck,
a South Carolina lawyer who made a detailed comparison between uses
of the death penalty in the U.S. and South Africa, noted, "during 1982-83,
for example, [South African] government figures show that a black
defendant was nearly nineteen times more likely to hang if convicted
of murdering a white than if his victim were black—[while] not a single
white was hanged for murdering a black." In making his comparison
of "justice" in the U.S. and South Africa, Bruck concludes that "racially
divided societies have a certain sameness about them."[31] In this sense,
if no other, Willie Darden joins the list of thousands of women and men
in the U.S. who have been racially murdered by the state.

Despite the emphasis on comparing black with white statistics, we
should remember that all people of color are subject to racist discrimination at trial and sentencing. The way in which government statistics
are compiled and published (i.e., "black and other") makes it difficult
to analyze if and how this varies for different groups. One significant
exception, however, is the case of all native people who live on "Indian
reservations." If, as seems likely, the Bush anti-crime wave succeeds
in dramatically expanding the use of the federal death penalty, these
residents of "federal lands" will comprise the majority of those destined
to be thereby executed. Senator Daniel Inouye, in calling for an
exemption for reservation inhabitants, recently projected that, as it
stands, eighty percent of the people to be affected by the federal death
penalty expansion will be Indians on reservations.[32]

As is true for all instances of inequality permeating the current
society, the interplay of color and class in determining who receives
the death penalty has been inadequately examined. This work is long
overdue, lest those of us seeking to correct injustice succeed only in
reinforcing the misconceptions and deliberate lies of the ruling elite
and its servants, who are determined to keep us divided along lines of
color, gender, and any other such factors useful for this purpose.[33] The
most relevant questions, however, concern the delegation of authority
to this government to determine who has committed murder and what
price should be paid for such an act, and also the possible ways in which
execution could be used to silence its most vocal critics. Such questions
were well addressed in a statement issued by a group of revolutionary
prisoners held at Leavenworth Federal Prison during their participation
in Fastathon 90, the 1990 observance of the annual fast sponsored by
the National Coalition to Abolish the Death Penalty:

> As revolutionaries, as prisoners, we have direct knowledge of
> how truly unjust, racist and corrupt the U.S. justice system can
> be and often is. . . . A government that screams about drugs while

it organized huge guns-for-drugs-for-money plots like Contragate, that preaches democracy while invading tiny nations like Panama, [to which now can be added, "that deplores murder while causing the deaths of hundreds of thousands of human beings in its Desert Storm adventure"], that is in violation of international law because of its vulture-like policies of interfering in and exploiting the lands and peoples of countries around the globe, has no moral or ethical right to murder-execute anyone! In particular, we join this fast to call attention to and give our total support to Mumia Abu-Jamal, an internationally recognized political prisoner who sits in a death row cell in Pennsylvania. Mumia, a lifelong advocate for justice and human rights for Black people and all oppressed people, was a very effective journalist in Philadelphia, who engendered the wrath of the racist police department and city power structure for his truthful coverage of the police attacks against the Move organization. As a result, he was attacked by the police, shot, arrested and convicted of killing a cop and sentenced to death. We feel his case demonstrates most clearly the unjust, racist and morally repugnant policy of official murder that the U.S. government practices.[34]

Mumia Abu-Jamal, known as the "voice of the voiceless" when he incurred the wrath of the system in Philadelphia, and who is continuing in that role on death row, has stated:

Perhaps we can shrug off and shred some of the dangerous myths laid on our minds like a second skin—such as the "right" to a fair and impartial jury of our peers; the "right" to represent oneself; the "right" to a fair trial even. They're *not* rights—they're privileges of the powerful and rich. For the powerless and the poor, they are chimera that vanish once one reaches out to claim them as something real or substantial. [F]reedom ain't in the interest of the system, efficiency is. The poor in the outer so-called "free" system are expendable, as they are perceived as inefficient. In the inner system efficiency is measured by the equation of control. The poor in the outer system, as expendable, are pushed into homelessness. The prisoners of the inner system, as expendable, are pushed into electric chairs. Cold, yet efficient, in a warped way that reminds one of that model of German efficiency known as the Third Reich.[35]

In early July, 1991, a statement entitled "Stop the Legal Lynching of Mumia Abu-Jamal!" was issued by a long list of "Prisoners of War, political prisoners, and politically conscious social prisoners" held by the U.S. It included these words:

We must put a stop to this genocidal agenda that has put more than 2400 Third World and white working class people on death rows around the country. The death penalty has already been used to kill children, the mentally retarded, and the innocent. Now, unless we stop it, it will again be used as a tool of political

revenge. The struggle against racism and injustice in this country
has had enough martyrs.

Justice Thurgood Marshall, one of the three remaining "liberal"
Supreme Court Justices and the only black member, resigned at the
close of the court's 1990-1991 term. His last opinion, given on the last
day of that term, was a dissent to the majority on *Payne v.
Tennessee*, discussed above, concerning the permissibility of "victim-impact"
evidence in death penalty sentencing. He closed his dissent as follows:
"Cast aside today are those condemned to face society's ultimate penalty.
Tomorrow's victims may be minorities, women or the indigent.
Inevitably, this campaign to resurrect yesterday's 'spirited dissents' will
squander the authority and the legitimacy of this Court as a protector
of the powerless." Justice Marshall began his opinion with the statement,
"Power, not reason, is the new currency of the Court's decision
making."[36] Marshall's words are reminiscent—surely intentionally—
of the declaration of anti-slavery leader Fredrick Douglass, "Power
concedes nothing without a demand." To refuse our responsibility to
make this demand could only leave us complicit in the type of "American
democracy" which—represented in Douglass' era by the institution of
slavery—now finds expression in the deaths of those human beings
executed by the state.

Notes

1. Michael E. Enders, *The Morality of Capital Punishment: Equal Justice
Under the Law?* (Mystic, CT: Twenty-Third Publications, 1985), pp. 8-9.

2. Gerald David Jaynes and Robin M. Williams, Jr. (eds.), *A Common
Destiny: Blacks in American Society* (Washington, D.C.: National Academy
Press, 1989), p. 478.

3. Amnesty International, *United States of America: The Death Penalty*
(London: Amnesty International Publications, 1987).

4. Endres, *op. cit.*, pp. 10-12.

5. Amnesty International, *op. cit.*, p. 15.

6. American Civil Liberties Union (ACLU), *Race and the Death Penalty:
Georgia and the Nation* (Washington, D.C.: ACLU, 1987).

7. Michael Kroll, *New York Times*, April 24, 1987.

8. Ron Kuby, quoted in *The Guardian*, November 14, 1987.

9. Kroll, *op. cit.*

10. Linda Greenhouse, "Thornburgh Goes to Court on Death Penalty
Precedents," *New York Times*, April 25, 1991.

11. *New York Times*, June 28, 1991.

12. *Rocky Mountain News*, April 18, 1991. As of mid-April, 1992, the
total number of people executed since the death penalty was reinstated in
1976 was one hundred sixty-eight. Characterized by "race/ethnic group,"
ninety-three were white, sixty-five were black, nine were "Hispanic [*sic*]—

who "can be of any race"—and one was Native. The two hundred-twenty-one victims included one hundred eighty-five were white, twenty-nine black, four "Hispanic," and three Asian people. (Sally Ann Stewart, "Execution debate entangles California," *USA Today*, April 15, 1992.

13. Kenneth B. Noble, "High Court to Decide Whether Death Penalty Discriminates Against Blacks," *New York Times*, March 23, 1987.

14. Stuart Taylor, Jr., "Court, 5-4, Rejects Challenge to Death Penalty," *New York Times*, April 23, 1987.

15. *Ibid*. In a scenario grimly reminiscent of the decision of the Eighth Circuit Court of Appeals to deny the appeal of Leonard Peltier, rather than consider the possibility of FBI misconduct, (see James Vander Wall, above), the political basis for the majority decision was made clear. Comments Mumia Abu-Jamal, ". . . Justice Powell noted with alarm that 'McCleskey's claim, taken to its logical conclusion, throws into serious question the principles that underlie our entire criminal justice system.' Precisely." (Mumia Abu-Jamal, "Teetering on the Brink Between Life and Death," *Yale Law Review*, vol. 100, no. 4, January 1991, p. 1000.)

16. Shabaku Sundiata Waqlimi, "Presumption of Guilt" in Ian Gray and Moria Stanley (eds.), *A Punishment in Search of a Crime: Americans Speak Out Against the Death Penalty* (New York: Avon Books, 1989), p. 215.

17. Lawrence Kilman, "86% in the U.S. Support the Death Penalty," *Rocky Mountain News*, January 12, 1987.

18. Akinshiju C. Ola, "Fight Goes on to Stop Racist Death Penalty," *The Guardian*, November 14, 1990.

19. Leigh Dingerson, "Rights Die too in Georgia Execution," *The Guardian*, October 30, 1991; also *New York Times*, April 17, 1991.

20. Editorial, *Denver Post*, April 18, 1991.

21. *New York Times*, April 25, 1991.

22. Diane R. Gordon, "Executioner's Song," *The Nation*, October 8, 1990, p. 374, quoting a study by the American Bar Association Task Force on Death Penalty Habeas Corpus.

23. *Ibid.*, p. 376.

24. Amnesty International, *USA Death Penalty: Briefing* (London: Amnesty International, 1987). It should be noted that the influence of race and class continue post-conviction: whites on death row are more likely than blacks to have their sentences commuted, but whether black or white, a person facing execution who as a private attorney is more likely to receive commutation than if defended by a court appointed lawyer; Marvin E. Wolfgang, Arlene Kelly, and Hans C. Nolde, "Comparison of the Executed and the Commuted Among Admissions to Death Row" in *Crime and Justice in Society*, Richard Quincy (ed.), pp. 508, 513. Quoted in Jeffrey Reiman, *The Rich Get Richer and the Poor Get Prison*, 3rd edition (New York: Macmillan Publishing Co., 1990), p. 102.

25. Marcia Coyle, Fred Strassner, and Marianne Lavelle, "Fatal Defense: Trial and Error in the Nations' Death Belt," *National Law Journal*, June 11, 1990, pp. 30-44.

26. *Ibid.*, p. 36.

27. *New York Times*, June 25, 1991.

28. *Ibid.*

29. David C. Leven, letter to the *New York Times*, July 3, 1991.

30. William Jasper Darden, taken from Michael I. Radelet, (ed.), *Facing the Death Penalty: Cruel and Unusual Punishment* (Philadelphia: Temple University Press, 1990).

31. David Brunch, "On Death Row in Pretoria Central," *Newsletter of the Colorado Coalition to Abolish the Death Penalty*," September, 1988.

32. "Crime Bill Conferees Agree on Death Penalty," *New York Times*, June 25, 1991. It should be noted that tin 1988, thirty-nine out of sixty-four cases of first degree murder prosecuted in federal courts involved Native people on their own land. (Nell Jessup Newton and Alex Tallchief Skibine, letter to the *New York Times*, July 19, 1991.) For more on this see, Colorado AIM, "American Indian Death Penalty Act," *New Studies on the Left*, vol. 14, nos. 1-2, p. 100.

33. One reasoned and sensitive study of this interplay has recently been published. See William King, *Going to Meet a Man: Denver's Last Legal Public Execution, 27 July 1886* (Boulder, University of Colorado Press, 1990).

34. "Leavenworth Prisoners Anti-Death Penalty Fast Statement," *Prison News Service Newsletter*, March-April 1990.

35. Partisan Defense Committee, *Class Struggle Defense Notes*, no. 10, April 1989.

36. Andrew Rosenthal, "Marshall Retires from High Court: Blow to Liberals," *New York Times*, June 28, 1991.

Ches-ne-o-nah-eh

Death Wing Days

I have spent a total of five years and nine months incarcerated, confined to a 5x8x8 foot isolation cell twenty-three and a half hours a day. The first two years were spent in the County Jail. I went through two trials. The first trial lasted nearly three months and resulted in convictions which have since been reversed. Then for three years and nine months I was housed in a place called "Ellis," a Texas Department of Corrections high-security prison, on Death Row. There is nothing unique about this as there are another half million people locked up in America and 1,300 or so on Death Rows awaiting execution.

On Death Row, some prisoners die by natural causes, some by suicide, while others are murdered by fellow prisoners or guards. Then execution claims its victims. Some simply crumble under the emotional strain and drift into another dimension. Prisoners who have done time before usually fare better in the long run. Some prisoners I have met were segregated from the general population because of their struggle to fight legally against dehumanizing prison conditions—issues such as health care, proper diet, educational programs, brutality and corruption and a system without true means of rehabilitation. These prisoners have suffered and many have paid the price with their lives. So to a great extent, they too are under the executioner's thumb. A strange balance exists between the extremes of the spectrum.

Death Row is a cruel place where sadistic games are played on prisoners. It is a place where life struggles to breathe and reach out, to restore harmony to one's being. Yet it is constantly being smothered. The keepers often treat Death Row prisoners as tiny insects trapped within a tin can. They laugh at the amusement of a match flaming beneath the toes as the prisoners scamper from side to side. Keeping one off balance in a constant state of confusion is the situation that the prison officials hope for. This is not to be confused with other more sophisticated brainwashing techniques applied to prisoners as well, on a daily basis.

Mental escape was something I personally relished but seldom reached. Escapism is a big part of survival. Reading books, writing letters and drawing and other such hobbies pass the time. And, oh yes, the t.v.s, the prison baby-sitters. There is limited expression available on Death Row. You may write letters, either personal or legal, and general correspondence, short stories and poems and other things. But this expression goes only so far. I have had many things simply disappear from letters, either articles or information that in some way might aid someone else or myself. Participation in active lawsuits against the prison system will surely mark you, with negative consequences.

Routinely, Sunday through Thursday from 9 a.m. until 11 p.m., the t.v.s run wide open. Friday nights and Saturdays they stay on till 1 a.m. No educational programming is offered. You can well imagine the assault on one's ears with t.v.s running at top volume. The whole building is constructed of steel and bricks so the reverberation shakes everything, including your body, physically.

What's worse is the systematic electronic signal fed through the cable. This method of mental torture is selected at random and specific times. It produces a high-pitched signal and a bouncy one as well which also distorts the t.v. picture. It can last for five minutes or be off and on throughout the day. When it continues for any length of time, the prisoners respond and the t.v.s are turned off, though not always. Experiencing this all day leaves you mentally and physically exhausted.

The weekend before Charles Brooks was executed, all the power was turned off. There was no water, nor lights. This happens often, any time there might be something over the radio or t.v. that prison officials believe prisoners should not view or hear. So disruption of t.v.s, radios and visits begin.

Total environmental control is the word in prison. Each morning at Ellis Unit showers begin after each group has exercised, with one prisoner at a time going to shower. (But this is often changed—depending on how the guards feel. They might let three people out at a time, which is against prison policy.) The shower stall is a converted cell made into a shower. Slimy green algae grows on the walls which are cleaned off once in a while. I was surprised that a group of mushrooms didn't sprout.

Showers are a head trip between the guards and prisoners each day. The plumbing is controlled from a "pipe chase," an area which runs the length of each row and tier. It holds the plumbing and electrical wiring and provides the guards with a spying tunnel, to peer through the vents in the back of the cells. The guard manipulates hot and cold water in a fast-surging action where the extremes between hot and cold could easily scorch you. Or might this be just another form of mind control meant for nothing more than to deprive you of a shower? All this adds to the tension, and being able to dodge the fluctuation of blasting cold and hot water is a trick for a magician. This is psychological warfare.

I am going to list twenty-four areas in which prison officials employ their brand of behavior modification, which were offered to social scientists and prison wardens in Washington, D.C., in 1962, by Dr. Edgar Schein. This list appeared in an article entitled "Breaking Men's Minds" by Eddie Griffen, a Marion Federal Penitentiary prisoner.

1) Physical removal of prisoners to areas sufficiently isolated to effectively break or seriously weaken close emotional ties.
2) Segregation of all natural leaders.
3) Use of cooperative prisoners as leaders.
4) Prohibition of group activities not in line with brainwashing objectives.
5) Spying on prisoners and reporting back private material.
6) Tricking men into written statements which are then shown to others.
7) Exploitation of opportunists and informers.
8) Convincing prisoners that they can trust no one.
9) Treating those who are willing to collaborate in far more lenient ways than those who are not.
10) Punishing those who show uncooperative attitudes.
11) Systematic withholding of mail.
12) Preventing contact with anyone non-sympathetic to the method of treatment and regimen of the captive populaces.
13) Disorganization of all group standards among prisoners.
14) Building a group conviction among the prisoners that they have been abandoned by and totally isolated from their social order.
15) Undermining of all emotional supports.
16) Preventing prisoners from writing home or to friends in the community regarding the conditions of their confinements.
17) Making available and permitting access to only those publications and books that are neutral to or supportive of the desired new attitudes.
18) Placing individuals into new and ambiguous situations for which the standards are kept deliberately unclear and then putting pressure to conform to what is desired in order to win favor and a reprieve from the pressure.
19) Placing individuals whose willpower has been severely weakened or eroded into a living situation with several others who are more advanced in their thought-reform whose job it is to further undermine the individual's emotional supports.
20) Using techniques of character invalidation, i.e., humiliations, revilements, shouting, to induce feelings of guilt, fear, and suggestibility; coupled with sleeplessness, an exacting prison regimen and periodic interrogational interviews.

21) Meeting all insincere attempts to comply with cellmates' pressures with renewed hostility.
22) Repeated pointing out to the prisoner by cellmates of where he has in the past, or is in the present, not even living up to his own standards or values.
23) Rewarding of submission and subserviency to the attitudes encompassing the brainwashing objective with a lifting of pressure and acceptance as a human being.
24) Providing social and emotional supports which reinforce the new attitudes.

These weapons and many more are employed against the prisoners each day. Often many prisoners never suspect they are the victims of this type of sophisticated brainwashing. As a result of this treatment, prisoners conform unwillingly, thereby providing the keepers an even more valuable tool against others.

The atmosphere often drifts onto people who come and visit with prisoners. The visitors themselves thus become part of this plan to alienate the emotional ties between families and friends. Rough treatment and searches, even strip searches, delaying visits, even going so far as to tell visitors that the prisoner doesn't wish a visit—all this contributes to mistrust and disruption of communication between families and friends. This policy is encouraged by officials. I remember a high Texas Department of Corrections official telling a reporter that prisoners' mothers were nothing more than whores, and that these inmates were used to sleeping on the floor and doing without baths and clean clothes, so he didn't see any need for the system to provide any better conditions.

Violence is a contagious element that thrives upon fear and submission. Capital punishment is a macabre law. Its supposed intent is to deter others from specified crimes of violence. It is true that executing individuals will definitely eliminate any further acts of violence from those people. Yet the very process is itself a positive reinforcement of violence. The old cliché applies so well. People kill people, so we will kill people. To illustrate this point, in the Texas Department of Corrections some inmates are labelled by term names: a) support service inmate, b) orderly, c) clerk, d) field service worker, e) turnkey, f) building tender, g) hall boy, h) floor boy.

These special jobs were created by prison officials for certain inmates as rewards in many forms for their violence against other prisoners: special privileges, possession of weapons, abusing other prisoners, controlling the movement of prisoners, making their cells "private property" and exemption from searches. These inmate-guards spy and steal sensitive materials such as personal letters and legal materials, and they have access to prison records and other related files. They spread rumors among prisoners to precipitate further violence, and they sexually abuse weaker prisoners for their greedy pleasures. The inmate-guards are far more dangerous than the guards, for they can kill you and receive more rewards. These inmates are part of the scheme of brainwashing techniques and assist with implementing these tactics as a responsibility towards their specially created job assignments.

In the last few years a number of death sentences have been reversed in appeal courts, after the defendants were found innocent by diligent investigative work and much money. This is overlooked more than anything associated with capital punishment. In some of these cases, the actual guilty party confessed and gave a statement. This work was accomplished by means of legal foundations, families working with journalists and even law enforcement agencies.

We are influenced by communications, such as newspapers and other printed media, t.v.s and radio, yet statistics have shown that right after the execution of John Spenkelnick in 1979, Florida's reported murder rate increased more than fourteen percent over the first six months of the year. Other truthful sources of media have been denied categorically access to Death Row prisoners. Interviews with some Death Row prisoners have been deliberately sabotaged with the media and prison administrations. Various morons have given statements saying that the whole Death Row population wishes to die. These people have converted to the system's self-destructive patterns.

We are influenced by what we see and hear, a part of the learning process and advancing in life. I have a strong feeling that the subliminal attacks on us through the media in the near future will prove we have all been, to our collective astonishment, guinea pigs. It is not surprising to learn that the murder rate has increased when an execution takes place. A society which encourages and uses capital punishment shouldn't be surprised that this psychologically breeds violent behavior. So you end with people killing people because people kill people, just a vicious circle.

It takes a great deal of courage, finances and faith to fight for one's life under a sentence of death. If you are innocent, a miracle at least must take place to free you from the bonds of the system. Some who prosecute capital cases are so insensitive that they'll overlook evidence in order to obtain a conviction and sentence of death merely because they have wagered a bet. When life becomes this cheap, it affects all of us in one fashion or another. It costs you more than dollars and most certainly costs us our right to live and exist as free human beings.

Heather Rhoads

The New Death Row—
Official Abuse of Prisoners with AIDS

On September 8, 1990, four prison guards suited up in full riot gear with thick rubber gloves, face shields, and protective clothing, and entered Donald Woods' cell at Waupun Correctional Institution, a Wisconsin state prison. Two guards carrying a hard plastic shield backed Woods to the rear of his cell. Two others followed with towels to prevent the prisoner from biting or spitting at them. The guards then handcuffed Woods, stuffed a towel in his mouth, placed him in a laundry cart, and wheeled him to the prison's "Adjustment Center." There the guards took Woods into a single cell and began strapping him to the bed. While they fastened and readjusted the restraints, one continued to hold the towel on Woods' mouth, keeping him from thrashing his head about, and another knelt on the victim's chest, forcing his body down to prevent him from arching his back.

"Most of the officers involved in this process report that at some point prior to the final securing of the chest restraint Mr. Woods ceased resisting completely and was lying totally still," read the twenty-three page investigative report from the District Attorney's office. "When . . . the officers left the cell, Mr. Woods remained completely still and it was observed that his head was tilted slightly to one side and that his mouth and eyes were partially open." Nine and a half hours later a nurse attempted to give him CPR, but Woods' "neck and jaw area were so stiff and rigid she was unable to do so," according to the report. The autopsy concluded that Donald Woods died of asphyxiation. Yet Special Prosecutor Royce Finne determined that the officers who caused Woods' death committed no crime. "The placing of a towel around the mouth of Mr. Woods . . . was not an unreasonable precaution against biting or spitting which the staff reasonably feared would risk their exposure to HIV virus," Finne wrote.

Public defender Mary Waitrovich, who is trying to reopen Woods' case, counters that the use of the towel was "obviously dangerous," prompted by an "unreasonable, irrational, and unwarranted fear of HIV exposure." She asserts that "it is virtually impossible for AIDS virus to be transmitted by spitting or even biting unless the victim's skin is broken and the biter has an open cut in his mouth." It would be completely impossible for Woods' saliva or blood to penetrate the guards' riot gear, made to withstand chemical agents such as Mace, she argues. Dan Savage of the AIDS Coalition To Unleash Power (ACT UP)/Madison charges Woods' death to the guards' ignorance and fear of AIDS. "To add insult to fatal injury, five months before Donald Woods' death, the governor's own AIDS Technical Advisory Committee recommended a complete overhaul in HIV/AIDS awareness and treatment in the prison system," he points out. "This still hasn't been implemented to this day. Had it been implemented upon recommendation, Donald Woods would be alive."

The 1990 Update on AIDS in Correctional Facilities by the National Institute of Justice, a branch of the U.S. Department of Justice, cites the Woods case to illustrate the danger of not providing HIV education for penal staff. "This is a clear example of a death that might have been avoided had updated information on HIV risk factors been disseminated to all staff on a regular basis," the report says. While Donald Woods' death is appalling, it is just one example of the horrendous treatment prisoners with AIDS endure across the nation. Those who are identified as HIV-positive face intimidation, physical harassment, and verbal abuse from staff and other prisoners, as well as breaches of confidentiality, segregation and isolation, substandard medical care, denial of privileges accorded other prisoners, and longer sentences. Fear of discovery keeps many from taking the AIDS antibody test; some are so afraid of the AIDS stigma they deny they are sick, even at the cost of not receiving treatment.

Ignorance and Repression

On June 11, 1989, one month before he was due to be released from the Camden County Jail in New Jersey, HIV-positive prisoner Gregory Smith allegedly bit a guard after doctors refused to x-ray his back. Camden County Judge John Mariano sentenced Smith to twenty-five years in prison for attempted murder and aggravated assault. The judge conceded that biting is extremely unlikely to transmit HIV, and indeed the guard in question had not contracted the virus. But what mattered, he said, was that Smith *believed* he could kill the guard with a bite. "Impossibility is no defense to a charge of attempted murder," Camden County prosecutor Harold Kasselman told the court. Mariano said he gave Smith the maximum possible sentences on both counts because he wanted to send a message that "criminal conduct of this nature will be met with swift and severe punishment."

Judy Greenspan, of the ACLU's National Prison Project, points out that cases classifying the intentional transmission of HIV as a felony are "springing up all over the country," sending "absolutely the wrong message" about infection through casual contact. Over a dozen transmission cases similar to Smith's have led to a dangerous "criminalization" of the disease, she says. In almost every case, HIV-positive defendants have been convicted of attempted murder and sentenced to long prison terms.

- In November 1989, Curtis Weeks, a twenty-eight-year-old HIV infected but asymptomatic Texas prisoner, was serving a two-year prison term when he received a life sentence for spitting on a guard. Although the Centers for Disease Control (CDC) have removed saliva from the list of bodily fluids which require universal precautions, the jury apparently believed a prosecution expert's testimony that transmission was possible.
- Another Texas prisoner, Jean Prysock, was indicted in February 1990 for biting a prison guard.
- In November 1990, a Georgia state appeals court upheld Gregory Scroggins' attempted-murder conviction for biting a police officer during an arrest; he was sentenced to ten years in prison. The court held that as long as scientists believe HIV transmission through biting is theoretically possible, "the jury was well within the evidence to consider the human bite of a person infected with the AIDS virus to be deadly."
- In Indiana, Donald Haines was convicted of attempted murder for intentionally spraying paramedics with blood and biting a police officer as they intervened in his suicide attempt. A state appeals court upheld the conviction; Haines was sentenced to thirty years in prison.
- Charges of reckless endangerment are still pending against a Tennessee woman who neglected to inform a rescue worker that her fiancé was HIV-positive before he performed mouth-to-mouth resuscitation. The woman, Connie Lewis, maintains that she panicked when her fiancé collapsed from a heart attack and told the ambulance officials he was infected as soon as she remembered. Police arrested Lewis right after her fiancé's funeral services; she was jailed for five days before she was released on a $2,500 bond. If found guilty, she faces five years in prison.

In February 1990, the CDC published the largest study to date concerning "casual transmission" through biting and the exchange of saliva. CDC researchers tested eighty-nine household members of HIV-positive children, many of whom had bitten noninfected siblings. They found no transmission of the virus. The National Institute of Justice reports that no prison guards or police officers have contracted HIV through on-the-job exposure. Nonetheless, people with HIV and AIDS continue to face criminal charges of attempted murder or assault with a dangerous weapon for acts that would be treated as routine misdemeanors or disciplinary infractions if the defendants were not infected. "The effect of these charges has been to cause unfounded and widespread fear in the general population," says Greenspan, "and to fan the flames of discrimination and abuse against people with AIDS and HIV."

Fear and Loathing Behind the Walls

The National Institute of Justice reports a 606 percent increase in confirmed AIDS cases in U.S. prisons and a large sample of jails from 1985 to 1989. AIDS is currently the leading cause of death in New York state prisons, where an estimated 9,000 of the state's 54,000 prisoners are HIV-positive. Health officials expect a surge in AIDS deaths in prisons across the country. Prisoners' advocates accuse penal facilities of causing needless pain and suffering and premature deaths. They call prison AIDS wards the "new death row." A 1987 study by the Correctional Association of New York found prisoners with AIDS to be dying at twice the rate of non-prisoners with AIDS. "Many prisoners with AIDS spend their last days in prison and alone, far from their families and loved ones," says Cathy Potler, director of the association's AIDS Prison Project.

The penal systems of New York, New Jersey, California, and Florida—states where poverty and IV-drug use have also reached epidemic proportions—have been hit hardest by the AIDS crisis so far. The New Jersey Department of Corrections estimates that thirty to fifty percent of its prisoners are HIV infected; in Broward County, Florida, more than fifty percent of prisoners who volunteered to take the test were diagnosed as seropositive. By choosing mass imprisonment as the official response to drug use, federal and state governments have created a de facto policy of incarcerating more and more HIV infected individuals. "Under the present policy, the percentage of drug offenders in the federal prison system will rise by 1995 from forty-seven percent to seventy percent," the National Commission on AIDS warns in its 1991 report. "With the amount of needle-sharing that goes on, we are sitting on top of a powder keg," says Doug Nelson, director of the Milwaukee AIDS Project. "We may well have an explosion of HIV infection. That will obviously have an effect on correctional systems." Prison and jail overcrowding further exacerbates the crisis. In the past decade, the United States has dramatically increased its prisoner population. The federal prison system alone holds double the number of prisoners it did in 1980. Chronic overcrowding increases prisoners' exposure to infectious diseases, a particularly grim situation for those who are immunodeficient.

Proper nutrition is often unavailable and experimental treatments and alternative therapies are virtually unobtainable in the nation's prisons and jails.

"Having AIDS in prison is an endless vigil to insure that you receive the medications and treatment you need," one inmate wrote in a letter to the National Commission on AIDS. "It is dealing with medical personnel who get a thrill out of putting your life and your well-being in jeopardy by revealing in sadistic and sinister ways that you are one of the 'accused.' It is being subject to assaults and 'burn-outs' (having your cell set on fire) by other prisoners. It is living with a debilitating fear that someone will find out that you're dying of AIDS and kick you. It's a horrible way to die."

Last spring, the Legal Aid Society Prisoners' Rights Project filed a lawsuit against New York State corrections officials, charging them with failing to deliver even nominal health care to prisoners with AIDS and violating the Eighth Amendment ban on cruel and unusual punishment. Among the ten plaintiffs is a prisoner who cannot walk or feed himself and who has no control over his bowels or bladder. For weeks, he was left to dehydrate and lie in his own urine and feces; nurses dismissed his incontinence as "manipulative" and "childish." "The situation today for many prisoners with HIV disease is nothing if not 'cruel and unusual,'" the National Commission on AIDS declares. "Too many correctional facilities subject inmates to a series of unnecessary, arbitrary indignities which fundamentally affect their basic human rights."

When fellow prisoners at the Minnesota state prison at St. Cloud found out last December that Todd Balow was HIV infected, they ordered him not to use "their" bathrooms, sprayed him with a water hose when he used the facilities anyway, told him not to go to lunch since he would not be allowed to sit anywhere, intimidated him from coming out of his cell, and threatened him with physical harm. "I'd lost a lot of weight and I looked real thin," Balow explains. "There were rumors I had AIDS, and a guard came up to me and said, 'Tell me confidentially. If it's true, maybe I can do some things to help you.'" However, according to Balow and signed statements by two other prisoners, the guard instead told other staff and prisoners about Balow's infection, and the news soon spread through the entire prison. "There is the atmosphere here that you can get AIDS from mosquito bites," Balow says. "Each time I get in line for dinner, it just kills me. You've got people saying stuff, people who won't come near me. You can accept some of that ignorance, but what gets me is that the guards were criminal gossips."

Balow's experience is not uncommon. "There are all sorts of ways confidentiality is violated," says Potler of New York's AIDS Prison

Project. "For example, many facilities exclude seropositive inmates from food-service work assignments. If you apply for a job in the mess hall and you don't get it, people say, 'Ah, you must have AIDS!'" At the Limestone Correctional Facility in Alabama, seropositive prisoners' clothes and laundry bags are stamped with the letters "HIV." Until the recent settlement of a prisoner's lawsuit, the Multnomah County jail system in Portland, Oregon, required prisoners with AIDS to wear red wristbands. "To say people with AIDS are treated insensitively would be putting it mildly," says Cruz Salgado, a prisoner in New York's Attica State Prison. "Once an inmate is diagnosed as HIV-positive, he is marked. Security, medical, and civilian staff have no respect for confidentiality laws."

The "rumor-mill" nature of prisons is a major drawback to voluntary testing, says Savage of ACT UP in Wisconsin. "It is widely known in the prisons in this state that it is not safe to be HIV-positive. You're not safe from the guards, you're not safe from other prisoners. The only way to get by is to not let anyone know you're HIV-positive, and the way to do that is not volunteering to take the test." According to the ACLU's Judy Greenspan, one-third of AIDS cases in New York are not diagnosed until the time of autopsy. In many states, prisoners suspected of prior high-risk activities are victims of mandatory testing policies; in seventeen states and the federal prisons, all prisoners are forced to undergo HIV tests. Several penal systems follow up testing with segregation or isolation of those determined to be HIV-positive, depriving them of work, recreation, vocational training, socialization, rehabilitation, parole and furloughs. The National Commission on AIDS determined segregation to be "wholly without public-health merit." Segregation effectively targets HIV-positive prisoners for "assaults, discrimination, and disparate treatment," the commissioners' 1991 report warned.

While segregation and breaches of confidentiality may discourage many prisoners from taking the AIDS test, visitation restriction is the biggest disincentive to getting tested, says Geri Pomerantz of New York's Prisoners Legal Services. Testing positive for HIV in California, New York and Mississippi means losing the privilege of taking part in family reunion programs, known as "trailer-visits," which allow prisoners to spend forty-eight hours with family members in separate units on prison grounds. "It doesn't matter if [the visitor] is a parent, a child, a sibling, or a spouse, prisoners who are diagnosed as HIV-positive are denied categorically from participation," says Potler. "This is a horrible public-health measure, because it makes people decide not to get tested."

Jane Miller (not her real name) has spent almost a year in jail, fearing that officials will discover she is HIV-positive. "They do have an idea, but they can't prove it," she says. "They've done things like pull me out and say they think I'm anemic and want a blood test. They put me on a scale twice a week, and I've lost fourteen pounds." Miller, still awaiting sentencing on a drug charge, knows that revealing her HIV status could buy her a delayed parole and a longer term, since judges often rule that HIV-positive prostitutes pose a public-health danger and should be kept off the streets as long as possible. "A girlfriend of mine in Milwaukee has been trying to deal with the system up there," says Miller. "She was into the line of life I was, prostitution and drugs. It came out that she had AIDS, and it turned on her in court. They wanted to keep her out of the population. Because with her lifestyle they were afraid she was going to sell her body again and infect a thousand more people. They gave her a maximum sentence, six years, which is a death sentence for her." Miller also knows her HIV status could mean a one-way ticket into solitary confinement, where she fears she would live in complete isolation until she dies. "Another person with AIDS I knew who was here about a year and a half ago was put in isolation, totally separated from the population, and kept from talking to anybody," she says. "The guards literally handled him with masks and gloves. He lost it up here. All his pride that he was struggling to maintain—he lost it in a two-month period. He was totally alone."

Miller's case is emblematic, not only because she has hidden her HIV infection, but because she is a woman. Infection rates among female prisoners are skyrocketing, the National Institute of Justice reports. A recent epidemiological study found higher seroprevalence rates for women than men in nine out of ten correctional systems. In New York City, 25.6 percent of female prisoners tested seropositive in a blind survey, compared to 16.1 percent of male prisoners. About thirty-five percent of the more than 400 women who chose to take the test at MCI-Farmingham in Massachusetts were found to be HIV-positive, compared to thirteen percent among male prisoners. According to Social Justice for Women, a non-profit prisoners' advocacy group in Boston, the higher seropositivity rates among women reflect the tendency of judges to sentence women for crimes related to poverty and substance abuse. More than ninety percent of incarcerated women have histories of chronic drug use and many have worked as prostitutes; most are serving short sentences for non-violent crimes related to their addictions. By contrast, relatively few male prisoners are IV-drug users, and they are more often convicted of violent crimes.

"This population of women is very slow to trust because of their life experiences," says Marianne Galvin of Social Justice. Like Miller, many female prisoners at high risk of HIV infection don't risk taking AIDS tests. "They are afraid of repercussions about parole eligibility and getting custody of their children." Social Justice maintains that as a group, women prisoners have more health problems than male prisoners. Yet many women's facilities have less adequate health-care systems than men's. At Farmingham, all incoming prisoners are initially confined in the Health Services Unit to be screened for communicable diseases before being transferred to the prison compound. "As many as seven women—some of whom are ill with infectious diseases—are locked twenty-two hours a day in a single dark, poorly ventilated ten-foot-by-sixteen-foot cell designed to accommodate one or two women" reports *Social Justice*. The women, many of whom are withdrawing from alcohol or drugs, share a common toilet. Although medical clearance can be completed in twenty-four hours, prisoners often remain in the Health Services Unit for several weeks before beds are available in the compound. Once they enter the general prison population, sick women must walk from their housing units to infirmary "med-lines"; some skip medications rather than endure the hardship, especially in cold and stormy weather. Symptomatic HIV-positive women are eligible for clinic visits at a nearby hospital, yet once there they may wait for a physician for as long as eight hours while handcuffed and confined in closet-sized, poorly ventilated cubicles.

Fighting Back

Between 1985 and 1987, the AIDS situation at Bedford Hills Correctional Facility in New York was characterized by "secrecy and denial, shame and fear, ignorance and ostracism, and poor medical care," according to Bedford Hills prisoners Judy Clark and Kathy Boudin. The prison's unwillingness to cope with the AIDS crisis prompted prisoners there to start their own self-help projects, education workshops, and counseling services. Now, the prisoner-run ACE (AIDS Counseling and Education) program at Bedford Hills has begun to improve conditions and create an atmosphere of trust and caring among HIV-positive prisoners. It has become a model for peer programs across the country. Still, prisoners face bureaucratic obstacles and opposition from prison officials in their efforts to motivate and empower one another. Prisoners who have been involved in organizing efforts have found themselves locked down or placed in "diesel therapy"—transporting shackled prisoners from institution to institution is a way in which officials quiet "troublemakers." James Magner, publisher of a newsletter called PWA—RAG (Prisoners With AIDS— Rights Advocacy Group), has been relocated more than twenty times in the past two-and-a-half years.

"It is really important for those of us on the outside to support the peer programs," Potler asserts. "A number of them end up going underground because they don't get support from the institutions." Several outside organizations have started support groups which help peer programs to function, providing resources and training for peer educators. The Southwest Minnesota AIDS Project runs one such group with prisoners at the federal penal medical center in Rochester, setting up "buddies" to provide emotional support to prisoners with AIDS. "They visit them, take them out on day passes, and get them information and literature about AIDS," says coordinator Ben Brager. "When [the prisoners] get seriously ill, they visit them at the hospital."

AIDS education in the prisons is woefully inadequate. Many facilities fail to provide even basic HIV/AIDS information to prisoners. Only 33 percent of the responding city/county jail systems in the Justice Institute's 1990 survey reported that half or more of their prisoners received an hour of live education on AIDS in the past year. Many prisons simply show the video *AIDS: A Bad Way to Die*, which contains outdated transmission information and no positive messages for HIV-positive prisoners. "It is far more productive to educate this 'captive' audience while incarcerated than to attempt to undertake such efforts on the streets," the New York AIDS Commission notes. Without education, prisoners continue to engage in high-risk behavior. In a Michigan survey, sixty to seventy percent said they engaged in sexual relations during incarceration.

In South Carolina, more than forty percent reported personal knowledge of needle sharing in the institution in the past year. Because syringes in prisons and jails are scarce, IV-drug users share them to a greater degree than on the outside. According to Judy Greenspan, a needle in prison may travel among fifty to eighty people. "For IV-drug users, it's more dangerous in jail than on the street," one prisoner told the AIDS Prison Project in New York. "On the street you can buy new needles or bleach to clean the works, but not in the prisons. You may not be able to stop the use of drugs for prisoners, but at least you can stop people from using the same needles." Most penal systems prohibit prisoners from having condoms and bleach to clean needles since sexual activity and drug use are prohibited. Prisoners who are educated about HIV transmission make do with the resources at hand. Matches are generally available and prisoners who work on cleaning assignments usually have access to bleach or alcohol solutions. In Wisconsin, some prisoners have been cutting the fingers off rubber gloves and distributing the makeshift condoms to others.

Some prison officials do see the value of ensuring that prisoners, especially those about to be released, know how to sterilize needles and feel comfortable wearing or requiring sexual partners to wear condoms.

Nicholas Freudenberg of the Montefiore Riker's Island Prison Health Service recommends that prisons provide one-to-one education for all prisoners through pre-release counseling sessions and prevention kits. Potler stresses that prisoners with HIV infection need to have health-care plans set up prior to release. "They need to know where they're going and to be able to connect their families with social services and entitlements," she says. "They should get the same discharge planning as people who are released from hospitals." Currently, many prisoners are released only to face a serious shortage of community resources. They encounter long waiting lists for substance-abuse treatment programs, housing, health care, and employment. "Correctional officials must resist the temptation to 'dump' prisoners with AIDS into the community without arrangements for their care and support," says the National Institute for Justice in its 1991 report.

Potler maintains that correctional departments could save a lot of money by granting early release to prisoners with advanced cases of AIDS. The Correctional Association of New York reports that treating a person with HIV infection costs prison facilities about $40,000 per year more than housing an uninfected prisoner. "People should not have to die in prison," says Nelson. "Those who are very sick with AIDS should be released to their families to receive better medical care and emotional support, to manage the devastation of the disease and the death process." But in the current "tough-on-crime" political climate, many policy-makers have blocked legislative proposals for medical clemency or parole and have even attacked prison furlough and work-release programs. In New Jersey and many other states, the only mechanism for early release—executive clemency—is such a prolonged process that prisoners who meet eligibility requirements frequently die before their applications reach the governor's desk. Compassionate release is perhaps the most pressing issue for prisoners with AIDS, Greenspan says. "It is time to change the unwritten policy that prisoners have to either be dead or on their death bed before they are considered for medical clemency."

As the crisis worsens, activists across the nation are taking up the cause of prisoners with AIDS. ACT UP chapters in New York, New Jersey, Minnesota, Wisconsin, California, and elsewhere have recently begun focusing on prisons as the central AIDS issue of today. Through creative direct actions, ACT UP-Madison has exposed the circumstances surrounding Donald Woods' death and publicized the treatment of other prisoners with AIDS. In April 1991, ACT UP members held a silent picket of the Department of Corrections (DoC) with towels tied around their mouths. In July, the activists carried a coffin to the DoC and staged a "die-in" to call attention to the questionable circumstances attending the sudden death of Ricardo Thomas, another Waupun prisoner with

AIDS. Savage and others have held long meetings with DoC officials, reviewing the status of each recommendation made by the governor's task force. Re-opening Woods' case is a crucial goal. "The same guards who murdered Donald Woods are still working at Waupun, guarding other HIV-infected inmates right now," Savage says. "Donald Woods was not sentenced to death, but they killed him. And nothing is being done about that."

In Memoriam

your honor
since i've been convicted of murder
and have taken the time to digest
just what that means
after noting what it means to my family
and how it affects people who read the newspapers
and all
i see now that i've made a terrible mistake!
and didn't approach this trial
in a respectful, deliberate or thoughtful manner
didn't take advantage of the best legal advice
and based my actions on irrelevant matters
which i can see now in a much more sober mind
had nothing to do with this case
i must have been legally insane thinking about:
the twenty-five murders of children in atlanta since
    Wayne Williams' capture
the recent murder of a man in boston by police
the recent murders of two in chicago by police
the shooting of a five-year-old little boy in suburban calif
the lynchings in alabama
the mob murder of a transit worker in brooklyn
the murders of fourteen women in boston
feeling that this is evidence of something
    and that there must be a lesson in all this — i thought
    murder was legal

—Kuwasi Balagoon

Kuwasi Balagoon (s/n: Donald Weams) was a defendant in the Panther 21 case of 1969-70, and a member of the Black Liberation Army. Captured and convicted of various "crimes against the State," he spent much of the 1970s in prison, escaping twice. After release, he went underground once again, and resumed BLA activity. He was captured in December 1981, charged with participating in an armored truck expropriation in West Nyack, New York, on October 21 of that year, an action in which two police officers were killed. Convicted and sentenced to life imprisonment, he died of AIDS-related illness (pneumocystis carninii pneumonia) on December 13, 1986.

David Gilbert

The Struggle for AIDS Education in Prison

Prisons, although more hidden from public view, are yet another arena where the AIDS epidemic is being allowed to spread because the authorities don't give a fig about human life when it comes to gays, third world people, and the poor. In 1987, one hundred-fifty New York state prisoners died of AIDS; two out of every three deaths in a system that holds 40,000 people. The death toll will continue to rise for years to come. Eighty-eight percent of New York prisoners with AIDS are Latino or Black. AIDS itself is bad enough, and it is heartbreaking to have to face death in prison. But for the prisoner with AIDS it is triple jeopardy because he or she might be completely isolated even from other prisoners.

The prisoner with AIDS is also likely to have a much shorter survival time. A recent New York Commission of Correction report shows that, for example, IV drug users with AIDS live for an average of 318 days after diagnosis in New York City but only 159 days in the state prisons. No one has put out a definitive analysis of this stark discrepancy; it is probably a combination of late diagnosis, poor medical treatment, and the depressing emotional atmosphere in prisons. It is shocking that this grim statistic of one half the survival time has not produced a public uproar. The deafening silence expresses how little value is placed on prisoners' lives by officials, the media, and sectors of the public.

Continued transmission of AIDS within prisons and to the communities to which most prisoners eventually return is both a dire and unattended problem. The most realistic estimate of the seropositive rate among New York State prisoners is twenty-five percent. (This figure is arrived at by correlating the percentage of New York IV drug users who are seropositive with the percentage of prisoners with IV drug histories. The figures for most other states would be much, much lower.) Tests of federal prisoners indicate that close to three percent are seropositive, and even this figure poses significant epidemiological dangers.

While sex and drugs are officially proscribed in prison, they are far from uncommon. Yet hard-to-come-by needles are likely to be widely shared, with little access to proper sterilization; condoms are a rarity.

(Condoms, needles, and disinfectants are all contraband in here.) There is no question but that *there is a grave problem of the continued spread of the epidemic in prison.* Yet the authorities stick by their official position of no "apparent" or "documented" spread. They claim that sharing needles and prison sex are now rare; we prisoners know better.

Quiet as it's kept, there is a way to prevent AIDS: education. The most effective approach is peer education. The peer aspect is doubly important in prison where inmates tend to distrust the authorities and are unlikely to discuss proscribed activities with staff. Some people take the cynical view that "dope-fiends" won't change. My experience is that working with people on the basis of respect and trust, in a consistent and day-to-day fashion, can bring significant changes away from high-risk practices. I've seen even more profound, and moving, changes in attitudes toward PWA's; once fears about casual contact are put to rest, people's compassion can blossom.

In June of 1987, three of us at Auburn Correctional Facility launched a Prisoner's Education Project on AIDS (PEPA). We were spurred into action by the AIDS death of our beloved fellow prisoner, and distinguished Black Liberation Army warrior, Kuwasi Balagoon. We developed our program by applying the example of the successful peer education in the San Francisco gay community to the very different prison context. Of course the Department of Correctional Services rejected our application to form an inmate organization. They rule by maintaining passivity and divisions among prisoners, so the type of initiative and unity intrinsic to a peer counseling program is an anathema to the authorities.

We were prepared for their opposition and had developed a good deal of outside support for our program—enough support to force through the compromise of a partial project. What we weren't prepared for was the role of the two white, male AIDS professionals who became the key to our outside training and sponsorship. They just didn't see prisoners—primarily third world and poor—as much of a priority, even though we had the highest concentration of seropositive people in their region. Their inordinate delays on promised work gave the prison authorities the space for a war of attrition against our project. These professionals also basically conformed with the administration's position that the program should first be worked out by the professionals and administration, with the prisoners then simply the recipients of the final product—some way to develop a "peer" project! Amidst the months of delays and constant hassles, I (the recognized "Inmate Coordinator" of the project) was suddenly shipped out to the most isolated Max A prison in the state. While several prisoners at Auburn, along with some dedicated outside AIDS volunteers, continue to make a valiant effort, the war of attrition has left a mere shell of the original project.

There is a bitter irony here, bitter with the taste of numerous deaths over time which could have been prevented. Probably the greatest initial obstacle to prisoner involvement was homophobia. Even though most prisoners with AIDS were exposed via needles, AIDS was defined as a "gay disease" and homophobia blocked prisoners from identifying with PWA's and from facing the issues forthrightly. On the other hand, the undoubted basis for how our efforts were undercut by AIDS professionals was their race and class bias. Meanwhile, the crucially needed prisoner peer education projects for New York and nation-wide continue to be stymied, at great cost to human lives.

My conclusions from this experience: 1) Thorough, consistent, and ongoing peer education can make a big difference in the attitudes and practices of prisoners; 2) The prison authorities will not accede to such programs without strong public pressure to do so; 3) There must be a powerful movement about AIDS to push the professionals (or supercede them) to be true to their professed ideals and put the fight against AIDS above careerism. To be effective against AIDS, the movement must consciously oppose race, class, gender and sexual-orientation biases.

Nancy Kurshan

Women and Imprisonment in the U.S.—
History and Current Reality

> They call us bandits, yet every time most Black people pick up
> our paychecks, we are being robbed. Every time we walk into
> a store in our neighborhood, we are being held up. And every
> time we pay our rent, the landlord sticks a gun into our ribs.
> —Assata Shakur, 1972

> These people in this judicial system, their concern is not for
> justice, as they claim. That is what they come in disguise of, to
> strip the people of everything. When I say strip, I mean rob,
> murder, exploit, intimidate, harass, persecute, everything to
> destroy the mind and body. They seek to take a person and make
> a complete vegetable of them.
> —Ruchell Cinque Magee, 1974

Prisons serve the same purpose for women as they do for men; they
are instruments of social control. However, the imprisonment of women,
as well as all the other aspects of our lives, takes place against a backdrop
of patriarchal relationships. We refer here to Gerda Lerner's definition
of patriarchy: "the manifestation and institutionalization of male
dominance over women and children in the family and the extension
of male dominance over women in society in general. It implies that
men hold power in all the important institutions of society and that
women are deprived of access to such power."[1] Therefore, the
imprisonment of women in the U.S. has always been a different
phenomenon than that for men; the proportion of women in prison has
always differed from that of men; women have traditionally been sent
to prison for different reasons; and once in prison, they endure different
conditions of incarceration. Women's "crimes" have often had a sexual
definition and been rooted in the patriarchal double standard.
Furthermore, the nature of women's imprisonment reflects the position
of women in society.

It an effort to examine these issues further, this essay explores how
prisons have historically served to enforce and reinforce women's
traditional roles, to foster dependency and passivity, bearing in mind

that it is not just incarcerated women who are affected. Rather, the social stigma and conditions of incarceration serve as a warning to women to stay within the "proper female sphere." Needless to say this warning is not issued equally to women of all nationalities and classes. For this reason, our analysis will also take into account the centrality of race in determining female prison populations, both in the North and the South and pre- and post-Civil War. We believe that white supremacy alters the way that gender impacts on white women and women of color. The final avenue of exploration of this chapter will thus concern the relationship between race and women's imprisonment. We will attempt to show that the history of the imprisonment of women is consistent with Audre Lorde's comment that in "a patriarchal power system where white skin privilege is a major prop, the entrapments used to neutralize Black women and white women are not the same."[2]

As long as there has been crime and punishment, patriarchal and gender-based realities and assumption have been central determinants of the response of society to women "offenders." In the late Middle Ages, reports reveal differential treatment of men and women. A woman might commonly be able to receive lenient punishment if she were to "plead her belly," that is, a pregnant women could plead leniency on the basis of her pregnancy.[3] On the other hand, women were burned at the stake of adultery or murdering a spouse, while men would most often not be punished for such actions. Such differential treatment reflected ideological assumptions as well as women's subordinate positions within the family, church, and other aspects of society. Although systematic imprisonment arose with industrialization, for centuries prior to that time unwanted daughters and wives were forced into convents, nunneries, and monasteries. In those cloisters were found political prisoners, illegitimate daughters, the disinherited, the physically deformed and the mentally defective.[4]

A more general campaign of violence against women was unleashed in the witch-hunts of sixteenth and seventeenth century Europe, as society tried to exert control over women by labelling them as witches. This resulted in the death by execution of at least tens of thousands, and possibly millions of people. Conservative estimates indicate that over eighty percent of all the people killed were women.[5] Here in the U.S., the witchcraft trial were a dramatic chapter in the social control of women long before systematic imprisonment. Although the colonies were settled relatively late in the history of European witch-hunts, the proved fertile ground for this misogynist campaign. The context was a new colonial society, changing and wrought with conflicts. There were arguments within the ruling alliance, a costly war with the indigenous people led by King Philip, and land disputes.[6] In the face of social uncertainty, unrest and "uncivilized Indians," the Puritans were determined to recreate the Christian family way of life in the wilderness and reestablish the social patterns of the homeland.[7] The success of their project was an open question at the time, and the molding of the role of women was an essential element in the defense of that project.

Hundreds were accused of witchcraft during the New England witchcraft trials of the late 1600s, and at least thirty-six were executed. The primary determinant of who was designated a witch was gender; overwhelmingly, it was women who were the objects of witch fear. More women were charged with witchcraft, and women were more likely than men to be convicted and executed. In fact, men who confessed were likely to be scoffed at as liars. But age, too, was an important factor. Women over forty were most likely to be accused of witchcraft and fared much worse than younger women when they were charged. Women over sixty were especially at high risk. Women who were alone, not attached to men as mothers, sister, or wives were also represented disproportionately among the witches.[8] Puritan society was very hierarchal, and the family was an essential aspect of that hierarchy. According to Karlsen, the Puritan definition of woman as procreator and "helpmate" of man could not be ensured except through force.[9] Most of the witches had expressed dissatisfaction with their lot, if only indirectly. Some were not sufficiently submissive in that they filed petitions and court suits, and sometimes sought divorces. Others were midwives and had influence over the well-being of others, often to the chagrin of their male competitors, medical doctors. Still others exhibited a female pride and assertiveness, refusing to defer to their male neighbors.

Karlsen goes on to offer one of the most powerful explanations of the New England witchcraft trials.[10] She argues that at the heart of the hysteria was an underlying anxiety about inheritance. The inheritance system was designed to keep property in the hands of men. When there were not legitimate male heirs, women inheritors became aberrations who threatened the orderly transmission of property from one male generation to the next. Many of the witches were potential inheritors. Some of them were already widowed and without sons. Others were married but older, beyond their childbearing years, and therefore no longer likely to produce male heirs. They were also "disposable" since they were no longer performing the "essential" functions of a woman, as reproducer and, in some cases, helpmeet. Many of the witches were charged just shortly after the death of the male family member, and their witchcraft convictions meant that their lands could easily be seized. Seen in this light, witchcraft was an attempt to maintain the patriarchal social structure and prevent women from becoming economically independent. These early examples of the use of criminal charges in the social control of women may be seen as precursors to the punitive institutions of the 1800s. Up until this time, there were few carceral institutions in society. However, with the rise of capitalism and urbanization come the burgeoning of prisons in the U.S.[11] It is to those initial days of systematic imprisonment that we now turn.

The Emergence of Prisons for Women

The relatively few women who were imprisoned at the beginning of the 19th century were confined in separate quarters or wings of men's prisons. Like the men, women suffered from filthy conditions, over-crowding, and harsh treatment. In 1838 in the New York City Jail (the "Tombs"), for instance, there were forty-two one-person cells for seventy women. In the 1920s at Auburn Penitentiary in New York, there were no separate cells for the twenty-five or so women serving sentences up to fourteen years. They were all lodged together in a one room attic, the windows sealed to prevent communication with men.[12] But women had to endure even more. Primary among these additional negative aspects was sexual abuse, which was reportedly a common occurrence. In 1826 Rachel Welch became pregnant while serving in solitary con-finement as a punishment and shortly after childbirth she died as a result of flogging by a prison official. Such sexual abuse was apparently so acceptable that the Indiana state prison actually ran a prostitution service for male guards, using female prisoners.[13]

In addition, women received the short end of even the prison stick. Rather than spend the money to hire a matron, women were often left completely on their own, vulnerable to attack by guards. Women had less access to the physician and chaplain and did not go to workshops, mess halls, or exercise yards as men did. Food and needlework were brought to their quarters, and they remained in that area for the full term of their sentence. Criminal conviction and imprisonment of women soared during and after the Civil War. In the North, this is commonly attributed to a multitude of factors, including men's absence during wartime, the rise of industrialization, as well as the impact of the dominant sexual ideology of the nineteenth century Victorianism.[14] The double standard of Victorian morality supported the criminalization of certain behaviors for women but not for men. In New York in the 1850s and 1860s, female "crimes against persons" tripled while "crimes against property" rose ten times faster than the male rate.

Black people, both women and men, have always been dispro-portionately incarcerated at all times and all places. This was true in the Northeast and Midwest prisons before the Civil War. It was also the case in the budding prison system in the western states, where blacks outstripped their very small percentage of the population. The only exception was in the South where slavery, not imprisonment, was the preferred form of control of Afroamerican people.[15] If the South had the lowest black imprisonment rate before the Civil War, this changed dramatically after the slaves were freed. This change took place for Afroamerican women as well as men. After the Civil War, as part of the re-entrenchment of Euroamerican control and the continuing sub-jugation of black people, the post-war southern states passed infamous Jim Crow laws which made newly freed blacks vulnerable to incarcer-ation for the most minor crimes.[16] For example, stealing a couple of chickens brought three to ten years in North Carolina. It is fair to say that many blacks stepped from slavery into imprisonment. As a result, southern prison populations became predominately black overnight. Between 1874 and 1877, the black imprisonment rate went up 300 percent in Mississippi and Georgia. In some states, previously all-white prisons could not contain the influx of Afroamericans sentenced to hard labor for petty offenses.[17]

These spiraling rates in both the North and South meant that by mid-century there were enough women prisoners, both in the North and South, to necessitate the emergence of separate women's quarters. This practical necessity opened the door to changes in the nature of the imprisonment of women. In 1869 Sarah Smith and Rhoda Coffin, two Indiana Quakers, led a campaign to end the sexual abuse of women in that state's prison, and in 1874 the first completely separate women's prison was constructed. By 1940 twenty-three states had separate women's prisons.[18] The literature refers to these separate prisons for women as "independent" women's prisons.[19] This is ironic usage of the word since they were independent only in their physical construction. In every other way they fostered all forms of dependency in the incarcerated women and were an integral part of the prison system. Although these prisons were not initiated as separate institutions until almost a century after men's prisons, it is not so much this time lag which differentiates the development of prisons for women from those for men. The difference comes from the establishment of a bifurcated (two-part) system, the roots of which can be found in the patriarchal and white supremacist aspects of life in the U.S. at the time. Under-standing this bifurcation is a step towards understanding the incarceration of women in the U.S.

On the one hand, there were custodial institutions which cor-responded by and large to man's prisons. The purpose of custodial prisons, as the name implies, was to warehouse prisoners. There was no pretense of rehabilitation. On the other hand, there were reformatories which, as the name implies, were intended to be more benevolent institutions that "uplifted" or "improved" the character of the women held there. These reformatories had no male counterparts. Almost every state had a custodial woman's prison, but in the Northeast and Midwest the majority of incarcerated women were in reformatories. In the South, the few reformatories that existed were exclusively white. However, these differences are not, in essence, geographical; they are racial. The women in the custodial institutions were black whether in the North or the South, and had to undergo the most degrading conditions, while it was mainly white women who were sent to the reformatories, institutions which had the ostensible philosophy of benevolence and sisterly and therapeutic ideals.[20]

The Evolution of Separate Custodial Prisons for Women

In the South after 1870, prison camps emerged as penal servitude and were essentially substituted for slavery. The overwhelming majority of women in the prison camps were black; the few white women who were there had been imprisoned for much more serious offenses, yet experienced better conditions of confinement. For instance, at Bowden Farm in Texas, the majority of women were black, were there for property offenses and worked in the field. The few white women who were there had been convicted of homicide and served as domestics. As the techniques of slavery were applied to the penal system, some states forced women to work on the state-owned penal plantations but also leased women to local farms, mines, and railroads. Treatment on the infamous chain gangs was brutal and degrading. For example, women were whipped on the buttocks in the presence of men. They were also forced to defecate right where they worked, in front of men.[21]

An 1880 census indicated that in Alabama, Louisiana, Mississippi, North Carolina, Tennessee, and Texas, thirty-seven percent of the 220 black women were leased out whereas only one of the forty white women was leased. Testimony in a 1870 Georgia investigation revealed that in one instance "There were no white women there. One started there, and I heard Mr. Alexander (the lessee) say he turned her loose. He was talking to the guard; I was working in the cut. He said his wife was a white woman, and he could not stand it to see a white women worked in such places."[22] Eventually, as central penitentiaries were built or rebuilt, many women were shipped there from prison farms because they were considered "dead hands" as compared with the men. At first the most common form of custodial confinement was attachment to male prisons; eventually independent women's prison evolved out of these male institutions. These separate women's prisons were established largely for administrative convenience, not reform. Female matrons worked there, but they took their orders from men.

Like the prison camps, custodial women's prisons were overwhelmingly black, regardless of their regionality. Although they have always been imprisoned in smaller numbers than Afroamerican or Euroamerican men, black women often constituted larger percentages within female prisons than black men did within men's prison. For instance, between 1797 and 1801, forty-four percent of the women sent to New York state prisons were Afroamericans as compared to twenty percent of the men. In the Tennessee state prison in 1868, one hundred percent of the women were were black, whereas sixty percent of the men were of African descent.[23] The women incarcerated in the custodial prisons tended to be twenty-one years or older. Forty percent were unmarried, and many of them had worked in the past.[24]

Women in custodial prisons were frequently convicted of felony charges; most commonly for "crimes" against property, often petty theft. Only about a third of female felons were serving time for violent crimes. Both the rates for property crimes and violent crimes were much higher than for the women at the reformatories. On the other hand, there were relatively fewer women incar-

Brixton Prison for Women (*A Just Measure of Pain*)

cerated for public order offenses (fornication, adultery, drunkenness, etc.) which were the most common in the reformatories. This was especially true in the South where these so-called morality offenses by blacks were generally ignored, and where authorities were reluctant to imprison white women at all. Data from the Auburn, New York prison on homicide statistics between 1909 and 1933 reveal the special nature of the women's "violent" crime. Most of the victims of murder by women were adult men. Of 149 victims, two-thirds were male: twenty-nine percent were husbands, two percent were lovers, and the rest were listed as "man" or "boy" (a similar distribution exists today). Another form of violent crime resulting in the imprisonment of women was performing "illegal" abortions.[25]

Tennessee Supreme Court records offer additional anecdotal information about the nature of women's violent crimes. Eighteen year old Sally Griffin killed her fifty year old husband after a fight in which, according to Sally, he knocked her though a window, hit her with a hammer, and threatened to "knock her brains out." A doctor testified that in previous months her husband had seriously injured her ovaries when he knocked her out of bed because she refused to have sex during her period. Sally's conviction stood because an eyewitness said she hadn't been threatened with a hammer. A second similar case was also turned down for retrial.[26] Southern states were especially reluctant to send white women to prison, so they were deliberately screened out by the judicial process. When white women were sent to prison, it was for homicide or sometimes arson; almost never did larceny result in incarceration. In the Tennessee prison, many of the African American property offenders had committed less serious offenses than the whites, although they were incarcerated in far greater numbers.[27] Of all the women tried, Frances Kellor, a renowned prison reformer, remarked that in this screening process the black female offender "is first a Negro and then a woman—in the whites' estimation."[28] A 1922 North Carolina report describes one institution as being "so horrible that the judge refuses to send white women to this jail, but Negro women are sometimes sent."[29] Hundreds of such instances combined to create institutions overwhelmingly made up of Afroamerican women.

The conditions of these custodial prisons were horrendous, as they were in prisons for men. The Southern prisons were by far the worst. They were generally unsanitary, lacking adequate toilet and bathing facilities. Medical attention was rarely available. Women were either left totally idle or forced into hard labor. Women with mental problems were locked in solitary confinement and ignored. But women suffered an additional oppression as well:

The condition of the women prisoners is most deplorable. They

are usually placed in the oldest part of the prison structure. They
are almost always in the direct charge of men guards. They are
treated and disciplined as men are. In some of the prisons children
are born . . . either from the male prisoners or just 'others'. . . .
One county warden told me in confidence, 'That I near kill that
woman yesterday. . . .' One of the most reliable women officials
in the South told me that in her state at the State Farm for women
the dining room contains a sweat box for women who are punished
by being locked up in a narrow place with insufficient room to
sit down, and near enough to be the table so as to be able to smell
the food. Over the table there is an iron bar to which women are
handcuffed when they are strapped.[30]

Generally speaking, the higher the proportion of women of color in
the prison population, the worse the conditions. Therefore, it is not
surprising that the physical conditions of incarceration for women in
the custodial prisons were abysmal compared to the reformatories (as
the following section indicates). Even in mainly black penal institutions,
Euroamerican women were treated better than Afroamerican women.

Early 20th Century Women's Reformatories

Reformatories for women developed alongside custodial prisons. These
were parallel, but distinct, developments. By the turn of the century,
industrialization was in full swing, bringing fundamental changes in
social relations: shifts from a rural society to an urban one, from a family
to market economy; increased geographic mobility; increased disruption
of lives; more life outside the church, family, and community. More
production, even for women, was outside the home. By 1910, a record
high of at least twenty-seven percent of all women in New York State
were gainfully employed.[31] Thousands of women worked in the New
York sweatshops under abominable conditions. There was a huge influx
of immigration from Southern and Eastern Europe; many of these were
Jewish women who had come straight from Czarist Russia and brought
with them a tradition of resistance and struggle. The division between
social classes was clearly widening and erupted in dynamic labor
struggles. For example, in 1909, 20,000 shirt-waist makers, four-fifths
of whom were women, went on strike in New York.[32] Racism and
national chauvinism were rampant in the U.S. at the turn of the century
in response to the waves of immigrants from Europe and black people
from the South. The Women's Prison Association of New York, which
was active in the social purity movement, declared in 1906 that:

If promiscuous immigration is to continue, it devolves upon the
enlightened, industrious, and moral citizens, from selfish as well

as from philanthropic motives, to instruct the morally defective
to conform to our ways and exact from them our own high
standard of morality and legitimate industry. . . . Do you want
immoral women to walk our streets, pollute society, endanger
your households, menace the morals of your sons and daughters.
. . ? Do you think the women here described fit to become mothers
of American citizens? Shall foreign powers generate criminals
and dump them on our shores?[33]

Also at the turn of the century various currents of social concern
converged to create a new reform effort, the Progressive movement, that
swept the country, particularly the Northeast and Midwest, for several
decades.[34] It was in this context that reformatories for women
proliferated. Reformatories were actually begun by an earlier generation
of women reformers who appeared between 1840 and 1900, but their
proliferation took place during this Progressive Era as an alternative
to the penitentiary's harsh conditions of enforced silence and hard
labor.[35] The reformatories came into being as a result of the work of
prison reformers who were ostensibly motivated to improve penal treatment for women. They believed that the mixed prisons afforded women
no privacy and left them vulnerable to debilitating humiliations.

Indeed, the reformatories were more humane and conditions were
better than at the women's penitentiaries (custodial institutions). They
did eliminate much male abuse and the fear of attack. They also resulted
in more freedom of movement and opened up a variety of opportunities
for "men's" work in the operation of the prison. Children of prisoners
up to two years old could stay in most institutions. At least some of
the reformatories were staffed and administered by women. They usually
had cottages, flower gardens, and no fences. They offered discussions
on the law, academics and training, and women were often paroled more
readily than in custodial institutions.[36] However, a closer look at who
the women prisoners were, the nature of their offenses, and the program
to which they were subjected reveals the seamier side of these ostensibly
noble institutions.

As with all prisons, the women in the reformatories were of the
working class. Many of them worked outside the home. At New York
State's Albion Reformatory, for instance, eighty percent had, in the past,
worked for wages. Reformatories were also overwhelmingly institutions
for white women. Fewer women of color were incarcerated in them.
Government statistics indicate that in 1921, for instance, twelve percent
of the women in reformatories were black while eighty-eight percent
were white.[37] Record keeping at the Albion reformatory in New York
demonstrates how unusual it was for black women to be incarcerated
there. The registries left spaces for entries of large number of variables,
such as family history of insanity and epilepsy. Nowhere was there a

space for recording race. When African Americans were admitted, the clerk penciled "colored" at the top of the page. Afroamerican women were much less likely to be arrested for such public order offenses. Rafter suggests that black women were not expected to act like "ladies" in the first place and therefore were reportedly not deemed worthy of such rehabilitation.[38]

It is important to emphasize that reformatories existed for women only. No such parallel development took place within men's prisons. There were no institutions devoted to "correcting" men for so-called moral offenses. In fact. such activities were not considered crimes when men engaged in them and therefore men were not as a result imprisoned.[39] A glace at these "crimes" for women only suggests the extent to which society was bent on repressing women's sexuality. Despite the hue and cry about prostitution, only 8.5 percent of the women at the reformatories were actually convicted of prostitution. More than half, however, were imprisoned because of "sexual misconduct." Women were incarcerated in reformatories primarily for various public order offenses or so-called "moral" offenses: lewd and lascivious carriage, stubbornness, idle and disorderly conduct, drunkenness, vagrancy, fornication, serial premarital pregnancies, keeping bad company, adultery, venereal disease and vagrancy. A woman might face charges simply because a relative disapproved of her behavior and reported her; or because she had been sexually abused and was being punished for it. Most were rebels of some sort.[40]

Jennie B., for instance, was sent to Albion reformatory for five years for having "had unlawful sexual intercourse with young men and remain[ing] at hotels with young men all night, particularly on July 4, 1893."[41] Lilian R. quit school and ran off for one week with a soldier, contracting venereal disease. She was hospitalized where she was then sentenced to the reformatory. Other women were convicted of offenses related to exploitation and/or abuse by men. Ann B. became pregnant twice from older men, one of whom was her father who was sentenced to prison for rape. She was convicted of "running around" when she was seven months pregnant.[42] One woman who claimed to have miscarried and disposed of the fetus had been convicted of murdering her illegitimate child. There was also the increasing practice of abortion which accounted for at least some of the rise in "crime against persons."[43]

The program of these institutions, as well as the offenses, was based on patriarchal assumptions. Reformatory training centered on fostering ladylike behavior and perfecting house-wifely skills. In this way it encouraged dependency and women's subjugation. Additionally, one aspect of the retraining of these women was to isolate them, to strip them of environmental influences in order to instill them with new values. To this end family ties were obstructed, which is somewhat ironic since the family is at the center of the traditional role of women. Letters might come every two months and were censored. Visits were allowed four times a year for those who were on the approved list. The reformatories were geographically remote, making it very difficult for loved ones to visit. Another thorn in the rosy picture of the reformatory was the fact that sentencing was often open-ended. This was an outgrowth of the rehabilitative ideology. The incarceration was not of fixed length, because the notion was that a woman would stay for as long as it took to accomplish the task of reforming her.

Parole was also used as a patriarchal weapon. Ever since the Civil War, there was a scarcity of working class women for domestic service. At the same time, the "need for good help" was increasing because more people could afford to hire help.[44] It was not an accident that women were frequently paroled into domestic jobs, the only ones for which they had been trained. In this way, vocational regulation went hand-in-hand with social control, leading always backwards to home and hearth, and away from self-sufficiency and independence. Additionally, independent behavior was punished by revoking parole for "sauciness," obscenity, or failure to work hard enough. One woman was cited for a parole violation for running away from a domestic position to join a theater troupe; another for going on car rides with men; still others for becoming pregnant, going around with a disreputable married man, or associating with the father of her child. And finally, some very unrepentant women were ultimately transferred indefinitely to asylums for the "feeble-minded."

Prison reform movements have been common; a reform movement also existed for men. However, all these institutions were inexorably returned to the role of institutions of social control.[45] Understanding this early history can prepare us to understand recent developments in women's imprisonment and indeed imprisonment in general. Although the reformatories rejected the more traditional authoritarian penal regimes they were nonetheless concerned with social control. Feminist criminologists claim that in their very inception, reformatories were institutions of patriarchy. They were part of a broad attack on young working class women who were attempting to lead somewhat more autonomous lives. Women's sexual independence was being curbed in the context of "social purity" campaigns.[46] As more and more white working class women left home for the labor force, they took up smoking, frequenting dance halls and having sexual relationships. Prostitution had long been a source of income for poor women, but despite the fact that prostitution had actually begun to wane about 1900, there was a major morality crusade at the turn of the century which attacked prostitution as well as all kinds of small deviations from the standard of "proper" female propriety.[47]

Even when the prisons were run by women they were, of course, still doing the work of a male supremacist prison system and society. We have seen how white working class women were punished for "immoral behavior" when men were not. We have seen how they were indoctrinated with a program of "ladylike" behavior. According to feminist criminologists such as Rafter and Freedman, reformatories essentially punished those who did not conform to bourgeois definitions of femininity and prescribed gender roles. The prisoners were to embrace the social values, although of course never to occupy the social station, of a "lady." It is relevant to note that the social stigma of imprisonment was even greater for women than men because women were supposedly denying their own "pure nature." This stigma plus the nature of the conditions of incarceration served as a warning to all such women to stay within the proper female sphere.

These observations shed some light on the role of "treatment" within penal practice. Reformatories were an early attempt at "treatment," that is the uplifting and improvement of the women, as opposed to mere punishment or retribution. However, these reforms were also an example of the subservience of "treatment" to social control. They demonstrate that the underlying function of control continually reasserts itself when attempts to "improve" people take place within a coercive framework.[48] The reformatories are an illustration of how sincere efforts at reform may only serve to broaden the net and extend the state's power of social control. In fact, hundreds and hundreds of women were incarcerated for public order offenses who previously would not have been vulnerable to the punishment of confinement in a state institution were it not for the existence of reformatories.

By 1935 the custodial prisons for women and the reformatories had basically merged. In the 1930s the U.S. experienced the repression of radicalism, the decline of the progressive and feminist movements, and the Great Depression. Along with these changes came the demise of the reformatories. The prison reform movement had achieved one of its earliest central aims, separate prisons for women. The reformatory building still stood and were filled with prisoners. However, these institutions were reformatories in name only. Some were administered by women but they were women who did not even have thee progressive pretenses of their predecessors. The conditions of incarceration had deteriorated miserably, suffering from cutbacks and lack of funding. Meanwhile, there had been a slow but steady transformation of the inmate population. Increasingly, the white women convicted of misdemeanors were given probation, paroled or sent back to local jails. As Euroamerican women left the reformatories, the buildings themselves were transformed into custodial prisons, institutions that repeated the terrible conditions of the past. As custodial prison buildings were physically closed down for various reasons, felons were transferred to the buildings that had housed the reformatories. Most of the women were not only poor but also were black. Increasingly, Afroamerican women were incarcerated there with the growth of the black migration north after World War I. These custodial institutions now included some added negative dimensions as the legacy of the reformatories, such as the strict reinforcement of gender roles and the infantilization of women. In the end the reformatories were certainly not a triumph for the women's liberation. Rather they can be viewed as one of many instances in which U.S. institutions are able to absorb an apparent reform and use it for continuing efforts at social control.

Women and Prison Today

Women are an extremely small proportion of the overall U.S. prison population, approximately five percent.[49] At the end of 1988, there were 32,691 women in state and federal prisons.[50] Although imprisonment rates for women are low, they are rising rapidly, after having remained more or less constant for the previous fifty years. According to government statistics, the number of women prisoners has mushroomed from 13,420 in just eight years, a 244 percent increase, as compared to an increase of 188 percent for men during the same period.[51] The rate for women has grown faster than that for men each year since 1981.[52] During 1987 alone, there was a 9.3 percent increase in the rate of imprisonment for women while the figure for men rose 6.6 percent.[53] In New York City jails, the rate for women rose a staggering thirty-three percent in the last year alone, more than twice the rate of men.[54] There is a good deal of speculation about the causes of this rate increase. Although the disproportionate rise in the imprisonment rate of women has not yet been satisfactorily explored, there are some existing explanations and hypotheses. Some say there has been a jump in violent crime perpetrated by women as a result of the women's movement and the associated empowerment of women. In other words, increased gender equality brings more violence by women. However, there is no evidence to support either the allegation that female violent crimes have increased, nor that equality leads to more violent crime by women.

In fact, by most if not all accounts, violent crimes by women have remained constant or, in some cases, actually declined. For instance, a comparison of female crime rates between 1977 and 1987 indicates that violent personal crimes actually declined while alcohol and drug-related crimes tripled.[55] A study by Weisheit specifically compared "gender equality" in various states with the female homicide rates in these states.[56] The results indicated that those states with the highest degree of gender equality also have the *lowest* rate of homicide by females. If feminism is not the explanation for those spiraling imprisonment rates, what is? The rising rates can be explained, to a large extent, by many of the same factors that influence the male imprisoned for substance abuse offenses. In one southern prison, seventy-seven percent of the women are there on drug or alcohol-related offenses. In another state, the number of new admissions for such offenses has jumped from five percent to fifty-six percent in the last ten years.[57] Not only are drug and alcohol-related offenses more frequent but the nature of the charges tends to be more severe. That is, we are now seeing felony drug charges as compared to past misdemeanors for substance abuse.[58]

Why the rates are rising more quickly for women remains an unanswered question. It is possible that deteriorating economic conditions are now pushing women to the brink faster than men; as the primary caretakers of children, women may be driven by poverty to engage in more "crimes" of survival. Changes in sentencing laws and practices, such as mandatory minimum-sentencing, are commonly referred to as a main factor in rising imprisonment rates for women.[59] Many commentators have indicated that judges are less hesitant than ever to send women to prison. Offenses which used to get probation are now drawing prison time and sentences are harsher. Some observers state that if there was ever a shred of "chivalry: in the white male criminal justice system, that is no longer true today. For instance, an administrator of a Texas women's prison was quoted by the *New York Times* as stating that "Chivalry is dead. . . . It's equal rights, dog eat dog, no woman at home with an apron on anymore."[60] Whatever the reason, it seems certain that women are being treated more punitively than in the past by the criminal justice system.

Who are the women in prison? The profile that emerges in study after study is that of a young, single mother with few marketable job skills, a high school drop-out who lives below the poverty level. Seventy-five percent are between the ages of twenty-five and thirty-four, are mothers of dependent children, and were unemployed at the time of arrest. Many left home early and have experienced sexual and physical abuse. Ninety percent have a drug or alcohol-related history.[61] Another extremely significant factor is the race of incarcerated women. In 1982:

> The population of women's prisons was 50 percent black, although blacks comprised only 11 percent of the total population in this

country; 9 percent Hispanic [*sic*, latino], when [they] were only 5 percent of the total population; and 3 percent Native American, although this group comprises only 0.4 percent of the total population.[62]

In fact, African-American women are eight times more likely than white women to go to prison. Although a greater proportion of white women are arrested, a smaller proportion are incarcerated. A 1985 Michigan study reported that 10.5 percent of all arrests were those of white women, while non-white women accounted for 6.1 percent of all arrests. On the other hand, Euroamerican women were 1.8 percent of those incarcerated while women of color were 4.5 percent.[63] It is not clear, of course, what other factors are involved, such as the distribution of arrestable offenses or the role of prosecutorial discretion. What seems certain is that there is a different set of dynamics at work for white and non-white women. And as Karl Rassmussen, Executive Director of Women's Prison Association of New York says, "150 years ago it was poor whites, their names often Irish—and alcohol abuse. Today, it's poor minorities and drug abuse."[64]

Numerous studies have indicated that women of color, black women in particular, are when compared with white women, over-arrested, over-indicted, under-defended and over-sentenced. African-American women are seven times more likely to be arrested for prostitution than women of other ethnic groups. A California study demonstrated that white women drug violators represent the primary group arrested for this offense (65.1 percent) but are far less likely to be imprisoned (39.4 percent) than any minority female group. Over a sixteen year period, black women incarcerated in Missouri received significantly longer sentences for crimes against property, and served longer periods in prison. White women were generally given much longer sentences for crimes against persons, in fact almost double those of black women. However, actual time served for Afroamerican women was longer. For both murder and drug offenses, Euroamerican women ended up serving one-third less time for the same offenses. The study concluded that "differential treatment is definitely accorded to female offenders by race."[65]

Assata Shakur, the once-imprisoned leader of the Black Liberation Army who was liberated from a New Jersey prison in 1979 and granted political asylum in Cuba, has offered this description:

> There are no criminals here at Riker's Island Correctional Institution for Women (New York), only victims. Most of the women (over 95 percent) are black and Puerto Rican. Many were abused children. Most have been abused by men and all have been abused by 'the system.' . . . There are no big time gangsters here, no premeditated mass murderers, no god mothers. There are no big time dope dealers, no kidnappers, no Watergate women.

> There are virtually no women here charged with white collar crimes like embezzling and fraud. Most of the women have drug related cases. Many are charged as accessories to crimes committed by men. The major crimes that women here are charged with are prostitution, pickpocketing, shop lifting, robbery and drugs. Women who have prostitution cases or who are doing 'fine' time make up a substantial part of the short term population. The women see stealing or hustling as necessary for the survival of themselves or their children because jobs are scarce and welfare is impossible to live on.[66]

As Shakur paints the picture, women's offenses are rarely vicious, dangerous, or profitable. Their crimes arise from difficult circumstances within society at large. Most women are in prison for relatively minor offenses; property crimes, sometimes referred to as poverty crimes, are the most frequent. According to 1983 Bureau of Justice statistics, forty-three percent of women were in for larceny, fraud, or forgery as compared with fifteen percent of men. Additionally, women are less likely to be imprisoned for violent offenses; thirty-five percent of the men were in for violent crimes as compared with twenty-four percent of women. In general, women are less likely to be involved in homicide than are men. For the years 1980-1984, women were found guilty of only fourteen percent of all homicides.[67]

Another important factor is that when women do engage in violent crime, it is often a fundamentally different sort of act. Women are much more likely to kill a male partner than to kill anyone else. Men are much more likely to perpetrate homicides against individuals outside the partner relationship, although the rate of male-perpetrated homicide against intimate partners is still nearly double the rate for female-perpetrated homicides of male partners.[68] Women are much more likely to kill in self-defense in response to their male partners' physical aggression and threats, and the recidivism rates for such crimes are extraordinarily low. That is, it is unlikely for a woman to repeat a homicide. This "female use of lethal counter-force" has been documented in numerous studies.[69] Other authors point out that besides the provocation that *immediately* triggers the female homicide and is recognized by the court of law, female homicide is often in response to preceding years of male abuse.[70]

According to Shelley Bannister, over one-third of all women have been or will be abused as children by males within and outside of their families. Annually, over two million women are battered by male partners.[71] Although no one knows exactly how many women are in prison for killing an abusing husband or boyfriend, Charles Patrick Ewing, a psychologist and attorney, believes that as many as a thousand women a year are convicted for such acts. He states that "This small but increasingly visible minority of battered women are in many cases doubly victimized: once by the men who have battered them and again by a system of criminal justice which holds them to an unrealistic standard of accountability." Moreover, Angela Brown, a Denver social psychologist who conducted research in this area, concludes that "women often face harsher penalties than men who kill their partners."[72]

In the early 1970s, when there was an activist women's movement, several strong campaigns were waged regarding individual cases in which women physically defended themselves and their children against attack. Yvonne Wanrow, a Colville Indian, was convicted by an all-white jury for the self-defense killing of a man who molested her nine-year-old son as well as several other children. Inez Garcia struck back against the men who raped her and threatened her life, while the judge insisted that the allegations of rape were not even an issue in the case.[73] Dessie Woods was found guilty of murder and robbery of a white insurance agent who tried to rape her and a friend.[74] The influence of feminist thinking and agitation can be seen today. Bannister argues in a current criminal justice journal that "women who kill or attempt to kill their abusers are incarcerated for several reasons: 1) to deter other women from believing that they can similarly resist; 2) to reinforce in women the belief that they have no right to their own bodies' integrity and no right to defend against or resist male attack; and 3) to protect and assert men's power over women."[75] Even the Governor of Ohio felt compelled to pardon thirty-five women who had been imprisoned as a result of violence towards husbands and other men who had abused them.

What are the conditions women face when they are imprisoned? Women are confined in a system designed, built and run by men for men, according to a fall 1990 issue of *Time* magazine. Prison authorities rationalize that because the numbers of women have been so relatively low, there are no "economies of scale" in meeting women's needs, particularly their special needs. Therefore, women suffer accordingly, they say. There are a wide range of institutions that incarcerate women and conditions vary. Some women's prisons look like "small college campuses," remnants of the historical legacy of the reformatory movement. Bedford Hills State prison in New York is one such institution; Alderson Federal Prison in West Virginia is another. Appearances, however, are deceptive. For instance, Dobash describes the "underlying atmosphere [of such a prison] as one of intense hostility, frustration and anger."[76]

Many institutions have no pretenses and are notoriously overcrowded and inadequate. The California Institution for Women at Frontera houses twenty-five hundred women in a facility built for 1,011.[77] Overcrowding sometimes means that women who are being held for trivial offenses are incarcerated in maximum security institutions for lack of other facilities. Women's prisons are often particularly ill-equipped and poorly financed. They have fewer medical, educational and vocational facilities than men's prisons.[78] Medical treatment is often unavailable, inappropriate, and inconsistent.[79] Job training is also largely unavailable; when opportunities exit, they are usually traditional female occupations. Courses concentrate on homemaking and low-paid skills like beautician and launderer.[80] Other barriers exist as well. In an Alabama women's prison, there is a cosmetology program but those convicted of felonies are prohibited by state law from obtaining such licenses.[81]

In most prisons, guards have total authority, and the women can never take care of their basic intimate needs in a secure atmosphere, free from intrusion. In the ostensible name of security, male guards can take down or look over a curtain, walk into a bathroom, or observe a women showering or changing her clothes.[82] In Michigan, for instance, male guards are employed at all women's prisons. At Huron Valley, about half the guards are men. At Crane prison, approximately eighty percent of the staff is male and there are open dormitories divided into cubicles. In one section the cubicle walls are only four feet high and there are no doors or curtains on any cubicles anywhere at Crane. The officers' desks are right next to the bathroom and the bathroom doors must be left open at all times. Males guards are also allowed to do body "shakedowns" where they run their hands all over the women's bodies.[83]

Incarceration has severe and particular ramifications for women. Eighty percent of women entering state prisons are mothers. By contrast sixty percent of men in state prisons are fathers and less than half of them have custodial responsibility. These mothers have to undergo the intense pain of forced separation from their children. They are often the sole caretakers of their children and were the primary source of financial and emotional support.[84] Their children are twice as likely to end up in foster care than the children of male prisoners.[85] Whereas when a man goes to prison, his wife or lover most often assumes or continues to assume responsibility for the children, the reverse is not true. Women often have no one else to turn to and are in danger of permanently losing custody of their children. For all imprisoned mothers the separation from their children is one of the greatest punishments of incarceration, and engenders despondency, feelings of guilt and anxiety about their children's welfare.[86]

Visiting with children often is extremely difficult or impossible. At county jails where women are awaiting trial, prisoners are often denied contact visits and are required to visit behind glass partitions or through telephones.[87] Prisons are usually built far away from the urban centers where most of the prisoners and their families and friends live. Where children are able to visit, they have to undergo frightening experiences like pat downs under awkward and generally anti-human conditions. When women get out of prison, many states are supposed to provide reunification services, but in fact most do not.[88] Although even departments of corrections admit that family contact is the one factor which most greatly enhances parole success, the prison system actively works to obstruct such contact.[89]

Reproductive rights are non-existent for the ten percent of the women in prison who are pregnant. Massachusetts is one of the few states to provide Medicaid funds for poor women to get abortions, but these funds are unavailable for imprisoned women.[90] All the essentials for a healthy pregnancy are missing in prison: nutritious food, fresh air, exercise, sanitary conditions, extra vitamins and pre-natal care. Women in prison are denied nutritional supplements such as those afforded by the WIC program.[91] Women frequently undergo bumpy bus rides, and are shackled and watched throughout their delivery.[92] It is no wonder than that a 1985 California Department of Health study indicated that a third of all prison pregnancies end in late term miscarriage, twice the outside rate. In fact, only twenty percent have live births. For those women who are lucky enough to have healthy deliveries, forced separation from the infant usually comes within twenty-four to seventy-two hours after birth.[93]

Many commentators argue that, at their best, women's prisons are shot through with a viciously destructive paternalistic mentality. According to Rafter, "women in prison are perpetually infantilized by routines and paternalistic attitudes."[94] Assata Shakur describes it as a "pseudo-motherly attitude . . . a deception which all too often successfully reverts women to children."[95] Guards call prisoners by their first names and admonish them to "grow up," "be good girls" and "behave." They threaten the women with a "good spanking." Kathryn Burkhart refers to this as a "mass infancy treatment."[96] Powerlessness, helplessness, and dependency are systematically heightened in prison while what would be most therapeutic for women is the opposite, for women to feel their own power and to take control of their lives. Friendship among women is discouraged, and the homophobia of the prison system is exemplified by rules in many prisons which prohibit any type of physical contact between women prisoners.[97] A woman can be punished for hugging a friend who has just learned that her mother died.[98] There is a general prohibition against physical affection, but it is most seriously enforced against known lesbians. One lesbian received a disciplinary ticket for lending a sweater and was told she didn't know the difference between compassion and passion. Lesbians may be confronted with extra surveillance or may be "treated like a man." Some lesbians receive incident reports simply because they are gay.[99]

Many prison administrators generally agree that community-based alternatives would be better and cheaper than imprisonment. However, there is very little public pressure in that direction. While imprisonment rates for women continue to rise, the public outcry is deafening in its silence. Ruth Ann Jones of the Division of Massachusetts Parole Board says her agency receives no outside pressure to develop programs for women.[100] However, around the country small groups of dedicated people are working to introduce progressive reforms into the prisons. In Michigan, there is a program that buses family and friends to visit at prisons. In New York, at Bedford Hills, there is a program geared towards enhancing and encouraging visits with children. Chicago Legal Aid for Imprisoned Mothers (CLAIM), Atlanta's Aid to Imprisoned Mothers and Madison, Wisconsin's Women's Jail Project are just some of the groups that have tirelessly and persistently fought for reforms as well as provided critical services for women and children.

The best programs are the ones that can concretely improve the situation of the women inside. However, many programs that begin with reform-minded intentions become institutionalized in such a way that they are disadvantageous to the population they are supposedly helping. Psychological counselors may have good intentions, but they work for the departments of corrections and often offer no confidentiality.[101] And of course even the best of them tend to focus on individual pathology rather than exposing systematic oppression. Less restrictive alternatives like halfway houses often get turned around so that they become halfway in, not halfway out. That is, what we are experiencing is the widening of the net of state control. The results are that women who would not be incarcerated at all wind up under the supervision of the State rather than decreasing the numbers of women who are imprisoned.[102]

Prison Resistance

One topic that has not been adequately researched is the rebellion and resistance of women in prison. It is only with great difficulty that any information was found. We do not believe that is because resistance does not occur, but rather because those in charge of documenting history have a stake in burying this herstory. Such a herstory would challenge the patriarchal ideology that insists that women are, by nature, passive and docile. What we do know is that as far back as 1943 there was a riot in Sing Sing Prison in New York which was the first woman's prison. It took place in response to overcrowding and inadequate facilities.[103]

During the Civil War, Georgia's prison was burned down, allegedly torched by women trying to escape. It was again burned down in 1900.[104] In 1888 similar activity took place at Framingham, Massachusetts, although reports refer to it as merely "fun." Women rebelled at New York's Hudson House of Refuge in response to excessive punishment. They forced the closing of "the dungeon," basement cells and a diet of bread and water. Within a year, similar cells were reinstituted. The story of Bedford Hills is a particularly interesting one. From 1915 to 1920 there were a series of rebellions against cruelty to inmates. The administration had refused to segregate Black and white women up until 1916, and reports of the time attribute these occurrences to the "unfortunate attachments formed by white women for the Negroes."[105] A 1931 study indicated that "colored girls" revolted against discrimination at the New Jersey State Reformatory.

Around the time of the historical prison rebellion at Attica Prison in New York State, rebellions also took place at women's prisons. In 1971, there was a work stoppage at Alderson simultaneous with the rebellion at Attica.[106] In June of 1975, the women at the North Carolina Correctional Center for Women staged a five day demonstration "against oppressive working atmospheres, inaccessible and inadequate medical facilities and treatment, and racial discrimination, and many other conditions at the prison."[107] Unprotected, unarmed women were attacked by male guards armed with riot gear. The women sustained physical injuries and miscarriages as well as punitive punishment in lockup and in segregation, and illegal transfers to the Mattawan State Hospital for the Criminally Insane. In February of 1977, male guards were for the first time officially assigned to duty in the housing units where they freely watched women showering, changing their clothes and performing all other private functions. On August 2, 1977, a riot squad of predominantly male guards armed with tear gas, high pressure water hoses and billy clubs attacked one housing unit for five hours. Many of the women defended themselves and were brutally beaten; twenty-eight women were illegally transferred to Mattawan where they faced a behavior modification program.[108] This short exposition of the rebellions in women's prisons is clearly inadequate. Feminist criminologists and others should look towards the need for a detailed herstory of this thread of the women's experience in America.

Conclusion

We began this research in an attempt to understand the way that patriarchy and white supremacy interact in the imprisonment of women.

We looked at the history of the imprisonment of women in the United States and found that it has always been different for white women and African American women. This was most dramatically true in the social control of white women, geared toward turning them into "ladies." This was a more physically benign prison track than the custodial prisons that contained black women or men. But it was insidiously patriarchal both in this character and in the fact that similar institution did not exist to control men's behavior in those areas. We also saw that historically the more "black" the penal institution, the worse the conditions. It is difficult to understand how this plays out within the walls of prisons today since there are more sophisticated forms of tracking. That is, within a given prison there are levels of privileges that offer a better or worse quality of life. Research is necessary to determine how this operates in terms of white and Afroamerican women prisoners. However, we can hypothesize that as womens' prisons become increasingly black institutions, conditions will, as in the past, come more and more to resemble the punitive conditions of men's prisons. This is an especially timely consideration now that black women are incarcerated eight times more frequently than white women.

Although the percentage of women in prison is still very low compared to men, the rates are rapidly rising. And when we examine the conditions of incarceration, it does appear as if the imprisonment of women is coming more and more to resemble that of men in the sense that there is no separate, more benign, track for women. Now more than ever, women are being subjected to more maximum security, control units, shock incarceration; in short, everything negative that men receive. We thus may be looking at the beginning of a new era in the imprisonment of women. One observation that is consistent with these findings is that the purpose of prisons for women may not be to function primarily as institutions of patriarchal control. That is, their mission as instruments of social control of people of color generally may be the overriding purpose. Turning women into "ladies" or "feminizing" women is not the essence of the mission of prisons. Warehousing and punishment are now enough, for women as well as men.

This is not to suggest that the imprisonment of women is not replete with sexist ideology and practices. It is a thoroughly patriarchal society that sends women to prison; that is, the rules and regulations, the definition of crimes are defined by the patriarchy. This would include situations in which it is "okay" for a husband to beat up his wife, but that very same wife cannot defend herself against his violence; in which women are forced to act as accessories to crimes committed by men; in which abortion is becoming more and more criminalized. Once in prison, patriarchal assumptions and male dominance continue to play an essential role in the treatment of women. As discussed previously, women have to deal with a whole set of factors that men do not, from intrusion by male guards to the denial of reproductive rights. Modern day women's imprisonment has taken on the worst aspects of the imprisonment of men. But it is also left with the sexist legacy of the reformatories and the contemporary structures of the patriarchy. Infantilization and the reinforcement of passivity and dependency are woven into the very fabric of the incarceration of women.

The imprisonment of women of color can be characterized by the enforcement of patriarchy in the service of the social control of people of color as a whole. This raises larger questions about the enormous attacks aimed at family life in communities of color, in which imprisonment of men, women and children plays a significant role. However, since this area of inquiry concerns the most disenfranchised elements of our society it is no wonder that so little attention is paid to dealing with this desperate situation. More research in this area is needed as there are certainly unanswered questions. But we needn't, we mustn't wait for this research before we begin to unleash our energies to dismantle a prison system that grinds up our sisters.

Notes

1. Gerda Lerner, *The Creation of Patriarchy* (London/New York: Oxford University Press, 1986), p. 239.

2. Audre Lorde, "Age, Race, Class, and Sex: Women Redefining Difference," in Paula S. Rothenberg (ed.), *Racism and Sexism: An Integrated Study* (New York: St. Martin's, 1988), p. 179.

3. It was the life of the fetus which had value, not the life of the woman herself, for "women were merely the vessels of the unborn soul." See Russel P. Dobash, R. Emerson, and Sue Gutteridge, *The Imprisonment of Women* (New York: Basil and Blackwell Publishers, 1986).

4. *Ibid.*

5. Carol F. Karlsen, *The Devil in the Shape of a Woman* (New York: W. W. Norton, 1987), p. xii.

6. William J. Chambliss and Milton Mankoff, *Functional and Conflict Theories of Crime* (New York: MSS Modular Publications, 1973).

7. John D'Emilio and Estelle B. Freedman, *Intimate Matters: A History of Sexuality in America* (New York: Harper and Row Publishers, 1988).

8. Karlsen, *op. cit.*

9. *Ibid.*

10. *Ibid.*

11. David J. Rothman, *The Discovery of the Asylum* (Boston: Little, Brown, and Co., 1971).

12. Nicole Hahn Rafter, *Partial Justice: Women in State Prisons, 1800-1935* (Boston: New England University Press, 1985).

13. Estelle B. Freedman, *Their Sisters' Keepers: Women's Prison Reform in America, 1830-1930* (Ann Arbor: University of Michigan Press, 1981), p. 15.

14. Victorian ideology maintained that women's world was a separate sphere, albeit a morally superior one. Women reportedly had little or no natural sexual desire; sexuality, on their parts, served only the function of reproduction. This was in contrast to men, who were viewed as being lustful. An interesting psychological speculation is that in the U.S. Jacksonian male reformers were obsessed with notions of sexual purity which stemmed from a deep fear of social disorder. As social and economic relations were transformed by capitalism, Jacksonians experienced "psychological tensions." "Uncontrolled" sexuality for women equalled chaos in the popular mind of this period; Jacksonians relied on "pure women to "keep the lid on" since men could not be expected to do so by their very "natures." See Freedman, *op. cit.*, pp. 19-20.

15. Rafter, *op. cit.*

16. W. E. B. DuBois, *Black Reconstruction in America* (New York: Atheneum Press, 1979).

17. Rafter, *op. cit.*

18. Freedman, *op. cit.*

19. *Ibid.* Also see Rafter, *op. cit.*

20. *Ibid.* In the West, little attention was paid by the authorities to systematic prison development until well into the 20th century. California established the only women's reformatory, which remained the region's sole independent prison for women until the 1960's. In 1930, Washington built a women's building.

21. *Ibid.*

22. *Ibid*, p. 151.

23. At least one-quarter of Tennessee's black women prisoners were recently emancipated slaves and part of the post-war northward migration. They were young, uneducated, separated from their families and unprepared for employment, *Ibid*, p. 139.

24. *Ibid.*, p. 128.

25. *Ibid.*, p. 112.

26. *Ibid.*, p. 110.

27. *Ibid.*, p. 144.

28. *Ibid.*, p. 134.

29. *Ibid.*

30. *Ibid.*, Chapter 4, Note 44, quoting Frank Tannenbaum.

31. Rafter, *op. cit.*, p. 160.

32. Richard O. Boyer and Herbert M. Morais, *Labor's Untold Story* (New York: UE Press, 1972).

33. Rafter, *op. cit.*, pp. 93-94.

34. Robert L. Allen, *Reluctant Reformers: Racism and Social Reform Movements in the United States* (Washington, DC: Howard University Press, 1974).

35. These women were middle to upper-class, of Protestant liberal sects, and from the Northeast. They belonged to women's religious and educational groups which fed their sense of sisterhood and fueled their mission. Some were abolitionists. Some were feminists. They were generally believers in

a separate women's sphere and did not seek equality in the public arena. These early reformers were, however, critical of the double standard for men and women, and called for women's solidarity. Their faith that women, with their moral superiority, could be redeemed led them to demand policy changes and eventually to fight for the establishment of allwomen's prisons, run by women. After the Civil War, the movement grew and changed, and eventually led to the founding of the women's reformatories. See Freedman, *op. cit.*

36. *Ibid.*

37. Custodial prisons, discussed earlier, were 64.5 percent black and 33.5 percent white during that time. An alternative explanation seems to be that the proportion of black women imprisoned in reformatories may have corresponded to their actual proportion within New York state society at large. The number seems small because we are accustomed to enormously disproportionate imprisonment rates for black women. See Rafter, *op. cit.*, p. 146.

38. *Ibid.*, p. 134.

39. Freedman, *op. cit.*

40. Rafter, *op. cit.*, p. 161.

41. *Ibid.*, p. 118.

42. *Ibid.*, p. 161.

43. Freedman, *op. cit.*, p. 13.

44. Rafter, *op. cit.*, p. 13.

45. Allen, *op. cit.*

46. Rafter, *op. cit.*, p. 164.

47. *Ibid.*, p. 118.

48. Dobash, *op. cit.*

49. U.S. Bureau of the Census, *Statistical Abstract of the United States, 1990* (Washington, DC: U.S. Government Printing Office, 1990). p. 198.

50. *Ibid.*

51. *Ibid.*

52. George J. Church, "The View from Behind Bars," *Time*, Fall 1990 (Special Issue).

53. Elaine DeCostanzo and Hellen Scholes, "Women Behind Bars, Their Numbers Increase," *Corrections Today*, June 1988.

54. *New York Times*, April 17, 1989.

55. DeCostanzo, *op. cit.*, p. 106.

56. Ralph A. Weisheit, "Structural Correlates for Female Homicide Patterns," unpublished paper delivered at the American Society of Criminology Annual Conference, Illinois State University, Normal, November 9, 1988.

57. DeCostanzo, *op. cit.*

58. William Bennett, statement on CNN News Program, August 23, 1989.

59. Linda Rocawich, "Lock 'em Up," *The Progressive*, August 1987.

60. Peter Appleborne, "Women in U.S. Prisons: Fast-Rising Population," *New York Times*, June 15, 1987.

61. See Imogene Moyer, "Mothers in Prison," *Journal of Contemporary Criminal Justice*, 1987, pp. 54-55. Also see Tatiana Shreiber and Stephanie Poggie, "Women in Prison: Does Anyone Out Here Hear?" *Resist Newsletter*,

no. 206, May 1988; and Jana Schroeder, "Fifth Annual Roundtable on Women in Prison: Advocates and Activists," *Off Our Backs*, October 1989.

62. Joycelyn M. Pollock-Byrne, *Women, Prison, and Crime* (Pacific Grove, CA: Brooks/Cole Publishing, 1990), p. 3. The author is citing R. B. Flowers, *Women and Criminality: The Woman as Victim, Offender, and Practitioner* (Westport, CT: Greenwood Press, 1987). p. 150.

63. See Sherrye Henry, "Women in Prison," *Parade Magazine*, April 10, 1988.

65. See Anon., *In U.S. Prisons and in Southern Africa, Women Fight a Common Enemy* (Berkeley, CA: Coalition for International Women's Week, 1989).

66. Assata Shakur, "Women in Prison: How We Are," *The Black Scholar*, vol. 9, no. 1, April 1978, p. 9.

67. See Angela Brown and Kirk Williams, "Resource Availability for Women at Risk," unpublished paper presented at the American Society of Criminology Annual Meeting, Chicago, November 1987.

68. *Ibid.*, p. 14.

69. *Ibid.*, p. 3. Also see Shelley Bannister, "Another View of Political Prisoners," *Critical Criminologist*, vol. 1, no. 4.

70. See Nancy Rubin, "Women Behind Bars," *McCall's*, August 1987. Also see Rocawich, *op. cit.*

71. *Ibid.*

72. Sandy Rovner, "Abused Women Who Kill," *Judgment*, vol. 10, no. 2, June 1987.

73. *In U.S. Prisons and South Africa, Women Fight a Common Enemy*, *op. cit.*

74. See *Bar None*, no. 7, Somerville, MA 1989.

75. Bannister, *op. cit.*, argues that women who respond to male violence with physical resistance, and are incarcerated as a result, should be viewed as political prisoners.

76. Dobash, et al. *op. cit.*, p. 5.

77. See George J. Church, "The View from Behind Bars," *Time Magazine*, Special Issue on Prisons, Fall 1990.

78. Dobash, et al., *op. cit.* Rubin, *op. cit.*

79. See Shreiber and Poggi, *op. cit.*

80. Church, *op. cit.*

81. See Schroeder, *op. cit.*

82. See Anon., *Resistance at Bedford Hills* (New York: Solidarity with Sisters Inside Committee, 1990).

83. Letter to the Editor, *Off Our Backs*, October 1989.

84. See Ellen Barry, "Children of Prisoners: Punishing the Innocent,: *Youth Law News*, March/April 1985.

85. Walters, *op. cit.*

86. See Phyllis Jo Baunach, *Mothers in Prison* (New Brunswick, NJ: Transaction Books, 1985).

87. Barry, *op. cit.*

88. Rubin, *op. cit.*

89. Schroeder, *op. cit.*

90. Schreiber, *op. cit.*; Schroeder, *op. cit.*

93. Walters, *op. cit.*

94. Rafter, *op. cit.*, p. 10.
95. Shakur, *op. cit.*, p. 10.
96. See Kathryn Burkhart, *Women in Prison* (New York: Doubleday Publishers, 1973).
97. Shroeder, *op. cit.*, p. 7; Burkhart, *op. cit.*, p. 377.
98. Shroeder, *op. cit.*
99. Schreiber, *op. cit.*, p. 5.
100. *Ibid.*, p. 3.
101. *Ibid.*, p. 5.
102. Rocowich, *op. cit.*
103. See Freedman, *op. cit.*, p. 48.
104. Rafter, *op. cit.*, p. 48.
105. *Ibid.*, pp. 80, 153, 170.
106. *In U.S. Prisons and South Africa, Women Fight a Common Enemy, op. cit.*
107. *Bar None, op. cit.*, p. 17.
108. *Resistance at Bedford Hills, op. cit.*

Susan Saxe

Telling Someone

It was difficult to know where or how to begin this article. Whatever I may have to say has already been said again and again, in books, articles, studies and reports. It has been said by radicals, liberals, even conservatives. It has been said by captives and by those who keep them captive, by impassioned advocates and by "detached" scholars and professionals. And so little changes. What has been said so many times is that the system doesn't work. Prisons don't prevent crime any more than nuclear weapons prevent war. The evidence is in, but we remain addicted to caging human beings very much in the same way we remain addicted to megabuck defense spending. These are false solutions that gorge on our limited resources while fueling and expanding the very problems they were meant to resolve. Perhaps it is because of my personal experience (I was on the inside of various prisons and jails from 1975 to 1982) that I am constantly confronting the connections between the "criminal justice" issue and other issues I work on, including gay/lesbian issues, reproductive rights, domestic violence and the rights of persons with disabilities. It seems to come up so often and so obviously that it is hard to imagine that others don't just naturally make the connection.

Here is just one example. A friend of mine who works for a shelter for abused women had to go to court with a client and watch her get a five-year mandatory sentence under Pennsylvania's gun law for shooting her abuser with his own gun. Where was the law when her abuser threatened her and her children with the same gun? The judge who sentenced her had no choice. She is actually working with others in the legal field to amend the law. Surely the legislature didn't intend it to have this effect . . . or did it? But this was not an isolated case. Other battered women are already serving mandatory sentences under this law. Some were even brought back to jail after serving and being released from lesser sentences handed down by judges who believed that the mandatory sentencing gun law was not meant to apply to battered women acting in self-defense. But the state, in its impersonal wisdom, appealed for its pound of flesh and won. And so women who had already suffered at the hands of their batterers and again at the hands of the courts, who had picked up the remnants of their lives and their children's lives, were without ceremony scooped up and deposited in jail for five years. These women represent no threat to anyone, or do they? Is it so threatening to the men who make our laws that women should want some alternative to abuse or death?

After all, who is it that goes to jail anyway? My own experience among women in prison tells me, as numerous studies and observations of others have shown, that an overwhelming majority of incarcerated women began as victims of child abuse. What differentiates them from all the rest of the abused women who do not go to jail? Not much, except that like the battered women who finally turned on their attackers, they sometimes fought back. They rebelled against their abusers, became throw-away or run-away children, were jailed, or were placed in institutions by parents who saw them as "crazy" or "delinquent." Again the message is the same: Submit to abuse in private by a parent, husband or boyfriend, or fall prey to abuse by strangers—the pimps and pushers on the street or the social workers, wardens, officers and attendants in the prisons, mental hospitals and detention centers.

For the past couple of years, in addition to working on a host of progressive issues ranging from Central America to abortion rights, I have been employed by agencies which advocate for persons with severe disabilities. We try to enhance their lives and eliminate the isolation, marginalization and abuse they have traditionally suffered at the hands of our society at large or in some of its many institutions. In one horrible case that recently came to light, Gary Heidnik, a man with a history of mental illness, preyed upon, imprisoned, tortured, and murdered several mentally retarded women over a period of years. I share every ounce of horror and outrage expressed by the media, the "experts" and the gawking public. But my knowledge of what happens daily to thousands of inmates in the modern-day snake pits that are our "hospitals," "training schools," and "homes" will not allow me to stop with mere anger toward an individual.

Every day people are starved, raped, beaten, and even killed in institutions. They are tied to chairs or lie naked—freezing or sweltering as the season dictates—in their own body wastes. They are drugged into oblivion or left to scream in physical or mental torment for years on end. But this is done by "professionals" licensed by the state: our taxes pay them to administer these legal torture chambers. When some of the worst cases are discovered we are shocked, maybe sickened, but where are the cries for revenge, for justice, for assurance that this will never happen again?

Frankly, I don't think most of us care. We don't know or don't want to know. We want "those people" kept out of sight and out of mind. And when an individual commits acts that we recognize as atrocities, we want him put out of sight with the rest of them. Well, Gary Heidnik was jailed before, and you can bet that prison did more to ensure that he *would* commit future violence than to deter him from it. And who was the target of his pent-up rage? Not the powerful, but the most needy and helpless people he could find. So Gary Heidnik carried out his revenge on his victims, and we are outraged. But the same abuses, committed in our names by those duly authorized, just make us a little uncomfortable for a while. State-sanctioned crimes are not crimes.

The Heidnik case also makes me wonder about the neighbors who heard noises, who smelled burning flesh, who were aware of suspicious disappearances, who saw the screaming women dragged into the car, but who did nothing. It makes me wonder about the police who were called and who couldn't seem to do anything. Where is it written that the odor of burning marijuana is probable cause to search a house but the smell of burning women is not? There's something we all have in common with the neighbors who "didn't know" or wouldn't notice the smell of burning flesh and the good Germans (and others) who "didn't know" what was being burned in those smoking furnaces outside their villages. It's that something that makes us deaf to the cries of an abused child next door, that enables us to step over a human being lying on a steam vent and go on about our business, that prevents us from identifying with a peasant being bombed in some village somewhere far away. We don't know because we don't want to know, because knowing demands action.

I am convinced that when the Heidnik case is finally unraveled, that somewhere there will be someone, a relative, a neighbor, a minister or teacher, someone who "didn't hear" the cries of little two-year-old or little five-year-old Gary Heidnik, a community that didn't respond because they "didn't know" that he was being abused. I am convinced that no one could do what he did without having experienced savage abuse himself. And I am equally convinced that when it happened, someone knew and did nothing. The Heidniks and the Hitlers come from our not wanting to get involved. They eventually get sent to places where we hope we won't ever have to think about them again—prisons, hospitals, history books. In the abuse prevention movement we teach children that if they are being abused, they should tell an adult, and they should tell and tell and keep telling until they get help. Children had better be prepared to tell and tell because in this world you have to do a lot of telling before help comes. I guess that's as good a reason as any for writing this article—to keep telling until someone hears, and to remind us all, myself included, to listen and to help.

Jennie Vander Wall

Thoughts on "Telling Someone"

Since Susan Saxe's article "Telling Someone" was first printed,[1] public concern about the very serious problem of child abuse—physical, psychological, and sexual—has escalated. Many adult women and men have realized that they were themselves victims of incest and other forms of abuse as children, and have become more open about discussing these traumatic experiences, both in small groups and in the media. There is now also a more widespread awareness, expressed both in the general media and in professional journals, that many people who are imprisoned, especially those guilty of committing truly heinous crimes, were themselves the victims of prolonged and extremely violent abuse as children. Since I'm particularly interested in this topic, I've been acquiring relevant material, from which I'd like to quote several passages.

Sharon Stricker, director of the Bright Fires Creative Writing Program at the California Rehabilitation Center (CRC), says, in her article "First We Create The Nightmare—Then We Build The Prison":

> When I first began at CRC, I had no idea that at least 90% of the women I would work with were victims of child abuse. Nor was I aware that at least 75% were victims of sexual child abuse. Child abuse, because it so often leads to self abuse, has played a major role in the lives of the women at CRC. As an adult, self abuse may take the form of drug addiction, suicide, mental illness and/or crime. Thus, child abuse is an integral part of the road to prison for most women with whom I have worked."[2]

Joel Norris, author of *Serial Killers*, states:

> Simply putting more police on the street and building more jails won't end the violence because the normal forms of deterrent don't work for serial killers. Executing convicted serial killers faster and closing down their avenues of appeal won't work either because most serial killers have a death wish to begin with. . . . The current knowledge of experts in the fields of neurology, internal medicine, psychology, and criminal justice shows that the disease of serial murder is generational. It is passed on through child abuse, negative parenting, and genetic damage. . . . [A]lmost two million children and adolescents are the victims

of physical violence each year, much of it in the form of sexual abuse committed by a relative or family member. This physical abuse directed against children is called multi-generational domestic violence, and it is one of the core causes of the epidemic of serial murder." Of particular relevance to Susan Saxe's article is Norris' reference to Gary Heidnick, who "repeatedly asked for but was *denied* psychological treatment while in prison. [emphasis added]."[3]

Ken Magrid and Carole McKelvey, in *High Risk: Children Without A Conscience*, also address this subject.[4] Unfortunately, despite its laudatory introduction by Colorado's "liberal" Congresswoman Pat Schroeder, this very popular book relies heavily on the regressive theories of Stanton E. Samenow, James Q. Wilson, and Richard J. Hernnstein. However, Magrid and McKelvey do include some useful material. For example, after stating—accurately enough—that "Charles Manson has been called the most dangerous, feared man alive" (although avoiding discussion of why Manson has acquired that reputation, when the number of homicides attributed to his direction is paltry, compared with the activities of various state-employed terrorists, of which Oliver North can serve as a notorious example), they go on to quote Manson himself:

Jails, courtrooms and prisons have been my life since I was 12 years old. . . . Most of the stories and articles written painted me as having fangs and horns from birth. They say my mother was a whore . . . would it change things to say I had no choice in selecting my mother? Or that, being a bastard child, I was an outlaw from birth? That during those so-called formative years, I was not in control of my life?. . . Hey, listen, by the time I was old enough to think or remember, I had been shoved around and left with people who were strangers even to those I knew. Rejection, more than love and acceptance, has been a part of my life since birth. . . . My feeling is, I've been raped and ravaged by society. . . . Sucked dry by the courts. Beaten by the guards and exhibited by the prisons. . . . My body remains trapped and imprisoned by a society that creates people like me.[5]

The question for the dominant society is whether it will continue to treat these former victims who are permanently scarred by childhood trauma in ways that are solely punitive. At what point or age does the abuse victim, recipient of the public's concern and compassion, change—in society's eyes—to the abuser, a subject for vilification and condemnation? Those of us who are activists, from reformers to revolutionaries, share, of course, the responsibility to stay aware, at all times, of what is happening to those children of today who could be tomorrow's Mansons and Heidnicks. But we also must face the very difficult question of what—if we had the power to open the prison doors—*we* would do with those prisoners who truly *are* "a menace to society" and with those people who are not currently in prison—who are perhaps holding high government offices or heading up multinational corporations—but who are also so psychologically warped as to pose, even when those positions of domination are eliminated, a societal threat *per se.*

We can take some comfort from the fact that much of the present situation is undoubtedly caused by the structure of the current system, the resurgence of overt racism, the widening economic gap between the rich and the poor, with the concomitant materialist consumption by the over-privileged and ongoing campaign to drug the underprivileged into submission, the sexist mentality which creates the role of prostitute and then denigrates the woman who fills that role, the patriarchal mind-set that declares a child, any child, to be "illegitimate." With the creation of a just and equitable society, all these problems—and the child abuse they give rise to, will indeed be history.

However, we—or if not us, those who come after us, the generation which sees our collective efforts succeed, will still have to deal with "the damage done," from the so-called "serial killers" to the fathers—and *mothers,* whose existence is a fact we must face,—who have seriously abused their children in the way that they were themselves abused. Since we have a healthy and valid distrust of those "experts" in whom, for example, Joel Norris appears to put some faith, we will have to develop our own answers to questions on the possibilities—and limits—of rehabilitation. Those of us who favor abolition, of the death penalty or of prisons in general, will have to discuss this subject now; because our opponents will take every available opportunity to attack us around it. Susan Saxe has again stimulated movement people to go beyond rhetoric to a serious discussion of the moral choices we ourselves are, or may in the future be, making. In this process, we ourselves, and our movements, will grow stronger.

Notes

1. First published in *Gay Community News,* August 23 -September 5, 1987.
2. Sharon Striker, "First We Create the Nightmare—Then We Build the Prison," *Heresies: A Feminist Publication on Art and Politics,* no. 22.
3. Joel Norris, *Serial Killers* (Garden City, NY: Doubleday, 1988)
4. Ken Magrid and Carole McKelvey, *High Risk: Children Without A Conscience* (New York: Bantam Books, 1988).
5. Magrid and McKelvey quoting from Noel Emmons, *Manson in His Own Words* (New York: Grove Press, 1986).

Laura Whitehorn

Preventive Detention
A Prevention of Human Rights?

> In our society liberty is the norm and detention without bail is
> a carefully limited exception.
>
> —Justice William Rehnquist
> *U.S. v. Salerno*
> 481 U.S. 739 (1987)

Justice Rehnquist's words describe an ideal that many of us would
like to believe is an integral part of the U.S. system of law. Ironically,
his pronouncement is from a Supreme Court decision that upheld the
constitutionality of preventive detention and thereby guaranteed that
the gap between the ideal and the reality of the criminal justice system
would widen. His words have given me little comfort during the five
and a half years I've spent in jail, only one year of which resulted from
a conviction. The rest of the time was spent on preventive detention
status, awaiting trial.

Being a "carefully limited exception" hasn't made it any easier to
be awakened at 4:30 a.m. every morning by clanging metal gates,
sometimes accompanied by a hostile "corrections officer" (guard) yelling,
"Hurry up! No talking! You're not at McDonald's, you're in jail!" I *know*;
I'm in jail, and I've known it since May 1985, when I was arrested in
a Baltimore apartment by the FBI. They were searching for a group
of revolutionaries, some of whom had been fugitives for a number of
years. Although I was not a fugitive, and had no outstanding charges,
I was immediately placed under arrest.

The initial accusation leveled against me was that I assaulted an
FBI agent during the raid, a charge so blatantly false that even the
magistrate who arraigned me questioned its veracity. That didn't stop
the U.S. Attorney from asking that I be held in preventive detention,
and it didn't deter the magistrate from granting her request.[1] In theory,
the government has the burden of showing why bail should be denied.
But, in practice, things are reversed. Magistrates and judges routinely
grant such requests by the government, and defendants inherit a new
burden of proving why they should be granted the fundamental right

of posting bail and thus remaining free until they have received a trial. In my case, over the following two months the prosecutor added charges of possessing two guns and false identification papers found in my apartment, and my preventive detention status was reaffirmed.

Under the so-called Bail "Reform" Act of 1984 (18 U.S.C. 3142), the law that authorized use of preventive detention in federal cases, the prosecution can supposedly request that an arrestee be placed on preventive detention only if a crime of violence is charged against him or her. In my case, the unproven and contrived—and ultimately petty— assault charge served as the requisite violent act. Under the law, the prosecution has to establish that the accused constitutes a *bona fide* "threat to the community," and/or could not be prevented from fleeing "any conditions or set of conditions" of her or his bail. To cast the necessary aura of "dangerousness" about me, all the U.S. Attorney was required to do was offer a pro forma recitation of the fact that I had a record of three prior arrests.

It was true, of course. I *had* been arrested before. Since the 1960s, when I became involved as a college student with the civil rights and anti-war movements, I've been involved in a broad range of human rights and social justice issues. I've picketed, protested, demonstrated, and defended myself and others when we've been attacked by the police. In 1969, I was arrested three times in anti-war demonstrations. None of the arrests were serious enough to result in a prison sentence. I was released on bail in each case, and appeared each time for all court dates. I violated none of the conditions of release, and, in one instance, I successfully completed two years of unsupervised probation. All this was also part of my record. Nevertheless, the magistrate decided I should be held in preventive detention. The fact that my father was willing to offer his home in lieu of cash bond, and offered to directly supervise my release, did not matter in the least.

At a later hearing, the judge articulated his own carefully-sculpted exception to my right to bail: I should be denied bond, he said, because I had stated in court that I chose to live by "revolutionary and human principles."[2] In other words, given the magnitude to which he felt such an attitude to be politically objectionable, the judge opted to leave me in lock-up without trial or bail. This decision was subsequently upheld twice by the Fourth Circuit Court of Appeals. Apparently no one in the federal judiciary was (or is) prepared to come to grips with the reality that once you begin to make these sorts of exceptions to basic rights— no matter how "carefully limited" by political considerations—the exceptions inherently destroy the right itself, for *everyone*, converting it into a mere "privilege" withheld at the whim of the state. Or maybe that's exactly the point they're trying to get across.

In May 1988, three years after my arrest in Baltimore, I was indicted along with five other political activists in Washington, D.C., on charges of conspiring "to influence, change, and protest policies and practices of the United States government in various international and domestic matters through violent and illegal means."[3] The policies and practices we were accused of protesting include the *contra* war against Nicaragua and the invasion of Grenada and shelling of Lebanon in 1983. The violent and illegal means at issue involved four bombings of government and military buildings, including the bombing of the U.S. Capitol Building itself following the assault on Grenada. No one was hurt in any of these bombings (unlike the U.S. actions, which resulted in thousands of deaths and tens of thousands of severe injuries, we were accused of protesting).

My co-defendants in what quickly became known as the "Resistance Conspiracy Case"[4] had been arrested at various points in 1984 and '85, and are now serving outrageously long prison terms for "offenses" which, for anyone else, would have resulted in far lighter sentences. Susan Rosenberg and Tim Blunk, for instance, were sentenced to serve fifty-eight years apiece for possessing explosives. Linda Evans is serving thirty-five years for charges involving the use of false identification to procure firearms. Marilyn Buck was sent up for a cumulative seventy years on a range of "offenses" centering in an alleged "RICO Conspiracy" to free Black Liberation Army leader Assata Shakur from prison and to expropriate funds from assorted banks and armored trucks. Alan Berkman was given twelve years and sent to the federal "super-maximum" prison at Marion, Illinois, merely for having provided medical treatment to Buck; this was construed as "harboring a fugitive."[5] Insofar as there are no counterparts to the severity of most of these sentences in U.S. juridical history, it seems that "carefully limited exceptions" in legal procedure extend well beyond questions of bail, at least where those charged with politically-motivated "offenses" are concerned.

In any event, because of these new charges, I was scheduled for a bail hearing in Washington, D.C., even though I was still being held on preventive detention in Baltimore. Here, too, I was ordered to be held without bond (the Justice Department then opted to hold the Baltimore charges in abeyance, apparently waiting to see the outcome of the much more serious Washington situation).[6] In April 1989, the judge in the Resistance Conspiracy case dismissed all charges against three of the co-defendants (Rosenberg, Blunk and Berkman) on grounds of double-jeopardy; they'd already been convicted of other charges in regard to exactly the same actions the government was attempting to try them for in this instance. The government appealed to have the charges reinstated. Because the appeal process could take up to a year,

I again requested bail. This time the judge ruled that arbitrary detention for more than a year constituted a violation of due process, and ordered my release on precisely the same grounds the Baltimore court had earlier rejected.[7]

At this point, the Justice Department simply trotted the Baltimore charges back to the fore, and was able to continue my detention without bond from that quarter. So, there I was: same defendant, essentially the same potential prison time facing me in each case, same bail conditions in each instance, and two diametrically opposed judicial decisions. The upshot was that I continued to sit in jail with neither bail nor trial, as the years passed. It was not until 1990 that an arrangement was arrived at in which I was actually ascertained to be "guilty" of anything at all, and then only by virtue of pleas I entered in exchange for federal agreement—since reneged upon—to the early release of my comrade and co-defendant Alan Berkman, suffering from Hodgkin's Disease (a form of lymphatic cancer) and in desperate need of the sort outside medical attention denied him in confinement.[8]

In the end, I was imprisoned much longer under such conditions— five and a half years, although about a year and half of this period came after I entered a plea on one count of the Baltimore charges and could be considered as serving time on that—than had I simply been tried, convicted and sentenced on the original assault charge, which carried a maximum penalty of only three and a half years. Certainly, I served far more time, without trial, in preventive detention, on fairly minor charges, than was served by ku klux klan leader Don Black, following his 1984 conviction for having stockpiled massive quantities of automatic weapons and explosives in preparation for invading and overthrowing the government of the Caribbean nation of Dominica.[9] Similarly, my preventive detention alone ultimately outstripped the forty-six months served by Michael Donald Bray, a right-wing fundamentalist convicted in 1985 of bombing ten abortion clinics.[10]

The 1984 Law in Practice

When the 1984 Bail Reform Act passed in Congress, a few members of Congress expressed the concern that preventive detention might prove to be open-ended in its application. They were assured by the Attorney General that the Speedy Trial Act would limit detention time to ninety days. But the Justice Department disingenuously neglected to mention that the same prosecutor and judge who were empowered to collaborate to deny bail under the first law were similarly empowered under the second to obtain exemptions from the speedy trial rule.[11] And that, to be sure, is precisely what the department's attorneys proceeded to do, once the law was passed. "Unless the right to bail before trial is preserved, the presumption of innocence, secured only after centuries of struggle, would lose its meaning," stated Justice Thurgood Marshall in an impassioned dissent in the *Salerno* case.[12] Justice Marshall warned that the erosion of any one of the hard-won rights of individuals faced with criminal charges would lead to others. He was right.

With the development of preventive detention, the presumption of guilt has replaced the presumption of innocence in U.S. law. Now, a detainee's guilt or innocence is decided, not by a jury of one's peers, but by a judge. The determination is made, not upon a full range of evidence, but upon a limited and selective presentation of information by the prosecution. The burden of rebuttal is placed squarely on the accused, and must be carried out within three days of his or her arrest, a point at which most defendants are lucky to have a lawyer, never mind having had time to prepare for a hearing. Indeed, beginning a case by having to defend her or his client from preventive detention leaves any defense attorney at a distinct disadvantage, because fighting for bail—including appeals in many cases—takes up much time and energy which could and should be spent preparing the case itself.

The implications of destruction of the presumption of innocence is, of course, most glaring in cases where the accused is later acquitted. Even if only ten to twenty percent of those held in preventive detention are eventually found not guilty—the Justice Department refuses to divulge the actual figures—hundreds, more probably thousands, of people who are never convicted of any crime are being arbitrarily imprisoned and otherwise punished in the United States every year. When the Bail Reform Act was debated in 1984, the Justice Department projected that it would be applied to only "a small group of detainees." But, by 1985, the first year in which the law was available to it, Justice, by its own statistics, used it against *twenty-nine percent* of all federal defendants. Every lawyer I've spoken with believes the percentage is far higher now (the rate is now estimated to be above forty percent; eds.)

The impact of preventive detention is even more far-reaching than is apparent from the above when it is considered that many studies have shown that defendants who are incarcerated prior to trial are, all other factors being equal, far more likely to be convicted by a jury than those who have been free on bond (or their own recognizance). That is partly a result of the deplorable conditions and escalating overcrowding in the country's jails, matters about which I am in a position to speak directly after extended periods in the Baltimore City Jail and Washington, D.C., Detention Center. Under such conditions, selecting an attorney becomes an almost impossible task for many prisoners; most pre-trial facilities will permit detainees to make collect phone calls only, and most lawyers won't accept them. There are, theoretically, provisions for the making of supervised, direct legal calls, but the demand is so great that guards often throw up their hands and refuse everyone rather than being forced to pick and chose among angry, desperate prisoners.

The Washington, D.C. Detention Center holds people accused of a crime and held without bail on preventive detention. (photo: Library of Congress)

The same conditions make it equally difficult to talk with a lawyer, once (or assuming) one can be retained. Phone calls are monitored by the authorities, and so attorney-client confidentiality is impossible. Additionally, as will be readily apparent to anyone who has ever had occasion to deal with an attorney, in the vast bulk of instances you are far more likely to be able to claim his or her "professional attention" if you are in a position to be able to walk into her/his office at his/her convenience. This is all the more true when jail visiting procedures require—as they typically do—that attorneys wait an hour or more for their clients to be brought down from the housing unit (assuming the visit occurs during one of the many "counts" of prisoners conducted every day, the wait can be extended to several hours). I have long since lost track of the number of women who have told me they met their lawyers for the first time upon entering the courtroom. Being imprisoned before trial also means that a defendant can't contact, interview, or select witnesses. You can neither coherently review the evidence to be entered against you, nor assemble evidence in your own defense. Nor can you hope to become even marginally proficient in the body of law pertaining to your case. In Baltimore, no law library facilities of any sort were available to the women incarcerated in the local jail, awaiting trial. In the D.C. jail, women were allowed to go to the law library for only fifteen minutes per week, a "privilege" which was frequently canceled for one reason or another.

When I was arrested in 1985, almost all the prisoners who were denied bond were either awaiting trial on first degree murder charges or had a clear history of bail-jumping and/or escape. Today, under the impact of the preventive detention statutes, the jails are filled beyond any definition of "reasonable capacity," largely with African American defendants awaiting trial on minor drug charges. It appears obvious that a large and increasing proportion of prosecutors and judges have arrived at the conclusion that simply being black and poor constitute *prima facie* evidence that one is either a "threat" to the community, a flight "risk," or both. Since it is an established fact that most prosecutors are more likely to request the death penalty in a capital case in which the defendant is poor and non-white, it follows that they are equally likely to request that preventive detention be imposed upon poor persons of color at disproportionately high rates.

Justice Rehnquist, in the *Salerno* decision, tried to distinguish preventive detention from imprisonment without trial through the absurd contention that pre-trial detainees are held under better conditions than sentenced prisoners. This, he asserted, made pre-trial detention "regulatory" rather than "punitive." This juridical sleight-of-hand—or patent falsehood, as it were—was intended to mask an entirely opposite reality. Like everyone else in the D.C. jail, I was locked in a tiny cell, intended to house one adult, with my cellmate at least fourteen hours per day, and often much longer. There were no real windows. The din of far too many people in far, far too little space became maddening. The noise, coupled to a "schedule" which began before dawn each morning, virtually precluded sleep. Several times each month, our cells would be turned insideout, papers strewn about or destroyed, and personal property trampled upon in an institutional effort to find "contraband." Visits with anyone other than attorneys and media representatives were restricted to two hours per week, and allowed to occur only by phone, with detainees separated from visitors by thick glass partitions. Outside recreation, the only time prisoners are allowed to see the sky or breath fresh air, was scheduled for three hours per week but, in practice, restricted to one or two.

The fact is that many, perhaps most, people held on preventive detention status, and who are subsequently convicted, experience a net *improvement* in their conditions of confinement once they are transferred to an outright prison. Moreover, after a few months of jail conditions, many pre-trial detainees are willing to cop a plea, just to get away from the zoo-like "regulatory" circumstances imposed upon them and into the relative sanity of a prison environment (this, in the context of the present volume, should give the uninitiated *some* idea of how bad contemporary jail conditions really are). The Rehnquist court inverted the facts—and one suspects it did so deliberately—in its desire to rationalize the "tool" of preventive detention for use by "law enforcement" agencies. In the doing, the majority of Justices took a giant step in creating the very conditions of overcrowding and other human misery which have made U.S. jails even more punitive than they were already. But, then, stripped of a veneer built upon prevarication and denial, this may well have been the motive underlying the majority opinion from the very outset.

Justice Marshall, in his dissent from the high court's "reasoning" in *Salerno*, advanced a view of the implications attending the Bail Reform Act and subsequent federal preventive detention practices with which no honest and thinking person can disagree. "Such statutes," Marshall wrote, "consistent with the usages of tyranny and what bitter experience teaches us to call the police state, have long been thought incompatible with the fundamental human rights protected by the Constitution."[13] Unfortunately, far too few honest and thinking people were paying attention at the time he penned his dissent, and things have moved very far in the direction the aging Justice most feared in the few years since.

Political Applications of the Law

One of the hallmarks of a police state is the conscious manipulation of the legal system to insure social and political control by a self-perpetuating élite.[14] Which modes of conduct are labeled criminal, and how severely they are treated as a result, are functions of the political agenda(s) of those in power, the status quo. Hence, it should come as no surprise to discover that, in the U.S., preventive detention and imprisonment are visited primarily upon the poor, the oppressed and political opponents of the government.[15] A clear example of the latter category may be found in the fact that my "co-conspirators" and I are in prison for our opposition to the contra war against Nicaragua while Oliver North—who made the war possible though what even the Congress and federal courts were forced to admit were entirely illegal means, including a blatant subversion of the constitution itself—was never required to serve a moment behind bars. Similarly, Marilyn Buck, Mutulu Shakur and other dissidents have been given huge sentences for "racketeering"—a term which is utterly inappropriate to describe either their actions or their motives—while Ivan Boesky, a man known to have masterminded a vast conspiracy to defraud others, and who *personally* benefited from his activities to the tune of $300 million, served less than three years.[16] Increasingly, it's not a matter of what you did, but of who you are—or what your politics are—that determines your legal status in America.

The preventive detention statute was used for the first time against eight African-American activists arrested by the FBI in 1984 and charged with planning a range of revolutionary activities, none of which actually took place.[17] As is always true in political cases, the Bureau orchestrated an hysterical media campaign branding the accused as the most dangerous "terrorists" ever apprehended in this country. And, as has become the Justice Department's standard operating procedure against left-wing defendants, the eight were labeled "perfect candidates" for the new law. The fact that most of them had no arrest record and had deep roots in the community carried no weight. Those "objective criteria" so carefully written into the law disappeared the very first time the FBI yelled "terrorist" and the defendants proudly acknowledged that the considered themselves to be revolutionary black liberationists.

The eight were held in preventive detention, some for many months. Only a massive outcry from the African-American community and a variety of international human rights organizations secured their release on bail. Contrary to the prosecution's warnings, they all appeared for trial and, after a lengthy process, were acquitted of all but the most minor charges. No one was sentenced to prison, and such "debt" as they were said to owe society was considered satisfied by short terms of community service.[18] Such was the verdict of a jury of their peers, a matter which prompted a considerable outpouring of opinion from propaganda mills like the *New York Times* to the effect that this was "proof" that "the system works." The fact remains, however, that each of the exonerated individuals had already served a substantial sentence of incarceration, imposed without a semblance of due process and for unabashedly political reasons. To the extent that the system that the system worked at all, it was in its unstated terms of visiting extra-legal punishment upon the "politically deviant" rather than in meeting its rhetorical goals of "securing justice."

An individual who has spent one of the longest periods in preventive detention (albeit, it was briefly interrupted), Filiberto Ojeda-Ríos, is also a political prisoner. He was one of twelve Puerto Rican *independentistas* arrested in a massive FBI sweep of the island on August 30, 1985, and accused with belonging to a revolutionary group called Los Macheteros. The Bureau contended that the organization expropriated more than $7 million from a Wells Fargo office in Hartford, Connecticut, on September 12, 1983, an action in which no one was hurt.[19] Again, FBI hype about "terrorists" and the defendants being "the most dangerous ever" abounded. This was particularly virulent in Ojeda's case because he had defended himself and his family from a Bureau SWAT team armed with machine guns and a bazooka during the FBI's raid upon his home. An agent was wounded in the resulting crossfire.[20]

The firefight figured prominently in Ojeda's bail hearing, and he and his co-defendants were all ordered held in preventive detention. Because of systematic FBI illegalities exposed during the pre-trial phase of the case, the trial itself was postponed for a year. One by one, the other defendants were granted bail. Finally, after almost three years incarceration, and after he underwent emergency heart surgery, Ojeda himself was released on bond in May 1988 (at that point, the Hartford case was projected as being at least another year away because of ongoing government appeals). Three months later, on the anniversary of his original arrest, he was rearrested by the FBI and charged with assault, a matter stemming from his defense against the Bureau's 1985 assault on his home. Although the court was fully aware of the facts surrounding this event when it finally granted him bail, a new judge in a different circuit again ordered that he be held in preventive detention. He spent another year in pre-trial lock-up until, on August 26, 1989, a jury in Puerto Rico acquitted him of all charges attending his conduct during the firefight. He had spent a cumulative forty-five months in jail without ever having been convicted of anything at all.[21]

While political prisoners constitute only a small percentage of those held in preventive detention, it is striking that the Justice Department requests—and invariably gets—it in virtually all cases involving radical left-wing activists. Obviously, the Bail Reform law has been molded to politically repressive purposes. Preventive detention, along with gag orders, anonymous juries, disproportionate sentencing, arbitrary denial of parole, and militarized courtrooms—the Resistance Conspiracy Case was the first in which certain high security measures, such as isolating defendants behind a massive plexiglass wall, were deployed—are all routinely applied in cases involving leftist political defendants at this point.[22] Such practices, when observed in other countries, often lead to outraged cries of "totalitarianism" by U.S. academics, journalists and political commentators. As these same measures have gathered increasing force and momentum in this country over the past several years, however, the situation has been faced by these same parties mainly with equivocation and denial, or with a thundering silence.

The government's "war on terrorism" has always concealed a political agenda of overseas aggression and domestic repression. The "war on international terrorism" was used to justify the invasion of Grenada, the contra war, continued support of the death squad regime in El Salvador, and, perhaps most spectacularly, the recent Gulf War. The "war on domestic terrorism" has been used to rationalize and justify the FBI's resurgent role as a political police force, the legalization of CIA operations at home, a vast buildup of state and local police power, and the passage of considerable repressive legislation to make it all "okay." Now, the "war on narcoterrorism" has been advanced as justification for the invasion of Panama and U.S. intervention in countries such as Columbia and Peru, as well as the overt militarization of U.S. society itself. Everywhere, we hear officials hailing indiscriminate sweeps of the streets in cities such as Los Angeles as an "important weapon" in the "war on drugs." Already, in places like Chicago and Washington, D.C., residents of public housing projects must produce official identity certificates to be able to enter their own homes (shades of South Africa's "pass laws"). How long can it be before the African-American and latino communities of North America are occupied and continuously patrolled by national guard or even army jeeps and helicopters?

There are no easy answers to the problems now faced by North American society. Having spent a few years in jail as one of the Supreme Court's "carefully limited exceptions," I *know* that these problems can not be "locked away." Unfortunately, far too many people have—however temporarily—bought into the lunacy of the government's "law and order" non-solution. Thus, given the realities of race and poverty, in combination with the dynamics of state power in the U.S., the prospect is that more

and more people who should be "innocent until proven guilty" will serve
long pre-trial sentences in the years ahead. The terrifying truth is that
we have already ventured almost the entire distance down the road to
the police state that Thurgood Marshall envisioned. One can only pray
that its possible for enough people to open their eyes in time, see the
beast which is now upon us, and to kill it before it devours us all.

Notes

1. Hearing, District of Maryland, May 14, 1985, before Magistrate Paul
D. Rosenberg.
2. Hearing, District of Maryland, June 24, 1985, before Judge Alexander
Harvey III.
3. *U.S. v. Whitehorn, et al.*, Crim. No. 88-0145 (HHG); Indictment, May
11, 1988.
4. *U.S. v. Whitehorn, et al.*, 710 F. Supp. 803 (S.D.C. 1985).
5. *U.S. v. Whitehorn, et al.*, Crim. No. 88-145-05 (HHG); "Defendants'
Motion to Dismiss the Indictment for Government Misconduct," January
3, 1989. "RICO" refers to the Racketeer Influenced and Corrupt Organizations Act, 18 USCS § 1961-1968.
6. Hearing, District of Washington, D.C., July 1, 1988, before Judge
Harold H. Greene.
7. *U.S. v. Whitehorn, et al.*, Crim. No. 88-0145, District of Washington,
D.C., June 8, 1989.
8. Whitehorn, Buck, and Evans each entered guilty pleas to one count
of conspiracy and one count of participation in the 1983 capitol bombing.
Whitehorn also entered a guilty plea with regard to the possession of false
identity papers in Baltimore. Whitehorn received an aggregate sentence
of fifteen years imprisonment; Buck and Evans received comparable
sentences tacked on to the ends of their existing prison terms. As of this
writing, fully a year after the fact, Alan Berkman—who has been eligible
for parole since 1987—remains in prison, despite the agreement, and despite
the fact that he has been near death several times since beginning treatment
in May 1990.
9. On Black, see "Defendants' Motion to Dismiss," *op. cit.*, p. 56.
10. *U.S. v. Bray*, Crim. No. 85-082, District of Maryland, 1985.
11. See *Congressional Record*, No. 130, February 3, 1984, pp. 139-40.
12. *Salerno, op. cit.*, at 2111, quoting *Stack v. Boyle*, 342 U.S. 1, 3.
13. *Ibid.*, at 2106.
14. A good analysis of the structural aspects of the police state may
be found in Issac D. Balbus, *The Dialectics of Legal Repression: Black Rebels
Before the American Courts* (New Brunswick, NJ: Transaction Books, 1973).
15. A dated but still useful examination of such trends can be found
in David Wise, *The American Police State: The Government Against the
People* (New York: Vintage Books, 1976). Also see Ward Churchill and Jim
Vander Wall, *The COINTELPRO Papers: Documents from the FBI's Secret
Wars Against Domestic Dissent* (Boston: South End Press, 1990).

16. Buck and Shakur were sentenced to fifty years apiece, Buck's sentence to run consecutively to a twenty year sentence for illegal possession of firearms by a convicted felon, and prison escape she was already serving. Her Resistance Conspiracy sentence was set to run consecutively to the preceding two.

17. *U.S. v. Chimurenga, et al.*, 609 F. Supp. 1070 (S.D.N.Y. 1984).

18. Convicted on minor weapons and possession of false identification charges were Coltrane Chimurenga, Omawale Clay, Ruth Carter, Yvette Kelly, Roger Wareham, and Robert Taylor.

19. *U.S. v. Gerena, et al.*, Crim. No. H-85-50 (TEC).

20. On the island-wide raid and Ojeda-Ríos' defense of home and family, see Ronald Fernandez, *Los Macheteros* (New York: Printice-Hall Press, 1987).

21. See "Filiberto is Free!" *La Patria Radical*, vol. 2, no. 2, September 1989.

22. For instance, Ojeda-Ríos was placed under a gag order which eliminated his ability to respond to government propaganda directed against him for the entire period in which his Puerto Rico case was pending and at trial. Similarly, Whitehorn was placed under a gag order with regard to her Baltimore case. On use of anonymous juries, see, as examples, *U.S. v. Ferguson* (758 F2d. 843 (2nd Cir. 1985)) and *U.S. v. Odinga, et al.* (F. Supp. 1043 (S.D.N.Y. 1983)). On militarized courtrooms, see *U.S. v. Whitehorn, et al.*, Crim. No. 88-0145-05 (HHG); "Defendants' Motion to Take Down Wall and Turn Off Cameras."

Richard Marquantte

Our Kids—
The New Revolutionaries

Two years ago I attended a party at a good friend's home. In attendance were college professors, like my friend, and all taught at the same local college. Others there were spouses of the professors, a principal and a minister. During a round-table discussion the subject turned to the state of the black revolution in America, as we all, except one, heralded our own little personal "war stories" from the revolution of the sixties. One had served time in the anti-Vietnam war campaign, and remembered the Kent State massacre vividly. Another had joined other black activists trekking to Ghana to experience Nkrumahism and dream the dream of a united motherland. And yet another had been involved, very actively, in the black struggle on a national level for over twenty years. One had done time and escaped, left the country and lived in a South American jungle. And there was one who said, "You know, I didn't do anything; I missed the whole revolution. I was going to college, you see. . . ."

We all had our own versions of "what had happened" to the movement, which meant we all blamed each other for what we came to believe was its demise. We looked at our middle-classness and wondered if it were true we were real revolutionaries. We blamed everybody in the movement without realizing at the time we were acting out the desired results of COINTELPRO launched by the FBI to clandestinely decimate the revolution of the sixties and leave it in a state of paranoia; which apparently lasts to this day. The professor who missed the revolution because she was going to college broke us out of our mourning by asking, "Where are the revolutionaries today?" Everybody today is into "doing their own thing," only caring about themselves. "From where will the next revolutionaries come?" Through the quiet I volunteered, "The 'new' revolutionaries are already here . . . the new revolutionaries are our kids . . . and they are rebelling against us."

They have tried to get our attention for the last ten years now and all we did was 'shine them on. Our parents taught us kids to be seen and not heard, and as liberated as we pretend to be in this age of high technology, we transferred what our parents taught on to our own kids as we dash about trying to accumulate security in an insecure world. They tried to tell us years ago that there was such an animal as family violence, that divorces were rising at an alarming rate, that a family breaking up caused great trauma to the children, that incest was on the rise, that there were a lot of "dirty 'ole men" out there. When we would not listen, they became runaways, and while we take another drink, pop another pill, take another hit off a joint or snort some more cocaine, hit the crack pipe, in our smugness and righteousness we say things like, "How dare they run away from home after all I've done for them."

Our kids go from runaways to prostitution to crime-in-general to dope to gangs to killing to dying. They go from school dropouts to overcrowded juvenile prisons. We wouldn't listen to them when they said something was wrong with the educational system, that racism had to go, we were destroying the environment, there were too many homeless in America, human beings were starving to death in Africa, that the threat of nuclear war frightened them, that religion was a fraud, politics a sham and Colonel North was a drug runner.

Our kids are the "new revolutionaries" because they are causing us to look at ourselves and the world we have created for them to inherit in ways we have failed to in the past. They are causing us to take closer looks at how alcohol and drug addiction affects the whole family, especially the kids; how child-abuse can be transferred from one generation to another; how parents transfer unresolved conflicts with their parents on to their spouses and kids; how the family structure, along with the extended-family structure, is disintegrating in America. They are causing us to take a closer look at the educational system in America and its shortcomings; that the near fifty percent school dropout rate is not so much reflective of this generation of kids, as it is of an education system unprepared to meet the needs of the kids of this generation. Young rap singers like Jazzy Jeff are telling us "Parents Just Don't Understand." L. L. Cool J says, "I Need Love." Bobby Brown's talkin 'bout "It's My Prerogative," and Ice T is exhorting all to beware "The Pusherman." These rappers are high tech, with hotlines to dissuade kids from gangs and drugs, and to give other bits of advice many kids obviously aren't getting from home. These kids, along with the thousands who are dying in the streets and going in and out of juvenile courts and detention centers across America all ask, "Why do we not value our kids?"

Listening to the media one would come to believe cocaine was manufactured in the ghetto. It grew there. Same thing with heroin. After all, the busts, killing and dealing go on in the ghetto. blacks have become synonymous with crack. When white America thinks of crack, they think of blacks automatically. And you can look all day long in the ghetto and not see any signs of the $100+ billion allegedly made off drugs, primarily cocaine. If the $100+ billion isn't in the ghetto, then where is it? And who's really making the money off this crack epidemic going down? Who's really behind supplying cocaine to the gangs: our kids?

The ghetto's being pimped, the gangs are being pimped, our kids are being pimped. The black community is being pimped by big-buck drug czars among whom you will find no blacks. The people at the top of this $100+ billion "industry" are not black. Cocaine flows into the ghetto and the cash it generates flows out, leaving broken families, high crime, gangs, killings, and more poverty in its departure. While Bush's modern day version of Elliot Ness, William Bennett, decided how best to attack black Washington, D.C., instead of launching a full assault on the czars bringing drugs into the country, one has to ask, "How do you stop drugs from coming into the country by arresting black people in Washington?"

Prisons are so overcrowded prisoners are being kept on floating barges. Bennett has advocated that military prisons are "ideal" for drug dealers. And what drug dealers was Bennett referring to? You got it: primarily black drug dealers, like those in Washington, D.C., the victims of cocaine. If he had drug czars in mind, one small sized penitentiary would hold them with room to spare. If nothing else convinces us, our prisons are rapidly becoming concentration camps, the possibility of using military prisons to hold drug "victims" should be ringing our bell: danger ahead!

I find it hard to believe a country that can clandestinely topple governments cannot topple a drug empire; how the FBI can way-lay the movement of the sixties with COINTELPRO but cannot generate that kind of machinery against the drug network. And if this country cannot defend its borders against cocaine, how is it going to defend itself against terrorism from abroad? These barges and ships carrying cocaine and marijuana could just as easily carry enough terrorists and hardware to bring America to a standstill.

With the amount of drugs coming into this country by the tons, it's obvious the only war on drugs is the war against victims of the drugs. There basically isn't a war of interdiction because regardless of the tons of cocaine confiscated from planes, barges and boats, each year there's more dope than ever. There is talk but very little action in the government busting money-laundering operations handling the $100+ billion a year made from drugs sold in America. Federal agents in "Operation Polar Cap" recently charged twenty-nine defendants with drug and currency violations in the U.S., Colombia and Panama. This group is supposedly a major U.S. money-laundering operation for the infamous "Colombian Medellín Cocaine Cartel." A Colombian bank and its Panamanian subsidiary were indicted on charges of conspiring on the shipment of more than $1 billion in U.S. drug proceeds to bank accounts controlled by the Cartel. A key defendant has escaped capture in Panama and is feared to be aided by Mañuel Noriega, Panamanian strongman indicted, arrested, and convicted on federal drug charges in Florida.

If this amount of money can change hands in one shipment, then we're talking about much more than a $100+ billion a year industry. We must also remember the Medellín Cartel is only selling the drugs to wealthy American drug czars who in turn make more money than the Cartel before paying off the Cartel. Most American drug czars pay cash for their product to get discounts on quantity. Drugs fronted usually cost more, and there is a lot fronted in this industry. Regardless, if it's cash or "on the cuff," around and around goes multi-billion dollars of cash, lining everyone's pockets but the pockets in the ghetto. Last month "Operation Polar Cap" busted alleged money-laundering organizations operating in California, New York and Florida. Drug money flowing through Los Angeles banks has produced a $3.8 billion cash surplus at the City's Federal Reserve Bank, a 2,200 percent jump since 1985.

It is not surprising the rise of gangs on the west coast coincides with the shift of drug trafficking from Miami to Los Angeles via Mexico. Los Angeles gangs have chapters in a phenomenal number of cities and states, but none in Florida. The traditional capital of the drug trade, Florida (even though Miami saw its Federal Reserve Cash surplus decline from $6 billion in 1985 to $4.8 billion last year) doesn't need gangs like the west coast does in opening new markets. The American drug czars open new markets and the gangs catch all the heat as the czars laugh all the way to the money-laundering banks.

How much longer are we going to allow this scenario to take place in our black communities, with the gangs that are comprised of our kids? How much longer are we going to think the drug problem is the kids' fault? Our kids are caught up in a conspiracy that's making drug lords at the top very big money. We must help extricate them from this system of self-destruction which lines the pockets of the American greedy.

Julio Rosado

Political Prisoners in the United States—
The Puerto Rican Charade

> Law has been threatened by the disintegration of public values
> in the larger society . . . and its future can be assured only by
> a reversal of those social processes. In order to save the law, we
> must look beyond the law. The analytical arguments wholly
> internal to the law can only take us so far. There must be
> something more—a belief in [fundamental human] values and
> the willingness to act on them.
>
> —Owen Fisk,
> *The Death of Law?*

One of the drawbacks most people experience in attempting to
understand the existence of a large number of political prisoners in the
United States, many of whom consider themselves to be prisoners of
war, is that they have no realistic view of what Puerto Rico is all about.
Puerto Ricans are certainly not a large body of people living in New
York City on drugs and welfare, struggling to achieve an education,
even an elementary school education. No, Puerto Ricans are a people
who were already existing in a vibrant European system a hundred
years before the English landed at Jamestown. We are a people who
evolved from a complex Afrocentric culture long before there was a
development of any sort of Anglo society in North America. And we
are certainly today a people who can count among ourselves some of
the finest lawyers, nuclear scientists, geneticists, and social and political
thinkers that Latin America has ever produced. To the extent that these
attainments have been ignored or are not a part of the body of knowledge
in places like Yale University, don't blame yourselves. Blame the fact
that Puerto Rico is a colony of the United States and that it has still
not achieved its independence.

In 1898, the U.S. imposed itself on Puerto Rico at a very opportune
moment, a moment when the Puerto Rican people and the people of
nearby Cuba were about to deal the death blow to Spanish colonialism
in this hemisphere. The struggle of the Puerto Rican people against
the U.S. imperial domination began from the very outset of the North

American military occupation of our island. And even with highs and lows in the struggle, it is one that has been consistent. As consistent, for example, as a week or two ago, when Puerto Ricans staged a general strike to prevent sale of the Puerto Rico Telephone Company, one of the few national resources still in the hands of the Puerto Rican people. We have produced many martyrs. There have been massacres in Puerto Rico; those who have fought for the independence of Puerto Rico have been the victims of massacres conducted by the North Americans on the island, under the leadership of some of the great legal minds of the United States, individuals who have come from universities like Yale to serve in Washington, D.C.

One of the particular dynamics of the struggle for national liberation waged by the Puerto Rican people is that we have very seldom sought refuge in the North American legal system. The reason for this is that for the people on the island who have waged the national liberation struggle, the North American legal system is itself representative of our oppression. It is the means by which the U.S. domination of our island has been rationalized and made to appear, if not just, then at least "legal." In other words, that legal system has been the instrument through which tyranny has been imposed upon the masses of Puerto Rico. And when I say "masses," please understand that I do not wish to exclude those who advocate statehood for Puerto Rico. Those who advocate statehood are as much victims of the North American occupation as those of us who advocate independence.

The present Puerto Rican prisoners emerged from the struggle of the 1960s, the first group having been captured on April 4, 1980. They were originally called the Puerto Rican Prisoners of War. Eventually, there were seventeen of them, with fourteen of them claiming the status of prisoners of war. This sounds strange to many people in the U.S., even those who don't hesitate to accept the idea that the individuals in question are political prisoners. But, prisoners of war? That's another story. Why? The issue of prisoners of war in the sense we employ the term comes from the context of international law, beginning with the protocols approved by the General Assembly of the United Nations, inspired by the struggle for Algerian independence and the decolonization of Africa. The importance of the protocols of the Geneva Convention of 1949 is that they acknowledge for the first time that to be a prisoner of war, a person, when captured, need not belong to a standing, recognizable army, or a fighter clothed in the usual garb of war. Because of the peculiar nature of national liberation struggles, the fighter, of necessity, must be dressed in the clothing of the civilian population in its everyday existence. Once captured, all that is required for such individuals to have a legitimate status as prisoners of war is that they advance a claim to that status and be identified with a recognized national liberation movement. Interestingly, when the additional protocols were updated, signed and approved in 1973, the Cuban delegation declared that they were signing with a clear understanding that the protocols would be automatically extended to Puerto Rican liberation fighters.

As prisoners of war, the Puerto Rican independence fighters have refused—as is their right under international law—to subject themselves to the North American judicial system. That is, when they were accused of and tried for specific "crimes" under U.S. law, they did not present a defense. The reason they assumed this posture is that the Puerto Rican national liberation struggle does not recognize the legitimacy of U.S. law or its jurisdiction over us. It is the rule of our colonizers. We, as a nation in our own right, have our own laws. Presenting a defense in U.S. courts would, by extension, serve the United States' claim of possessing a right to adjudicate our political status, thus denying our right to national self-determination.

While clearly understanding why the Puerto Rican nationalists were (and are) unwilling, by participation in its court procedures, to legitimate U.S. claims to "rightful" hegemony over us, the United States simply refused to deal with the position advanced by the prisoners. "Trials" were conducted even without the participation of the accused. Ultimately, all of them were summarily imprisoned on criminal charges, with sentences running from thirty-five to a hundred and thirty-five years. The outcomes would be laughable in some instances, were real people not doing real time as a result. For instance, in the case of Alicia Rodríguez and Luis Rosa, they were charged with and convicted of stealing a vehicle, tying a person up, and then using the vehicle in commission of a felony. For this, they were sentenced to *one hundred and thirty-five years*. In other instances, conspiracy charges—often "seditious conspiracy," formulated as a plot to overthrown the government of the U.S. in Puerto Rico through actions undertaken on the mainland—has been advanced. Now, when you think about it, the whole idea is absurd. But, again, the penalties imposed have been most severe.

In most countries, there would be absolutely no question that the actions contemplated or carried out by these Puerto Rican nationalists were of a political nature and that the people involved were therefore guilty of, if anything, political "crimes." Even under a penal regime such as that of Pinochet in Chile, which all of us must agree was of a fascist character, political actions were acknowledged as such and the people who committed such "offenses" were periodically released. In fact, in most countries of the world—even in the worst dictatorships— people imprisoned for their political actions are periodically released.

Only in the United States, where deviation from political orthodoxy is typically presented as common criminal conduct, and where the act of resisting the objectives of the status quo is cast as something unnatural, akin to child molestation, selling drugs or running a prostitution ring, do we find a refusal to recognize any category of political "criminality." Thus, it is the official position of the government and, unfortunately, much of the citizenry, that there can be no such thing as a political prisoner, much less a prisoner of war, held by the United States. It follows that it is impossible to create the environment necessary to obtain amnesty for such persons.

Yet, and there is no lack of intentionality involved in this apparent paradox, political prisoners are treated much worse in U.S. prisons than are other prisoners. While denying the very possibility of their existence, the authorities insure that political prisoners and prisoners of war are isolated and repeatedly transferred from one prison to another, beaten, and attacked in a variety of ways. They have been consistently denied visits, denied mail in settings where for non-political or "social" prisoners, such things are no problem. The political people are constantly harassed in this country's penal institutions. In sum, the government conducts an official charade, refusing to acknowledge the category of "political prisoner" on the one hand, while, behind the walls, it deferentially treats people according to their political status. Such a systematic approach cannot be "coincidental" or "accidental." It is the result of an official policy of duplicity and cynicism in the most extreme form.

Puertorriqueño Political Prisoner—
Nelson Ramirez Speaks

I was born in the City of New York, raised in the ghettoes of the South Bronx during the "Decade of the Fires" (the 1950s). I am a 31-year-old Puerto Rican *independentista*, son of Lydia Almadovar, a small-town *jibaro* with enormous pride in herself and her people. It is from her that I received such passionate feelings for our people and our homeland, Puerto Rico. She is a woman of amazing strength and courage. I grew up in a single-parent home in which there were four children to feed. We defied the onslaught of drugs and violence that surrounded us and followed our mother's orders; I finished high school and went on to college.

Since the 1970s, when I attended Hunter College, I have participated in various organizations, such as the Committee to Free Puerto Rican POWs, dedicated to the independence of Puerto Rico. I also became president of the Puerto Rican Student Union on campus, where we battled the administration for such things as day care for students with children, "registration" for the draft, and institutional complicity in U.S. policies abroad. We sponsored numerous activities in support of our POWs and, on several occasions, were honored with the presence of Don Juan Antonio Corretjer and his compañera, Consuelo Lee Corretjer.

Some time after leaving the university, I became an emergency medical technician and joined the Emergency Medical Service of the City of New York, where I was awarded numerous medals and awards for saving lives. During my tenure there, I was placed in the front line of a society at war with its people, a society in decline. I witnessed incredible levels of violence and resultant pain—drug addiction and overdoses, rapes, murders, stabbings, assaults, the list is endless—inflicted upon the people in utterly cynical fashion through conditions imposed by the routine functioning of the State. I was often left feeling powerless to help the victims of such atrocities. Indeed, there was little I could do to help, given the nature of the system in which I was imbedded, and the constraints it placed upon me. Such genuine assistance as I could provide had to come through my political activities—that is, my efforts to help change the structure of this society in radical and constructive ways—outside the sphere of my "professional" existence.

On May 23, 1988, as I left work, I was confronted by four misfits, supreme losers in life, who were agents of the FBI. They desired to

question me about involvement in the Puerto Rican independence movement and various persons within that movement. When I refused to
cooperate in any way, I was issued a subpoena to appear before a grand
jury investigating the independence movement. On June 15—because
of continuing refusal to testify or otherwise collaborate with the forces
of the State—I was politically interned in a maximum security setting
at MCC New York for an indefinite period.

It is important to note that my incarceration was ordered at a moment
when my wife was in the final stages of a very difficult and high-risk
pregnancy. It was obvious that the State was seeking to use her condition,
complicated by her anxiety over my arbitrary imprisonment—and my
own natural concern as to her and our unborn child's well-being—as
psychological means to compel my collaboration. Their belief—and they
said as much, openly and repeatedly—was that I would ultimately "cooperate" rather than "abandon" my wife in her moment of need.
Apparently, they never once factored in the support that those who
struggle for liberation will inevitably receive from their people. In the
end, I was able to rely with full confidence upon such support to see
my family through the trying circumstances which the State—not me
or my compañeros—had deliberately contrived.

Since my incarceration, my wife has given birth to a beautiful baby
girl, born on August 30, 1988. It was an extremely difficult delivery,
lasting more than thirty hours and culminating in a cesarean section.
That, despite the best efforts of the authorities, I was present during
this ordeal was due solely to a massive expression of outrage by the
Puerto Rican community and its allies that I, who was convicted of no
crime, and my wife, who was accused of none, should be denied the
fundamental right of being together during such a crucial period. Ten
days after the birth of my daughter—whom we named Lydia Haydeé
in honor of Haydeé Beltran, a Puerto Rican POW whose courage before
a U.S. court I once had the privilege of witnessing—I was returned to
maximum security, apparently under the misguided assumption that
continued incarceration will eventually break my will to resist.

In lock-up, I often have occasion to witness what is being done to
our national hero, Filiberto Ojeda Ríos, who is kept in an isolation cell
near mine. The longest-held prisoner in U.S. history never to have gone
to trial, he is often dragged past my cell, shackled like an animal, on
his way to a legal visit. Such experiences cause me to say, often aloud,
"Any cooperation with the process of colonization is not an alternative,
no matter what the circumstances." Upon my release, my commitment
to the cause of decolonization will have been renewed with many times
the force and depth a felt before I went inside. The system which does
such things as I have witnessed must be destroyed.

The Free Puerto Rico Committee

To Free a Homeland—
An Interview with Puertorriqueña
POW Alicia Rodríguez

The following is an interview with *Puertorriqueña* Prisoner of War Alicia Rodríguez. Alicia was captured on April 4, 1980 along with her sister Ida Luz and other comrades in the FALN. She is currently serving a thirty-year state charge and also has a five-year federal sentence on charges of seditious conspiracy.

FPR: What oppression do you experience as a Puerto Rican Prisoner of War in a U.S. prison?

Alicia: The kind of oppression I experience extends over a total of nine years incarceration. That means nine years in which our positions as POWs has been completely ignored. We've not been recognized as POWs—instead it's been nine years in which the prison administration has continued to treat us as common criminals. So that oppression is an extension of everything that the POW status represents. Throughout these nine years, another form of oppression is having to deal with the reality that there is repression inside jails. For example, the control units with Oscar Lopez in Marion, and Alejandrina Torres in the Lexington Women's Control Unit. But this repression also exists to the extent that other comrades have been charged and sentenced. There is a sense of indignation in seeing so many inside prisons, because they represent the potential that could definitely be put to work outside.

You're in a daily struggle against the administration when you're behind bars. One struggles against the monotony and drudgery to re-affirm your political identity because for most of us who do not have fellow comrades with us we lack someone to serve as a mirror of ourselves. It's a political tool and a way to measure and to be able to self-criticize or to have a dialogue, to discuss and dissect issues. I'm saying that from experience because for four years, I had comrades incarcerated in the same jail with me. For the past five years, I've been alone. It's an uphill battle. It's an unpredictable battle. There are periods when there is no confrontation with the prison administration. The prison bureaucracy probably feels that it has successfully mellowed you out until a prison guard gives a direct order or the administration does something that you know violates your principles and you respond. For example, strip searching is a common experience for each and every one of us. But, since it is done randomly, it can be done out of vengeance. Procedures for strip searching can be arbitrary, depending on the mood of that particular guard. Because of the arbitrary moves, it is a reminder that we must be on guard.

Recently, during a strip search two female prison guards demanded that I do something that was totally outside prison regulations. After my refusal, they both began to threaten to take action. This action entailed calling the guards and dragging me off to segregation. Such threats are nothing new nor do they serve to intimidate me. After a heated argument, one of the guards stepped out to confer with the supervisors. That particular guard was well aware of my position—that if they continued to try to carry out such a humiliating order, I would be searched only in the presence of a nurse. After a period of fifteen minutes, the officer came back and shut the door without saying a word. I questioned; none of my questions were answered. She just maintained a stern and foreboding stare. The next knock was from the nurse. The strip search was carried out, but it was not done under the threats and humiliations that were originally attempted by the guards. By forcing them to call the nurse, their unjustifiable harassment was revealed.

I'm the longest held prisoner with guard escort-status at Dwight. Simply put, guard-escort entails having each and every movement continuously monitored by a prison guard. Each and every time I am transported from one unit to the next, I have to wait an indefinite amount of time, sometimes a few minutes or as long as an hour. Besides what that implies, being a guard-escorted prisoner is a psychological tool utilized by the bureaucracy to make the guards think that no matter what I'm doing they have to be constantly watching me. The prison also plays around with my correspondence. They will deny any correspondence between me and my comrades. But they will send me approved notices to correspond with other male prisoners who don't write to engage in political dialogue, but rather penitentiary romance. And the bottom line, what is really oppressive is not being able to contribute to the needed development of clandestine work. That's the hardest. That's the hardest separation. This may not be the place to develop politically, but nine years have proven that it is neither a setback nor a total loss.

FPR: Could you talk some about women's oppression in prison?

Alicia: Until colonialism is dismantled, issues such as women's liberation cannot fully mature. But in the meantime, I see the need for revolutionary work to develop among women. In each different culture there are women and it is an enriching experience to be able to learn from each culture and its unique problems. It is also enriching to learn about the differences and how one has gone about struggling against sexual discrimination. An example would be the recent MLN trip to Japan and how the women's movement in Japan felt a solidarity with the Puerto Rican POWs because our oppression was an oppression they could easily identify. This commonality has resulted in a recent dialogue. In the U.S. there are many issues which the the women's movement has become involved with such as the abortion issue, the nuclear arms issue, sexual discrimination, pornography and violence against women— all issues that must be publicized and need our support. Even behind prison bars we are still subjected to sexual discrimination. We don't take this lightly. One thing I've noticed here at Dwight is that the male guards and staff will try to find out how long the women have been here. They think that the longer a woman has been here, the more likely she will be willing to be "turned on" by them. Whether it be by the looks, the jokes, the innuendos, and touching, these "pea-brain" guards think we're just physical objects, sex objects. They honestly believe we have the "hots" for them.

FPR: At this point, could you tell us about the impact that prison has had on you?

Alicia: It's taught me that I cannot divorce the past. That the past is ever so present. I agree with what has been said: if I were here for any other charge, it would be a very frightening experience. Nine years confirms the ability to politically analyze one's experience and one's purposes. One's future goals should derive not from selfish interests but from unselfish love. It's not an easy task, in fact, it's a daily struggle to shed selfish, individualistic tendencies. It stems from the fact that we're human. A lot of these needs get suppressed either consciously or unconsciously. The way I deal with it only reaffirms that I'm just like everybody else—I'm not separate from the human race. You learn to keep yourself in focus and develop priorities. Most of the time this allows you to be patient. You're not here because you wish to be here, it has been imposed on you because of your beliefs and political aspirations.

People ask me, "what do you do all day?" I'm so busy. In reality, I don't have enough time. After four and a half years of struggle, I've finally managed to engage in vocational and academic programs. After four and a half years of janitorial duties (not to belittle janitorial work, because my father was a janitor who took pride in his work and from his salary supported five children), I managed to find a loophole within the bureaucracy to engage in intellectually stimulating courses. In the beginning, it was overwhelming because I spent most of my time in those four and one half years in a cell and in an unstructured environment. So, finding myself in a classroom with responsibilities outside of political ones, it took time to get used to it. At first, I felt that it was incorrect to deviate from my political tasks. But, after several discussions with comrades, I realized that I was wrong. Regardless of the situation, if the opportunity arises to learn one should not close doors. Since then, I've managed to develop a passion for photography. Photography helped me open up a new perspective towards life. Behind a view-finder, one develops a keen eye towards details which can easily cross over to everyday life. It was also an opportunity to realize how important it is for a prisoner to find an outlet in which to nurture creativities.

The monotony of prison life can sometimes make you stir crazy. It can also numb the brain. Therefore, one has to develop a self-discipline to challenge oneself. It is easy to flow with the majority, which means sitting for hours in front of a t.v. watching soap operas and sit-coms, or engaging in several hours of card games, or hours of grooming and letting time pass with no demands on anyone. I find myself going against the grain. Out of a population of seven hundred women, there are only seven women that are engaged in academic courses in a four year academic program. Even though we have no choice over the courses that will be offered, and are uncertain our studies will lead towards a specific degree, I view this as a challenge. A challenge because I am forced to study an area that I may never have found myself taking classes in if I were on the outside. In other words, we make the most of what's available. After each and every quarter, I may feel mental fatigue, but I also feel a sense of accomplishment that is necessary in this environment.

In looking back on these nine years, I feel that instead of developing any symptoms of depression, of cynicism or tiredness, I feel, instead, that I've developed more patience, more self-assurance and a positive outlook. I must admit that this fountain of dynamic energy that I draw strength from comes from within the other prisons that hold captive my comrades, and from the unselfish work on the outside. I'm aware that we still have a long way to go, but the small and major victories keep us surefooted and confident of the future.

Puertorriqueño Political Prisoner—
Filiberto Ojeda Ríos Speaks

I am the third and youngest of three brothers and sisters born to Inocencio Ojeda and Gloria Ríos, all natives of Naguabo, Puerto Rico. I was born in 1933. My father was a teacher in the public instruction system. My mother administered what was then the rural post office, which consisted of a room in the house where I was born in Río Blanco, a small community about five miles from Naguabo. I have been married for thirty-four years [as of 1989] to Blanca Serrano Serrano, and am the father of four children.

During the early years of my life, Puerto Rico experienced some of its worst social and economic crises. Unemployment, malnutrition, abandonment of children, and the propagation of highly contagious diseases was destroying a large portion of our population. My grandparents, on both my mother's and father's sides, were farmers. Their land and agricultural properties were lost and businesses ruined when the established system of production changed hands and the North American sugar monopolies took over the Puerto Rican economic structure. These were years in which many thousands of *macheteros—* sugar cane cutters—were enslaved by the North American absentee companies. These companies controlled all productive agricultural land in Puerto Rico. The wages paid to the Puerto Rican people guaranteed nothing but misery and abject poverty.

These were also years of great struggles for the freedom of my homeland. The names of Don Pedro Albizu Campos, Elias Beauchamp, Hiram Rosado, and such criminal acts of colonial repression as the Ponce Massacre, could not possibly escape the attention of the *Puertorriqueño* children of the era. During my early years, my father was a Cadet of the Republic, an organization which at that time had as its primary purpose the recruiting of volunteers for a Puerto Rican army, sometimes called the Liberation Army. My early education was heavily influenced by this sociopolitical context. The English language was forced upon all Puerto Rican students as the main vehicle of learning. Many teachers in those days expressed open resentment of this fact, and their resentment carried an *independentista* message directly to we students. The preservation of our national language became an important tool against colonialism in the absence of sufficient strength to oppose the fierce repression through other means.

When I was eleven, in 1944, my mother emigrated to New York. It was then that I was confronted, for the first time in my life, with all the elements of racism, social discrimination and social oppression that characterized the life of Puerto Rican migrants, and which prevail to this day. I went through my junior high school years in different schools in Manhattan and Brooklyn, returning to Puerto Rico in 1947. This was due mainly to my inadaptability and unacceptance of the humiliating and degrading U.S. education system, with its highly institutionalized mechanisms of discrimination.

During the early 50s, I worked in various factories in New York City while I undertook musical studies. It was my contact with other *Puertorriqueños* in the factories that finally helped me to understand the true nature of exploitation, racism, and colonialism. I discovered what life in the ghettoes really meant; the reasons my people were systematically denied decent education, health and housing opportunities, and equal work opportunities. In sum, I was able to establish in my mind the connection between workers' exploitation and the dominant politicoeconomic system, including colonialism. This understanding led me, among other things, to oppose the military recruitment and conscription of Puerto Ricans to be used by the United States as cannon fodder in its wars of aggression against other Third World peoples. I refused to be drafted during the Korean War, and had the misfortune of losing beloved family members while receiving others who returned spiritually and emotionally wounded by their forced involvement in that war, a war they neither understood nor condoned.

In 1957, I joined the *Puertorriqueño* independence movement through participation in a number of activities. My membership in the *Movimiento Liberator de Puerto Rico* was formalized in 1959 and, through it, I engaged in intensive studies of my people's history and politics. In 1961, I went to revolutionary Cuba, taking my family with me. Once there, I joined the *Movimiento Pro-Independencia* (MPI). I entered the University of Havana in 1964, and studied political science until 1965. In the latter year, I became subchief of the permanent mission of the MPI in Cuba. In 1966, I was appointed alternate delegate to the Organization of Solidarity for the Peoples of Asia, Africa and Latin America (OSPAAL). From 1966-1969, I also served as a member of the directorate of the Association of Puerto Rican Residents in Cuba, and was editor of the Puerto Rican publications directed at our own community and to other Latin American communities in Cuba.

In 1969, I returned to my own country, engaging in diverse political activities as part of the *Puertorriqueño* revolutionary movement and our struggle for independence from U.S. colonialism. I witnessed first-hand the police attack against the central offices of the MPI and, in 1970, I was arrested, accused of being an organizer of the *Movimiento Independentista Revolucionario en Armas* (MIRA), a formation involved in armed struggle at that time. I was never convicted of these charges, which were finally dismissed in 1980 for lack of evidence. From 1970 until my next arrest on August 30, 1985—accused of being a leader of the armed formation *Los Macheteros*—during the massive anti-*independentista* FBI raid on the island, I lived in clandestine fashion in my country. The persecution of *independentistas* by the federal colonialist forces, the numerous attacks and assassinations carried out by right wing forces—including police "death squads" and other vigilante groups organized or encouraged by the CIA and FBI—and repeated threats against my life allowed me no option to assume a more open political role in our struggle.

This personal experience confirmed for me the significance of the concept of "clandestinity," which is unfortunately a necessary response to the consistent repression by the U.S. of national liberation movements in general, and the *independentista* movement in particular. My present circumstance of being held for years on end in North American jails with recourse to neither bail nor trial has merely reinforced once again the correctness of this view. Insofar as the system by which we are oppressed no longer offers us even the illusions of justice or "due process," we have no alternative but to pursue our liberation by any and all means available to us.

Puertorriqueña Political Prisoner—
Lucy Berríos Berríos Speaks

I am known as Lucy, but my full name is Luz Berríos Berríos. I was born on March 5, 1949 in the mountains of Naranjito, under the light of an oil lamp. I am the fourth of five children, three girls and two boys. My father is a farmer and although he is 78 years old, he is still working the land he inherited from my grandparents. My mother dedicated herself to caring for our family and home. I have the same two surnames because my parents are children of two brothers. I lived in those mountains during my infant years, with dogs, horses, and nature, close to the people and land that I love. I lived among humble people: my family, brothers and sisters, aunts and uncles, grandparents, cousins, neighbors. When I was eight years old, we moved to Barrio Lomas Jaguas, close to the road and the local school. My parents live in this house today. Although my brothers and sisters have since left home, we are a closely knit family.

I went to grammar school in my barrio and junior high and high school in my home town. I was a good student, with good discipline. I attended the University of Puerto Rico at seventeen and earned a BA in Occupational Therapy. Although I had pro-independence sympathies in high school, it was not until my second year in college that I became an *independentista*, after the police killed Antonia Martinez, a classmate. During the Vietnam War, I began to realize my true feelings about independence, but it wasn't until I finished college that I became a member of the Puerto Rican Independence Party (PIP). After the 1972 elections, I became a member of the Puerto Rican Socialist Party (PSP). It was in the PSP that I educated myself as an *independentista*. I was in the PSP during their days of major marches and demonstrations, when we had a record membership and competed with the PIP.

During that time, I met my *compañero*, Juan E. Segarra, whom I called "Papo." We fell in love the first time we saw each other, when I was visiting friends in Boston. Although we were living in different countries, he in the U.S. and I in Puerto Rico, we visited one another a few times. We tried to develop other relationships, but were unable to forget one another. I married Tomás Perez in 1974 and had my first child on March 30, 1975. We named her Luriza. When she was two years old, Tomás and I were divorced. I met Papo again when he returned to Puerto Rico and, since then, we have never been apart. My son, Ramon Enrique, was born on September 3, 1979.

When the PSP decided to become part of the electoral process every four years, an internal situation developed that touched many of us. I started to become involved with other groups that supported the Sandinistas in Nicaragua and Vieques. I also devoted much time to working as an occupational therapist in my own labor center. We organized and developed awareness in other workers through union activities. In 1981, I decided to change jobs, after working ten years in the center. For a while I was unemployed. Then I started working as a therapist making home visits. In 1984, I studied communications at the Sacred Heart College in Santruce, Puerto Rico. I later moved to Vega Baja, but was unable to continue my studies. So I rejoined the PIP and began working in the *Graficos El Caribe* print shop.

In June 1985, I moved with my *compañero* to Mexico because we wanted to develop a clothing business. But, on August 30 of the same year, back in Puerto Rico, the FBI detained me and my children during a massive island-wide raid of the independence movement which occurred on that date. Agents, who never identified themselves, kidnapped us and threatened our lives. The day of my son's birthday, September 3, they took us to Miami, never following any legal procedure for our extradition and even ignoring a writ of *habeas corpus*. That day I began my life as a political prisoner of the United States. I was imprisoned without bond until my release on December 23, 1986. I remained out on bond until December 1, 1988, when I turned myself in at the Federal Correctional Institution for Women at Lexington, Kentucky.

During the preparations for trial, I worked with other *compañeros* involved in the case. I feel partly responsible for the eventual suppression of electronic evidence which the government used to divide its case into two groups of defendants and charges. Papo and I were part of the first group to stand trial. Being tried before a North American jury for acts intended to liberate my homeland from the colonial domination of the United States—I believe in the axiom that "when you violate the law of empire, you execute the law of your own nation"—did not represent any sort of justice for me or the other defendants. Further, I did not wish to deny my involvement with the "conspiracy" to distribute toys to *Puertorriqueño* children on the mainland during the 1985 Three Kings Day celebration Hartford, Connecticut. This was and is my position despite the fact that my participation in distributing the toys implied, according to the U.S. government, that I was involved in the handling and transportation of money "stolen" by the *Los Macheteros* organization from a Wells Fargo facility in Hartford on September 9, 1983.

All things considered, and after a lot of internal and emotional struggle, I decided to plead guilty to one of the lesser charges before the trial began on September 6, 1988. I made this decision to insure that our children would have at least one parent with them during their youth. In the alternative, both Juan and I would have been locked away for extremely long prison terms. My *compañero* therefore represents me, our children, and our people through his sacrifice in the federal court at Hartford. They can jail our bodies, but never our spirits, the spirit of the battle for liberation and basic human dignity embodied in our efforts to throw off the yoke of colonial oppression. This spirit of resistance will continue, no matter the intensity of the repression visited upon us, until final victory is achieved.

Let it be said that I made the decision to make my obligations as a mother my highest priority without putting aside my belief in and commitment to the Puerto Rican independence struggle. Before I entered my guilty plea, the prosecution was required to agree that neither it nor the State it represented would not attempt to call me as a witness against my *compañeros*, nor seek any other form of collaboration from me. I hold a revolutionary conception of motherhood. I will, upon my release, continue to raise my children as *independentistas* (a third child was born in May 1989, after I had begun my sentence). Thus, the struggle *will* continue. Puerto Rico will be free. All oppressed people will be free. *Venceremos!*

Puertorriqueña Political Prisoner—
Carmen Valentín Speaks

I was born in Arecibo, Puerto Rico, in 1946, and attended school on the island until my parents were forced to migrate to the mainland in 1956. Because of dire socioeconomic circumstances, we were forced to relocate from the small farm where we had been living in our homeland to Chicago's West Side. It was in this predominantly black neighborhood that Martin Luther King led a crucial march during the period of civil rights agitation of the mid-60s. By 1969, the Black Panther Party headquarters was located just two blocks away from my home. On December 4, 1969, Party leaders Fred Hampton and Mark Clark were assassinated by police in the same immediate area. These events became the basis for my political formation and development. The racism, discrimination and social oppression, so emphatically denounced by leaders such as King, Clark, and Hampton, served as the context from which I launched my search for equality and social justice.

I attended parochial schools during my elementary and secondary years in Chicago. My education continued at Northeastern Illinois University, where I obtained a BA in Spanish. Later, I earned an MA in Secondary School Administration from Roosevelt University. I had completed about half the courses required for a doctoral degree in psychology when I was captured by the forces of the State. In any event, after I graduated from Northeastern, I returned to the West Side community and began teaching at Tuley-Clemente High School, a predominantly Puerto Rican institution. My political awareness grew, due in large part to the hard studying and continuous practical experience I gained every day I was at Tuley-Clemente. I acquired a relentless interest in helping my people learn about their cultural heritage, understand the nature of their oppression, and therefore to identify their real enemy.

During this period, I was not only involved in educational efforts in the public school system and the José de Diego Bilingual Center, but in combatting "Plan 21," the Chicago city government's plan to physically disperse our West Side community. I was also very active in fighting police brutality against the Puerto Rican community, and in programs designed to support Puerto Rican and other Latin American prisoners at Statesville Prison, in Joliet, Illinois. For several years, I was totally committed to attempting to help bring positive change to U.S. institutions. It was not until later, overwhelmed by the futility of the task in the face of official rejection of any constructive alteration to the status quo, that I had seen I had been squandering my energy in pursuit of empty reforms. All was not wasted, however, as this was an instrumental part of my political education, something which could never have been learned in any other fashion, at least not by me.

Suffice it to say that, by the late 1970s, the nature of my political consciousness and, consequently, of my political activities, had undergone a considerable evolution. On April 4, 1980, I was captured in Evanston, Illinois, along with nine of my comrades in the Armed Forces for National Liberation of Puerto Rico (FALN). We were charged with an array of "offenses" involving sedition and armed insurrection. Eventually, I was sentenced to serve ninety-eight years in prison. As a consequence, I have been separated from my beloved son, Antonio, now 21 and a student at De Paul University, in Chicago. I am, however, proud to say that he has grown into a perfect example of the revolutionary intellect I tried for so long to instill among our youth.

During the festivities which celebrated the 120th anniversary of the Lares Uprising in Puerto Rico, the Unitary Committee Against Repression (CUCRE) awarded the "Mariana Bracetti Order" to us, the *Puertorriqueña* women prisoners of war. Antonio was present at the celebration as my personal representative, as well as the representative of Dylcia Pagán and a whole new generation of *independentistas* (see his message in *Libertad*, vol. IX, nos. 21-22). As of December 1988, he was also appointed to represent the Puerto Rican independence movement at a human rights conference held in Japan. Although my body may now be encapsulated within this cage of steel, it is obvious that my spirit, and therefore our struggle, lives on in my son. This continuity of resistance from one generation to the next is, and has always been, the irrepressible strength of our movement. It is this strength, this power, which guarantees that ultimately we will win.

We are ready to continue our until the final victory—not only against colonialism, but against capitalism, racism, sexism and all other forms of oppression—is secured. Wherever I may be, and under whatever circumstances of confinement, I will always be honored to have served, and to continue to serve, as a fighter and, hopefully, as a useful example to the oppressed masses of humanity everywhere. My belief in the communist future of my country, and ultimately of the world, remains firm. My faith in you, my people, remains equally firm.

Jim Campbell

New Jersey Prisoners Under Attack

The Afrikan National Ujamaa (ANU), a Pan Afrikan Nationalist group that has been educating and organizing black prisoners in New Jersey for several years, is under full attack by the state of New Jersey. Last summer the state prison administration and guards blamed the ANU for two major disturbances which left many guards injured. On May 30, 1991, seven prisoners at Trenton were indicted for allegedly attempting to murder three guards, as well as fourteen counts of aggravated assault on seven injured guards. They could face an additional fifty to a hundred years.

The immediate cause of the incidents in which black prisoners fought it out with white guards was ongoing racial and political harassment. In retaliation, suspected leaders of ANU were exiled to other state prison systems as far away as Oregon. Other prisoners were sent to the Management Control Unit (MCU) or into the notorious VROOM Re-adjustment Unit, a control unit used as punishment. There was the usual round of beatings and destruction of personal property that one can expect anytime prisoners act to protect themselves in a collective manner. Attempts are still being made to charge ANU people who were in the MCU at the time with responsibility for the "attacks" on the guards— even thought the MCU is completely cut off from the general populations.

Further developments suggest that the state is not content to leave the repression up to the outside courts, or their own kangaroo internal courts. On May 9, 1991, Dinard Pinkney was arrested in Philadelphia after he had allegedly purchased weapons and explosives from an undercover cop. According to the media, the police had set up the purchase after an informant in Trenton State Prison told authorities of a planned escape involving automatic weapons and explosives that was linked to Pinkney's brother-in-law, William Stovall, being held at the state prison. In spite of protest by Ajamu U. Kafele, one of the founders of the ANU, that Stovall was not part of the ANU, the police insisted that he was an active member and that Pinkney was a minor player in the group.

In the last week of May, 1991, Hatari Wahaki was arrested for allegedly possessing an assortment of "escape" tools, including wire cutters, needle nose pliers, an ice pick, a screwdriver, and a set of visegrips. These were "found" in the insulation cavity of an ice cooler in Wahaki's cell in the VROOM Readjustment Unit. Again the authorities said that the search was conducted after they had received information from an informant that an escape was being planned. Wahaki was transferred to the MCU. Wahaki's involvement with the ANU was also played up.

The prison officials were also suggesting that some staff members were negligent or criminally involved in getting the "escape tools" to Wahaki. One can understand the attempt at "logic," since Wahaki could not pick the tools up at the local hardware store. But considering that the whole matter seemed like a set-up from the beginning, it raised the possibility that some of the black guards shielded a group of African prisoners from white guards seeking to extract revenge for the thumping they had just taken. An internal report confirmed that there had been a stand-off between the two groups of guards along racial lines. While VROOM is physically separated from the main body of the Trenton State Prison, it is nonetheless likely that the tensions between the white and black guards carry over to the VROOM unit.

In both instances, the ANU was linked in the media to the Black Liberation Army (BLA), a group which developed out of the Black Panthers and which waged armed resistance during the seventies and early eighties. The BLA had several shoot-outs with the police, including one with the New Jersey state police in which Assata Shakur was wounded and captured, and Zayd Malik Shakur was killed along with one of the (storm) troopers. Assata was later freed from a state prison when four armed comrades went for a short visit. In spite of the denials by the ANU that they are connected to the BLA, the media reports make repeated references to just such a connection. It serves as further evidence that the ANU, according to corrections officials, is "terrorist in nature" and "violence prone."

The ANU is one of the new generation of radical prisoner groups to emerge in the last few years. To prison officials, a politically and socially conscious organization with an ability to reach other prisoners, to educate, to help develop a sense of dignity and self-worth is more dangerous to the smooth running of the prisons than the existence of the usual prison gangs. The gangs, with their focus on power, on turf, on drugs, and money, are easily understood by bureaucrats. Their existence is often tolerated as a means of keeping the prison functioning. And there is always the hole or the control units for any of them who get too far out of line.

But a political group that shows any sign of gaining strength will be met with severe reprisals. The authorities are able to draw on their

402 • Jim Campbell

years of experience in attacking groups such as the Black Panthers and the American Indian Movement. One of the most effective tools is to link any such group in the public mind with violence, and, more recently, with "terrorists." And in using this tactic, the groundwork is also created for more repressive conditions in prison, especially for anyone engaged in political organizing. At the same time, the severe punishment inflicted on the activist prisoners serves as a warning to other prisoners.

The police, politicians, and prisoncrats all know that the prisons are a powder keg, ready to blow at any time. Indeed, they themselves predict major riots will be coming by the mid-nineties and they're already preparing for this both politically and technologically. They will be carefully studying the past, even if we don't. And what they know very well is that they must smash any emerging political consciousness before it has a chance to develop.

Excerpts from, The Verdict of the International Tribunal on Political Prisoners and Prisoners of War in the United States

> Whereas it is essential, if man is not to be compelled to have recourse, as a last resort, to rebellion against tyranny and oppression, that human rights should be protected by the rule of law.
> —*Preamble to the Universal Declaration of Human Rights*
> December 10, 1948

The Special International Tribunal on the Human Rights Violations Against Political Prisoners and Prisoners of War in the United States, sponsored by a wide coalition of eighty-eight organizations from the civic, religious, anti-imperialist, labor and national liberation sectors, was held in New York City from the 7th to the 10th of December, 1990. This successful event held at Hunter College included the active participation of various jurists and renowned international figures: Frank Badohu (Barrister, Solicitor of the Supreme Court and member of the Association of African Jurists in Ghana), Jawad Boulus (Palestinian attorney), Lord Anthony Gifford (British Barrister and member of the House of Lords), Norman Paech (Professor of Public International Law and Constitutional Law at the University of Hamburg, Germany), José R. Rendùn (Solicitor and Professor of Law at the University of San Marcos, Perù), Celina Romany (Professor of Jurisprudence and Human Rights at the City University of New York Law School), Toshi Yuki Tanaka (Professor of Political Science at the University of Melbourne, Australia), George Wald (Professor Emeritus of Biology at Harvard University and winner of the Nobel Prize in Biology). The event was coordinated by Dr. Luis Nieves Falcón, renowned sociologist, lawyer, writer and member of the Pen Club.

At the start of the tribunal, which was attended by more than 1,200 persons from ten countries representing every continent and fifteen states of the U.S., the above-named jurists stated that the tribunal assumed jurisdiction under international law approved by appropriate international organs, specifically Resolution 1503 (XLVIII), adopted by the Economic and Social Council of the United Nations. Article 38 of the

Statutes of the International Court of Justice recognizes the authoritative effect of such tribunals on contemporary standards of international law. Additionally, jurisdiction is conferred upon such bodies pursuant to accepted principles of international law approved and adopted by the world community in convening such extraordinary tribunals as that established in Nuremberg, Germany, and Tokyo, Japan, during the period 1946-1949. Finally, it is a universally-accepted principle of international jurisprudence that, once all "domestic" legal remedies have been exhausted, victims of fundamental human rights violations should have recourse to appropriate international tribunals.

It should be noted that the tribunal is satisfied that all necessary steps were taken to inform the defendant government and its agencies of the nature and purposes of the tribunal hearings, including service of the indictment of President George Bush and other appropriate federal and state officials, and that every opportunity was afforded the defendants to attend and present testimony in their own behalf. Although the defendants failed to avail themselves of the opportunity to testify, many of the documents and expert witnesses indicated fairly the basis of the government's opposition [to altering its policies in relevant connections], and the tribunal duly noted such views in reaching its findings.

The tribunal examined the situation of the New Afrikan, Native American, Mexicano-Chicano and Puerto Rican sectors [of territory directly claimed by the United States] and ascertained that the U.S. is in violation of the 1960 United Nations General Assembly Declaration on the Granting of Independence to Colonial Countries and Peoples (Resolution 1514 (XV)) with regard to its assertion of continuing control and jurisdiction in these areas. Additionally, the tribunal found the U.S. to be in violation of the Universal Declaration of the Rights of People (the "Algiers Declaration") and United Nations Resolution 2625 (XXV), known as the "Declaration on the Principles of International Law Concerning Friendly Relations and Cooperation Among States in Accordance with the Charter of the United Nations," passed by consensus in 1970. Hence, the sectors in question are fully entitled to exercise self-determination under various elements of international law, including the above-noted declarations and resolutions, and Common Article 1 (1) of the International Human Rights Covenants, 1966. It follows that individuals and organizations pursuing self-determining status for the sectors in question must be considered as *bona fide* and legitimate national liberation movements within the meaning of Article I, Paragraph 4, Additional Protocol I of the Geneva Conventions Relative to the Treatment of Prisoners of War, of 12 August 1949 (Additional Protocol I, General Assembly Resolution 3103 (XXVIII) was signed on

12 December 1973, and effected in 1977) and "are to be accorded the status of prisoners of war and their treatment should be in accordance with the Geneva Convention."

The U.S. has refused POW status to these anti-colonialist fighters, claiming that it is not a signatory to the Additional Protocols of the Geneva Convention. This refusal to accept universally recognized humanitarian protections for peoples fighting colonialism, apartheid and alien domination, should not and does not preclude the according of those protections [a principle of international jurisprudence firmly established—by the United States, among other parties—at Nuremberg, Tokyo, and elsewhere]. Ironically, the U.S. government has expressed strong support, albeit selectively, for the freeing of political prisoners throughout the world. At the same time, however, [this same government] vociferously denies the existence of political prisoners at home and resolutely echoes a familiar refrain that those who claim to be political prisoners and prisoners of war are simply "terrorists" and "criminals." The tribunal was mindful that the U.S. judicial system is promoted by many as one of the most progressive and protective of individual rights. The claim that the U.S. does not hold political prisoners has therefore gone generally unchallenged. The tribunal believes that the evidence presented before it overwhelmingly establishes an opposite case. The U.S. government uses its judicial system to repress legitimate political movements which are opposed it it.

Following the presentation and review of numerous documents provided to the jurists [of particular interest were the government's own secret documents concerning the Counterintelligence Program of the Federal Bureau of Investigation, known as COINTELPRO, showing that agency's concerted and illegal operations to disrupt and neutralize leaders and organizations of the New Afrikan, Puerto Rican, Native American and Mexicano-Chicano struggles for self-determination], and after hearing testimony from various representatives of the national liberation movements at issue concerning the circumstances of certain of their incarcerated members, the tribunal declared the U.S. must be held to the same standard of international law and human rights safeguards that it subscribes for other countries in the world. The panel of judges established parallels between the struggles and conditions of political prisoners and prisoners of war from these movements [against U.S. denials of rights to national self-determination for Native America, New Afrika, Occupied Mexico and Puerto Rico] with those who suffer imprisonment under despotic regimes such as that of South Africa, jailed for their activism against apartheid. The tribunal therefore concluded that any U.S. denial of the existence of political prisoners and prisoners of war in its jails, and consequent failure to afford such prisoners the fundamental protections of humanitarian international law, constitute serious violations of human rights [requiring] immediate attention of world public opinion and rectification by the U.S. government.

Criminalization and Denial of the Rule of Law

It is a violation of international law for a state to attempt to criminalize the struggle of peoples to achieve self-determination. According to the authoritative United Nations Resolution 2625 (XXV) of 1970, "Every State has the duty to refrain from any forcible action which deprives peoples . . . of their right to self-determination and freedom and independence." U.N. Resolutions 33/22 and 33/24 (1978) also condemn the detention and imprisonment of people fighting colonialism. [The tribunal has] heard testimony of the development of a system of repression in the United States which uses the judicial system as a key element in denying peoples' rights to self-determination and to disrupt people organizing to oppose illegal U.S. government policies. The use of the judicial system to repress political activists violates Articles 6, 7, 8, 9 and 10 of the Universal Declaration of Human Rights and Articles 9 and 14 of the International Covenant on Civil and Political Rights. Further, [since the majority of political prisoners and prisoners of war held by the U.S. are persons of color,] such conduct further violates Article 5 of the International Convention on the Elimination of All Forms of Racial Discrimination, 1966.

The evidence shows that the [federal] government is using a strategy which parallels those of certain other states—e.g., those of South Africa, Israel, and the British administration in northern Ireland—in confronting insurgent movements through repressive, anti-democratic modifications of the legal system aimed at the suppression of radical political opposition. This counter-insurgency strategy allows for the enhancement or expansion of the power of law enforcement agencies to surveil and infiltrate political groups as well as to coerce the cooperation of individuals with police investigations and to criminalize political association. The testimony [and government documents] showed that federal agents are authorized to spy on and infiltrate political, community and religious groups in the United States. The tribunal was also informed of highly sophisticated electronic technology to carry out video and audio surveillance at the homes and workplaces of members and supporters of [national liberation movements]. Additionally, we were informed of litigation in Puerto Rico [comparable cases having already been litigated with regard to other movements] that has recently revealed the existence of more than 100,000 dossiers collected by the police on activists and supporters of the cause of Puerto Rican independence, and who have been correspondingly labeled "subversives" by the authorities because of their legitimate desire and work for an end to colonization.

It has been shown that the FBI also uses an internment power through the grand jury process, a secret proceeding under direction and control of the government, to force cooperation with investigations into political activities under pain of arbitrary imprisonment for refusal. In this procedure, the government issues subpoenas to a secret hearing in which there is no judge, and from which defense counsel is barred. Witnesses can be [and are] stripped of their constitutional right to remain silent and forced [under pain of a "contempt" citation carrying a penalty of indeterminate jail time; up to eighteen months for "civil" contempt, an unlimited sentence for "criminal" contempt] to answer all questions concerning their political associations and activities. Scores of activists have been imprisoned over the past fifteen years through this process. The government has even resubpoenaed activists who have already served time in prison for refusing to collaborate with grand juries, in full knowledge they will refuse again [and thus be returned to prison]. This effectively constitutes internment without trial or demonstration of just cause.

Those charged with politically-motivated offenses are frequently held in preventative detention. Specifically, the evidence shows the U.S. government's use of the Bail Reform Act of 1984 violates international law by designating as "dangerous to the community" those persons who most actively struggle for self-determination. This statute enables the government to jail its opponents for years without trial by means of indefinite detention, thus denying the right either to a speedy trial, or to release pending trial. . . . Excessive pretrial detention violates Article II (1) of the Universal Declaration of Human Rights and Article 9 (3) of the 1969 International Covenant on Civil and Political Rights.

The evidence further shows that political activists are often charged with violation of broad conspiracy laws which rely on evidence of political associations and beliefs to prove "criminal" agreements. The tribunal heard testimony about two special statutes, that pertaining to Seditious Conspiracy, and the Racketeer Influenced and Corrupt Organizations (RICO) Act, which specifically allow for criminalization of membership in political organizations and national liberation movements. These statutes have been used to incarcerate political activists with lengthy sentences. The Seditious Conspiracy law specifically criminalizes opposition to U.S. policy [particularly with regard to colonialism]. Under this law, a mere agreement to oppose U.S. policy with force, without proof of any act taken in furtherance of that agreement, is subject to twenty years imprisonment.

[Substantial evidence has been received to demonstrate that] political prisoners in the U.S. have also been victimized by false charges and prosecutions in which evidence favorable to the accused is deliberately suppressed [by the government]. The tribunal was presented with evidence of three particularly serious cases: those of Geronimo ji Jaga Pratt, Leonard Peltier and Dhoruba Bin Wahad, in which the government consciously concealed or destroyed evidence which would have established their innocence of the charges against them. [Other cases in which this may well pertain include, among others, those of Mumia Abu Jamal, David Rice and Edward Poindexter, and the so-called "New York Three": Herman Bell, Anthony "Jalil" Bottom and Albert "Nuh" Washington.] We find most disturbing that the U.S. government continues to incarcerate such prisoners despite documentary and other proof, disclosed after conviction, conclusively establishing that they did not commit the offenses for which they have been tried.

The tribunal also received evidence of a series of repressive measures employed in the conduct of political trials. Of particular concern is evidence indicating a calculated attack by the U.S. government on the independence and impartiality of jury trial procedures. [Plainly and repeatedly] the media have been used to poison attitudes in the communities from which juries are selected. Just as disturbing is the use of "anonymous" trial juries. Under the latter system, by declaring the necessity [for their own "protection"] of keeping jurors' identities secret, those same jurors are inherently prejudiced into believing they have cause to [personally] fear the defendants. This fear is often exacerbated by intentional, ostentatious and excessive militarization of courtroom security.... The tribunal was informed of the use of multiple metal detectors, concrete bunkers, [large and prominent forces of] armed marshals, sharpshooters [visibly displayed on] roofs adjacent to court-houses and, in one instance, the erection of a special bullet-proof glass partition to separate the accused from the public. Evidence showed that trial venues are also manipulated, particularly in the cases of Puerto Rican activists, to deny [defendants] a trial by their peers. Finally, politically-accused persons are routinely denied the right to present a full defense, including issues of necessity, ["lesser evil"] and other justifications for their actions available under international law.

Excessive and Inhuman Sentences

The evidence shows that the Unites States metes out the longest sentences of any country in the world to its political prisoners. Most political prisoners and prisoners of war in the U.S. are serving the equivalent of natural life in prison. Leonard Peltier has served over thirteen years of two consecutive life sentences; Sundiata Acoli is serving life plus thirty years; Herman Bell, Nuh Washington and Jalil Bottom are each serving twenty-five years to life [as was Dhoruba Bin Wahad, before the New York high court was finally forced to overturn his conviction. Rice and Poindexter continue to serve life sentences in Nebraska. The list, obviously might be continued at length.] The Puerto Rican POWs—Carlos Torres, Adolfo Matos, Dylcia Pagán, Ida Luz Rodríguez, Carmen Valentín, Elizam Escobar, Alejandrina Torres, Ricardo Jiménez, Alicia Rodríguez, Luis Rosa, Edwin Cortéz, Alberto Rodríguez, and Oscar López Rivera—many of whom have already spent more than ten years in prison, have sentences averaging sixty-seven years. The judge who sentenced them stated that, had it been within his power, he would have sentenced them to death. Mumia Abu-Jamal currently sits on Pennsylvania's death row, awaiting imposition of the ultimate penalty.

Evidence was presented demonstrating that political beliefs have been used to impose, in many instances, life terms of imprisonment. Moreover, it is abundantly clear that the sentences imposed upon [many left-wing prisoners] are grossly disproportionate to sanctions imposed upon members of right wing and/or racist organizations convicted of similar offenses. For example, an assassin [Michael Townley] of Chilean diplomat Orlando Letelier [a research assistant, Ronnie Moffit, also died in the September 1976 car-bomb blast in Washington, D.C. which killed Letelier] was permitted in a plea agreement, wherein most charges against him were dropped, to receive a sentence of only twelve years. Conversely, [Japanese activist] Yu Kikumura, arrested in the United States with three pipe bombs in his car, was charged with twelve separate offenses and sentenced to an aggregate of thirty years. There are several other instances in which comparable disparities are evident, to wit:

• In 1986, a man convicted of planning and carrying out bombings, without warning calls, of ten occupied health clinics where abortions were performed received a sentence of ten years and received parole after 46 months. By contrast, [left-wing activist] Raymond Luc Levasseur was convicted of bombing four unoccupied military targets in protest of U.S. foreign policies and was sentenced to a total of 45 years.

• Another acknowledged abortion clinic bomber received seven years following his arrest in possession of over 100 pounds of explosives in a populous Manhattan apartment building. By comparison, [left-wing activists] Tim Blunk and Susan Rosenberg, charged with keeping explosives in an unpopulated storage facility, were each sentenced to serve fifty-eight years, far and away the longest sentences for this offense in U.S. history.

• A ku klux klansman, charged with violations of the Neutrality Act and with possessing a boatload of explosives and illegal weapons to be used in a planned invasion of Dominica, received an eight year sentence and was freed after serving only two. In contrast, [left-wing activist] Linda Evans was convicted of purchasing four weapons while using false identification and was sentenced to forty years imprisonment, again the longest sentence [by far] ever imposed for this conviction in U.S. history.

The evidence also established plainly that prisoners [such as Geronimo ji Jaga Pratt] have been denied parole as a penalty for refusing to renounce their political beliefs and associations. Such excessive and disproportionate sentences imposed on persons active in self-determination struggles, and in support of those struggles, constitute inhuman and degrading treatment which violates [not only most of the Resolution, Covenants and Declarations cited above, but] Article 1 of U.N. Resolution 3452 (XXX), the Declaration of Protection from Torture, 1975. Unfortunately, a number of additional violations of the latter can also be discerned with regard to U.S. treatment of political prisoners and prisoners of war.

Torture and Cruel, Degrading, and Inhuman Treatment

The tribunal heard considerable testimony [and received substantial corroborating documentation] that the United States government uses its prisons as a key element in efforts to deny various peoples the right to self-determination, and to disrupt or neutralize those organizing to oppose U.S. policies. The evidence established that the government uses political beliefs and associations as a basis for classification of prisoners and consequent placement of them in highly punitive and restrictive facilities, especially isolation units. Of the fact that such treatment can be extraordinarily damaging to those subjected to it, there can be little doubt.

The testimony of Dr. Stuart Grassian, a psychiatric expert on the serious and harmful effects of long-term isolation and solitary confinement, made a profound impression on the tribunal. Evidence was also received demonstrating that in the early 1960s U.S. prisons adopted a policy [centering in the use of isolation units] putting into effect brainwashing practices designed to "modify" the behavior and attitudes of political prisoners and resisters. [The obvious implication is that] with full knowledge that conditions of solitary confinement, "small group isolation," and restricted sensory stimulation cause adverse psychopathological effects, the government has created and maintained prisons and "control units" embodying precisely these features. Examples include the U.S. prison at Marion, Illinois; the federal Women's High Security Unit at Lexington, Kentucky; and New York State's Shawangunk Correctional Facility [as well as, among other places, the California State facility at Pelican Bay, and at least some portion of the federal prison at at Florence, Colorado, presently under construction].

The U.S. prison at Marion, condemned by Amnesty International as violating virtually every one of the United Nations Standard Minimum Rules for the Treatment of Prisoners, holds more political prisoners and prisoners of war than any other prison in the United States. [It has been conclusively shown that] prison officials [systematically and arbitrarily] place political prisoners at Marion and retain them there for years although they do not meet the stated criteria for assignment to that facility. A U.S. court which found the conditions at Marion to pass constitutional muster [that is, the court found the conditions at Marion not to be "cruel" or "unusual"] was nonetheless forced to describe them as "sordid" and "depressing in the extreme." The Women's High Security Unity at Lexington, which was closed in 1988 as the result of national and international human rights campaigns, was also condemned by Amnesty International, which found that the federal Bureau of Prisons deliberately placed political prisoners there under cruel, inhuman and degrading conditions because of their political beliefs. Expert medical testimony revealed that the conditions were calculated to destroy the women psychologically and physically.

The evidence also shows that, in addition to the use of isolation in control units, the government also uses other prison conditions as a means of "breaking" political prisoners and prisoners of war. These conditions include censorship, denial of religious worship, harassment of families and limitations of visits, false accusations of [and unwarranted punishment for] infractions against prison rules, punitive transfers, strip and cavity searches (including regular searches of female prisoners by male staff). Sexual assault, physical torture, and [at least occasionally] assassination. Denial of medical care is also used as a technique in this regard, apparently routinely. Several political prisoners suffering from cancer have been subjected to lengthy and punitive delays in diagnosis and treatment. For example, Alan Berkman, afflicted with Hodgkins Disease, has nearly died several times when prison officials withheld necessary medical treatment and refused to place him in an appropriate hospital facility. Silvia Baraldini's palpable abdominal lumps were ignored for months, despite the fact that she later revealed to suffer an aggressive form of uterine cancer. Similarly, Kuwasi Balagoon, suffering from AIDS, was not diagnosed [despite his repeated requests for medical attention] until ten days before his death.

In sum, the tribunal finds the U.S. government's handling of political prisoners and prisoners of war constitutes torture, and cruel, inhuman and degrading treatment in violation of Article 6 of the Universal Declaration of Human Rights, and in contravention of the United Nations Standard Minimum Rules for Treatment of Prisoners. Additionally, the tribunal finds for the same reasons that the U.S. government is in substantive violation of the Declaration on the Protection of All Persons from being Subjected to Torture and other Cruel, Inhuman or Degrading Treatment or Punishment; the Convention Against Torture and Other Cruel, Inhuman or Degrading Treatment or Punishment; the International Covenant on Civil and Political Rights; the American Declaration of Human Rights; and the Geneva Convention and Protocols thereto. Finally, in the same connection, the tribunal finds that U.S. government's policies regarding political prisoners and prisoners of war violate the First, Eighth and Fourteenth Amendments to its own Constitution, as well as equivalent provisions within the Constitutions of the various States of the Union.

Verdict

Based on the factual and legal foundations stated above, the Special International Tribunal on the Human Rights Violations Against Political Prisoners and Prisoners of War in the United States declares:

1. Within the prisons and jails of the United States exist substantial numbers of political prisoners and prisoners of war.

2. These prisoners have been incarcerated for their opposition to U.S. government policies and actions that are illegal under domestic and international law, including denial of the right to self-determination, genocide, colonialism, racism and militarism.

3. The U.S. government criminalizes and imprisons persons involved in the struggles for self-determination of Native Americans, Puerto Ricans, Black/New Afrikan and Mexicano-Chicano activists within the borders of the United States.

4. Those peoples legitimately struggling for national liberation are not to be treated as criminals, but must be afforded the status of prisoners of war under the Additional Protocol I of the Geneva Convention.

5. The U.S. government also criminalizes and imprisons white North Americans and others who have worked in solidarity with struggles for self-determination, as well as for peace and against nuclear arms, against racism, sexism and other forms of discrimination.

6. The criminal justice system of the U.S. is being used in a harsh and discriminatory way against political activists in the United States.

7. The U.S. government's use of surveillance, infiltration, grand juries, preventative detention, politically-motivated criminal conspiracy charges, prejudicial security and anonymous trial juries deprive political activists of the fair trials guaranteed them under domestic and international law.

8. Political activists have been systematically subjected to disproportionately lengthy prison sentences and to torture and cruel, inhumane and degrading treatment within the U.S. prison system.

The tribunal therefore calls upon the U.S. government to:

1. Release all prisoners who have been incarcerated for the legitimate exercise of their rights to self-determination or in opposition to U.S. policies and practices illegal under international law.

2. Cease all acts of interference and repression against political movements struggling for self-determination or against U.S. policies and practices illegal under international law.

Current Addresses of U.S. Political Prisoners and Prisoners of War

Puertorriqueno Prisoners

Edwin Cortez, No. 92153-024
Ricardo Jiminez, No. 88967-024 A2
Alberto Rodríguez No. 92150-024 B-3
FCI Lewisburg
P. O. Box 1000
Lewisburg, PA 17837

Carlos Alberto Torres
No. 88976-024
FCI Oxford
P. O. Box 1000
Oxford, WI 5952-1000

Alicia Rodrígues, No. NO7157
P. O. Box 5007
Dwight, IL 60420

Luis Rosa, No. NO2743
P. O. Box 711
Menard, IL 62259

Oscar López-Rivera, No. 87651-024
USP Marion
P. O. Box 1000
Marion, IL 62959

Juan Segarra-Palmer
No. 15357-077
FCI Marianna
PMB 7007
Unit Navajo B
Marianna, FL 32446

Eliam Escobar, No. 88968-024
FCI Colorado Unit
P. O. Box 1500
El Reno, OK 73036

Adolfo Matos, No. 88968-024
USP Lompoc
3901 Klein Blvd.
Lompoc, CA 93436

Antonio Camacho, No. 03587-069
FCI McKean, Unit 2
Bradford, PA 16701

Dylcia Pagán, No. 88971-024
Lucy Rodríguez, No. 88973-024
Alejandrina Torres, No. 92152-024
Carmin Valentín, No. 88974-024
Haydeé Beltran, No. 88462-024
FCI Pleasanton
5701 8th Street
Camp Parks
Dublin, CA 94568

Norma Ramirez Talavera
No. 03171-069
FCI Danbury
Pembroke Station
Danbury, CT 06811

Luis Cólon Osorio, No. 03172-069
FCI Otisville
P. O. Box 1000
Unit 5
Otisville, NY 10963

Juan Segarra-Palmer No. 15357-077
FCI Marianna
PMB 7007
Unit Navajo B
Marianna, FL 32446

Roberto José Maldonado
No. 03588-069
Federal Medical Facility
3150 Horton Road
Fort Worth, TX 79119

New African/Black Prisoners

Herman Ferguson, No. 89-A-4621
c/o Center for Constitutional Rights
Attn: Joan Gibbs
666 Broadway
New York, NY 10012

Herman Bell, No. 89-C-262
P. O. Box 338
Napanoch, NY 12458-0338

Abdul Haqq, No. 89-T-1710
(s/n: Craig Randall)
Greenhaven State Prison
Drawer B
Stormville, NY 12582

Teddy (Jah) Heath, No. 75-A-0319
Mohaman Gekua Koti, No.80-A-808
Jalil A. Muntaquin, No. 77-A-4283
(s/n: Anthony Bottom)
Shawagunk Correctional Facility
P. O. Box 700
Wallkill, NY 12589

Abdul Majid, No. 83-A-483
(s/n: Anthony LaBorde)
Sullivan Correctional Facility
Box A-G
Fallsburg, NY 12733

Bashir Hameed, No. 82-A-6313
(s/n: James York)
Maliki Shakur Latine
No. 81-A-4469
Clinton Correctional Facility
P. O. Drawer B
Dannemora, NY 12929

Albert Nuh Washington
No. 77-A-1528
Auburn Correctional Facility
135 State Street
Auburn, NY 13024

Robert Seth Haynes, No. 74-A-2280
Wende Correctional Facility
1187 Wende Road
Alden, NY 14004

Robert Taylor, No. 10376-054
Attica Correctional Facility
P. O. Box 149
Attica, NY 14011

Thomas Warner, No. M3049
Drawer R
Huntington, PA 16652

Kojo Bomani Sababu, No. 39384-046
(s/n: Grailing Brown)
FCI Lewisburg
P. O. Box 1000
Lewisburg, PA 17837

Cecilio Chui Ferguson
No. 04372-054
Drawer K
Dallas, TX 18612

Martin Rutrell, No. 042600
FCI Raiford
UCI 68-2018 Box 221
Raiford, FL 32083

Richard Mafundi Lake, No.79972-X
100 Warrior Land 4-93B
Bessemer, AL 35023

Sekou Kambui, No. 113058
(s/n William Turk)
P. O. Box 56 7E-2-18
Elmore, AL 36025-0056

Charles Scott, No. C-19320
San Quentin Prison
Tamal, CA 94974

Ojore N. Lutalo, No. CN-861-59860
MCU
Trenton, NJ 08625

William Allen, No. 66843
RMSI
7475 Cockrell Bend
Indian Road
Nashville, TN 37243-0471

Ahmad Abdur Rahman, No. 130539
141 First Street
Coldwater, MI 49036

Sekou Odinga, No. 05228-054
(s/n Nathaniel Burns)
Richard Thompson-EL, No. 155229
USP Marion
P. O. Box 1000
Marion, IL 62959

Sundiata Acoli, No. 39794-066
(s/n: Clark Squire)
Mark Cook, No. 20025-148
USP Leavenworth
P. O. Box 1000
Leavenworth, KS 60048

Mondo Langa
(s/n: David Rice)
P. O. Box 2500
Lincoln, NE 68520

Gary Tyler, No. 84156
Ash 4
Louisana State Prison
Angola, LA 70712

Rikke Green, No. 84244
DCCC
Box 220
Hominy, OK 74502

Haki Malik Abdullah, No. C-56123
(s/n Michael Green)
Corcoran Prison
P. O. Box 3456
Corcoran, CA 93212

Kalima Aswad, No. B24120
(s/n Robert Duran)
CMC
P. O. Box 8108
San Luis Obispo, CA 93409

Tariq James Haskins, No. 40075-133
Mutulu Shakur, No. 83205
(s/n Jeral Wayne Williams)
USP Lompoc
3901 Klein Blvd.
Lompoc, CA 93436

Geronimo ji Jaga, No. B40319
(s/n Elmer Gerard Pratt)
P. O. Box 1902B 1C-211U
Tehachapi, CA 93581

Ruchell Cinque McGee, No. A92051
Pelican Bay CF
P. O. Box 7500 SHU 4C-105
Crescent City, CA 95531

Hugo Pinell, No. A88401
Pelican Bay CF
P. O. Box
Crescent City, CA 95531

Awali Stoneman, No. B-98168
Soledad Prison
P. O. Box 100
Soledad, CA 93960

On Death Row

Mumia Abu-Jamal, No. AM-8335
Drawer R
Huntington, PA 16652

MOVE Prisoners

Charles Simms Africa, No. AM-4975
P. O. Box 99901
Pittsburgh, PA 15033

Michael Davis Africa, No. AM-4973
Drawer R
Huntington, PA 16652

William Phillips Africa
No. AM-4984
RFD 3
Bellfonte, PA 16823

Edward Goodman Africa
No. AM-4974
P. O. Box 200
Camp Hill, PA 17001-0200

Delbert Orr Africa, No. AM-4985
Carlos Perez Africa, No. AM-8400
Drawer K
Dallas, PA 18612

Debbi Sims Africa, No. 006307
Consuella Dotson Africa
No. 006434
Janine Phillips Africa, No. 006309
Merle Austin Africa, No. 006306
Janet Holloway Africa, No. 006308
Sue Leon Africa, No. 006325
P. O. Box 180
Muncy, PA 17756

Virgin Island 5

Malik El-Amin, No. 96557-131
(s/n Meral Smith)
FCI Lewisburg
Lewisburg, PA 17837

Hanif Shabazz Bey, No. 9654-131
(s/n Beaumont Gereau)
USP Marion
P. O. Box 1000
Marion, IL 62959

Abdul Azis, No. 96521-131
(s/n Warren Ballentine)
USP Leavenworth
P. O. Box 1000
Leavenworth, KS 66048

Raphael Kwesi Joseph
No. 96558-131
UPS Lompoc
3901 Klein Blvd.
Lompoc, CA 93436

American Indian Prisoners

Eddie Hatcher, No. DL213
Odom Correctional Center
Rt. 1, Box 35
Jackson, NC 27845

Leonard Peltier, No. 89637-132
USP Leavenworth
P. O. Box 1000
Leavenworth, KS 66048

Standing Deer, No. 83947
(aka Robert Hugh Wilson)
DCCC
Box 220
Hominy, OK 74502

Norma Jean Croy, No. 14293
CIW Chochilla
P. O. Box 1501
Chowchilla, CA 93601

Mexicano Prisoners

Alberto Aranda, No. 300823
Ellis Unit 1
Huntsville, RX 77343

Luis Rodrígues, No. C 33000 SQ
San Quentin Prison
Tamal, CA 94974

Cubana Prisoners

Aria Lucia Gelabert, No. 384484
Rt. 2, Box 800
Gatesville, TX 76528

Irish Prisoners

Gerard Hoy, No. 17480-038
Richard Johnson, No. 17422-038
P. O. Box 900
Raybrook, NY 12977-0300

Martin P. Quigly, No. 41064-U3A
P. O. Box 8000
Bradford, PA 16701

Brian Fleming, No. 08022-002
P. O. Box PMB
Atlanta, GA 30315

Kevin McKinley, No. 27801
FCI Jesup
Jesup, GA 31545

Seamus Moley
MCC Miami
15801 S. W. 137th Avenue
Miami, FL 33177

Joseph McColgan, No. 27803-004
FCI Talladega Unit G
565 E. Renfroe Road
Talladega, AL 35160

Chuck Malone, No. 48310-097
FMC Rochester, PMB 4600
Rochester, MN 55903

Noel O. Murchu
FCI Oakdale
Oakdale, LA 71463

Ciaron O'Reilly, No. 103810-052
Reeves County Law Center
P. O. Box 1560
Pecos, TX 79772

Chris Reid
FCI Pleasanton
5701 8th Street
Camp Parks
Dublin, CA 94568

Japanese Red Army Prisoners

Yu Kikumura, No. 09008-050
USP Marion
P. O. Box 1000
Marion, IL 62959

Italian National Prisoners

Silvia Baraldini, No. 05125-054
FCI Marianna
PMB 7007
Shawnee Unit
Marianna, FL 32446

Euroamerican Political Prisoners

Richard Picariello, No. 05812
Walpole State Prison
P. O. Box 1000
South Walpole, MA 02071

Kathy Boudin, No. 84-G-171
Judy Clark, No. 83-G-313
P. O. Box 1000
Bedford Hills, NY 10507

David Gilbert, No. 83-A-6158
Great Meadow Correctional Facility
P. O. box 51
Comstock, NY 12821

Tim Blunk, No. 09429-050
FCI Lewisburg
P. O. Box 1000
Lewisburg, PA 17837

Roy Bourgeois, No. 01579-017
PMB 1000
Tallahassee, FL 32310

Marilyn Buck, No. 00482-285
Susan Rosenberg, No. 03684-016
FCI Marianna
PMB 7007
Shawnee Unit
Marianna, FL 32446

Carol Manning, No. 10375-016
Laura Whitehorn, No. 22432-037
FIC Lexington
3301 Leestown Road
Lexington, KY 40511

Alan Berkman, No. 35049-006
FMC Rochester
PMB 4600
Rochester, MN 55903

Bill Dunne, No. 10916-086/3K
P. O. Box 33
Terra Haute, IN 47808

Ray Luc Levasseur, No. 10376-016
Thomas Manning, No. 20873-SH
Richard Williams, No. 79372-SH
USP Marion
P. O. Box 1000
Marion, IL 62959

Larry Giddings, No. 10917-086
Jaan Laaman, No. 10372-016
USP Leavenworth
P. O. Box 1000
Leavenworth, KS 66048

Linda Evans, No. 19973-054
FCI Pleasanton
5701 8th Street
Camp Parks
Dublin, CA 94568

Ed Mead, No. 251397
P. O. Box 777
Monroe, WA 98272

Paul Wright, No. 930783
Box 500 HC63
Clallam Bay, WA 98320

Plowshares/Disarmament Prison

Randy Kehler
Keets Road
Deerfield, MA 01342

William Frankle-Strait
No. 03809-052
P. O. Box 1000
Unit 5
Otisville, CA 10963

Moana Cole, No. 91-891
Blair County Prison
419 Market Square Alley
Hollidaysburg, PA 16648

Margaret Millett, No. 32118-008
FPC
37900 North 4th Avenue
Dept. 1785
Phoenix, AZ 85027-7066

Mark Davis, No. 23106-008
FCI
RR 2, Box 9000
Safford, AZ 85546

Military Resisters

Jody Anderson, No. 243-43-8434
Robert Beard, No. 568-31-3629
Kenneth Boyd, No. 384-76-9367
Paul Cook, No. 500-64-1670
Shane Fisher, No. 545-79-7908
Kendall Langley $437-49-1308
Glen Mulholland, No. 147-54-5186
Jean Claude Rainey, No.215-06-4430
Ken Sharpe, No. 307-72-5424
Marine Corps Brig
Bldg. 1041 MCB
Camp Lejune, NC 28542

Michael Bell
Fort Knox Box A
Fort Knox, KY 48121

William Allen
David Childress
Faith Grasso
Tracy Robb
MP Co. Bldg. 1390
Fort Sill, OK 73503-5020

William Walker
8320-1 Smith Drive
Fort Hood, TX 76544

Tim Silvey
Fort Lewis, Bldg. 1450
Fort Lewis, WA 98433

Sources of Further Information

Organizations

Anti-Repression Resources
P. O. Box 122
Jackson, MS 39205

Center for Constitutional
Rights/Movement Support
666 Broadway, 7th Floor
New York, NY 10012

Committee to End the Marion
Lockdown (CEML)
343 S. Dearborn, Suite 1607
Chicago, IL 60604

Commission to Fight Repression
Box 1435, Cathedral Station
New York, NY 10025

Emergency Committee for
Political Prisoners
P. O. Box 28191
Washington, D.C. 20038

Free Puerto Rico Committee
P. O. Box 022512, Cadman Plaza
New York, NY 11202

Freedom Now!
5249 N. Kenmore Street
Chicago, IL 60640

Friends of Political Prisoners
P. O. Box 3113
Madison, WI 53704

Justice for Geronimo Campaign
214 Duboce Avenue
San Francisco, CA 94103

National Alliance Against
Racist/Political Repression
126 W. 119th Street
New York, 10026

National Committee Against
Repressive Legislation
501 C Street, NE
Washington, D.C. 20002

National Committee to Free
Puerto Rican Prisoners
P. O. Box 476698
Chicago, IL 60647

National Emergency Civil Rights
Committee
175 Fifth Avenue
New York, NY 10010

National Lawyers Guild
55 Avenue of the Americas
New York, NY 10013

The National Prison Project
1616 P Street, NW
Washington, D.C. 20035

New African People's
Organization
P. O. Box 11464
Atlanta, GA 30310

Nuclear Resister
P. O. Box 43383
Tucon, AZ 85733

Partisan Defense Committee
c/o R. Wolkensten, Esq.
P. O. Box 99, Canal Street Sta.
New York, NY 10013

Peltier Defense Committee
P. O. Box 583
Lawrence, KS 66044

People's Law Office
633 S Dearborn, No. 1614
Chicago, IL 60604

Political Rights Defense Fund
P. O. Box 649, Cooper Station
New York, NY 10003

Prairie Fire Organizing
Committee
P. O. Box 747
Allston, MA 02134

P. O. Box 18044
Atlanta, GA 30316

P. O. Box 1442
San Francisco, CA 94114

2520 N. Lincoln
Chicago, IL 60614

Prison Book Program
c/o Redbook Bookstore
92 Green Street
Jamaica Plain, MA 02130

Saxifrage Action Group
P. O. Box 18717
Denver, CO 80218

The Sentencing Project
918 F Street, N.W., Suite 501
Washington, D.C. 20004

Publications

Breakthrough
c/o John Brown Education Fund
220 9th Street, No. 443
San Francisco, CA 94103

Bulldozer/Prison News Service
P. O. Box 5052, Station A
Toronto, Ontario
M5W 1W4 Canada

Can't Jail the Spirit
Editorial El Coqui Publishers
1671 N. Claremont Street
Chicago, IL 60647

Gay Community News
62 Berkeley Street
Boston, MA 02116

The Progressive
409 E. Main Street
Madison, WI 53703

The Real Dragon
P. O. Box 3294
Berkeley, CA 94703-9901

Notes on Contributors

Biographical information concerning many of the contributors to this volume appears in the main text. These include Kuwasi Balagoon, Alan Berkman, Lucy Berríos Berríos, Dhoruba Bin Wahad, Tim Blunk, Marilyn Buck, Filberto Ojeda Ríos, George Jackson, Ray Luc Levasseur, Sekou Odinga, Leonard Peltier, Geronimo ji Jaga Pratt, Nelson Ramirez, Bob Robideau, Susan Rosenberg, Carmin Valentín, Karen Wald, Albert Nuh Washington, and Karen Wald. The following biographical sketches provide data on the others involved.

Daoud Ahmed is the pseudonym of a former member of the Black Panther Party who is presently serving heavy time for "crimes against the state." He does not wish to be further identified at this time, for reasons of personal security.

Jim Campbell is a long-time Canadian activist working for the rights of prisoners and native peoples. He is a member of the Bulldozer collective in Toronto and edits Prison News Service.

Ches-ne-o-nah-eh (Claude Wilkerson) bas been released from prison and continues to work as a speaker and artist on behalf of death row and native prisoners.

Ward Churchill is associate professor of American Indian Studies and Communications with the Center for Studies of Ethnicity and Race in America, University of Colorado at Boulder. He serves as co-director of the American Indian Movement of Colorado and vice chair of the American Indian Anti-Defamation Council. A prolific writer on indigenous rights and other progressive issues, Churchill has authored, co-authored, or edited eight books and more than a hundred articles.

Fay Dowker works with the Committee to End the Marion Lockdown (CEML), an organization devoted not only to correcting prevailing conditions at USP Marion, but to preventing replication and intensification of such conditions elsewhere, notably at the new federal facility under construction near Florence, Colorado.

Dan Debo is a long-time Bay Area activist involved mainly with Philippine and Palestine liberation support work, as well as rights movements for prisoners and indigenous people. He has contributed writings and photography to a number of progressive publications.

Bill Dunne is a committed warrior in the cause of human liberation, held as a Prisoner of War at USP Marion for more than seven years. During his stay "in the belly of beast," he wrote numerous articles on prison conditions, sparks which ignited the work in Colorado which ultimately produced *Cages of Steel*. In March of 1992, Dunne was transferred to USP Terre Haute, where he continues to function as an activist and author.

Cecilio Chui Ferguson is a former member of the Black Panther Party and Black Liberation Army (BLA), and was a defendant in the notorious "Panther 21" trial of 1969-1970. Along with BLA members Edward Joseph and Sekou Odinga, and May 19th Communist Organization member Silvia Baraldini, he was convicted in 1983 of RICO conspiracy in connection with an alleged series of bank and armored car robberies. He is serving a forty year sentence.

David Gilbert is a former member of SDS and the Weather Underground Organization. On September 15, 1985, he, along with co-defendants Judy Clark and Kuwasi Balagoon, was convicted of robbery and murder in connection with the failed 1981 highjacking of a Brinks truck in West Nyack, New York, during which a guard and a police officer were killed. All were sentenced to life imprisonment in New York state facilities. Gilbert is active in the prisoner's rights movement, with an emphasis on AIDS education.

Glenn Good is an activist with CEML.

M. Annette Jaimes is a lecturer with the Center for Studies of Ethnicity and Race in America, University of Colorado at Boulder and a Humanities Fellow at Cornell University. The author of numerous articles on indigenous rights and related matters, she is an Associate Editor of *New Studies on the Left*. Her books include *The State of Native America: Genocide, Colonization, and Resistance*.

Richard Korn is a psychologist specializing in the effects of coercion and isolation on human consciousness and personality. The material included here is excerpted form a report prepared for the American Civil Liberties Union.

Nancy Kurshan is a former SDS member and was a founder of WITCH (Women's International Terrorist Conspiracy from Hell), the feminist equivalent of YIPPIE! during the early 1970s. She currently works with CEML.

Richard Marquantte is editor and publisher of the prison journal *Blind Lady Quarterly* and *Takin' It to the Streets: A Literary Showcase of Incarcerated Writers*. A cultural nationalist, he served five years in the Indiana prison system after a political conviction in 1967.

Marc Mauer is assistant director of the Sentencing Project, a national non-profit research group that evaluates criminal justice policies and promotes sentencing reform. He has testified extensively before Congress and is a recipient of the Helen L. Buttenwelser Award from the Fortune Society for "bringing to national attention the injustice and human damage created by our criminal justice system."

Mary O'Melveny is a progressive attorney working in the Washington, D.C. area. She as been involved in such major cases as the Resistance Conspiracy defense and the Freedom of Information Act suit pressed by Geronimo ji Jaga Pratt.

Heather Rhoads is a prisoners' rights and AIDS activist and has been an intern with *The Progressive* magazine.

Julio Rosado is an activist in the Puerto Rican independence movement and head of the prisoners' rights organization Freedom Now!

Mike Ryan, a Montréal-based activist, has long been involved in prison-related issues particularly in support of native prisoners struggling to have their rights recognized. A regular contributor to *New Studies on the Left*, Ryan's treatment of the Stammheim Prison in Germany in that publication stands as the best study of the facility presently available in North America.

Fukoka Sano is an activist with CEML.

Susan Saxe is a former political prisoner, incarcerated from 1975 to 1982 for participating in expropriations (bank robberies) in Boston and Philadelphia, as well as the theft and destruction of property at the Massachusetts National Guard Armory. Prior to her capture, she and co-conspirator Kathy Power were on the FBI's "Ten Most Wanted" list. Her contribution to this volume originally appeared in *Gay Community News*, an excellent source of information on current work concerning the rights of prisoners with AIDS.

Mutulu Shakur (s/n: Jeral Wayne Williams) was director of the Lincoln Detox Program in South Bronx and founder of the Black Acupuncture Advisory Association of America (BAAANA). He is also accused of heading the BLA section which freed Assata Shakur from prison in 1978, and which is alleged to have conducted a lengthy series of armed expropriations from banks and armored trucks in the Northeast (the proceeds going to fund drug rehab efforts in the African American community). Along with co-defendant Marilyn Buck, he was convicted of RICO conspiracy in 1987, and sentenced to fifty years incarceration.

Standing Deer (formerly Robert Hugh Wilson) is currently serving time on a range of convictions related to bank robberies in Oklahoma and Texas. In 1973, he was involved in a $27 million riot in which the Oklahoma state prison was burned to the ground, and spent the following year in the hole. On April 29, 1975, he highjacked a prison bus and escaped. Upon his re-capture, Standing Deer was designated by the FBI as "the most dangerous individual ever captured in Chicago." In 1977, while he was incarcerated at USP Marion, the FBI tried to recruit him to assassinate AIM activist Leonard Peltier in exchange for medical treatment and dropping of charges pending against him. Instead, he warned Peltier of the plot. Back in state facilities, Standing Deer remains an eloquent advocate of prisoner's rights.

Jennie Vander Wall, a long-time Denver activist in gay/lesbian, indigenous peoples' and prisoners' rights movements, she is an associate editor of *New Studies on the Left* and head of the Saxifrage Action Group.

Jim Vander Wall is head of the Denver area Leonard Peltier Support Group and an associate editor of *New Studies on the Left*. He is co-author with Ward Churchill of *Agents of Repression: The FBI's Secret Wars Against the Black Panther Party and the American Indian Movement* and *The COINTELPRO Papers: Documents from the FBI's Secret Wars Against Dissent in the United States.*

Index

Convict Mathias Maccumsey died after this "iron gag" was locked on his mouth
while imprisoned in the Eastern State Pennitentiary of Pennsylvania. While
the U.S. Constitution prohibits cruel and unusual punishment, the history of
imprisonment in the U.S. proves otherwise. The handbill reproduced above was
presented to Congress and the District Court of Eastern Pennsylvania in 1855
by James Akin. It reads: "In open defiance of all known maxims of Law and
Contrary to Legislative enactments, a convict was compelled to endure the
appalling tortures of this infernal contrivance for merely speaking to a fellow
prisoner. In a Land too, where Tyranny and Oppression, is held in utter
abhorrence, and Liberty, Equality, and a just enjoyment of rights are the
constant boasting of the people!!! The Spanish inquisitions cannot exhibit a
more fearful and barbarous mode beyond all human endurance! It ought to
be forever abolished!!!" (photo: Library of Congress)